CLINICAL
MICROBIOLOGY

Dr. Sheeana Gangadoo

ALLIED
HEALTH
PRESS

Clinical Microbiology

Author: **Dr. Sheeana Gangadoo**

Allied Health Press
4164 Lakeshore Road
Burlington ON L7L 1A4
Canada
www.alliedhealthpress.com
Email: orders@arclereducation.com

ISBN: 978-1-77956-209-8

ABOUT THE AUTHOR

Dr. Sheeana Gangadoo was awarded her PhD in Microbiology and Agricultural Sciences, where her work focused on the influence of nanoparticles to improve the gut microbiota and overall health of broiler chickens. As a postdoctoral researcher, she focused on the investigation of antimicrobial materials to reduce the spread of antibiotic resistant microbes and was trained on various spectroscopic and microscopy techniques. She was later employed as a microbiologist in collaboration with Australian biotechnology company, Biomebank, and successfully optimised a novel anaerobic bioreactor for the production of probiotics in treating gut diseases.

Word Roots, Prefixes, and Suffixes by Chapter

Chapter 1 Introduction to Clinical Microbiology

Acet-, Aceto- Pertaining to Acetic Acid

Anti-, Ant Against- Antimicrobial

Bacteri-, Bacterio- Denoting Bacteria

micro- Microbiology

Nucleo- Nucleotides

Glyco- Glycolipids

Chapter 2 Tuberculosis

tubercul-osis-, Tuberculosis

Tub- Referring to a structure shaped like a tube.

-er- (Infix)- Connecting vowel.

-cul- (Infix)- Denoting a small structure.

-osis (Suffix)- Indicating a diseased or abnormal condition.

Together- Tub(er)cul- + -osis = Tuberculosis

Chapter 3 Infections of the Blood and Respiratory Tract

Hemat- Referring to blood

Hemo- Denoting blood

Emia- Suffix indicating a condition of the blood

Pulmo- or Pulmon, Referring to the lungs

Naso- or Nas, Referring to the nose

Ectomy- Denoting surgical removal

Chapter 4 Infections of the Urinary Tract and Alimentary Canal

Chole-cholecystectomy

Cysto-cystitis

Hepato- hepatitis

Nephr-nephrotoxic

Chapter 5 Infections of the Liver and Biliary Tract

hepat-, hepatic-hepatology, hepatitis

-ary-biliary tract, coronary

-pepsia-dyspepsia

bil(i)-, chol(e)-cholaemia (UK)/cholemia (US), cholecystitis

cholecyst(o)-cholecystectomy

Chapter 6 Infections of the Skin, Soft Tissues, Joints and Bone

cutane/o –skin

derm/o-(skin)

ossi-bone

ost(e)-, oste(o)- bone

Cutane(o) skin

Cut- skin

pelv(i)-, pelv(o)- hip bone

Chapter 7 Infections of the Central Nervous System

Cerebellum, cerebella or cerebellums- little brain

Neuro- nerve

Cerebro-, enceph-brain

Phlebitis, venitis- inflammation of a vein

Crani-skull

Mening-, membrane

Ventriculo-, cavity

Chapter 8 Infections of the Eye

Oculo-, Eye

Ophthalm/o- Eye

Retin- Retina (of the eye)

Kerat/o- Cornea (eye or skin)

Lacrim/o- Tear (from your eyes)

Table of Contents

LIST OF FIGURES

LIST OF TABLES

PREFACE

In medical microbiology, microorganisms are identified to diagnose infectious diseases and to predict how a given therapeutic intervention will be received. The following are important groups of organisms: fungi, viruses, bacteria, mycobacteria, and parasites. Microbiological techniques are used in conjunction with clinical symptoms, extra laboratory testing, and imaging methods to differentiate between a true infection linked to the disease and colonization with normal flora or other conditions, such as autoimmune disorders, inflammatory diseases, or malignancies, each of which has a different prognosis and course of treatment for the patient. Traditional microscopy and culture techniques are combined in laboratories with a rapidly developing set of molecular and proteomic techniques.

Diagnosing microbial infections remains crucial for many patients, as evidenced by the rise in immunocompromised patients from transplants, the epidemic of HIV, and the use of immunosuppressive drugs to treat autoimmune disorders. Knowledge of clinical microbiology and infectious diseases is critical as new pathogens are identified, infectious outbreaks increase, microorganisms develop resistance mechanisms, and increasingly advanced laboratory techniques are used. Clinical microbiology laboratories are critical to the success of antimicrobial stewardship programs due to their ability to provide data that enables accurate diagnosis and supports the treatment of patients. Rapid diagnostic tests such as peptide nucleic acid fluorescence in situ hybridization technique (PNA-FISH), matrix-assisted laser desorption ionization time-of-flight mass spectrometry (MALDI-TOF-MS), multiplex nucleic acid testing and quantitative polymerase chain reaction (qPCR) have been developed in the last decade. Compared to traditional tests, these techniques can all more quickly provide information about the type of pathogen involved in the infectious process, as well as the presence of resistance genes.

This book "Clinical Microbiology" is intended to explore the principles and practices of microbiology as they pertain to the diagnosis, treatment, and prevention of infectious diseases in clinical settings. Through a meticulous examination of microbial identification, pathogenesis, host-pathogen interactions, and laboratory techniques, the book aims to equip healthcare professionals, microbiologists, and students with the knowledge and skills necessary to understand, manage, and combat infectious diseases. The book is focused on the practical application of microbiological concepts in the clinical realm, and aims to bridge the gap between theory and real-world healthcare scenarios, adopting a deeper understanding of the role of microorganisms in human health and disease.

Chapter 1

INTRODUCTION TO CLINICAL MICROBIOLOGY

Contents

Unit Introduction

The field of clinical microbiology is diverse in terms of the organisms it studies and the techniques employed to isolate and characterize them. It also includes a wide range of testing procedures. The identification of culture organisms in clinical microbiology is still largely dependent on phenotypic and culture-based methods, despite notable advancements in testing methodologies. Microbiological testing is difficult due to the large range of pathogens and testing techniques available; as a result, error detection and correction are crucial elements of high-quality microbiology laboratory testing.

Errors can occur in all testing stages (pre-analytical, analytical and post-analytical; an error in one testing phase is likely to overlap and/or lead to errors in other phases (e.g., incorrect sampling can lead to the culturing, identification and reporting of organisms not involved in the disease process, resulting in the incorrect or unnecessary antimicrobial therapy).

Orientation and Directional Terms

Term	Definition	Illustration
Gram staining	A laboratory technique that categorizes bacteria based on their cell wall composition. Bacteria are classified as either Gram-positive or Gram-negative, which has implications for treatment and identification.	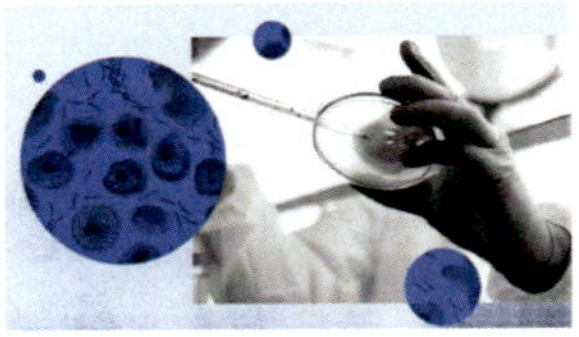
Nosocomial Infection	An infection acquired in a hospital or healthcare setting. Clinical microbiologists focus on identifying and preventing nosocomial infections to improve patient safety.	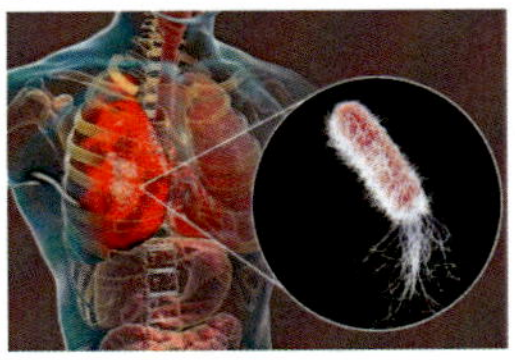
Serology	The study of blood serum, particularly in the context of identifying antibodies or antigens. Serological tests are crucial in diagnosing infectious diseases and monitoring immune responses.	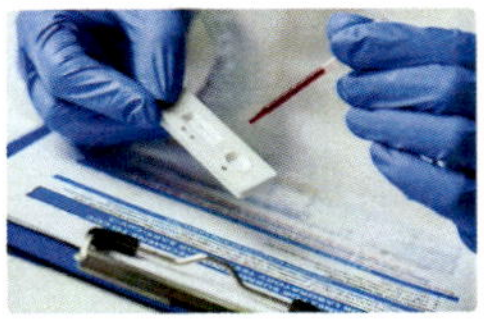
Molecular diagnostics	The use of molecular biology techniques, such as PCR and DNA sequencing, in diagnosing diseases. In clinical microbiology, molecular diagnostics offer rapid and accurate identification of pathogens.	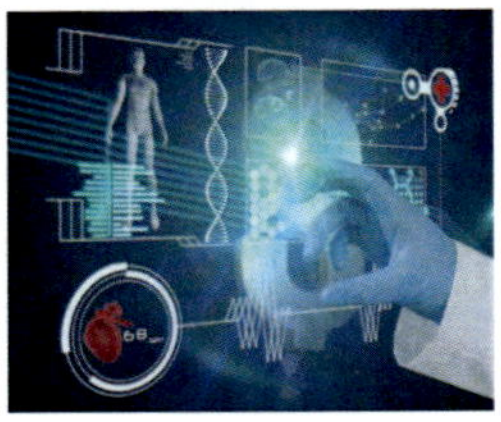
Penicillin-binding proteins.	These are membrane-associated proteins involved in the biosynthesis of peptidoglycan (PG), the main component of bacterial cell walls.	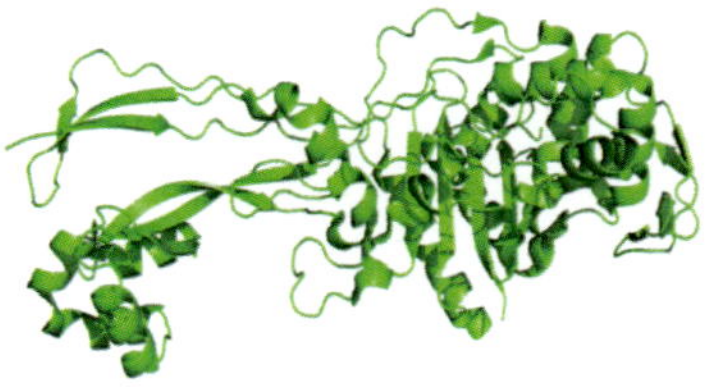
Cell membrane	Protect and organize cells. All cells have an outer plasma membrane that regulates not only what enters the cell, but also how much of any given substance comes in. Unlike prokaryotes, eukaryotic cells also possess internal membranes that encase their organelles and control the exchange of essential cell components.	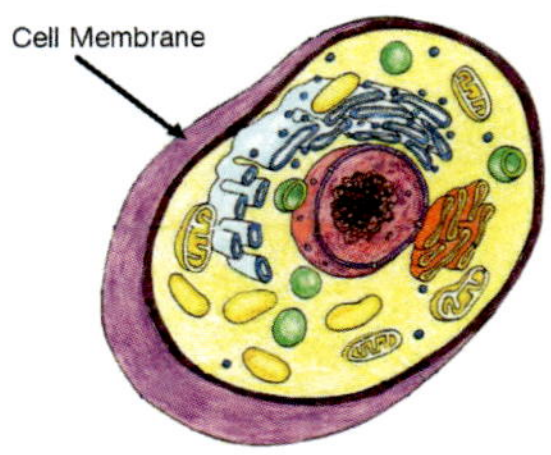

1.1. Bacteria

Bacteria are single-celled, microscopic living things. The term "bacterium" refers to just one microbe. There are millions, if not billions, of different kinds of bacteria in the world, and your body is one of them. They are in your mouth, in your airways, and on your skin. They are also present in your urinary tract, reproductive system, and digestive system.

The majority of bacteria are either harmless or beneficial to your health, and can be found in your gut or on your skin. These are collections of microbes that live in and on your body; they are referred to as resident flora or your microbiome. By assisting with nutrition absorption, food digestion, and the inhibition of the growth of pathogenic bacteria, gut bacteria maintain your good health.

Microorganisms that can cause disease are known as pathogens, and a category of these pathogens include bacteria that can cause illness. They can proliferate swiftly within your body and release toxins, or poisons, which can lead to infection.

Examples of harmful bacteria include:

i. ***Streptococcus***: Bacteria that cause strep throat.

ii. ***Staphylococcus***: Bacteria that cause staph infections.

iii. ***Escherichia coli***: Bacteria that cause *E. coli* infections.

When the germs mentioned above enter your bloodstream, they trigger the following infections, causing sepsis, or blood poisoning. Sepsis can occur when bacteria spread throughout the blood, sparking a widespread infection in the body that leads to a systemic overreaction.

Other examples of pathogenic bacteria include:

i. **Aerococcusurinae:** Bacteria in urine that cause urinary tract infections.

ii. ***Chlamydia trachomatis***: Bacteria that cause a sexually transmitted infection (STI) called chlamydia.

iii. ***Bordetella pertussis***: Bacteria that cause whooping cough.

While most bacterial infections are treatable with antibiotic, the likelihood that your body will develop an immunity to an antibiotic increases with usage. In addition, failure to take antibiotics as directed increases the risk of developing bacterial resistance.

1.1.1. Cell Wall

In the majority of bacteria, the maintenance of cell shape and structural integrity depends on the intricate, mesh-like bacterial cell wall structure. Since most bacteria require the cell wall to survive, and eukaryotic organisms lack this component, some of our strongest antibiotics have been historically directed towards it, raising significant research interest. Furthermore, bacterial cell wall fragments may be cytotoxic and immunostimulatory, which means they are important players in the pathophysiology and disease.

The primary component of the cell wall is peptidoglycan (PG), a network of polysaccharide strands cross-linked by brief peptide bridges joined to the MurNAc residues. PG is produced on the outside of the cytoplasm, and the steps involved in synthesis are as follows: lipid-linked disaccharide-pentapeptide precursor lipid II is generated cytoplasmically; flippases (MurJ and/or Amj) translocate lipid II to the outside of the cell; and penicillin-binding proteins (PBPs) and Shape, Elongation, Division, and Sporulation (SEDS) proteins assemble the cell wall.

The process of assembly can be further broken down into two parts: the polymerization of the GlcNAc-MurNAc-pentapeptide through glycosyltransferase reactions, which are catalyzed by class A PBPs and SEDS proteins; and the (as of yet) poorly understood crosslinking of the peptide sidestems into a taut meshwork by class A and B PBPs and L,D-transpeptidases. Furthermore, secondary cell wall polymers, such as capsule polysaccharides covalently attached to PG or wall teichoic acids (polyol-phosphate polymers), can be used to decorate the PG mesh. The cell wall structure of mycobacteria is further complex by the addition of layers of long-chain lipids and polysaccharides to the PG layer.

The cell wall needs to be both flexible and rigid in order to permit cellular expansion as well as high intracellular pressures and resistance to external stresses. The result is that the cell wall is continually disassembled, turned over, and remodeled in addition to performing synthesis functions. This is made possible by an amazing and little-known class of enzymes that together have the ability to cleave and/or alter a wide range of PG structures. For instance, a functionally diverse class of enzymes known as "autolysins" breaks PG crosslinks (endopeptidases), peptide sidestems (amidases, carboxypeptidases), or the sugar backbone (lytic transglycosylases, muramidases). To elaborate, PG-acetyltransferases add acetyl residues to the backbone structures of MurNAc molecules, increasing their resistance to lysozyme. L,D-transpeptidases catalyze D-amino acid (DAA) exchange reactions, which can be used to label PG with fluorescent compounds by substituting a range of alternative DAAs for terminal D-Ala residues. Numerous of these systems carry out crucial tasks like recycling polymeric groups, daughter cell separation, sacculus expansion during growth, and insertion of macromolecular trans-envelope protein complexes.

1.1.2. Gram-Positive Cell Walls

PG is the main component of gram-positive bacteria's cell walls, and with layer upon layer of peptidoglycan accumulating around the cell membrane, it can make up as much as 90% of the cell wall. With a peptide interbridge, the NAM tetrapeptides are usually cross-linked; complete cross-linking is frequent. An extraordinarily robust cell wall is the result of all of this combined.

Teichoic acid is an extra component found in gram-positive cell walls. It is a glycopolymer that is encased in PG layers. Teichoic acid is thought to have a number of vital functions for the cell, including producing the net negative charge necessary for the development of a proton motive force.

Teichoic acid plays a role in the overall rigidity of the cell wall, which is crucial for maintaining the shape of the cell, especially in organisms that resemble rods. Teichoic acids have been shown to interact with the machinery involved in PG biosynthesis to contribute to cell division.

Finally, it seems that teichoic acids contribute to resistance against β-lactam antibiotics and unfavorable environments like high salt and temperature concentrations. Teichoic acids are known as lipoteichoic acid when they are attached to the cell membrane via a lipid anchor or covalently linked to PG (wall teichoic acids, or WTA) (Figure 1.1).

Most substances can easily pass through the gram-positive cell wall due to the relatively porous PG. However, some nutrients are too big, and the cell must therefore use exoenzymes to break them down. These extracellular enzymes are produced in the cytoplasm of the cell and are subsequently released through the cell wall, and beyond the cell membrane, to break down big macromolecules into smaller parts outside of the cell.

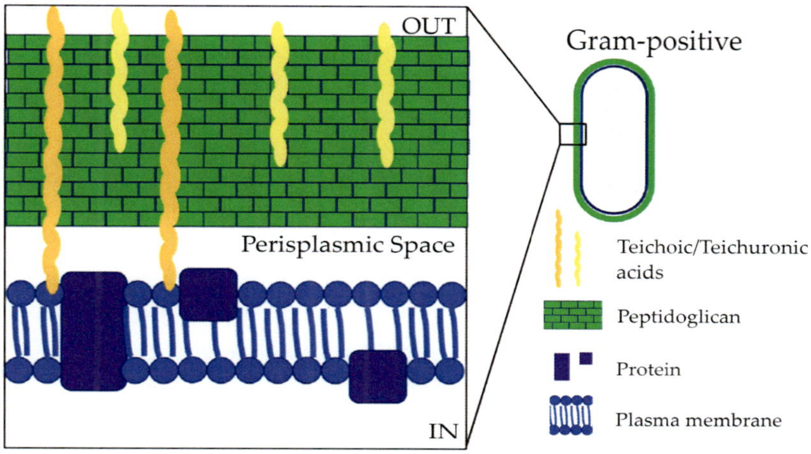

Figure 1.1. *The structure of gram-positive bacteria wall.*

Source: Franco, D., Calabrese, G., Guglielmino, S. P. P., & Conoci, S., (2022). Metal-based nanoparticles: Antibacterial mechanisms and biomedical application. Microorganisms, 10(9), 1778. https://doi.org/10.3390/microorganisms10091778.

1.1.3. Gram-Negative Cell Walls

Gram-negative bacteria have more components overall in their cell walls, making them more complex than gram-positive bacteria. Even though they only make up a few layers—between 5% and 10% of the entire cell wall—PG is present. The outside membrane, or plasma membrane, which is found outside of the PG layers, is the most distinctive feature of the gram-negative cell wall. The gram-negative cell wall is mostly composed of polar heads, fatty acid tails, and integral proteins, and the lipid bilayer that makes up the outer membrane is remarkably similar to the cell membrane. Unlike the cell membrane however, it contains lipopolysaccharide (LPS), which are big molecules that protrude from the cell into the surroundings and are anchored into the outer membrane. Three distinct parts are comprised of LPS:

- The O-antigen or O-polysaccharide, representing the outermost part of the structure;
- The core polysaccharide; and
- Lipid A, which anchors the LPS into the outer membrane.

LPS is known to perform a wide range of tasks for the cell, including stabilizing the outer membrane, adding to the cell's net negative charge, and protecting the cell from certain chemicals by physically obstructing access to other areas of the cell wall. Additionally, it is recognized that LPS may contribute to the way a host—a human or another animal—responds to an infection caused by a pathogenic gram-negative bacterium. In particular, the O-antigen component of LPS causes the host to mount an immunological defense, which results in the production of antibodies that recognize a specific O-antigen (consider *E. coli* O157:H7). It is also known that lipid A has the ability to act as an endotoxin in humans, which can result in common illness symptoms like fever and diarrhea. A significant quantity of lipid A discharged into the bloodstream may cause endotoxic shock, a potentially fatal inflammatory reaction affecting the entire body (Figure 1.2).

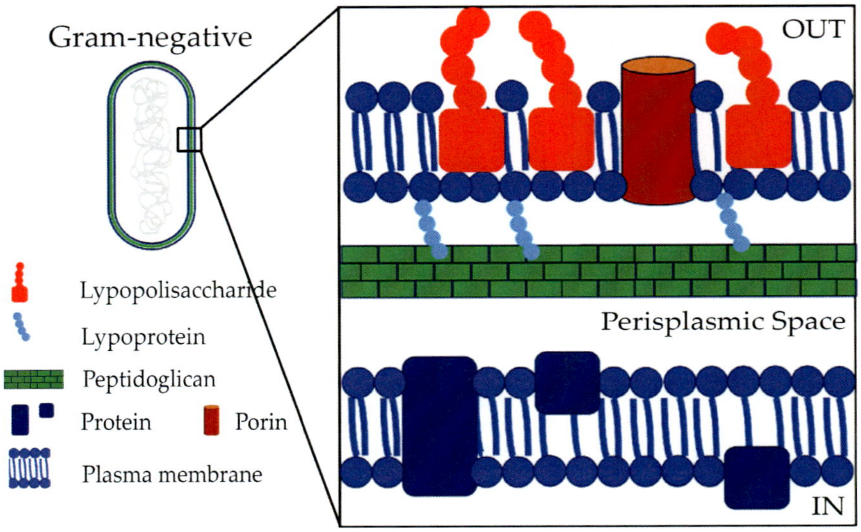

Figure 1.2. *The cell wall cycle of gram-negative bacteria.*

Source: Franco, D., Calabrese, G., Guglielmino, S. P. P., & Conoci, S., (2022). Metal-based nanoparticles: Antibacterial mechanisms and biomedical application. Microorganisms, 10(9), 1778. https://doi.org/10.3390/microorganisms10091778.

Regarding the outer membrane, it acts as a barrier for the cell, and selectively regulates the passage of nutrients, allowing some to enter while preventing others from exiting. The presence of the extra lipid bilayer creates a strong barrier that allows specific nutrients to enter, and enzymes are used to break down large molecules so they can pass through the lipophilic barrier (LPS). Gram-negative bacteria use periplasmic enzymes instead of exoenzymes, as do gram-positive bacteria, and are kept in the periplasm. If you're wondering where the gram-negative peptidoglycan is found, it's in the periplasm, which is the area that lies between the inner and outer surfaces of the cell membrane.

The periplasmic enzymes must still carry the nutrients across the lipid bilayer, including the outer membrane, in order for them to pass through the LPS after they have broken down into smaller molecules. Porins, found in gram-negative cells, are transmembrane proteins made up of a trimer of three subunits that create a pore across the membrane. Certain porins are specific and only move molecules that they recognize through the use of a binding site; other porins are non-specific and move any molecule that fits. Molecules pass through the porous PG layers in the periplasm and outer membrane before being carried across the cell membrane by integral proteins.

The outer membrane and the PG layers are connected by a lipoprotein called Braun's lipoprotein, (ol' Dr. Braun). The lipoprotein is covalently attached to the PG at one end, while its polar head is embedded into the outer membrane at the other end. The connection between the two layers increases the overall strength and structural integrity of the cell wall.

1.1.4. Bacterial Physiology

The study of the essential mechanisms and functions that keep bacteria alive is known as bacterial physiology. Bacterial physiology primarily studies the different metabolic pathways, cellular architectures, and regulatory systems that allow bacteria to live and grow in a variety of settings. Single-celled microorganisms, such as bacteria, are known for their extraordinary adaptability, and can thrive in a variety of harsh environments and use a broad range of energy sources. Important steps in the synthesis of energy are performed by their metabolism, which includes oxidative phosphorylation, the tricarboxylic acid cycle, and glycolysis. A variety of nutrient-acquisition mechanisms are also demonstrated by bacteria, such as passive diffusion and active transport.

One area of biology called bacterial physiology studies the general principles of cellular reproduction. Bacterial physiology involves a lot of quantitative problems, and its leading lights have frequently combined methods and ideas from other academic fields.

1. **Bacterial Physiology:** It consists of studying the nutrition, metabolism and growth of bacteria according to variations (natural or controlled) in the environment in which they live.
2. **Bacterial Nutrition:** It is the analysis of the elementary, energetic and specific needs necessary for the functioning and growth of the bacterium, as well as the physico-chemical factors likely to influence them.
3. **Bacterial Biochemical Metabolism:** It is the set of chemical transformations (anabolism or biosynthesis and catabolism or degradation) that ensure the development of bacterial constituents and their functioning.
4. **Bacterial Growth:** In an optimal environment, the bacterial cell, thanks to its highly developed enzymatic system, will give birth in a short time (20 minutes for the majority of bacteria in the environment), to two daughter bacteria that are identical to it: We are talking about bacterial growth. It is manifested by a numerical increase in bacterial cells and not an increase in size as in higher organisms (Human, animal, plant).

1.1.5. DNA Synthesis

Genes that code for instructions on how to synthesize proteins are found in a large molecule called DNA (deoxyribonucleic acid). Repeating subunits, or nucleotides, make up the code, and each nucleotide is composed of three parts (Figure 1.3):

- A phosphate group (an acid);
- A sugar (in the case of DNA, deoxyribose); and
- A ring of carbon and nitrogen atoms (the nitrogen can form a bond with hydrogen so the nucleotide is basic).

The phosphate group of one nucleotide is joined to the sugar of an adjacent nucleotide to form a chain of nucleotides, or nucleic acids, and the phosphate-sugar backbone's side is where the bases protrude. For DNA, the third component—the base, which is made up of a ring of carbon and nitrogen atoms—occurs in four different forms. These bases fall into two classes: the pyrimidine bases (cytosine and thymine), which have only one ring, and the purine bases (adenine and guanine), which have double rings of nitrogen and carbon atoms. Two polynucleotide chains that are wound around one another to form a double helix make up a DNA molecule. Hydrogen bonds between purine and pyrimidine bases—more precisely, adenine and thymine and guanine and cytosine—keep the chains together. As a result, each double helix chain is complementary to the other.

In the context of a lab, in synthetic biology, DNA synthesis is both a limiting step and a potent enabling technology. Reducing the cost of synthesizing DNA will open up new possibilities and project ideas that most scientists would not be able to carry out at their current level. During the previous 15 years, the price of column-synthesized oligonucleotides has decreased tenfold, and it is currently between USD 0 and USD 02 per nucleotide. Gene synthesis is a more costly procedure that creates longer DNA constructs by layering oligonucleotides together. The market price of gene synthesis was roughly USD 10 per base in 2000. Since then, with average error rates of roughly 1 in 300–600 bases, prices have decreased nearly 50 times in 10 years, to as low as USD 0.2 per base pair. Like Moore's law, prices continue to decline by a factor of 1.5 annually. There were 39 gene synthesis vendors in the world by 2005, and that number has since gone up. More businesses have started to surface in the last few years to take on the task of bringing new synthesis technologies to market. In the near future, it would be interesting to see significant changes in the gene synthesis market.

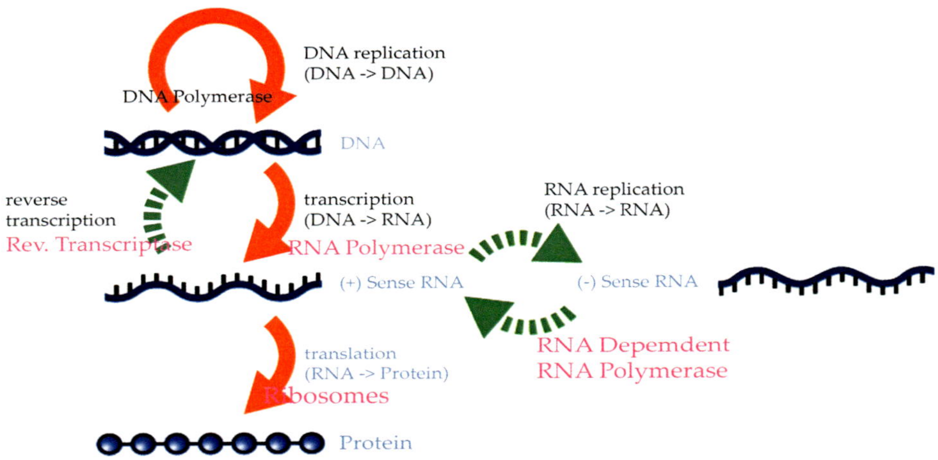

Figure 1.3. *DNA transcription and translation: synthesis of proteins.*

Source: By User:Dhorspool, CC BY-SA 3.0, https://commons.wikimedia.org/w/index.php?curid=26070240.

1.1.6. RNA Synthesis

RNA polymerases are the type of enzymes that synthesize RNA. There are three primary RNA polymerases in higher organisms, denoted I, II, and III (or occasionally A, B, and C). Every protein is a complex structure made up of numerous subunits. Since three of the four types of ribosomal RNA (rRNA)—referred to as 18S, 28S, and 5.8S RNA—are synthesized by RNA polymerase I, it is active in the nucleolus, which is home to the genes that encode these rRNA molecules. Though its initial products are larger precursors known as heterogeneous nuclear RNA, which are completed later, rather than mature RNA, RNA polymerase II synthesizes messenger RNA (mRNA) (see Processing of mRNA below). Translator RNA (tRNA) and 5S RNA, the fourth RNA component of the ribosome, are the byproducts of RNA polymerase III.

The RNA synthesis is initiated by each of the three polymerases at distinct locations on DNA. They then move along the molecule, sequentially joining specific nucleotides until they reach the end of the gene, which stops the RNA chain from growing. High-energy phosphate linkages found in the RNA nucleotide precursors provide energy for RNA synthesis. The final RNA product is basically made up of one phosphate, one base, and one sugar.

When a nucleotide is incorporated into RNA during synthesis, two phosphates are broken down and discarded. The nucleotides are joined by the energy that is released from the phosphate bonds. The key aspect of RNA synthesis is that the sequence of nucleotides in the DNA template determines the sequence of nucleotides joined into an expanding RNA chain: every adenine in DNA specifies uracil in RNA, every cytosine in DNA specifies guanine, every guanine in DNA specifies adenine, and every thymine in DNA specifies adenine. This is how each gene's information is translated from RNA and I further translated by the cytoplasm's protein-synthesizing apparatus.

The nucleotide sequence of DNA contains additional information to define the amino acid sequence that is to be polymerized into proteins. For instance, brief nucleotide sequences identify each RNA polymerase's initiation site, indicating the location and timing of RNA synthesis. The sequences defining the initiation sites for RNA polymerases I and II are located immediately in front of the genes.

In contrast, the gene—that is, the section of DNA that needs to be converted into RNA—contains the corresponding information for RNA polymerase III. In a DNA segment, the promoter is the location of the initiation site, and while some nucleotide sequences are shared by the promoters of distinct genes, others are unique. Transcription factors are specialized proteins that are required for the expression of specific gene types. They are able to detect sequence variations. A factor contributing to the variations in gene expression across various cell types is transcription factor specificity.

1.1.7. Protein Synthesis

DNA is "read" by creating "words" out of three-base sequences that control the synthesis of particular amino acids.

These three-base segments, also referred to as codons or triplets, are positioned along the DNA molecule in a linear fashion. Genes are segments of linear DNA that code for particular proteins. The human genome is the collection of all the genes found in the human population.

The majority of protein synthesis takes place in the cell's cytoplasm, but the majority of DNA is found in the nucleus (a tiny amount is found in the mitochondria).

The genetic information must be transferred from the nucleus into the cytoplasm by a message because DNA molecules are too big to fit through the nuclear membrane. mRNA molecules are tiny, single-stranded nucleic acids carrying the coding information of specific genes, are responsible for carrying this message. The process by which information is converted from DNA to mRNA in the nucleus is known as transcription since each gene's DNA sequence is converted into an RNA that corresponds to it.

After that, the mRNA enters the cytoplasm and initiates the process known as translation, which assembles a particular amino acid sequence to create the gene's protein.

On ribosomes that are either free in the cytoplasm or affixed to the endoplasmic reticulum, translation takes place. With the aid of mRNA and tRNA, the information contained in a protein's DNA controls the synthesis of that protein (Figure 1.4), where the tRNA assists in converting the mRNA message from the nucleus into a protein at the ribosome in the cytoplasm.

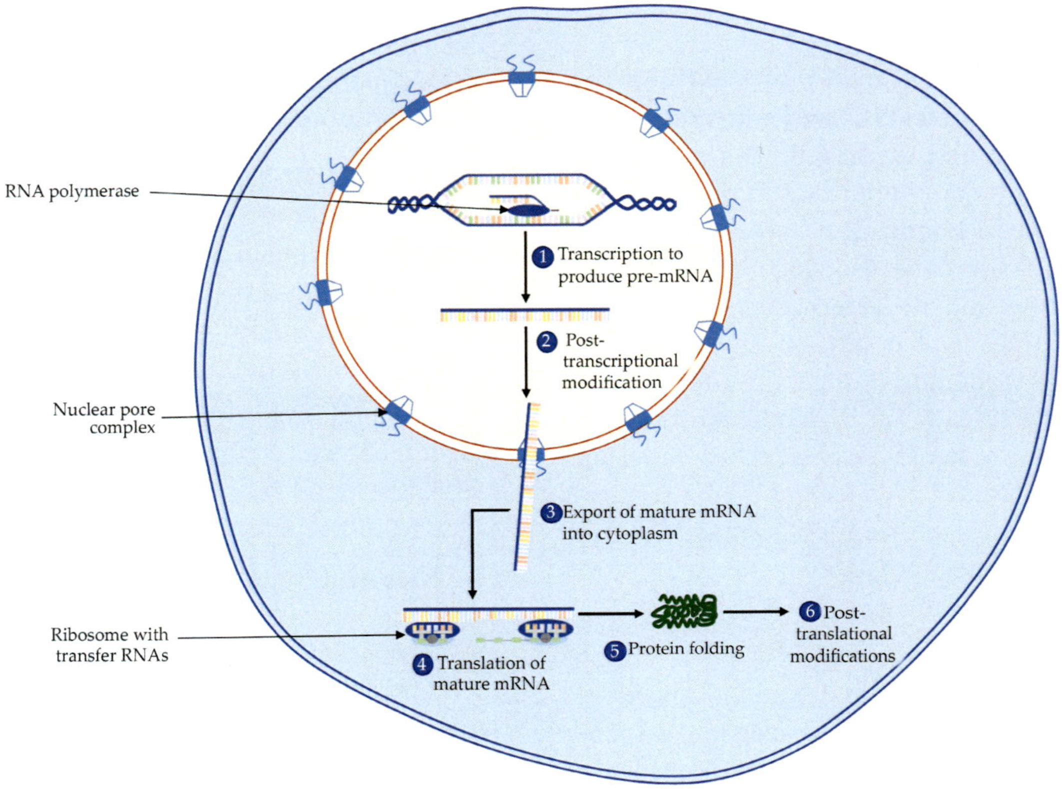

Figure 1.4. *Protein synthesis and translation.*

Source: By Kep17 - Own work, CC BY-SA 4.0, https://commons.wikimedia.org/w/index.php?curid=89042835.

1.1.8. Cytoplasmic Membrane and Its Few Functions

The membrane that lines the inside of a cell and keeps it safe from the outside world (the extracellular space) is called the cell membrane, sometimes known as the plasma membrane, cytoplasmic membrane, or plasmalemma in the past (Figure 1.5).

Furthermore, it contains complex lipids known as steroids, which are absent from prokaryotic membranes (apart from certain mycoplasmas) and resemble the cholesterol molecules found in cell membranes. Sterols help stabilize the membrane, reduce the membrane's permeability to the majority of biological molecules, and possibly give the membranes more rigidity, which helps eukaryotic cells that lack a cell wall withstand osmotic lysis.

The proteins and glycoproteins in the cytoplasmic membrane are quite diverse and function as (Figure 1.6):

- Channel proteins to form pores for the free transport of small molecules and ions across the membrane.

- Carrier proteins for facilitated diffusion and active transport of molecules and ions across the membrane.
- Cell recognition proteins that identifies a particular cell.
- Receptor proteins that bind specific molecules such as hormones and cytokines.
- Enzymatic proteins that catalyze specific chemical reactions.

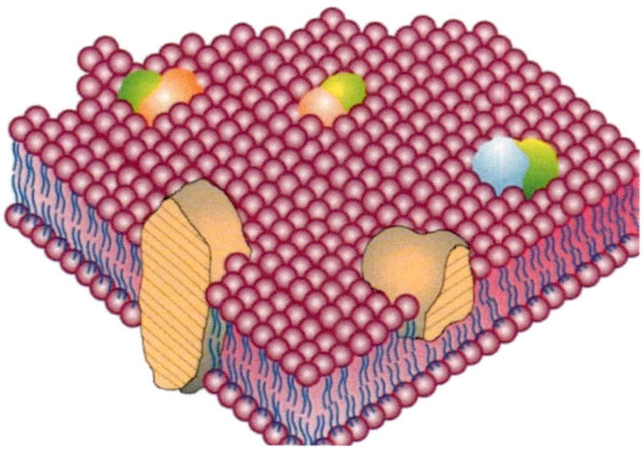

Figure 1.5. *Diagram of a cytoplasmic membrane.*

Source: Nicolson, G. L., & Ferreira, de M. G., (2021). A brief introduction to some aspects of the fluid–mosaic model of cell membrane structure and its importance in membrane lipid replacement. Membranes, 11(12), 947. https://doi.org/10.3390/membranes11120947.

Kinetic energy, or the energy of motion, is present in all molecules and atoms. A concentration gradient is created when molecules or atoms are not equally distributed on both sides of a membrane; this gradient is a type of potential energy or stored energy. Since these particles are moving from an area of higher concentration to one of lower concentration, their net movement will be down their concentration gradient. Metabolic energy is not needed for diffusion to occur because it is driven by the potential energy of a concentration gradient.

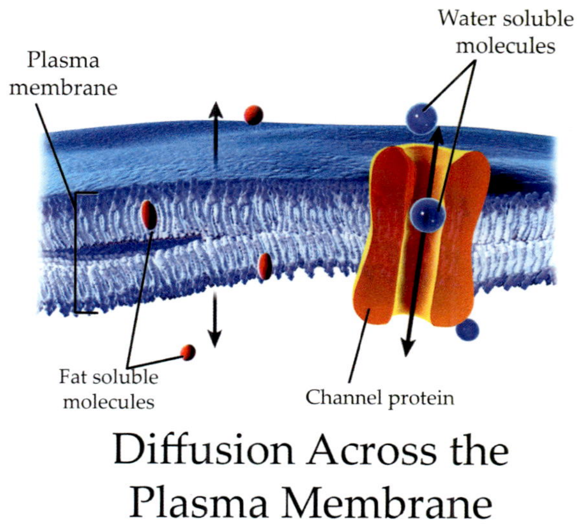

Figure 1.6. *Passive diffusion, Step 1. Passive diffusion is the net movement of gases or small uncharged polar molecules across a phospholipid bilayer membrane from an area of higher concentration to an area of lower concentration. Examples of gases that cross membranes by passive diffusion include N_2, O_2, and CO_2; examples of small polar molecules include ethanol, H_2O, and urea.*

Source: Blausen.com staff (2014). "Medical gallery of Blausen Medical 2014." WikiJournal of Medicine, 1(2). doi: 10.15347/wjm/2014.010. ISSN: 2002-4436 - Own work, CC BY 3.0, https://commons.wikimedia.org/w/index.php?curid=29140354.

1.1.9. Capsules

A capsule is typically a hydrated polysaccharide complex that covers the outermost part of the cell wall and is composed of monosaccharides joined together by glycosidic linkages in most bacteria (Figure 1.7).

Role of bacterial capsules:

- They keep phagocytosis from ingesting and destroying the bacterial cell.

- Capsules make the bacterial surface constituents slippery.
- They allow germs to adhere to surfaces and hide from the immune system by mimicking host tissues,
- They make them resistant to complementing their invasiveness.
- The capsule protects the cell from desiccation and harmful byproducts.

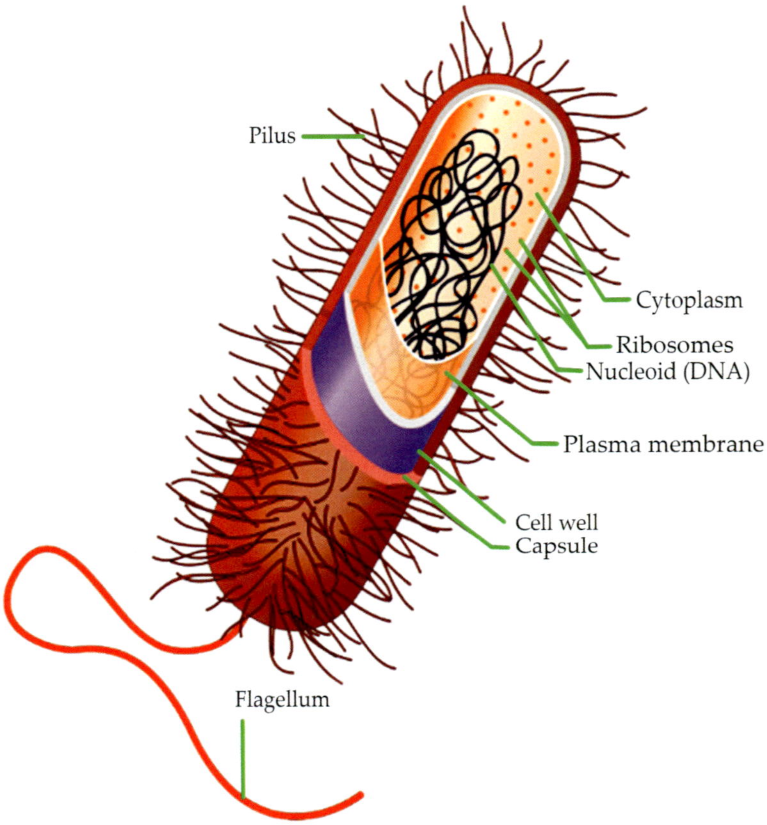

Figure 1.7. *Diagram of a typical prokaryotic cell (cell wall capsule).*

Source: Wikipedia; https://upload.wikimedia.org/wikipedia/commons/thumb/c/c5/Prokaryote_cell.svg/800px-Prokaryote_cell.svg.png.

Gram-negative bacteria's LPS is covered by repeating polysaccharides that are found outside of their cell membranes. These polysaccharides are the usual components of bacterial capsules. Owing to its position as the initial bacterial component to engage with the host, the bacterial capsule performs a variety of functions and is frequently essential in evading host defense mechanisms. In particular, sugar-coated capsules prevent complements from binding to the bacterial surface and cover immunogenic membrane proteins that could otherwise activate immune cells to destroy the pathogen. Although *Francisella tularensis* was reported to have a capsule, it took many years to isolate and characterize the polysaccharide found inside.

The development of a monoclonal antibody that was able to identify the capsule in the F strains Type A and Type B. Studies focused on *F. tularensis* enabled the characterization of this carbohydrate as the F-associated capsule, and since the bacteria contains the same sugars as the O-antigen linked to F, it is regarded as an O-antigen capsule. LPS from *Francisella tularensis*. Utilizing the monoclonal antibody specific to the capsule to screen sizable transposon libraries of *F. tularensis* mutants with replication errors made it possible to identify these mutants in capsules. These findings have identified several loci and genes involved in capsule formation.

It's significant that these studies have also shown that a capsule is necessary for successfully dodging intracellular and extracellular defense systems. First of all, when opsonized and used to infect primary macrophages, capsule mutants are extremely susceptible to removal by serum components. It has been suggested that the mutants' inabillity to avoid being taken up and destroyed by the autophagic machinery of the host cell is the reason why the absence of a capsule initially hinders the replication of unopsonized bacteria in the host cell. Additionally, capsule mutants are slightly attenuated *in vivo* due to their low capacity for replication and sensitivity to serum component-induced killing. Thus, for initial host defense network evasion, the *F. tularensis* capsule is a crucial element.

1.1.10. Sporulation

Sporulation helps organisms adapt to harsh growth conditions and disperse to new, more hospitable environments. It happens in a wide range of organisms, from bacteria and protozoa to plants and fungi. Spores are generally stress-resistant, metabolically quiescent, and ready to proliferate (germinate) under the right growth conditions. These characteristics have been found in eukaryotes and eubacteria, as evidenced by the discovery of culturable fungal spores in arctic ice and ocean sediments that date back hundreds of thousands of years, as well as viable bacterial spores embedded in amber that is tens of millions of years old. It has even been demonstrated that a number of bacterial spore species can endure the vacuum of space. These remarkable qualities demonstrate how spores help a wide range of organisms survive in a wide range of settings.

Spores have been thoroughly studied in several model systems to comprehend how they are endowed with such resilient survival traits. The bacterial sporulation systems that are best understood are those in which cellular differentiation and environmental adaptation are driven by distinct developmental programs. Members of three classes of Gram-positive bacteria, Bacilli, Clostridia, and Negativicutes, produce endospores that are significantly more resistant to a variety of environmental stresses, including heat, desiccation, and ultraviolet (UV) light.

These organisms' resistance to severe environmental conditions stems from their distinct spore composition as well as their specialized, multi-layered surface structures. Critical compositional properties in the extensively researched *Bacillus subtilis* system include a low core water content, high concentrations of dipicolinic acid (DPA) in chelation with divalent cations like Calcium or Ca (CaDPA), a large number of small acid-soluble spore proteins (SASP), and the intrinsic stability of spore proteins as a whole. Theoretically, each of these unique characteristics functions in unison to support spore stability and resistance against adverse environmental circumstances.

Spores therefore have the chance to resume vegetative growth in response to favorable circumstances because of their remarkable capacity for persistence, where they can germinate or return to growing cells when given the right stimulus. During spore germination in. *subtilis*, a number of significant processes occur, such as the release of monovalent cations and CaDPA, the breakdown of PG, and the expansion of the spore core.

Proteomic studies conducted on *B. subtilis* spores reveal that the spores contain proteins necessary for anabolism, stress resistance, and cell signaling. These findings are consistent with the theory that the spores are resistant to environmental stresses and are ready to grow quickly when they receive germination signals. These classes of spore protein components seem to be fairly consistent amongst different species of bacteria; on the other hand, the molecular components that sense and signal germination vary greatly, as do the conditions and compounds that provide the signal to germinate.

Nutrient-stimulated spores can vary significantly in how long it takes to germinate, from minutes to hours or even days, even within the same population. This variant exemplifies the knowledge gaps in bacterial spore biology and is likely to affect the outcome of spore survival. It has been and will remain crucial to comprehend the characteristics of bacterial spores and the circumstances in which they resume vegetative growth in order to ascertain not only the survival of bacteria but also the adaptability of microbes and other spore-forming organisms throughout the branch of life.

Protist and fungal sporulation are also common, but bacterial systems provide the majority of the knowledge about spore biology. Fungi actually make up the majority of the spore-forming organisms on Earth. Fungi are the undisputed masters of spore dispersal because they have developed sophisticated and reliable spore production techniques. It has been demonstrated that fungi can spread throughout the world on wind currents, which explains why fungi are present in almost every ecosystem on Earth.

The model yeast *Saccharomyces cerevisiae* has been used to study sporulation in detail. In this model, sporulation is triggered when diploid cells lack nitrogen while being exposed to a non-fermentable carbon source. Several planned events are included in this developmental program, which combines meiosis with spore biogenesis inside a single mother cell. These events are as follows:

- Chromosome alignment, recombination, and segregation;
- Prospore membrane formation to envelope four newly-produced haploid nuclei; and
- Cell wall assembly outside the four maturing spores.

Although this is one of the best understood processes for creating spores, there are thousands of other ways that fungi can create spores.

For instance, sporulation happens in Aspergillus species through both sexual and asexual development, resulting in thousands of ascospores or conidia per fruiting body. Spores are produced during sexual reproduction in some mushrooms, including *Coprinopsis cinerea*, and are discharged through the gills of fruiting bodies. Diploid spores are produced in planta and disperse before meiosis in plant pathogens like *Ustilago maydis*. Hence, fungal spores can be haploid, diploid, or multinucleate; they can be produced in chains or individually; they can be contained within an ascus; and they can represent mitotic or meiotic products. As they are all adapted to endure harsh environments in their own environmental niches, they all share a number of essential spore characteristics, such as relative metabolic quiescence, stress resistance, and germination ability.

Similar to bacterial spores, fungal spores can be classified into two general categories based on the components that contribute to their unique characteristics and functions: structural and compositional. The spore wall of *S. cerevisiae* is made up of four layers: mannan, β-1,3-glucans, chitosan, and dityrosine molecules. The outer two layers, which are absent from vegetative yeast cell walls, are primarily responsible for the spores' resistance to heat, digesting enzymes, and organic solvents.

Spores have protective small molecules such as betaine, amino acids, glycerol, mannitol, and sugars like trehalose in addition to their relatively thick coat. Lastly, proteins that offer a general advantage in terms of resistance to different kinds of fungal spores under environmental stress include hydrophilins and heat shock proteins.

Spore production can be a lifesaver for certain microorganisms, but the ability to reproduce and survive depends on their ability to germinate or resume vegetative growth in response to favorable environmental factors. Similar to the process of bacterial differentiation, fungal germination is a crucial process that transforms spores from a comparatively dormant particle into a vegetatively growing cell. Typically, a particular set of events occurs during fungal germination, such as modifications to the weight and absorbance of the cells (water uptake), the breakdown of trehalose and mannitol, cell wall remodeling, and the expansion and elongation of the densely packed spore contents.

Different environmental signals (either germinants or inhibitors) elicit different effects on spore germination, depending on the type of spore. For instance, when uredospores from certain rust fungi come into contact with pure water, they begin to germinate. A volatile compound produced by *Penicillium paneum* conidiospores itself prevents their untimely germination.

S. cerevisiae spores germinate easily when a fermentable carbon source is present, while Talaromycesmacrosporus spores need nutrients in addition to a strict external trigger, such as a high temperature of 85°C or a pressure of 400–800 MPa. These signals all reflect the various conditions that fungi must grow in and they sum up the diversity of fungal biology as a whole. The overall conservation of the molecular mechanisms underlying fungal spore germination, as well as the degree to which each strategy is universal or specialized, remain unknown.

Global gene expression profiling of germinating spores has been conducted in several fungi to start understanding molecular events that occur during germination. In *Aspergillus fumigatus* and in *Aspergillus niger*, during conidia germination, there are increases in the transcript levels of genes related to respiratory metabolism, RNA turnover, and protein biosynthesis. Similar transcriptional changes were observed in *S. cerevisiae* during germination, with an overall trend showing up-regulation of genes related to protein folding and transport, and increases in genes involved in the metabolism of glucose and other nutrients. The release from stress responses and the shift to cellular proliferation were both indicated by these changes in gene expression.

The changes in gene expression that occur when *S. cerevisiae* cells grown to stationary phase are transferred to fresh medium and reenter vegetative growth closely resembled the changes in gene expression that were observed. The possibility that germination is primarily a regulated metabolic adaptation rather than a specific differentiation process from one cell type to another is suggested by this metabolic similarity and the apparent absence of germination-specific gene groups.

The fact that the few genes in fungi that have been found to be crucial for spore germination—such as those involved in the Ras/mitogen-activated protein kinase pathway and the transcription factor Ume6—all have vital functions during other phases of the life cycle and are not germination-specific lends further credence to this theory. Furthermore, genes involved in meiotic chromosome behavior, carbon metabolism, vesicle transport, nutrient sensing, and cell wall integrity were among the 158 strains with defects in growth from the spore state that were found by a large-scale genetic screen of the *S. cerevisiae* deletion set. However, it is unclear what specific roles these genes play during germination.

Two novel genes, TRF4 and ERG6, which are involved in the biosynthesis of ergosterol and the degradation of mRNA in the TRAMP complex, were found in a more recent screen for germination mutants. Both genes are involved in the growth of plants. Therefore, it appears that in *S. cerevisiae*, either 1) there may not be specifically germination-specific molecular machinery; rather, fungal spore germination may be facilitated by adaptation of already-existing signaling pathways and regulatory components, or 2) certain germination-process components are so crucial to this survival process that there exists system redundancy that prevents their detection in screens conducted thus far.

In any scenario, gaining a basic understanding of the particular elements, or combinations of already-existing elements, that control germination will offer important new perspectives on how eukaryotes adapt to shifting environmental circumstances and how new cell types are developed as a result.

1.1.11. Genetic Exchange in Bacteria

Bacteria do not have a mandatory sexual reproduction stage in their life cycle, and can therefore exchange genetic information quite actively. From one cell to another, genetic information can be transferred through DNA, however, since only one partner receives the new information, this is not a true exchange. A tiny portion of the chromosome is typically the only DNA that is transferred as well. This is accomplished through multiple mechanisms. Bacteria gather free DNA fragments floating in the medium and use them for transformation.

Bacteria must be in a competent state in order to take up DNA efficiently. This state is characterized by the bacteria's ability to bind free fragments of DNA and is only naturally present in a small number of bacteria, including Haemophilus, Neisseria, *Streptococcus*, and Bacillus. Other bacteria, such as *E. coli*, for example, can be artificially made competent in a lab setting by subjecting it to calcium chloride ($CaCl_2$) solutions. The fragments of DNA from an organism can be absorbed by another, enabling the second organism to take on new traits - transformation is therefore a key tool in recombinant DNA technology.

Transduction is the process by which DNA is transferred from one bacterium to another using a virus known as a bacteriophage. As DNA enclosed in bacteriophages is injected directly into cells by the bacteriophage and is shielded from both physical decay and environmental enzyme attacks, transduction is an effective method of transferring DNA between bacteria. The efficient packaging of bacterial DNA into a virus and the generally narrow range of bacterial species that bacteriophages can infect make widespread gene transfer through transduction. However, this process is of limited significance, resulting in the uncommon practice of transduction-based DNA transfer between species.

DNA is transferred between cells directly through a process called conjugation, which is facilitated by plasmids, known as nonchromosomal DNA molecules. The highly effective mechanism that conjugative plasmids encode allows them to mediate their own transfer from a donor cell to a recipient cell. However, since only the donor cells have the conjugative plasmid, the process is unidirectional. The sex pilus, a plasmid-coded structure that connects donor and recipient cells, is produced by donor cells in gram-negative bacteria. A conjugal bridge forms when the two cells are directly connected, allowing the DNA to be transferred from the donor to the recipient. Numerous different gram-negative bacterial species are capable of accepting and reproducing conjugative plasmids. The number of base pairs in a plasmid can range from a few 1,000 to over 100,000; the latter are sometimes referred to as megaplasmids.

Conjugation can also result in the transfer of the bacterial chromosome, though this is less common than plasmid transfer. Large gene inheritance is made possible by conjugation, which may also be the cause of multi-species-combining traits in bacteria. Although conjugation has also been seen in the gram-positive genus Enterococci, the process by which DNA is transferred and cells are recognized differs from that of gram-negative bacteria.

1.2. Viruses

Microscopic organisms known as viruses are capable of infecting humans, plants, and animals. They are tiny bits of genetic material (DNA or RNA) encased in a capsid, which serves as protective barrier. Moreover, some viruses have an envelope, and require a host in order to reproduce.

Viral infections are caused by viruses, can be contracted by animals, plants, fungi, and humans, and are host-specific. Viral infections in humans can result in either no symptoms or make the host extremely ill. Types of diseases they can cause include:

- Respiratory illnesses;
- Diarrhea and vomiting;
- Sexually transmitted infections (STIs);
- Skin conditions.

Since viruses are not composed of cells, they lack all the machinery that cells have to divide to make new copies of themselves. Rather, they transport instructions and utilize the resources of a host cell to multiply the virus. It is comparable to someone breaking into your home to utilize the kitchen. The virus carried its own recipe with it, but to make it, it needs your dishes, measuring cups, mixer, and oven. Regretfully, when you eventually kick them out, they typically leave behind a huge mess.

1.2.1. General Features

Viruses are classified as a distinct taxonomic group because they do not belong to the same kingdom as plants, animals, or prokaryotic bacteria, which are single-celled organisms without distinct nuclei. In fact, viruses should not even be considered organisms, in the strictest sense, because they are not free-living—i.e., they cannot reproduce and carry on metabolic processes without a host cell. Protein and nucleic acid, either deoxyribonucleic acid (DNA) or ribonucleic acid (RNA), are present in all true viruses. Each virus's specific genetic information is encoded in its nucleic acid. The virion is the infectious, extracellular (found outside the cell) form of a virus, and itt has at least one distinct protein that is produced by particular genes in the virus's nucleic acid. Almost all viruses have at least one of these proteins that envelops the nucleic acid in a shell known as a capsid.

There are additional proteins that are contained within the capsid of some viruses. These proteins frequently function as enzymes when the viral nucleic acid synthesizes. "Virus-like" organisms, or "viroids," are defined as having no structural proteins and only nucleic acid. Proteins and tiny nucleic acids are tightly complexed to form the main component of other virus-like particles known as prions. The degenerative brain disease that prions appear to cause in mammals, including humans, is highly resistant to inactivation. Viruses are classic parasites because they rely almost entirely on their host cell to survive. Viruses lack ribosomes, the cell organelles that facilitate the translation of viral messenger RNA (mRNA) and directs protein synthesis, and are therefore unable to synthesize proteins, in contrast to true organisms. Viral mRNA must be translated into viral proteins by the virus using the ribosomes of their host cells.

Viruses, like cells, are parasites that consume energy. Unlike cells, they are unable to produce or store adenosine triphosphate (ATP), and relies on the host cell to provide the virus with energy and perform their metabolic processes. The invasive virus synthesizes its proteins and nucleic acids using the host cell's nucleotides and amino acids, respectively. Certain viruses utilize the host cell's lipids and sugar chains to create their membranes and glycoproteins, which are proteins connected to brief polymers made up of multiple sugars.

Nucleic acid, which can be either DNA or RNA but never both, is the actual infectious component of any virus. When a virus is stripped of its capsid, the nucleic acid alone—though much less effective than when the virus is intact—can infect (transfect) cells in many, but not all cases.

The capsid of the virion serves three purposes: (i) it shields the viral nucleic acid from being broken down by specific enzymes (nucleases); (ii) it provides sites on the surface of the virus that allow it to attach itself (adsorb) to receptors on the surface of the host cell; and (iii) in certain viruses, it contains proteins that are part of a specialized component that allows the virion to pass through the cell surface membrane or, in rare circumstances, inject the infectious nucleic acid into the interior of the host cell.

1.2.2. Host Range and Distribution

Initially, it made sense to identify viruses based on the hosts they infected. The host range and distribution of viruses is just one criterion for their classification; in many cases, this is justified, but not in others. Viruses that infect bacteria, plants, or animals are still traditionally categorized into three groups.

Almost all plant viruses are spread by insects or other plant-eating animals, or vectors whereas animal viruses can have a variety of hosts, including humans and protozoans, which are single-celled organisms. Many viruses only affect vertebrates, but only some affect invertebrate animals. Arthropods are carriers of certain viruses that can inflict serious illness on humans and animals, and these viruses can spread and proliferate in both their invertebrate vector and their vertebrate host.

Some viruses can only infect different orders of vertebrates as their hosts. Perhaps because they can only reproduce at low temperatures, some viruses seem to be exclusively adapted for growth in ectothermic vertebrates, or cold-blooded animals like fish and reptiles. Other viruses can only infect endothermic vertebrates, or warm-blooded animals like mammals, as their host range.

1.2.3. Size and Shape

The size and shape of viruses are determined by the composition and quantity of their proteins and nucleic acid. A structure known as a nucleoprotein, or nucleocapsid, is formed by the nucleic acid and proteins of each class of viruses assembling together. While the nucleic acid of certain viruses is surrounded by multiple protein layers, the nucleocapsid core of other viruses is surrounded by an envelope, or lipoprotein membrane, that is derived from the host cell's membrane.

Additional proteins that penetrate the membrane control how specific the virus is to its host cells. Each class of virus is distinguished by the characteristics of its constituent proteins and nucleic acids, which, when combined, define the class-specific virus's dimensions and form. Among the largest viruses currently known to science, the genomes of mimiviruses and pandoraviruses range from 1 to 2 point 5 Mb (1 Mb is equal to 1 million base pairs of DNA).

The majority of viruses range in size from 20 nanometers (nm; 0.0000008 inch) to 250–400 nm; the largest, on the other hand, have a diameter of roughly 500 nm and a length of roughly 700–1,000 nm. Under a light microscope, only the largest and most complex viruses can be seen at the highest resolution. Given that different virus classes have unique shapes, any assessment of a virus's size must also consider its shape.

Virus shapes primarily consist of two types: spheres, which are actually 20-sided (icosahedral) polygons, and rods, also known as filaments because of the linear arrangement of the protein subunits and nucleic acid. Like most bacterial viruses, the majority of plant viruses are tiny and either polygons or filaments. Conversely, the larger and more complex bacteriophages combine filamentous and polygonal shapes with double-stranded DNA as their genetic material. A polygonal head housing the DNA genome and a rod-shaped tail with long fibers serving a specific purpose make up the traditional T4 bacteriophage. These structures can only be found in bacteriophages.

Viral organisms can vary greatly in size and form. The smallest animal viruses are comprised of members of the families Paraviridae and Picoraviridae and are approximately 20 nm and 30 nm in diameter, respectively. Icosahedron viruses belonging to these two families have limited genetic information in their nucleic acids. Viruses in the Poxviridae family have the longest lengths of between 250 and 400 nm and have neither filaments nor polygons. Even though they resemble simple bacteria, poxviruses are structurally more complex.

Included in the families Paramyxoviridae, Orthomyxoviridae, Coronavirides, and Rhabdoviridae are animal viruses with envelope-enclosed nucleocapsids that have a rod-shaped (helical) nuclear structure. Herpesviridae, Retroviridae, and Togaviridae viruses are examples of enveloped viruses that have polygonal nucleocapsids rather than helical ones. Rhabdoviruses are long, cylinder-shaped viruses, but the majority of enveloped viruses seem to be spherical.

The criteria used for classifying viruses into families and genera are primarily based on three structural considerations: (i) the type and size of their nucleic acid; (ii) the shape and size of the capsids; and (iii) the presence of a lipid envelope, derived from the host cell, surrounding the viral nucleocapsid.

1.2.3.1. The Nucleic Acid

As is the case with all living forms, every virus's nucleic acid contains the genetic code needed to synthesize every protein. The genetic material of nearly all free-living organisms is double-stranded DNA, which is arranged as a spiral lattice and joined at the bases all the way along the molecule (a double helix). However, genetic material can exist in viruses in a number of forms, such as single- or double-stranded DNA or RNA.

Virion genomes are composed of their nucleic acids. All double-stranded DNA viruses are made up of a single large molecule, but the majority of double-stranded RNA viruses have genomes that are divided into segments, each of which typically contains a single gene that codes for the synthesis of a single protein. Viruses that possess single-stranded genomic DNA typically have a small genetic information content. Certain viruses that only contain one strand of complementary single-stranded DNA have two populations of virions, one of which has the opposite polarity to the other.

Single-stranded RNA makes up the majority of plant viruses' virions as well as those of numerous animal and bacterial viruses. Because the genomic RNA functions as mRNA for the direct synthesis (translation) of viral protein, it is known as a positive strand in the majority of these viruses. However, genomic single-stranded RNA, also known as a negative strand, is complementary to mRNA and can be found in several large families of animal viruses, including the Rabdoviridae, which includes both plant and animal viruses. The synthesis of complementary mRNA from the virion genomic RNA is a prerequisite for the synthesis of viral proteins in all of these negative-strand RNA viruses. This enzyme is known as an RNA-dependent RNA polymerase (transcriptase). These differences in virus nucleic acids serve as a primary classification criterion for all viruses. Retroviridae is the name of a unique, large family of single-stranded RNA viruses. Although the RNA strands of these viruses are positive, they possess an enzyme called reverse transcriptase, which copies the RNA strands to create double-stranded DNA.

1.2.3.2. The Protein Capsid

The second primary criterion for classifying viruses is provided by their protein capsule. Capsomeres, a limited number of protein subunits that typically bind to or are present in close proximity to the virion nucleic acid, make up the capsid, which envelops the virus.

Based on the protein capsid, viruses fall into two main categories: (i) those in which a single (or segmented) linear nucleic acid molecule with two free ends is more or less completely extended, forming a helix; and (ii) those in which the nucleic acid, which might or might not be a covalently closed circle, is tightly wound into a condensed configuration, resembling a ball of yarn. These two virus classes assume an extended, long rod-like structure in the first instance and a symmetrical polygon in the second.

The tobacco mosaic virus, which was crystallized by Wendell Stanley in 1935, is by far the most researched example of a helical rod-shaped virus. With 2,130 molecules of a single protein encasing a genome of single-stranded RNA, the tobacco mosaic virus has 161/3 protein molecules for every turn of the RNA helix, or three nucleotides for every protein molecule.

Protein and RNA molecules from viruses in liquid suspension will combine to form a fully functional and contagious virus in the correct conditions. Since the nucleic acid molecule serves as the structural foundation for the assembly of the capsid protein, the length of the helical virus capsid is determined by its length. The variations in the mass and shape of the protein molecule, nucleic acid size, and other factors, result in the production of helical viruses differing in length and width. Depending on the characteristics of the assembled proteins, certain helical viruses result in stiff rods and others in flexible rods.

Polygonal viruses range widely in diameter from 20 to 150 nm, which is roughly proportional to the size of the coiled nucleic acid molecule inside the virion. As with a geodesic dome, the majority, if not all, of polygonal viruses are icosahedral, formed by 20 equilateral triangles.

These protein subunits, known as capsomeres, make up each triangle, and are the fundamental units of the capsid which are frequently hexons, or multiples of six.

A penton (five subunits) is comprised of each of the 12 vertices, which are the apical junctions of these 20 triangles. The three axes of rotational symmetry of these icosahedral virions are threefold, threefold, and twofold. These virus families are categorized taxonomically based on the number of capsomeres they contain. Intracellular proteins that cling to the nucleic acid in some icosahedral viruses—typically the more complex ones—are inaccessible at the virions' surface.

1.2.3.3. The Lipoprotein Envelope

The unit membranes of two lipid layers containing protein molecules (lipoprotein bilayer) that surround viruses with helical or icosahedral symmetry. Budding is the process by which these viruses create their neutral lipids, mostly cholesterol and phospholipids, from cell membranes.

Nevertheless, during budding, almost all of the proteins in the cell membrane are changed out for proteins that come from viruses. Although the cell is the source of all viral envelope lipids, the viral proteins selectively choose specific lipids during budding, causing differences in their relative proportions from those in the cell membrane.

"Peripheral" matrix proteins border the inner surface of the lipid bilayer and "integral" glycoproteins that span the entire bilayer are linked to the virion membrane. Regions of amino acids found in the glycoproteins are responsible for the initial recognition of host-cell receptors by the virus during infection. Matrix proteins seem to have a role in both helping the virion enter cells and choosing which areas of the cell membrane to use as the viral membrane.

1.2.4. The Cycle of Infection

A virus can replicate only in the host cell, and many progeny produced by the parental virus (virion), are typically structurally and genetically identical to the parent virus. The virus's behavior is determined by the environment as well as its propensity for causing harm to a particular host cell. Progeny viruses can multiply quickly during the vegetative phase of a viral infection, and this infection cycle frequently causes the cell to die and releases a large number of virus progeny.

Since some viruses, especially bacteriophages, do not cause cell death right away, they are referred to as temperate (or latent) viruses. The genetic material of the virus either stays dormant or gets incorporated into the host cell's genome. The term "lysogenic" refers to cells infected with temperate viruses because these cells have a propensity to degrade in response to chemical or physical stimuli, such as ultraviolet light.

Furthermore, a lot of plant and animal viruses, whose genetic material is not incorporated into the DNA of their hosts, can remain dormant in tissues for extended periods of time without doing much, if any, harm to the tissues. Not all viral infections cause tissue damage or cell death; in fact, the majority of viruses either remain dormant in tissue for a long time without ever causing pathological effects, or they only do so in response to other, frequently environmental, stimuli.

There are some fundamental ideas and a specific sequence of events in the infection cycle for the majority of viruses, if not all of them, despite the fact that the reproductive pathways of different viruses vary greatly. The invasive parental virus (virion) must first adhere to the host cell's surface through a process known as adsorption in order to begin the infection cycle.

In the second stage, the intact virion either injects the virus's genetic material into the interior of the cell while the protein capsid (and envelope, if present) stays at the cell surface, or it breaks through the outer membrane and enters the cytoplasm of the cell. When whole-virion penetration occurs, the genetic material from the capsid and envelope, if any, is released by a later step called uncoating. In either scenario, the genetic material of the virus cannot start producing protein until it has detached from the envelope or capsid.

A complex process of infection has evolved in certain bacterial viruses, like the T4 bacteriophage. The flexible tail of the virus contracts and pierces the cell wall and underlying membrane to inject virus (phage) DNA into the cell after its tail has been adsorbed and firmly attached to the bacterium surface by proteinaceous "pins." Various methods are used by other bacteriophages to breach the cell membrane, such as injecting nucleic acid through the bacterium's male (sex) pili. Viral nucleic acid is transmitted through the stiff bacterial cell wall by penetration in all bacterial viruses.

Additionally, plant viruses are typically unable to penetrate the tough cell walls found in plant cells. In contrast, plant viruses are spread by the proboscis of insects that feed on plants because they lack the ability to transfer nucleic acids into host cells on their own. Plant viruses can enter laboratory plants if the walls of the cells have been worn down by sandpaper or if the cell protoplasts—the nucleus, cytoplasm, and plasma membrane—have no walls.

Since animal cells lack cell walls and are instead surrounded by a flexible lipoprotein bilayer membrane, there are distinct processes involved in the penetration of viruses into animal cells. The majority of animal viruses use a process known as endocytosis to enter cells in an intact state, whether or not they are covered in lipid envelopes. A virus particle that has been adsorbed onto a cell is typically invaginated and engulfed by the membrane in an area known as a coated pit, which is lined by a unique protein called clathrin.

A coated vesicle is created when the coated pit is pinched off in the cytoplasm during invagination. The coated vesicle merges with lysosomes and cytoplasmic endosomes, which are membrane-enclosed vesicles containing enzymes. The viral nucleocapsid is released into the cytoplasm when the membrane of an enveloped virus fuses with the endosome membrane in an acidic environment. Similar processes, involving the degradation of the protein capsid and the release of the naked viral nucleic acid into the cytoplasm, are probably followed by nonenveloped viruses.

Several virus classes have different sequences for the phases of viral replication that come after the genome is uncoated. Viral mRNA is produced by transcription of the virus's genome and occurs in the third stage of the infection cycle of many virus families, while translation of the viral mRNA into proteins occurs in the fourth stage.

In the case of viruses where the genomic nucleic acid is an RNA intermediate (i.e., positive-strand RNA viruses), the RNA is translated into viral proteins in the third step. Some of these newly created viral proteins are polymerase enzymes, which synthesize nucleic acids and carry out the transcription of additional mRNA from the viral genome in the fourth step.

In the case of more complex DNA viruses, like adenoviruses and herpesviruses, specific genomic regions produce "early" mRNAs. These mRNAs are then translated into polymerases, which start the transcription of "late" DNA regions into mRNAs that are subsequently translated into structural proteins.

Replication is the fifth stage in the infection cycle, and it happens regardless of how the third and fourth steps go. Replication is the process of reproducing the parental genome to create progeny genomes. The assembling of the freshly replicated progeny genomes with structural proteins to create fully formed progeny virions is the sixth step.

Seventh and final step: depending on the type of virus, extrusion or budding may be used to lyse the host cell and release progeny virions. This seventh-step can occur repeatedly in a host animal or cell culture; the progeny virions released from the initial infection site subsequently spread to other locations or to different people.

All cytoplasmic replication processes occur for the majority of RNA viruses found in plants and animals; in fact, a large number of these viruses can proliferate in host cells that have had their nuclei removed. The majority of DNA viruses found in plants and animals, along with the RNA influenza virus, replicate in the nucleus. These viruses have a nucleus for transcription, a cytoplasm for mRNA translation, and a nucleus for the assembly of newly replicated progeny genomes with the help of these viral proteins. Generally speaking, certain amino acid sequences known as "signals" are responsible for the migration of freshly translated viral proteins from the cytoplasm to the nucleus. These signals can cause the protein to move through pores in the nucleus membrane.

1.3. Fungi

Living things that are categorized differently from plants and animals are called fungi. They can travel by dispersing or releasing spores—reproductive parts—into the atmosphere or surrounding areas,. Numerous fungi are naturally found in our bodies including in the mouth, GI tract, and skin, and in some situations, they can proliferate uncontrollably. Only a tiny percentage of the millions of fungi that are thought to exist in the world are known to be harmful to humans, according to scientists. Mycosis, or fungus-related infections, are illnesses brought on by mold or yeast. Though they can affect your mouth, throat, lungs, urinary tract, and many other areas of your body, fungi (plural of fungus) are most commonly found infecting skin and nails.

Skin infections caused by fungi can appear red, swollen, or rough, and they may resemble a rash or be visible as a lump beneath your skin. A result of fungus infections may include your nails becoming thick, cracked, or discolored (yellow, brown, or white) and the presence of white coating or patches in your mouth or throat.

A fungal infection can strike anyone, particularly if it affects the skin or nails. Fungal infections are more prevalent in areas of the body where there is a lot of friction or moisture retention. If you have diabetes, poor circulation, or a compromised immune system, you're more vulnerable to infections, especially the severe ones, including:

- HIV/AIDS;
- Cancer or cancer treatments;
- Immunosuppressant medications (for autoimmune conditions or organ, stem cell or bone marrow transplants).

Nowadays, one of the hardest diseases to treat in humans is fungal infections. Certain types of fungi can cause disease in healthy individuals, but the majority of fungal infections happen to people who are already seriously ill. These infections often compromise the effectiveness of the most recent medical advancements in the treatment of cancer, solid organ and hematopoietic stem cell transplantation, neonatal medicine, autoimmune disease therapies, trauma and intensive care, and advanced surgery. Actually, the very nature of these medical advancements frequently leaves their recipients open to fungal illness. In patients who are susceptible, such as very preterm newborns who survive long enough to contract a fungal infection, treatment options may include suppressing normal immune functions.

1.4. Parasitism in Humans

Diseases in humans and other animals have been linked to numerous pathogenic fungi, which are parasitic on humans. The most common way for parasitic fungi to enter a human body is through an epidermal (skin) wound. These wounds could be scratches, cuts, or bruises that happened by accident, or they could be insect bites. A fungal disease (ergotism) that affects humans is caused by *Claviceps purpurea*, which is the cause of ergotism (sometimes referred to as St. rye-bread consumption, such as Anthony's fire), and a disease that was common in northern Europe during the Middle Ages.

Fungal spores of ergot are carried by the wind to the rye flowers, where they germinate, infect and destroy the plant's ovaries, and replace them with masses of microscopic threads cemented together into a hard fungal structure resembling a dark, hard rye kernel. Several toxic organic substances known as alkaloids are found inside this structure, which is known as an ergot.

In addition to non-infected kernels, a mature head of rye may contain multiple ergots. A portion of the ergot stays on the plants and is combined with the grain after the grain is harvested, with the majority falling to the ground. Modern grain-cleaning and milling techniques have all but eradicated the disease, but if the ergot is not removed prior to milling, contaminated flour could find its way into bread and other food products.

Cattle that are allowed to graze in rye fields following harvest may also eat the ergot that falls to the ground, and can result in death in both cattle and fetuses alike. A fresh round of infections is initiated in the spring, when the rye is in bloom, by the tiny, black, mushroom-shaped bodies of ergot that remain on the ground and release a lot of spores.

Ringworm, aspergillosis, histoplasmosis, coccidioidomycosis, and athlete's foot are among the other human illnesses brought on by fungi. If the yeast *Candida albicans* is in ecological balance with other digestive system microbes, it does not cause disease as it is a normal resident of the human mouth, throat, colon, and reproductive organs. That being said, it can also result from age, illness, or hormonal changes. The body's defense mechanisms are unable to stop *C. albicans* from growing, which causes candidiasis, also known as thrush, when it affects the mouth. The symptoms of candidiasis range from persistent inflammatory skin lesions or elevated white patches on the tongue to a potentially fatal invasive infection that harms the brain or heart lining. Fungal disease in humans has become more common as a result of better diagnosis and more international travel, the latter of which has allowed tropical pathogenic fungi to spread. Furthermore, medication-assisted immune system management in cancer and transplant recipients compromises the body's resistance to fungi. A number of AIDS-related deaths are brought on by fungal infections, particularly those caused by *A. fumigatus*. Patients infected with the human immunodeficiency virus (HIV), the agent responsible for causing acquired immunodeficiency syndrome (AIDS), also have similarly compromised immune defenses against fungi.

1.4.1. What Do Parasites Do to Your Body?

Microorganisms that lie in, on, or live in another organism (host) are called parasites. They require their host to survive and inflict damage when they feed, grow, or multiply. Although they rarely kill their host, they frequently spread diseases that can be fatal.

The three main types of parasites that cause disease in people include:

1. **Ectoparasites:** An ectoparasite is a parasite that lives on the outside (exterior) of its host. They're vectors (living things that carry diseases between animals and humans) that usually carry infections through blood. Many creatures that healthcare providers classify as vectors feed on your blood. They generally include:
   - **Fleas:** These are small, wingless insects with strong back legs that they use to jump long distances. Infected fleas can spread disease when they bite their host or if a host accidentally swallows an infected flea.
   - **Head Lice and Pubic Lice (Crabs):** Lice are tiny, flat insects that travel by crawling. Head lice live on the hair on your head. Pubic lice live in your pubic hair, near your genitals. Both types of lice travel from person to person through close contact, which may include sexual intercourse or sharing personal items like sheets, pillows or towels.
   - **Mites:** These are small arachnids (eight-legged arthropods) that are relatives of spiders and ticks. They're smaller than 1 millimeter (0.04 inches, about as tall as a stack of 10 sheets of paper). Certain types may cause scabies.
   - **Ticks:** These are arachnids. Their bites usually don't cause pain or itchiness. They typically bite you and then burrow into your skin. They're common in wooded areas or grassy fields.
2. **Helminths:** The parasitic worms known as helminths typically reside in the gastrointestinal (GI) tract. Your GI tract consists of your stomach, small intestine, and large intestine, as well as other hollow organs that join together from your mouth to your anus. When helminths reach adulthood, they can be seen with the unaided eye. Their sizes vary from over 1 millimeter to overthan 1 meter, or slightly longer than 39 inches and narrower than a doorway.

   The main types of helminths that affect people include:
   - **Flukes (Trematodes):** Flukes are a type of flatworm. They can spread through contaminated water or aquatic animals, including snails, crabs and fish. There are many different types of flukes, and they may infect your blood, urinary bladder, liver, lungs, intestines and other organs.
   - **Tapeworms (Cestodes):** Adult tapeworms are long, flat worms that live in the intestines. They feed off the nutrients that their host gets from eating food. They spread by laying eggs in their host's body. The eggs then leave the host's body when the host poops. The eggs spread through infected food and water or undercooked meat.
   - **Roundworms (Nematodes):**

These are small parasites that live in your intestines. They spread from infected poop or soil. There are many different types of roundworms.

3. Protozoans: The organisms known as protozoa are unicellular, and a microscope is required to see them. Your intestines, blood, and tissues could be home to them. Contaminated food or water, direct contact between individuals, or vector bites are some of the ways in which they can spread.

   There are tens of thousands of different types of protozoans. Experts classify them according to how they move. The main types that affect people include:

   - **Amoeba:** These form temporary "false feet" (pseudopods) to move. The amoeba *Entamoeba histolytica* causes dysentery.
   - **Ciliates:** These use many short, hairlike structures (cilia) to move and gather food. *Balantidium coli* is the only ciliate that affects people. It causes dysentery.
   - **Flagellates:** These use one or many whip-like structures (flagella) to move and sense their surroundings. The flagellate *Giardia intestinalis* causes giardiasis, and *Trypanosoma brucei* causes sleeping sickness.
   - **Sporozoans (Apicomplexan):** In their adult stage, sporozoans aren't capable of moving. They eat the food their host is digesting or their host's body fluids. The sporozoan *Plasmodium* causes malaria, and *Cryptosporidium* causes cryptosporidiosis.

It is common to have parasites and parasite infections. Around the globe, they have an impact on millions of people. Since most infections have minimal symptoms, many people might not even be aware that they have one, in contrary there could be others that may cause grave illnesses.

1.4.2. Symptoms and Causes

1.4.2.1. What Are Parasite Symptoms in Humans?

There are many different types of parasites, so their symptoms can vary. Common parasite symptoms may include:

- Diarrhea;
- Nausea and vomiting;
- Abdominal pain;
- Unexplained weight loss;
- Increased appetite;
- Muscle aches;
- Fever;
- Chills;
- Problems sleeping (insomnia);
- Fatigue;
- Weakness;
- Skin rash.

You may have a parasite and no symptoms, or the symptoms may appear a long time after infection. You may also not have any symptoms and accidentally pass a parasite to another person who develops symptoms.

1.4.2.2. What Foods Cause Parasites?

Common food sources of parasites include:

- Raw or undercooked meat, including fish;
- Raw or unwashed fruits and vegetables;

- Raw aquatic plants, such as watercress;
- Unpasteurized milk and juices.

1.4.2.3. How Do People Get Parasites?

Common causes of parasitic infections include:

- Spending time in areas with known parasites.
- Contaminated water, foods, soil, blood or feces (poop).
- Not washing your hands before eating or drinking.
- Washing or bathing infrequently.
- Having a weak immune system.
- Contaminated bug bites.
- Sexual contact.

A Closer Look

Perspective of Clinical Microbiology

The clinical specialty of clinical microbiology is the study of diseases that affect humans and are brought on by microorganisms such as bacteria, viruses, fungi, and parasites. It is associated with the study of disease pathology and immunology and encompasses the study of microbial pathogenesis and epidemiology. It is a specialty that includes clinical management and prevention of microbial diseases in addition to laboratory diagnostic aspects.

The goal of the Clinical Microbiology curriculum is to give students a thorough education in medical virology, medical microbiology, infection prevention and control, and infectious diseases. Clinical Microbiology trainees need to learn a few fundamental skills that are necessary for practicing medicine well in addition to these specialty-specific components. The curriculum's general components are made up of these.

In order to control and treat infectious organisms in patients, clinical microbiology focuses on isolating and characterizing them. Bacteria, fungi, viruses, and parasites can all cause infections. Patient samples must be taken at a site where the presence of a pathogen or related biomarkers is likely to indicate disease to diagnose an infection. The specimen needs to be delivered to the lab in a way that will protect it for the planned tests. Next, a sensitive and specific test for the suspected disease-causing organism must be performed on the specimen. In order for a clinician to properly interpret and respond to these findings, they must be returned to them.

One could argue that the field of clinical microbiology was the pioneer of personalized medicine. For instance, a patient may exhibit increased urgency, frequency, and pain during urination, all of which are indicative of a urinary tract infection. A sample of urine is taken, and it is quantitatively cultured. The clinical microbiology lab reports the type and amount of bacteria found in the urine in less than a day. A couple of days later, the lab reports on the patient's bacterial isolate's resistance to a range of antibiotics that are authorized for the treatment of UTIs. The doctor treating the patient can then select an antibiotic based on the likelihood of effectiveness against the patient's infection.

Summary

- Clinical microbiology is a discipline that encompasses a broad range of testing methodologies, and it is complex in terms of organisms and methods used to isolate and identify them.
- Bacteria are microscopic living organisms that have only one cell. The word for just one is "bacterium." Millions (if not billions) of different types of bacteria can be found all over the world, including in your body.
- The bacterial cell wall is a complex, mesh-like structure that in most bacteria is essential for maintenance of cell shape and structural integrity.
- The cell walls of gram positive bacteria are composed predominantly of peptidoglycan. In fact, peptidoglycan can represent up to 90% of the cell wall, with layer after layer forming around the cell membrane.
- The cell walls of gram negative bacteria are more complex than that of gram positive bacteria, with more ingredients overall. They do contain peptidoglycan as well, although only a couple of layers, representing 5-10% of the total cell wall.
- Bacterial physiology encompasses the study of the vital processes and functions that sustain bacterial life. At its core, bacterial physiology explores the diverse metabolic pathways, cellular structures, and regulatory mechanisms that enable bacteria to thrive in various environments.
- The cell membrane (also known as the plasma membrane or cytoplasmic membrane, and historically referred to as the plasmalemma) is a biological membrane that separates and protects the interior of a cell from the outside environment (the extracellular space).
- Bacterial capsules are typically made up of repeating polysaccharides located outside the cell membranes and in the case of gram-negative bacteria cover the lipopolysaccharide (LPS).
- Sporulation occurs in organisms across the tree of life from bacteria and protozoa to plants and fungi and facilitates both survival in response to adverse growth conditions and dispersal to new, more hospitable environments.

References

1. Forbes, B. A., Sahm, D. F., & Weissfeld, A. S., (2007). *Bailey & Scott's Diagnostic Microbiology*. Mosby.
2. Garcia, L. S., (2015). *Clinical Microbiology Procedures Handbook.* ASM Press.
3. Jawetz, M., Adelberg, E. A., & Brooks, G. F., (2019). *Jawetz, Melnick & Adelberg's Medical Microbiology.* McGraw-Hill Education.
4. Leboffe, M. J., & Pierce, B. E., (2018). *A Photographic Atlas for the Microbiology Laboratory*. Morton Publishing Company.
5. Mahon, C. R., Lehman, D. C., & Manuselis, G., (2014). *Textbook of Diagnostic Microbiology*. Saunders.

6. Murray, P. R., Baron, E. J., Jorgensen, J. H., Landry, M. L., & Pfaller, M. A., (2015). *Manual of Clinical Microbiology*. ASM Press.
7. Murray, P. R., Rosenthal, K. S., & Pfaller, M. A., (2021). *Medical Microbiology*. Elsevier.
8. Tille, P. M., (2017). *Bailey & Scott's Diagnostic Microbiology.* Elsevier.
9. Versalovic, J., Carroll, K. C., Funke, G., Jorgensen, J. H., & Landry, M. L., (2018). *Manual of Clinical Microbiology*. ASM Press.
10. Wilson, B. A., & Salyers, A. A., (2011). *Bacterial Pathogenesis: A Molecular Approach*. ASM Press.

Chapter

TUBERCULOSIS

2

Contents

Unit Introduction

The infectious disease tuberculosis (TB) is a potentially fatal illness that is caused by the *Mycobacterium tuberculosis* bacteria. Although it can affect other organs in the body, the lungs are the primary organ affected by this airborne pathogen. Even with tremendous progress in medicine and healthcare, TB continues to be a major global health issue, especially in developing nations. According to the World Health Organization (WHO), TB affects about 10 million people annually worldwide and is still one of the top 10 causes of death worldwide.

M. tuberculosis are present in respiratory droplets that can be inhaled and cause TB. People nearby may get infected when an infected person coughs, sneezes, or talks because these droplets are released into the air. The transmission of tuberculosis more likely occurs in situations where there is inadequate ventilation, living quarters that are packed, and immune systems that are weakened. A major obstacle to the efficient control and treatment of TB is the emergence of drug-resistant strains of the bacterium. The fact that TB is an infection that can be both active and latent is one of its unique characteristics. People with active TB may have fever, night sweats, weight loss, and a chronic cough, and if left untreated, the disease can advance quickly and result in serious complications, and possibly death. On the other hand, latent TB arises when people carry the bacteria but do not show any symptoms. Although it is not communicable, it has the potential to become active over time, particularly in cases where the immune system is compromised.

Beyond the individual level, TB has an impact on society and the economy. Vulnerable groups are disproportionately affected by TB, such as the impoverished, those with weakened immune systems, and marginalized communities. Due to its tendency to affect people who are already socioeconomically disadvantaged, the illness perpetuates a cycle of poverty. Moreover, the extended TB treatment regimen may lead to a decrease in earnings and efficiency, thereby intensifying the financial strain on impacted individuals and societies.

A multimodal strategy is used to fight TB, which includes early detection, quick treatment, and preventive measures. The identification of people with latent or active TB depends heavily on diagnostic instruments like the tuberculin skin test and more recent molecular tests. In order to prevent the emergence of drug-resistant strains, treatment usually entails a combination of antibiotics administered over an extended period of time. It is crucial to ensure patient adherence to the entire course of medication.

One example of a preventive measure is the Bacillus Calmette-Guérin (BCG) vaccine, which is given in many nations where tuberculosis is highly prevalent. The vaccination does not, however, offer lifetime immunity, and its effectiveness varies. Research and development activities are still concentrated on developing more potent vaccinations and treatment plans, as well as approaches to deal with drug-resistant tuberculosis.

The goal of global programs like the WHO's End TB Strategy is to lower the incidence and mortality of TB. These initiatives include improving research and development, fortifying healthcare systems, and tackling socioeconomic factors that contribute to tuberculosis, such as deprivation and substandard housing. Given that TB is a global disease, cooperation between governments, international organizations, and the private sector is essential.

Millions of people and communities worldwide are still impacted by TB, which continues to be a major global health concern, and it is a formidable adversary due to the complex interplay of medical, social, and economic factors. To achieve meaningful progress in its prevention, diagnosis, and treatment, comprehensive and collaborative efforts are required. The burden of TB needs to be addressed as a top priority on the global health agenda as the world works toward health equity.

Orientation and Directional Terms

Terms	Definition	Illustration
BCG	A vaccine for TB named after the French scientists who developed it, Calmette and Guérin. BCG is rarely used in the United States, but it is often given to infants and small children in other countries where TB is common.	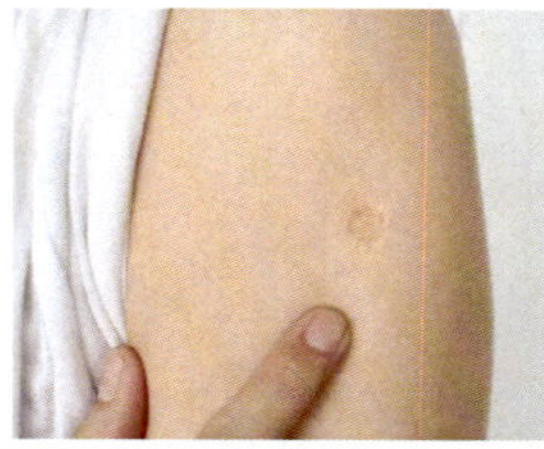
Chest X-ray	A picture of the inside of your chest. A chest X-ray is made by exposing a film to x-rays that pass through the chest. A doctor can look at this film to see whether TB bacteria have damaged the lungs.	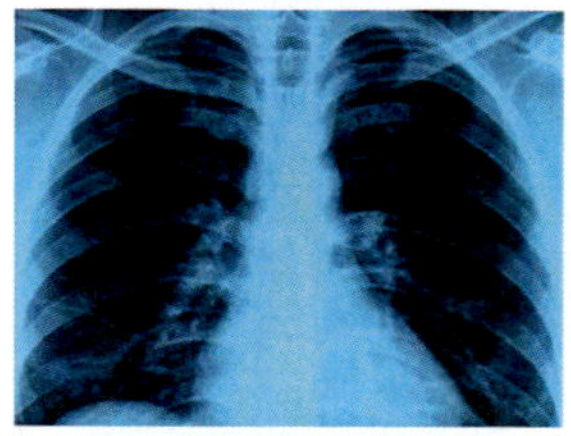
Extensively drug-resistant TB (XDR TB)	XDR TB is a rare type of TB disease that is resistant to nearly all medicines used to treat TB.	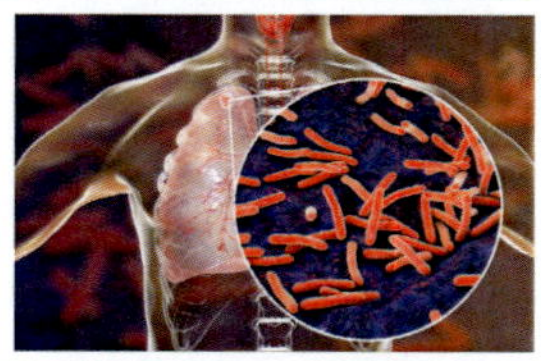
Extrapulmonary TB	TB disease in any part of the body other than the lungs (for example, the kidney, spine, brain, or lymph nodes).	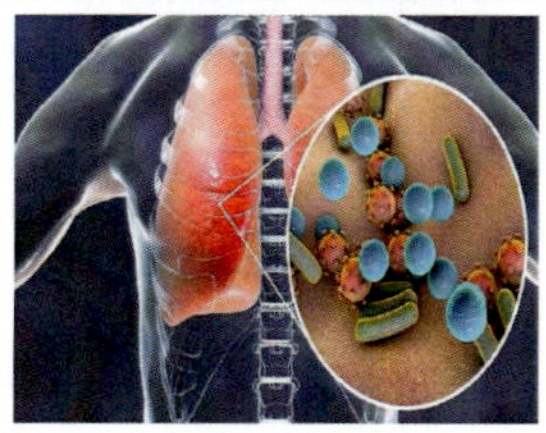
Latent TB infection	A condition in which TB bacteria are alive, but inactive in the body. People with latent TB infection have no symptoms, don't feel sick, can't spread TB to others, and usually have a positive TB skin test or positive TB blood test reaction. However, they may develop TB disease if they do not receive treatment for latent TB infection.	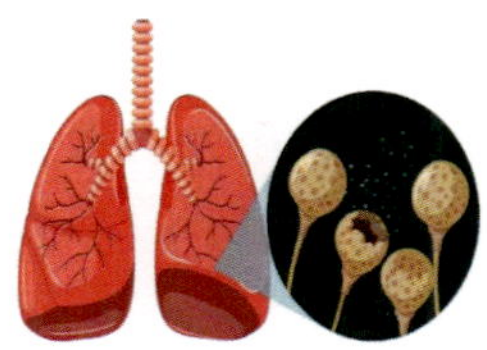
Pulmonary TB	TB disease that occurs in the lungs, usually producing a cough that lasts 3 weeks or longer. Most TB disease is pulmonary.	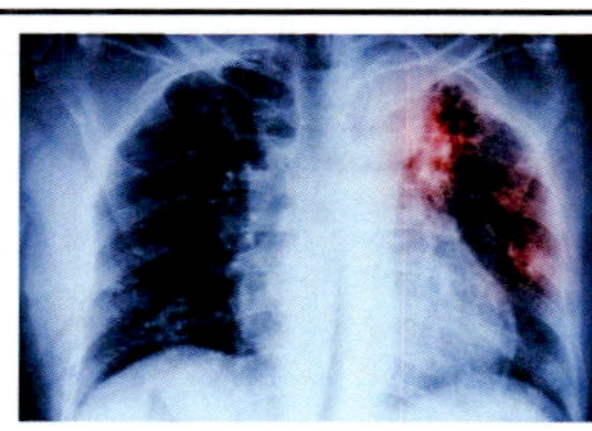

2.1. Overview of Tuberculosis

M. tuberculosis (MTB) bacteria is typically the cause of TB, and was previously referred to as "white death" or "consumption". Although it can affect other parts of the body as well, TB usually affects the lungs. While most infections are referred to as latent TB when no symptoms are present, approximately 10% of dormant infections develop into active illnesses, which kill roughly 50% of victims if treatment is not received. Frequent signs of active TB include fever, night sweats, weight loss, and a persistent cough with blood-containing mucus. A wide range of symptoms can arise from infection in other organs.

TB is spread through the air from one person to another when people with active TB in the lungs cough, spit, talk, or sneeze. People with latent TB do not spread the disease, while active infections occur more frequently in people with HIV/AIDS and in smokers. The diagnosis of active TB is based on chest x-rays and microscopic examination, and the culture of body fluids, while the diagnosis of latent TB is based on the tuberculin skin test (TST) or blood tests.

The prevention of TB includes immunizing against the bacillus Calmette-Guérin (BCG) vaccine, early case detection and treatment, and screening of high-risk individuals. A person's home, place of employment, and social contacts who have active TB are among those who are at high risk. An extended course of treatment necessitates the use of several antibiotics, however as the rates of multiple drug-resistant tuberculosis (MDR-TB) rise, antibiotic resistance becomes an increasingly pressing issue.

An estimated 21.0 billion people worldwide, or one-third of the population, have TB caused by *M. tuberculosis*, and over 9 million new cases are reported each year. Among all infectious agents combined, TB is the leading cause of death. Approximately 10 cases per 100,000 people are affected by the disease annually in countries like the UK, whereas over 200 cases per 100,000 people are affected in Africa. The rate in the countries of origin is reflected in a breakdown of incidence among various ethnic groups in the UK. The rates of ethnic minorities categorized as Black African, Indian subcontinent, and Caribbean are >150, >50, and 20–30 per 100,000, respectively.

TB treatment is lengthy—it takes at least six months. Under-resourced treatment delivery and monitoring services can lead to significant problems with patient compliance and the breeding ground for bacteria resistant to antibiotics. After two months of treatment with isoniazid (INH), rifampicin, pyrazinamide, and ethambutol, INH and rifampicin are continued together for 4 to 10 months, depending on the infection site.

Resistance to rifampicin and INH is the minimum requirement for MDR-TB; occasionally, resistance to ethambutol and/or pyrazinamide is also present. TB that is highly resistant to drugs (XDR-TB) can withstand at least INH, rifampicin, and two second-line medications, including a fluoroquinolone (e.g., moxifloxacin), as well as an injectable medication (capreomycin, kanamycin, or amikacin). Concerns about treatment and infection control in the hospital and community are paramount when it comes to patients with MDR or XDR TB.

In addition to affecting the individual, TB has complicated medical and social ramifications for family, the workplace, the hospital, and social networks. Human immunodeficiency virus (HIV) infection is a significant risk factor for the development of active TB. That being said, the highest case rates are found in nations where this virus is highly prevalent. It is imperative to promptly identify the individual suffering from open pulmonary disease to stop the organism from spreading to other people. The clinical diagnosis of tuberculosis can be clearly seen in a patient who has a persistent cough, weight loss, fever, and a chest X-ray that is typical of the disease. The diagnosis can be verified by a positive microscopy result. A chest X-ray is reviewed belatedly or when a chronic cough is noticed, but sadly, patients are still admitted to the hospital for other reasons, and it is not until days later that pulmonary TB is finally diagnosed. Anyone with a persistent cough needs to have TB taken into consideration. Although certain patients have no obvious risk, others may have risk factors such as living in a high-incidence area, being of African descent, having HIV, or being an alcoholic. Patients and staff may have been exposed to open pulmonary TB for weeks before the infection is recognized and diagnosed. This happens frequently in healthcare professionals who have a persistent cough.

2.1.1. History of Tuberculosis

Since ancient times, there has been TB. The earliest *M. tuberculosis* that has been conclusively identified indicates that the disease existed in bison remains found in Wyoming approximately 17,000 years ago. But it's still unclear if TB infection begun in cows and further spread to humans, or if TB in humans and cattle diverged from a common ancestor. Contrary to what was previously thought, humans did not acquire MTBC from animals during animal domestication, according to a comparison of the genes of the *M. tuberculosis* complex (MTBC) in humans and MTBC in animals. There is a common ancestor between the two strains of TB bacteria, and this ancestor may have infected people before the Neolithic Revolution. Researchers have discovered tubercular decay in the spines of Egyptian mummies dating from 3000 to 2400 BC, and skeletal remains indicate that some prehistoric humans (4000 BC) suffered from TB. Genetics research indicates that tuberculosis TB was present in the Americas as early as AD 100.

2.1.1.1. Identification

Due to the wide range of symptoms, TB was not recognized as a single disease until the 1820s, despite the fact that Richard Morton established the pulmonary form associated with tubercles as a pathology in 1689. In 1720, Benjamin Marten postulated that microbes transmitted by individuals residing in close proximity to one another were responsible for consumption. René Laennec asserted in 1819 that pulmonary TB was caused by tubercles. J. L. In 1832, Schönlein published the term "tuberculosis" (German: Tuberkulose) for the first time.

John Croghan, who had owned Mammoth Cave in Kentucky from 1839 onward, brought several TB patients into the cave between 1838 and 1845 in the hopes that the consistent temperature and pure air would cure the illness; all of the patients passed away within a year. In 1859, Hermann Brehmer established the first TB sanatorium in Görbersdorf, Silesia (now Sokołowsko). In 1865, it was shown by Jean Antoine Villemin that animals could contract TB from one another and from humans through inoculation.

2.1.1.2. Development of Treatments

In Europe, TB rates peaked in the 1800s, accounting for almost 25% of all deaths, after starting to rise in the early 1600s. During the 18th and 19th centuries, TB had spread throughout Europe and was exhibiting a seasonal trend. As the disease spread among the urban poor in the 19th and early 20th centuries, TB became a major public health concern. In England, "consumption" accounted for one out of every four deaths in 1815. In 1918, TB accounted for one in six fatalities in France. Following the discovery that TB was contagious, it was listed as a notifiable disease in Britain in the 1880s. Public health campaigns were launched to discourage public spitting and to "encourage" infected individuals to enter prison-like sanatoria, which provided superior medical care and round-the-clock care to middle-class and upper-class residents. Even in the best of circumstances, half of those who entered the sanatoria died within five years, regardless of the advantages of the "fresh air" and labor there (c. 1916).

Robert Koch postponed identifying contaminated milk as a source of infection because he did not think the diseases caused by TB in cattle and humans were similar. Following the application of the pasteurization process, the risk of transmission from this source was significantly decreased during the first half of the 1900s.

In 1890, Koch introduced "tuberculin," a glycerine extract of the tubercle bacilli, as a "treatment" for TB. It was later successfully modified as a screening test for the presence of pre-symptomatic tuberculosis, despite its initial ineffectiveness. Every year on March 24, the anniversary of Koch's initial scientific announcement, people celebrate World Tuberculosis Day. In 1913, the British Medical Research Council was established with a primary focus on TB research.

In 1906, Albert Calmette and Camille Guérin used attenuated bovine-strain TB to achieve the first real success in TB immunization. It was referred to as BCG or bacille Calmette-Guérin. After World War II, the BCG vaccine was finally widely accepted in the US, Great Britain, and Germany.

It was first administered to humans in France in 1921, however approximately 90% fewer people died in Europe by the 1950s. Even before the discovery of streptomycin and other antibiotics, advances in vaccination, sanitation, and other public health initiatives started to dramatically lower TB rates, though the illness was still a serious concern. Effective TB treatment and curing became possible in 1946 with the discovery of the antibiotic streptomycin. The "pneumothorax technique," which included collapsing an infected lung to "rest" while allowing TB lesions to heal, was one of the only treatments available prior to the introduction of this medication.

2.1.1.3. Current Reemergence

Surgery has been reinstated for some TB infections due to the rise in MDR-TB. In order to decrease the amount of bacteria and increase the exposure of the remaining bacteria to antibiotics in the bloodstream, it entails the removal of infected chest cavities ("bullae") in the lungs. When drug-resistant strains of TB emerged in the 1980s, hopes of its eradication were dashed. The WHO declared a global health emergency in 1993 as a result of the subsequent resurgence of TB.

2.1.1.4. Signs and Symptoms

TB most frequently affects the lungs (pulmonary TB), however it can also develop outside of the lungs (extrapulmonary TB) where the two variation can coexist. Fever, chills, night sweats, appetite loss, weight loss, and exhaustion are examples of general signs and symptoms of TB. Importantly, nail clubbing might also take place (Figure 2.1).

The following lists the primary symptoms of TB at different variations and stages. Many of these symptoms are shared by multiple variants, while some are more (though not totally) unique to a particular variant. It is possible that more than one variation exists at once. A TB infection occurs when the germs from the disease survive and grow in the lungs. There are three stages to a TB infection and every stage has a different set of symptoms.

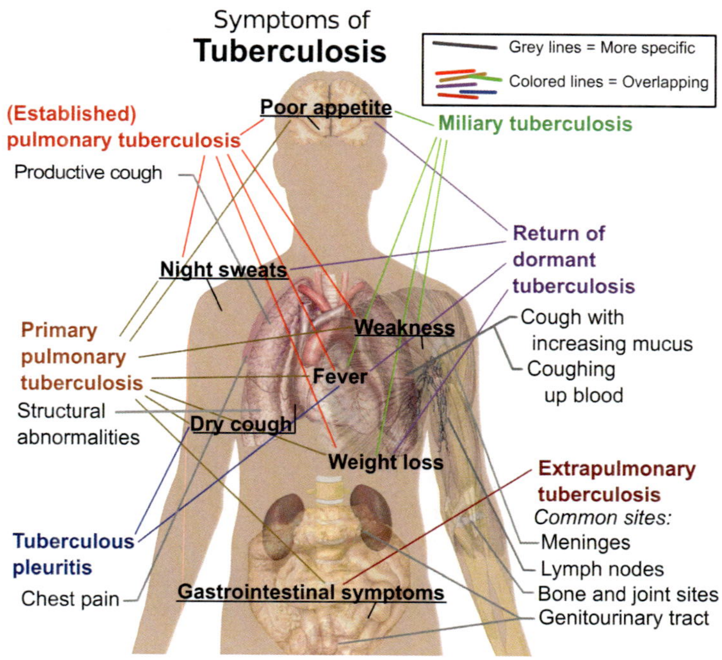

Figure 2.1. *Symptoms of tuberculosis.*

Source: Häggström, M., (2014). "Medical gallery of Mikael Häggström 2014." WikiJournal of Medicine, 1(2). doi: 10.15347/wjm/2014.008. ISSN: 2002-4436. Public Domain or By Mikael Häggström, used with permission. All used images are in public domain. Public Domain, https://commons.wikimedia.org/w/index.php?curid=6919871.

1. **Primary Infection with TB:** The initial phase is referred to as the primary infection. Immune system cells locate and seize the pathogens. The germs might be entirely destroyed by the immune system. However, some trapped germs might continue to exist and proliferate. A primary infection usually causes no symptoms at all for most people. Some persons may experience flu-like symptoms, like the following.
   - Low fever;
   - Tiredness;
   - Cough.

i. **Active TB Illness:** When an infection gets out of hand, the immune system becomes active and causes TB. The disease spreads throughout the body, including the lungs, due to germs, and following a primary infection, active TB disease may develop. However, latent TB infection lasting months or years is usually the cause. Active TB symptoms in the lungs typically start out mildly and get worse over a few weeks. Some of them might be:
   - Cough;
   - Coughing up blood or mucus;
   - Chest pain;
   - Pain with breathing or coughing;

- Fever;
- Chills;
- Night sweats;
- Weight loss;
- Not wanting to eat;
- Tiredness;
- Not feeling well in general.

ii. **Active TB Disease Outside the Lungs:** TB infection can spread from the lungs to other parts of the body (extrapulmonary TB). Symptoms vary depending on what part of the body is infected. Common symptoms may include:

- Fever;
- Chills;
- Night sweats;
- Weight loss;
- Not wanting to eat;
- Tiredness;
- Not feeling well in general;
- Pain near the site of infection.

Active TB disease in the voice box is outside the lungs, but it exhibits symptoms more similar to that of the diseased lungs.

Common sites of active TB disease outside the lungs include:

- Kidneys;
- Liver;
- Fluid surrounding the brain and spinal cord;
- Heart muscles;
- Genitals;
- Lymph nodes;
- Bones and joints;
- Skin;
- Walls of blood vessels;
- Voice box, also called larynx.

iii. **Active TB Disease in Children:** Symptoms of active TB disease in children vary. Typically, symptoms by age may include the following:

- **Teenagers:** Symptoms are similar to adult symptoms.
- **1- to 12-Year-Olds:** Younger children may have a fever that won't go away and weight loss.
- **Infants:** The baby doesn't grow or gain weight as expected. Also, a baby may have symptoms from swelling in the fluid around the brain or spinal cord, including:
  - Being sluggish or not active.
  - Unusually fussy.
  - Vomiting.
  - Poor feeding.
  - Bulging soft spot on the head.
  - Poor reflexes.

2. **Pulmonary TB:** If a TB infection does materialize, it usually affects the lungs (about 90% of cases). Chest pain and a persistent cough with sputum production are possible symptoms. About 25% of individuals might not exhibit any symptoms at all (i.e., they don't exhibit any symptoms). Rarely, the infection may erode into the pulmonary artery or a Rasmussen's aneurysm, causing massive bleeding. People may occasionally cough up small amounts of blood. Extensive scarring in the upper lobes of the lungs can result from TB, which can further develop into a chronic illness. More often than not, TB affects the upper rather than the lower lung lobes. This cause of this discrepancy is still unclear, but it is believed it might be the result of either inadequate

lymph drainage in the upper lungs or improved air flow.

3. **Extrapulmonary TB:** In 15%–20% of active cases, the infection spreads to the lungs and results in the development of different types of TB, where all of these conditions are referred to as extrapulmonary TB. The latter is more common in young children and those with compromised immune systems. This happens in more than 50% of cases involving HIV-positive individuals. The lymphatic system (in scrofula of the neck), the genitourinary system (in urogenital TB), the pleura (in TB pleurisy), the central nervous system (in TB meningitis), the bones and joints (in Pott disease of the spine), and others are notable extrapulmonary infection sites. "Disseminated tuberculosis," also referred to as "miliary tuberculosis," is a potentially more dangerous and common type of TB. Currently, 10% of extrapulmonary cases of TB are attributed to miliary cases.

Under a microscope, researchers can identify MTB from expectorated samples of phlegm (also known as sputum) using histological stains. MTB is categorized as an acid-fast bacillus since some strains can remain after being exposed to an acidic solution. The most popular methods for staining acid-fast bacteria are the Ziehl-Neelsen stain and the Kinyoun stain, which give the bacteria a vivid red color that contrasts with a blue background. Fluorescence microscopy and uramine-rhodamine staining are also employed. Four additional mycobacteria that cause tuberculosis are included in the *M. tuberculosis* complex (MTBC): *Mycobacterium bovis*, *Mycobacterium africanum*, *Mycobacterium canettii*, and *Mycobacterium microti*. While *M. africanum* is not common, except in some regions of Africa, it is a major cause of TB. In developed nations, the prevalence of TB caused by *M. bovis* has nearly completely disappeared since pasteurized milk was introduced. *M. canettii* is uncommon and appears to be restricted to the Horn of Africa, though some African immigrants have reported having the condition.

Mycobacterium microti is also uncommon and almost exclusively observed in immunocompromised individuals; however, the prevalence of this condition may be greatly underestimated. The pathogenic mycobacteria *Mycobacterium leprae*, *Mycobacterium avium*, and *Mycobacterium kansasii* are among the other known varieties. The last two species are categorized as atypical mycobacteria or "nontuberculous mycobacteria" (NTM). Leprosy and TB are not caused by NTM, but they do cause lung conditions that mimic TB.

2.1.1.5. Transmission

Individuals with active pulmonary TB cough, sneeze, speak, sing, or spit out infectious aerosol droplets that range in diameter from 0.5 to 5 µm. Up to 40,000 droplets can be released with a single sneeze. As the infectious dose of TB is very low (the inhalation of fewer than 10 bacteria may cause an infection), each of these droplets has the potential to spread the disease.

2.1.1.6. Risk of Transmission

With an estimated 22% infection rate, people who have close, frequent, or prolonged contact with TB patients are particularly vulnerable to contracting the disease. A person who has active but untreated TB has the potential to infect 10–15 or more people annually. Only individuals with active TB can transmit the disease while latent infections are not considered transmissible. The number of infectious droplets expelled by the carrier, the efficiency of ventilation, the length of exposure, the virulence of the *M. tuberculosis* strain, the degree of immunity in the uninfected person, and other factors all affect the likelihood of transmission from one person to another. Person-to-person transmission can be prevented by placing individuals with active (or "overt") TB in isolation and starting them on anti-TB medication regimens. Subjects with nonresistant active infections typically stop being contagious following two weeks of effective treatment. In most cases, it takes three to four weeks for an individual to contract the disease and become contagious enough to spread to other people.

2.1.1.7. Risk Factors

A number of factors make individuals more susceptible to TB infection and/or disease:

1. **Active Disease Risk:** Concurrent HIV infection is the major risk factor for developing active tuberculosis (TB); 13% of patients with TB also have HIV infection. Given the high prevalence of HIV infection in sub-Saharan Africa, this is a particularly problematic area. About 5–10% of people with TB who are not HIV positive go on to develop active disease during their lifetimes; in contrast, 30% of people develop the active disease when co-infected with HIV. Using specific drugs, like anti-αTNF monoclonal antibody infliximab and corticosteroids, is another significant risk factor, particularly in developed nations.

   Additional risk factors include: alcoholism; diabetes mellitus (three times higher risk); silicosis (30 times higher risk); tobacco smoking (2 times higher risk); indoor air pollution; malnourishment; early age; recent TB infection; recreational drug use; severe kidney disease; low body weight; organ transplant; head and neck cancer; and genetic susceptibility (the relative importance of genetic risk factors is still a matter of debate).

2. **Infection Susceptibility:** Tobacco smoking increases the risk of infections (in addition to increasing the risk of active disease and death). Additional factors increasing infection susceptibility include young age.

2.2. Organisms

Throughout billions of years, organisms—the fundamental units of life on Earth—have developed into a remarkable diversity. Organisms come in a wide variety of shapes, sizes, and functions, ranging from microscopic bacteria to enormous trees and intricate animals. Biology is the study of living things. It focuses on their traits, interactions, and behaviors to reveal the complex web of life. Cellular structure is the foundation of every organism. Many times regarded as the fundamental building block of life, the cell is actually a complex system that performs vital tasks for the organism's survival and procreation. In contrast to eukaryotic cells, which have a distinct nucleus and are found in plants, animals, fungi, and protists, prokaryotic cells lack a defined nucleus and are represented by bacteria and archaea. The diversity of cells found in organisms is a reflection of the many ways that life has adapted to occupy various ecological niches and environments.

Organisms are classified using a hierarchical framework comprising domains, kingdoms, phyla, classes, orders, families, genera, and species. This methodical process, called taxonomy, offers a framework for comprehending the shared traits and evolutionary relationships between organisms. The diversity that exists both within and across these taxonomic groups is indicative of the processes of evolution that have molded life on Earth.

An essential idea in organism life is adaptation. Natural selection, a process driven by environmental pressures, causes organisms to change over generations in terms of behaviors and traits. Advantageous traits increase an individual's chances of surviving, procreating, and passing those traits on to their progeny. The extraordinary diversity and complexity found in the natural world are the result of this never-ending cycle of adaptation. Organisms engage in complex interactions with their surroundings. Ecological relationships that characterize the interdependence of species within ecosystems include mutualism, commensalism, parasitism, and predation. These interactions emphasize the delicate balance that keeps life on Earth alive. Two important aspects of these interactions are the flow of energy and the cycling of nutrients in ecosystems. An organism's ability to reproduce is what makes it unique and ensures the survival of its species.

Sexual reproduction adds genetic diversity by combining genetic material from two parent organisms, whereas asexual reproduction creates offspring without the fusion of gametes. The different ways that organisms reproduce are a reflection of their evolutionary history.

Genetic drift, selective pressures, and genetic mutations all play a dynamic role in the evolution of organisms. The existence and disappearance of innumerable species are revealed by the fossil record, which offers a window into the evolutionary history of life. Our comprehension of the mechanisms underlying evolutionary change has been further enhanced by research in molecular biology and genetics.

The impact of human activity on ecosystems and organisms is growing in the modern era. Threats to biodiversity include overexploitation, pollution, climate change, and habitat destruction. Aiming to protect threatened species and their environments, conservation efforts highlight the significance of preserving ecological balance and the interdependence of all living things. The creatures, sculpted over enormous periods of time by evolutionary processes, stand for the astounding diversity of life on Earth. All types of organisms, from microscopic to massive, are vital to ecosystems and the complex web of life. Preserving biodiversity and maintaining the sustainability of our planet require an understanding of their biology, interactions, and adaptations.

Mycobacterium is a genus of bacteria that includes several significant species. Table 2.1 classifies these organisms along with some of the diseases they can cause. Gram-positive or gram-negative, all mycobacteria are rod-shaped, obligate aerobic, non-spore-forming organisms. Because mycobacteria are "acid fast" and stain a deep magenta color when exposed to Ziehl-Neelsen (ZN) stain, they are also known as acid-fast bacilli (AFB). Figure 2.2 shows the steps involved in ZN staining. The composition of the cell wall, which consists of complex lipids and mycolic acids, renders the material acid-fast.

The carbol-fuchsin stain is forced into the cell by heating, which then forms a complex with mycolic acid to prevent acid alcohol from decolorizing the organism. A photomicrograph of *M. tuberculosis* in a sputum specimen stained using the ZN technique is displayed in Figure 2.3. Figure 2.4 depicts an outline of the cell wall structure of *M. tuberculosis*, where the pathogenic characteristics of TB caused by the bacteria is attributed to components of the cell wall.

Table 2.1. *Mycobacteria are Broadly Grouped into Tuberculous and Non-Tuberculous Groups**

Organism	Diseases Usually Associated with
Tuberculous – these are a public health risk *Mycobacterium tuberculosis.*	Tuberculosis (pulmonary, miliary, etc.).
Mycobacterium bovis	Bovine-derived tuberculosis.
Non-tuberculous – are not a public health risk Mycobacterium avium/ intracellulare.	All these organisms are ubiquitous in the environment Pulmonary disease in patients with pre-existing lung disease (COPD, bronchiectasis), plus disseminated disease in HIV patients; AIDS-defining illness.
Mycobacterium chelonae	Can cause disease in the lung, skin, soft tissue, or bone in individuals who are immunocompromised or following trauma. A 'rapid grower.'
Mycobacterium kansasii	Chronic pulmonary lung disease simulating tuberculosis, can be disseminated in HIV patients.
Mycobacterium malmoense	Pulmonary disease of patients with pre-existing lung disease.
Mycobacterium marinum	Skin and joint infections from salt or fresh water, especially of the hands of those who keep tropical fish. Considered to be more common in lifeguards as well. Can disseminate to other joints in immunosuppressed individuals.

*Some features of important members are outlined.

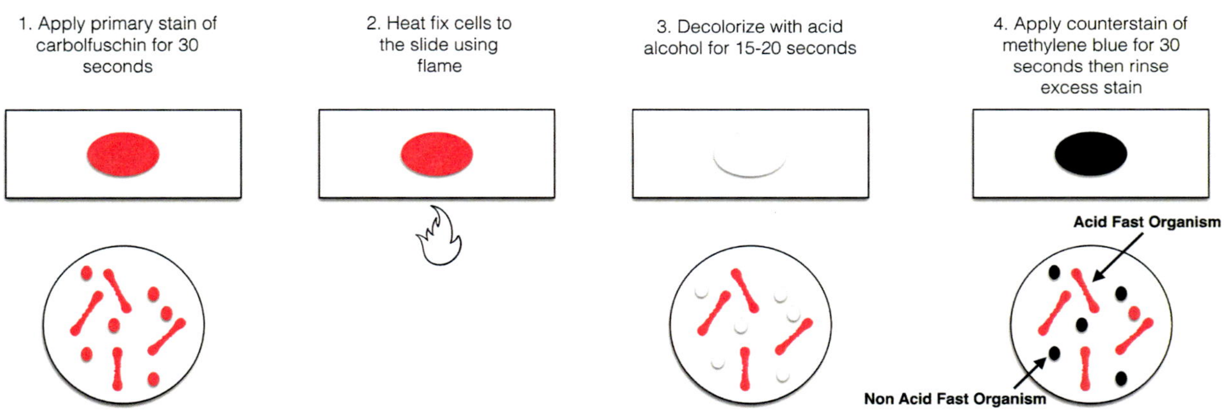

Figure 2.2. *The Ziehl–Neelsen stain. Carbol fuchsin enters the organism in the heating process. The subsequent decolorization step is unable to remove the stain.*

Source: By Elizabeth Gray – File: CC BY-SA 4.0, https://commons.wikimedia.org/w/index.php?curid=135137580.

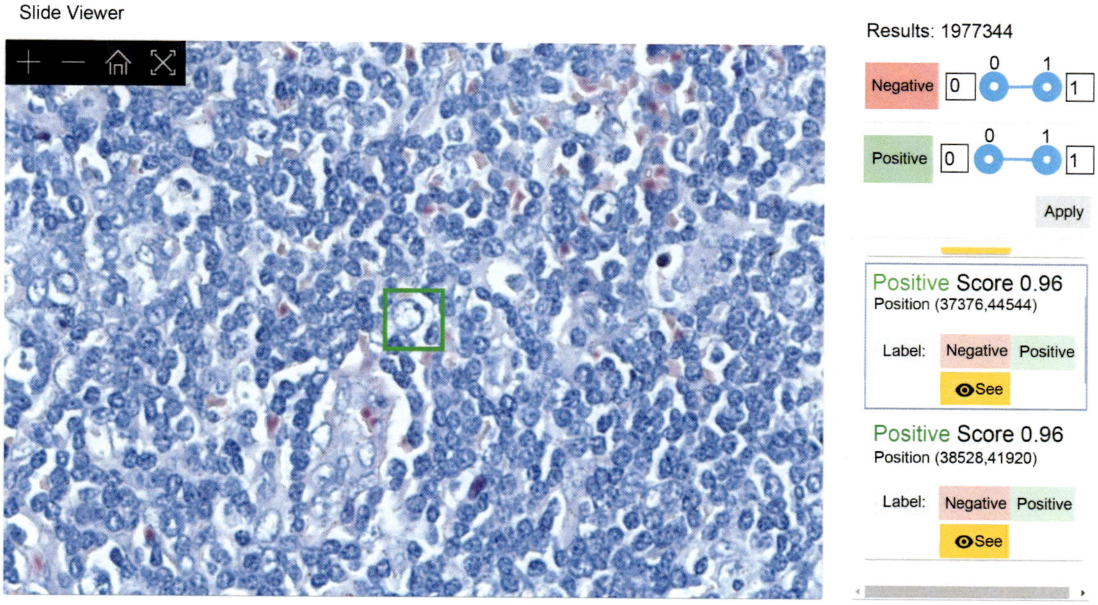

Figure 2.3. *A photomicrograph of a sputum specimen stained by the Ziehl–Neelsen method. Numerous acid-fast bacilli are seen against the blue background.*

Source: Zurac, S., Mogodici, C., Poncu, T., Trăscău, M., Popp, C., Nichita, L., Cioplea, M., Ceachi, B., Sticlaru, L., Cioroianu, A., et al., (2022). A new artificial intelligence-based method for identifying Mycobacterium tuberculosis in Ziehl–Neelsen stain on tissue. Diagnostics, 12(6), 1484. https://doi.org/10.3390/diagnostics12061484.

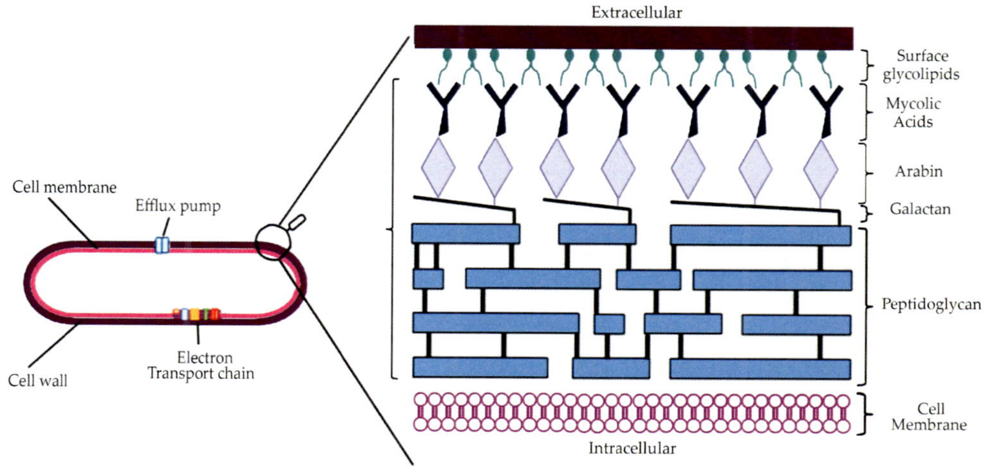

Figure 2.4. *The structural components of the cell wall are important pathogenic properties of Mycobacterium tuberculosis.*

Source: Capela, R., Félix, R., Clariano, M., Nunes, D., Perry, M. D. J., & Lopes, F., (2023). Target identification in anti-tuberculosis drug discovery. International Journal of Molecular Sciences, 24(13), 10482. https://doi.org/10.3390/ijms241310482.

2.2.1. Active TB

It is challenging to diagnose active TB based solely on signs and symptoms, as well as to diagnose the illness in people with compromised immune systems. However, individuals exhibiting symptoms of lung disease or experiencing constitutional symptoms for more than two weeks should be evaluated for a TB diagnosis. The initial evaluation usually includes multiple sputum cultures for acid-fast bacilli and a chest X-ray. Most of the developing world finds little use for tuberculin skin tests and interferon-γ release assays (IGRA). IGRA limits are comparable for HIV-positive individuals.

A definitive diagnosis of TB is made by identifying *M. tuberculosis* in a clinical sample (e.g., pus, sputum, or a tissue sample). However, blood or sputum cultures for this slow-growing organism can be challenging and require two to six weeks to complete. As a result, therapy frequently starts before cultures are verified. Adenosine deaminase testing and nucleic acid amplification tests may enable a speedy diagnosis of tuberculosis. Antibody-detecting blood tests are not advised because they are neither sensitive nor specific.

2.2.1.1. Latent Tuberculosis

Individuals who are at a high risk of TB can be screened using the *Mantoux* skin test. Test results from those who have previously received the BCC vaccine however could be falsely positive. Those suffering from *sarcoidosis*, *Hodgkin's lymphoma*, malnourishment, and most significantly, active TB, may have a false negative test result. It is advised to perform *interferon gamma release assays* on a blood sample in individuals who test positive for the *Mantoux* virus. These produce fewer false-positive results because they are unaffected by vaccination or the majority of environmental mycobacteria.

On the other hand, *Mycobacterium szulgai*, *Mycobacterium marinum*, and *M. kansasii* have an impact on them. When combined with the skin test, *IGRAs* have the potential to enhance sensitivity; however, when used in isolation, they may have the opposite effect. People who are highly susceptible to latent TB should be screened using either *interferon-gamma release assays* or *tuberculin skin tests*, according to the *US Preventive Services Task Force (USPSTF)*. Although testing healthcare workers has been suggested by some, there is currently little evidence to support this as of 2019. The annual testing of health certificates is no longer advised by the *Centers for Disease Control and Prevention (CDC)*.

2.3. Pathogenesis

Pathogenesis is the term used to describe the intricate process by which diseases start and spread within the body. This process includes interactions between the infectious agent, the host, and the environment. For efficient diagnosis, treatment, and preventative measures, it is essential to comprehend the pathophysiology of diseases. A pathogen's introduction into the host organism frequently marks the start of the pathogenesis process. Microorganisms such as bacteria, viruses, fungi, parasites, and others that have the capacity to spread disease, are referred to as pathogens and are determined by their virulence factors or characteristics that make it easier for it to infiltrate and get past the host's defenses. Adhesion molecules, poisons, and immune-evading techniques are a few examples of these.

An important part of pathogenesis is the host's reaction to the pathogen. As the first line of defense, the immune system identifies and eliminates infections. Nonetheless, a pathogen's capacity to thwart or elude the host's immune system frequently determines how well it can spread illness. Important roles are played by variables like the host's overall health, immune system, and genetic predispositions in determining how this interaction turns out. Pathogens may cause collateral damage during the pathogenesis process by inducing a heightened immune response or by directly damaging host tissues. Numerous diseases share the characteristic of inflammation, and the degree of the illness can be influenced by the fine balance that exists between the immune response's beneficial and detrimental components. The pathogenesis can also be attributed to environmental factors, which could include the general living environment, lifestyle decisions, and exposure to toxins and pollutants. Environmental factors can influence a person's susceptibility to infections or play a role in the emergence of chronic illnesses. The idea of the "disease continuum" captures pathogenesis's dynamic character, where diseases often worsen over time.

A complex process that involves interactions between hosts, pathogens, and the environment is called pathogenesis. Understanding the mechanisms underlying diseases through the study of pathogenesis paves the way for the development of focused treatments and preventative measures. The more we learn about pathogenesis, the more equipped we are to prevent and lessen the effects of a wide range of diseases on human health. When a pathogen such as pneumococcus enters the lung, it can be eliminated by the phagocytosis and destruction of the bacteria by cells like activated macrophages. Certain acute phase proteins, complements, and antibodies that neutralize the pathogenic potential of the encapsulated pneumococcus improve the capacity of macrophages to absorb the bacteria. It is unknown what part the robust antibody response that develops in TB plays in the illness process.

The immune system has to deal with TB due to the mycobacterial cell wall that contains peculiar components preventing T cells and macrophages from activating their cytokines. Mycobacteria enter the macrophage and prevent the phagosome and lysosome from fusing, which allows them to escape into the cytoplasm and avoid the intracellular death apparatus. As mentioned in the introduction, *M. tuberculosis* infects roughly one-third of the world's population, although only a small percentage of those people are present symptoms. Figure 2.5 depicts a summary of the process that takes place in the exposed person. Inhaled aerosol-borne organisms settle in the alveoli of the lungs. Alveolar macrophages phagocytose the bacteria, but they are not yet capable of killing them. Mycobacteria multiply both inside and outside of macrophages and when they proliferate, they travel to the perihilar lymph nodes through infected macrophages. Organisms that enter the bloodstream spread throughout the body, and this procedure, which takes several weeks, is indicative of the mycobacteria's slow 18-hour division rate.

A cell-mediated immune (CMI) response starts to form after roughly 4 weeks. T cells have stimulated macrophages to produce enough enzymes and other metabolites in sufficient quantities for them to eliminate the bacteria within. These activated macrophages form granulomas and are referred to as epithelioid cells. They unite as multinucleate giant cells, also known as Langerhans cells, in the center. This efficient killing device is surrounded by fibroblasts and T cells. Cell-to-cell contact and cytokines tightly regulate the entire T cell-macrophage cooperative process as well as the level of macrophage killing activity. The ultimate outcome is the cessation of the infection at every location within the body where the organism has penetrated. This is a fruitful result. It is known, nevertheless, that some dormant bacteria can live for decades inside of macrophages. These bacteria can proliferate and result in reactivated disease if immune control is impaired. The Mantoux and Heaf tests can detect the emergence of the cell-mediated response in TB several weeks post-infection. This response is also known as the delayed type hypersensitivity (DTH) response (Figure 2.5).

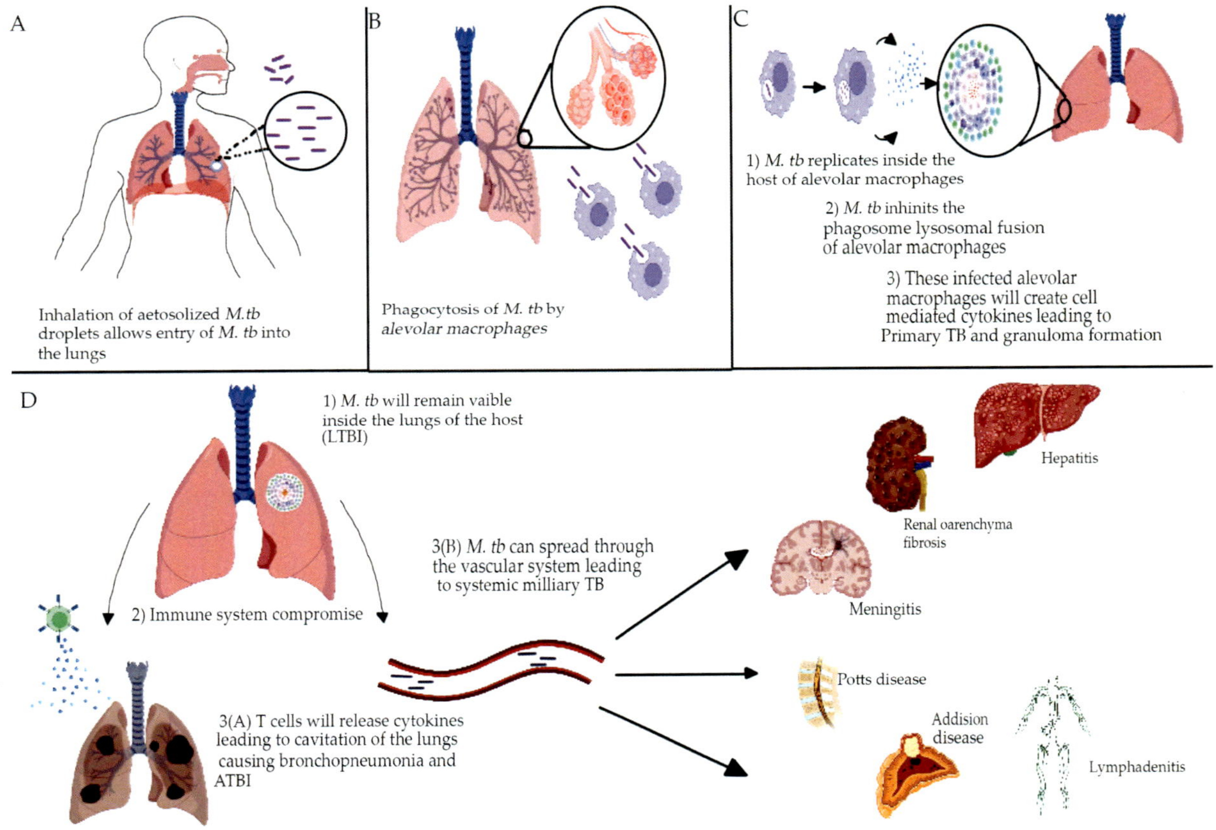

Figure 2.5. *The first exposure to Mycobacterium tuberculosis usually results in a cell-mediated immune response (delayed type hypersensitivity) that kills the bacteria.*

Source: Stewart, P., Patel, S., Comer, A., Muneer, S., Nawaz, U., Quann, V., Bansal, M., & Venketaraman, V., (2023). Role of B cells in mycobacterium tuberculosis infection. Vaccines, 11(5), 955. https://doi.org/10.3390/vaccines11050955.

A compromised cell-mediated immune system is one of the main causes of a poor outcome from infection at primary exposure, reactivated disease, or re-infection. Therefore, it is not unexpected that immunosuppression—such as that caused by HIV infection—pushes the infection in the direction of a worse prognosis. A very young age and malnutrition are additional risk factors. This highlights the fact that eliminating this organism requires a healthy, well-functioning cell-mediated immune system. Figure 2.6 compares the above-described "good" outcome of infection with a "poor" outcome. The level of hypersensitivity is higher in the "bad" scenario. When the immune system mediated by cells is weak, effective elimination is impeded, leading to an abundance of the organism. The fact that mycobacteria's cell wall components function as adjuvants, attracting T cells and macrophages to the infection site, exacerbates the issue. When macrophages lyze uncontrollably, a lot of enzymes and metabolites are released, which damage nearby tissue. Unstable caseous necrosis patches in the lung melt into the surrounding tissue. Cavities develop and fuse.

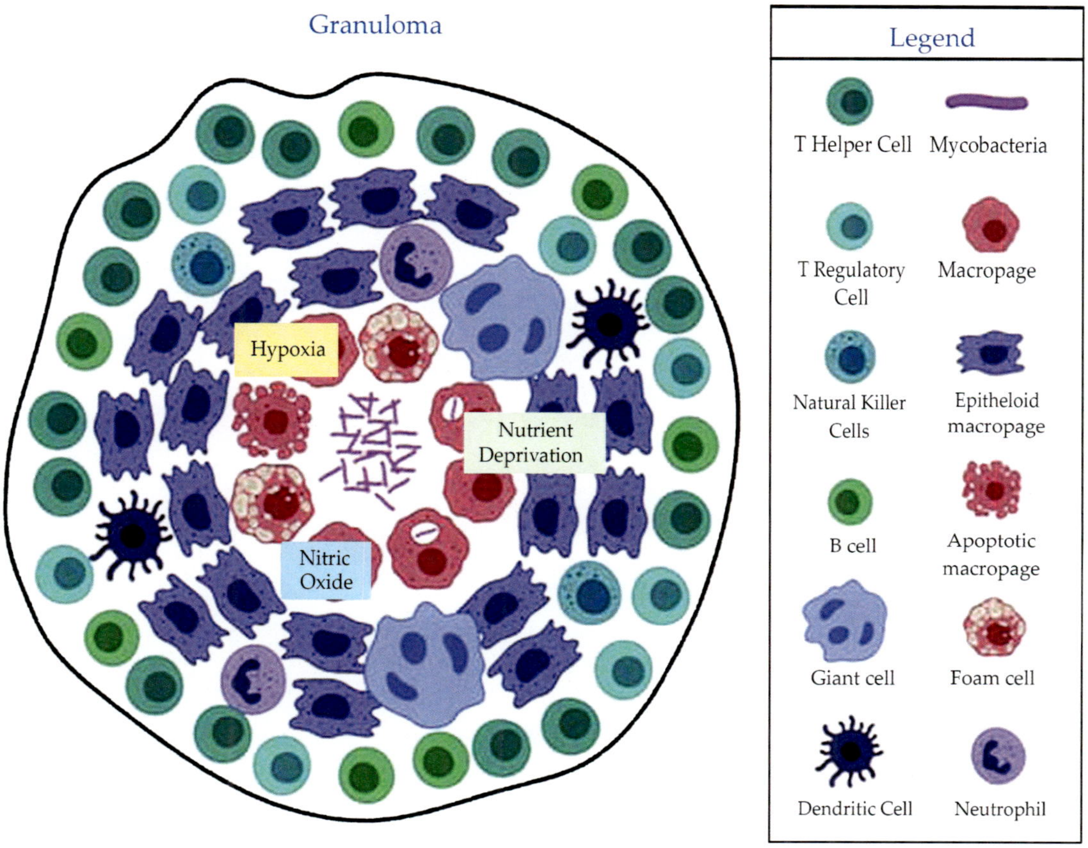

Figure 2.6. *(a) The end result of a good outcome is an effective organization in a granuloma. (b) A poor outcome arises as a result of some defect in the cell-mediated response.*

Source: Stewart, P., Patel, S., Comer, A., Muneer, S., Nawaz, U., Quann, V., Bansal, M., & Venketaraman, V., (2023). Role of B cells in mycobacterium tuberculosis infection. Vaccines, 11(5), 955. https://doi.org/10.3390/vaccines11050955.

A clinical disease can be classified into two main categories. After the first exposure to the organism, primary TB develops, and is followed by the secondary or reactivated disease which manifest itself years after. Figure 2.7 depicts an outline of infection and disease over time. The ensuing cell-mediated response manages the infection wherever the organism is located in the body if the initial infection has a positive outcome. If the result is negative, the organism's growth will not be regulated, and the primary disease may appear. Particularly in young children, there can be a great deal of inflammation in the hilar lymph nodes, which can compress the bronchi and cause symptoms like stridor and cough. Meningitis is caused by germs that infect the meninges of the blood. A pleural effusion occurs when a lung granuloma bursts into the pleural space due to an allergic reaction. The multiple "millet seed"-sized lesions visible on chest X-rays are the defining characteristic of miliary TB, a form of disseminated primary disease. The organism leaves its infection focus and made its way to the lungs through the systemic circulation.

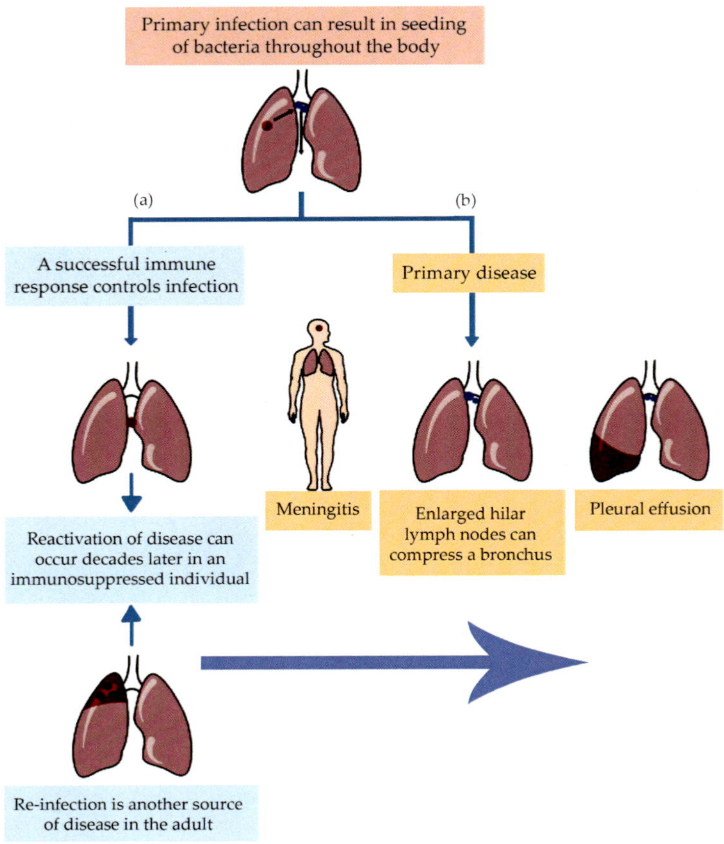

Figure 2.7. *During primary infection, the organism can spread to all organ systems. (a) The optimum outcome of the hypersensitivity response is control of the organism at all sites. (b) During the primary infection stage, clinical diseases such as meningitis and pleural effusion can occur.*

Source: Stewart, P., Patel, S., Comer, A., Muneer, S., Nawaz, U., Quann, V., Bansal, M., & Venketaraman, V., (2023). Role of B cells in mycobacterium tuberculosis infection. Vaccines, 11(5), 955. https://doi.org/10.3390/vaccines11050955.

Organisms can live in tissue for many years after the initial infection is under control, during which time they may reactivate. Reactivation, or secondary disease, happens when a person's CMI declines and latent bacteria proliferate to overpower the weakened immune system. Reactivated disease occurs in the lung's upper, highly oxygenated lobes. When the infection cannot be controlled, the lesions break down and eventually fuse together to form cavities large enough to be visible on a chest X-ray. It is crucial to recognize that in older patients residing in areas with low TB incidence, reactivation is most likely the disease's mechanism. The most likely mechanism in high-incidence areas is re-infection. Once more, the patient with a compromised immune system stands to gain the most from an active illness.

2.4. Diagnosis and Management

Effective healthcare relies heavily on diagnosis and management, which include a methodical approach to recognizing and treating medical conditions. Technological developments have greatly improved the diagnostic process in modern medicine, enabling the more accurate and prompt identification of illnesses. Usually, the diagnostic process starts with a comprehensive medical history and physical examination. These preliminary actions offer insightful information about a patient's condition and direct medical personnel toward focused investigations. A thorough diagnostic profile is aided by laboratory testing, imaging studies, and, in certain situations, genetic analysis. The speed and accuracy of obtaining diagnostic information have been revolutionized by emerging technologies like point-of-care testing and molecular diagnostics.

After a diagnosis is made, it is critical to implement effective management. Treatment plans are customized to meet the unique requirements of each patient as well as the unique features of the ailment. In severe situations, immediate medical attention may be needed to stabilize the patient's condition. This will be followed by continuing care and modifications to the treatment plan. The management of chronic conditions frequently requires long-term approaches. To address different facets of the patient's well-being, healthcare professionals work together in a multidisciplinary manner. The management plan may include medication, lifestyle changes, and

, to maximize the patient's quality of life and minimize the condition's impact on day-to-day activities. A key element of efficient management is patient education. Giving patients information about their illnesses encourages them to take an active role in their treatment. This entails being aware of available treatments, any possible side effects, and lifestyle adjustments that can improve general health continuous dialog between patients and medical professionals.

The idea of personalized medicine has become more well-known in diagnosis and treatment in recent years. This method acknowledges the distinct genetic, environmental, and lifestyle elements that impact a person's well-being. Treatment plans that are customized with these factors in mind will be more accurate and effective, producing better results. Furthermore, the use of digital health technologies is essential to contemporary diagnosis and treatment. Healthcare providers can share information more easily thanks to electronic health records, which also guarantee continuity of care. Platforms for telemedicine make it easier to have remote consultations, increasing access to medical care and tracking long-term illnesses. With the help of wearable technology and smartphone apps, people can take an active role in their own health care by accessing real-time data that can guide medical decisions.

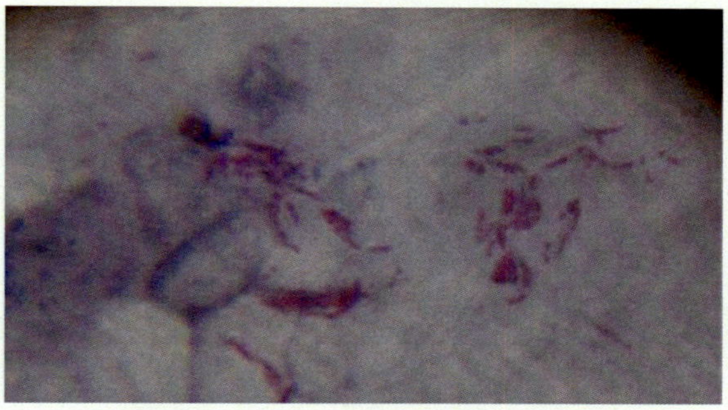

Figure 2.8. *To obtain secretions that have accumulated in the lungs during sleep, it is crucial that the sputum specimens be taken "first of the day." For the best possible isolation of the organism, samples must be taken over the course of three days.*

Source: https://commons.wikimedia.org/wiki/File:M_tuberculosis_sputum.jpg.

In the field of healthcare, diagnosis and management constitute a dynamic and interrelated process. The development of efficient and comprehensive healthcare practices is largely attributed to the convergence of patient-centered strategies, personalized approaches, and technological advancements. Precision, individualization, and patient involvement will continue to be crucial for obtaining the best results in diagnosis and treatment even as the medical field changes. Three consecutive days of early morning sputum specimen collection are necessary for the laboratory diagnosis of pulmonary TB (Figure 2.8). Both the ZN stain and the auramine stain are used in the microbiology lab. Auramine is a fluorescent dye that attaches itself to mycobacteria's cell wall components, and is used for screening a lot of smears due to its higher senstibity compared to the ZN stain. ZN stain is then used to confirm auramine-positive smears (Figures 2.2 and 2.3).

Two more specimens are required even if the first specimen tests positive for microscopy; all three are processed to guarantee that the organism is grown. On rare occasions, bacteria from the oral flora may outgrow the existing mycobacteria and survive the decontamination procedure (described below). Since culture is more sensitive than microscopy, three negative smears do not rule out pulmonary TB. A "first-of-the-day" midstream urine specimen (MSU), collected into a white-topped container, and blood in two citrated "blue-topped" (citrated) bottles, which are used to inoculate specific blood culture bottles at the Reference laboratory, are additional specimens that should be collected from the patient with suspected (military) TB. Figure 2.9 illustrates the frequency of involvement of different organs and sites in TB infection, along with the specimens that need to be collected. A recreational exposure history is an important laboratory alert to include on the request form. *M. marinum* grows best at 30°C in the laboratory, where it causes "fish tank-associated" infections of the hand joints.

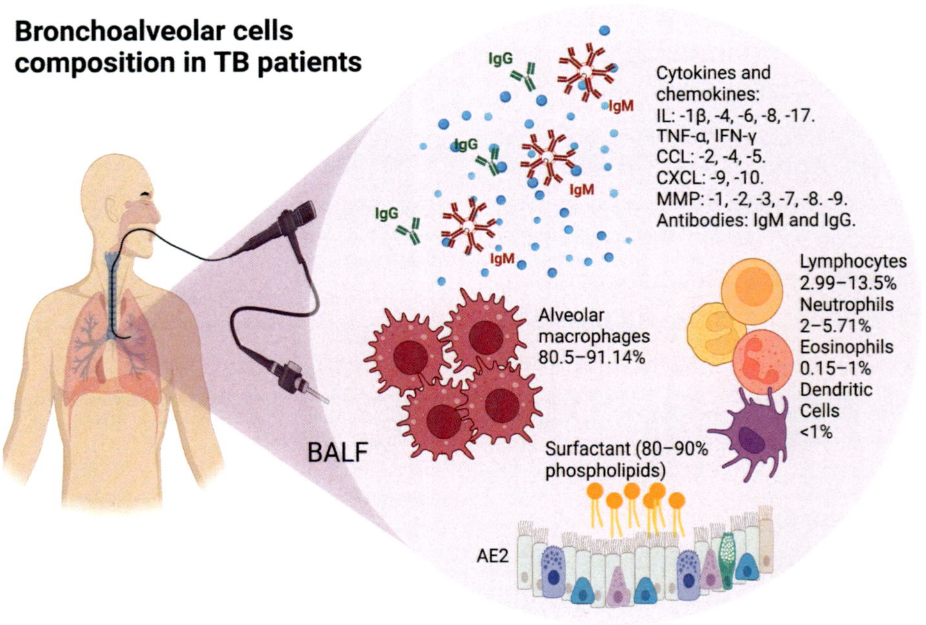

Figure 2.9. *Pulmonary tuberculosis is the most common presentation of the disease, but the disease may arise at any site.*

Source: Herrera, M. T., Guzmán-Beltrán, S., Bobadilla, K., Santos-Mendoza, T., Flores-Valdez, M. A., Gutiérrez-González, L. H., & González, Y., (2022). Human pulmonary tuberculosis: Understanding the immune response in the bronchoalveolar system. Biomolecules, 12(8), 1148. https://doi.org/10.3390/biom12081148f.

TB specialists are contacted and Public Health is informed when a patient has been diagnosed or is suspected of having TB. HIV testing has to be additionally done on the infected patients. Single-room nursing is imperative for cases of confirmed or suspected "open" pulmonary TB. These rooms ought to have negative-pressure ventilation systems to lower the organism load within the patient's surroundings and stop the spread of infection to other patients. Negative pressure in a single room is crucial for the nursing care of patients with MDR or XDR TB.

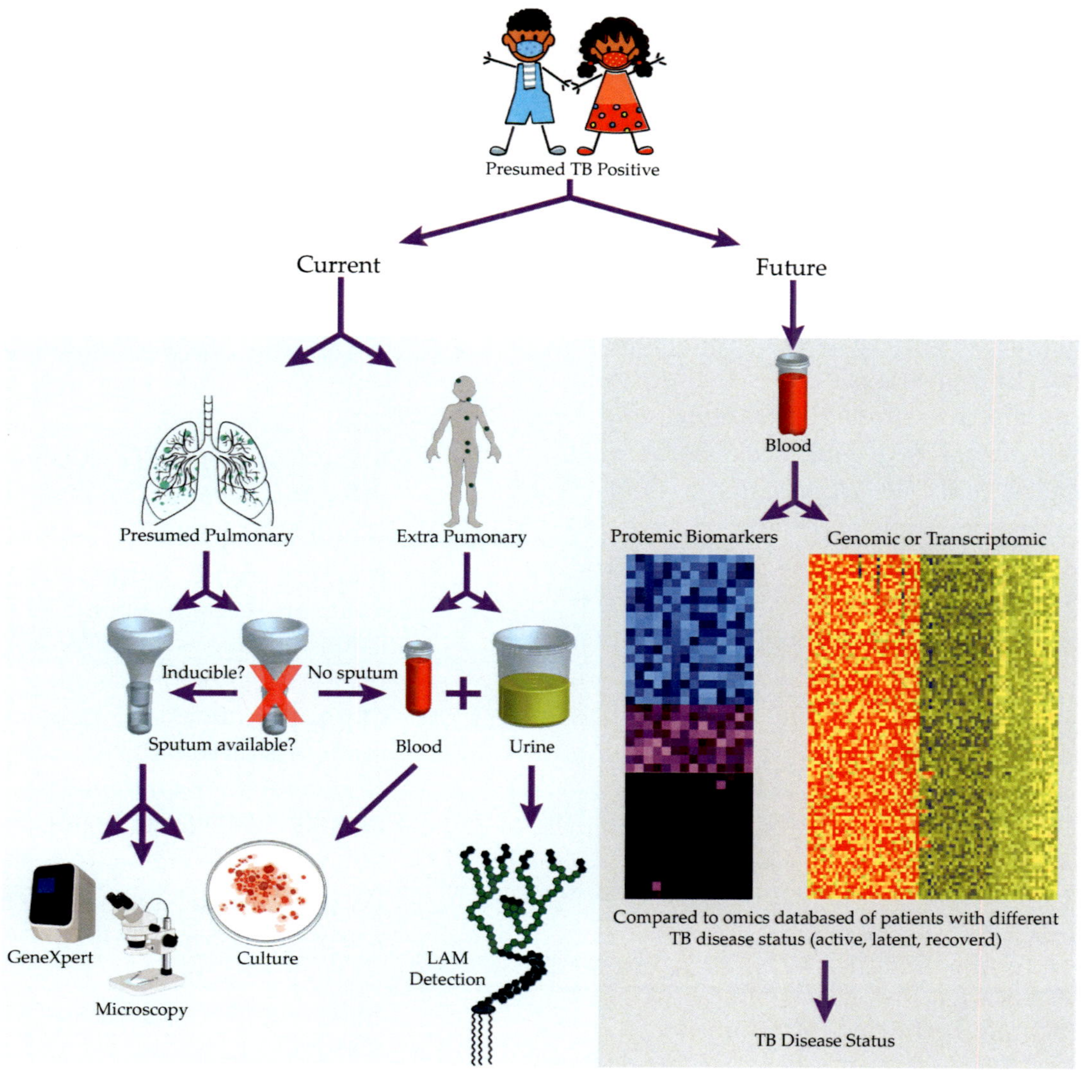

Figure 2.10. *An outline of laboratory tests for tuberculosis.*

Source: Jakhar, S., Bitzer, A. A., Stromberg, L. R., & Mukundan, H., (2020). Pediatric tuberculosis: The impact of "omics" on diagnostics development. International Journal of Molecular Sciences, 21(19), 6979. https://doi.org/10.3390/ijms21196979.

Figure 2.10 shows a summary of the laboratory procedure. Sodium hydroxide is used to decontaminate sputum samples to render other bacterial contaminants inactive. Mycobacteria are resistant to this decontamination process because they are comparatively hardy organisms. Sputum samples and all other specimens are centrifuged to concentrate any mycobacteria present after the alkaline step to be neutralized. Agar medium is inoculated using the centrifuged deposit (Lowenstein–Jensen [LJ]). Mycobacteria divide roughly every 15 to 20 hours, and compared to other bacteria, they take longer to produce visible growth. For up to 10 weeks, inoculated agar "slopes" are thus examined once a week.

Standard culture is used with "rapid" liquid culture systems. In the bottle base of the BD Bactec™ system, there is a fluorescent substance, and the liquid's oxygen causes this compound to evaporate. The oxygen levels decrease, the oxygen quenching effect is gradually lessened, and a fluorescent signal is produced as the aerobic mycobacteria multiply. When using a solid LJ medium, growth typically takes 3–5 weeks, whereas liquid culture shows results in 1–2 weeks. Mycobacterium isolates are forwarded to the Reference lab for thorough identification and susceptibility testing. Examined are INH, rifampicin, pyrazinamide, and ethambutol as first-line antibiotics. Antibiotic susceptibility testing and identification are expected to be routinely performed using whole genome sequencing (WGS).

2.4.1. Molecular Testing

Molecular testing is now advised for at least one sputum sample submitted for TB investigation, regardless of the ZN/auramine stain result, in order to check for the presence of *M. tuberculosis* and rifampicin resistance. The ribonucleic acid (RNA) polymerase (rpoB) gene is amplified in the Cepheid Xpert MTB/rif polymerase chain reaction (PCR) assay, which includes the nucleotide where a point mutation results in resistance to rifampicin. By using the molecular test, about 60% of sputum specimens that are culture-positive but microscopy-negative are positive.

Clinical microbiology's revolutionary use of molecular testing has revolutionized the diagnosis and treatment of infectious diseases. With its focus on the identification and characterization of microbial DNA, RNA, and proteins, this advanced set of techniques offers quick and accurate insights into pathogen identity, genetic composition, and even antibiotic resistance profiles. In clinical microbiology, several important molecular testing techniques are used.

1. **Polymerase Chain Reaction (PCR):** A key method for amplifying particular DNA sequences and detecting pathogens with high sensitivity is PCR. Target DNA can be quantified using real-time PCR, which helps with infection severity assessment and treatment response tracking.
2. **Nucleic Acid Sequencing:** Next-generation sequencing (NGS) and other advances in DNA sequencing technologies enable thorough analysis of entire microbial genomes. This method is very useful for understanding the evolution of microbial populations, identifying newly emerging pathogens, and researching genetic variations.
3. **Loop-Mediated Isothermal Amplification (LAMP):** It is an isothermal amplification method that amplifies DNA quickly while maintaining a steady temperature. Because it's easy to use and requires little equipment, it's especially helpful in environments with limited resources.
4. **Microarray Technology:** Several microbial targets can be detected simultaneously in a single assay thanks to microarrays. This high-throughput

method is useful for figuring out which pathogens are present and what their resistance profiles are.

5. **Reverse Transcription Polymerase Chain Reaction (RT-PCR):** RNA is amplified and detected using RT-PCR, which makes it possible to identify RNA viruses and measure the expression of certain genes in microorganisms. It is essential for identifying viral infections and tracking their development.
6. **Fluorescent *In Situ* Hybridization (FISH):** FISH binds selectively to microbial nucleic acids in clinical samples using fluorescently labeled DNA probes. When identifying and localizing pathogens directly in tissue specimens, this technique is especially helpful.
7. **Matrix-Assisted Laser Desorption/ Ionization Time-of-Flight Mass Spectrometry (MALDI-TOF MS):** MALDI-TOF MS analyzes the distinct protein profiles of microorganisms to enable the quick and precise identification of these entities. It is now a common tool in clinical microbiology labs for identifying bacteria and fungi.

There are many benefits to using molecular testing in clinical microbiology. Timely and accurate diagnoses are facilitated by high sensitivity, specificity, and rapid turnaround times. Furthermore, pathogens that may be difficult to identify or cultivate using conventional methods can now be detected thanks to molecular techniques. Molecular testing is essential for antimicrobial resistance surveillance in infectious disease management. Clinicians can optimize treatment outcomes and reduce the risk of antibiotic resistance by customizing antibiotic therapy to each patient's unique microbial profile through the identification of specific resistance genes.

Furthermore, the applications of targeted infection control measures and outbreak investigations are facilitated by the improved understanding of microbial epidemiology that molecular testing provides. Tracking the movement of particular strains within a hospital or community is crucial for controlling and averting infectious disease outbreaks. By offering quick, accurate, and targeted techniques for identifying and characterizing microbial pathogens, molecular testing has completely transformed clinical microbiology. As technology develops, molecular testing is probably going to become more and more important for diagnosing infectious diseases, optimizing treatments, and promoting public health.

2.4.2. The Histopathology Specimen

It is imperative that a sample be sent to the microbiology laboratory when TB is suspected during a surgical biopsy. A few milliliters of saline solution should be added to the sample and placed in a sterile, white-topped container. An organism's ability to grow, identify itself, and ascertain its susceptibility profile is lost if the specimen is fixed in formalin in its entirety. The microscopic structure of tissues and organs can be understood through the use of histopathology specimens, which are essential in the field of diagnostic medicine. Within this field of pathology, tissues are examined at the cellular level in order to detect anomalies, evaluate the course of the disease, and inform treatment choices. The careful gathering and preparation of patient tissue samples is the first stage in the pathology specimen's journey, and it is an essential part of the diagnosis process.

The tissue that is taken from a patient during a biopsy or surgical procedure is preserved in a fixative, usually formalin, to stop it from degrading. In order to preserve morphological details and prevent post-mortem changes, the fixation process stabilizes cellular structures. The tissue is processed further, including dehydration, clearing, and embedding in paraffin wax, after fixation. Slices from microtomy, a technique that creates thin tissue sections, are normally 4 to 5 micrometers thick. Following the mounting of these sections onto glass slides, histological slides that can be stained and viewed under a microscope are produced. Hematoxylin and eosin (H & E) is one staining method that highlights cellular structures and helps distinguish between normal and aberrant tissue components.

The slides are examined under a microscope by histopathologists, qualified medical professionals who specialize in the interpretation of tissue specimens. They can recognize cellular features, evaluate tissue architecture, and diagnose a variety of illnesses, from benign tumors to malignant cancers, thanks to this visual analysis. The interpretation of histopathology results is essential for figuring out the type of disease, how far along it is, and whether it will progress or come back. Technological developments have added methods like immunohistochemistry and molecular pathology to conventional light microscopy, improving diagnostic precision. Using particular antibodies, immunohistochemistry helps characterize tumors and identify different cell types in tissues by detecting proteins. The study of genetic and molecular changes within tissues is made possible by molecular pathology techniques like PCR and NGS. This information is crucial for targeted therapies and personalized medicine.

Histopathology specimens, which offer vital information about the microscopic structure of tissues, are the foundation of diagnostic medicine. Histopathology is essential for guiding treatment decisions and advancing medical research, from cancer diagnosis to comprehending the complexities of different diseases. A vast range of medical conditions can be accurately diagnosed and treated thanks to the careful handling and inspection of these specimens by knowledgeable histopathologists.

2.4.3. Treatment

Antibiotics are used in TB treatment to destroy the bacteria. The unique structure and chemical makeup of the mycobacterial cell wall make it difficult to treat TB effectively because it prevents drugs from entering the body and renders many antibiotics ineffective. Combining multiple antibiotics is the most effective way to treat active TB and lower the likelihood that the bacteria will become resistant to them. As of 2007, there was no evidence to support the routine use of rifabutin rather than rifampicin in HIV-positive TB patients. It has been demonstrated that giving patients with pulmonary TB 100 mg of acetylsalicylic acid (aspirin) daily improves clinical signs and symptoms, decreases cavitary lesions, lowers inflammatory markers, and increases the rate of sputum-negative conversion. When treating pulmonary TB in a patient with a sensitive organism, quadruple therapy is administered. This entails two months of INH, pyrazinamide, rifampicin, and ethambutol, followed by an additional four months of INH and rifampicin. To treat TB meningitis, a 12-month course of treatment consists of 10 months of INH and 10 months of rifampicin. Pyridoxine is taken daily to counteract the vitamin B6 deficiency caused by INH.

The patient receiving anti-TB treatment must be continuously observed. Long-term compliance issues can be resolved with directly observed therapy (DOT). In this case, the patient visits the clinic every day and is seen taking the medication. Because pyrazinamide, rifampicin, and INH have the potential to be hepatotoxic, baseline liver function tests (LFTs) are carried out prior to the initiation of treatment. An index of suspicion is crucial, and the patient's liver functions need to be examined if they have nausea and tenderness in the right upper quadrant. When a patient has a bilirubin level greater than 60 µmol/L and elevated levels of AST and ALT, it is necessary to promptly assess the patient and review the treatment plan. Since both of these medications have the potential to be nephrotoxic, an alternate combination to consider in the case of deranged LFTs is ethambutol and streptomycin. Ethambutol side effects include optic neuritis. Hepatitis B and C infections are checked for in all TB patients receiving treatment.

2.4.3.1. Latent TB

Treatment options for latent TB include isoniazid or rifampin alone, or isoniazid plus either rifampicin or rifapentine. Depending on the drugs taken, the course of treatment lasts three to nine months. To stop latent infections from developing into active TB disease later in life, treatment is given to those who have them. Treatment completion rates for latent TB may be raised by counseling or education.

2.4.3.2. New Onset

As of 2010, a combination of antibiotics comprising rifampicin, isoniazid, pyrazinamide, and ethambutol for the first two months and just rifampicin and isoniazid for the final four months is the recommended treatment for new-onset pulmonary TB. As a backup, ethambutol may be added for the final four months in cases where isoniazid resistance is high. Even though the difference is marginal, treatment with anti-TB drugs for at least six months leads to higher success rates than treatment for less than six months. For patients who struggle with compliance, a shorter treatment plan might be suggested. When compared to a 6-month treatment regimen, there is no evidence to support shorter anti-TB treatment regimens. A four-month daily treatment regimen comprising high-dose, or "optimized," rifapentine with moxifloxacin (2PHZM/2PHM) is, however, as safe and effective as the current standard six-month daily regimen at curing drug-susceptible TB disease, according to recent results from an international, randomized, controlled clinical trial.

2.4.3.3. Recurrent Disease

It is crucial to test for antibiotic sensitivity in order to determine the appropriate course of treatment if TB recurs. If more than one drug-resistant strain of TB is found, it is advised to treat the patient for 18 to 24 months with at least four capable antibiotics.

2.4.3.4. Medication Administration

The WHO suggests that in an effort to lower the number of people who do not take antibiotics as directed, having a healthcare provider watch the patient take their medications could be helpful. This approach, however, is not well supported by the evidence when compared to people who take their medications on their own. Research does not support the notion that more patients receiving DOT will be cured or will finish their prescribed course of treatment. A family member or a medical professional observing a patient at home or in a clinic appears to have no bearing on the outcome, according to evidence of moderate quality. A minor but significant improvement could come from strategies to remind people of the value of appointments and treatment. Additionally, there is insufficient data to establish that twice or three times a week intermittent rifampicin-containing therapy is as effective as a daily dose regimen in terms of increasing cure rates and lowering relapse rates. When it comes to treating TB, there is insufficient data to determine whether a daily dosing regimen or an intermittent twice or three times weekly short course regimen is more effective.

2.4.3.5. Medication Resistance

When a person contracts a resistant strain of TB, primary resistance sets in. When receiving therapy for fully susceptible MTB, a patient may acquire secondary resistance due to insufficient treatment, improper adherence to the recommended regimen, or the use of substandard medication. Drug-resistant TB poses a significant public health risk in numerous developing nations due to its prolonged treatment course and higher drug costs. MDR-TB is characterized by resistance to isoniazid and rifampicin, the two first-line TB medications that are most effective.

Additionally resistant to three or more of the six classes of second-line drugs is TB that is extensively drug-resistant. TB that is completely drug-resistant is resistant to every medication in use today. It was first discovered in Italy in 2003, but reports of it were scarce until 2012. It has since been discovered in Iran and India. While linezolid has some efficacy in treating XDR-TB patients, medication discontinuation and adverse effects were frequent outcomes. The use of bedaquiline in MDR-TB is provisionally supported. XDR-TB, which accounts for 10% of MDR-TB cases, is a term that is occasionally used to describe extensively resistant tuberculosis. More than 90% of the countries have reported cases of XDR TB. Molecular tests like the Genotype MTBDRsl Assay, which are conducted on culture isolates or smear-positive specimens, can help identify second-line anti-tubercular drug resistance in patients with known rifampicin or MDR-TB.

2.4.3.6. Infection Control

Patients with laryngeal or pulmonary (open) TB who are suspected or confirmed should be cared for in a single room, ideally with negative pressure. In a negative-pressure single room where staff members are wearing FFP3 masks, MDR-TB or XDR-TB is a mandatory requirement for nursing. If the compliant patient needs to stay in the hospital, they can be nursed on the open ward and should be non-infectious within two weeks, provided there is no underlying immunocompromise or resistance concerns. It is comforting that during the first few days of treatment, the symptoms have resolved. This decision is further supported by the lack of cavitation on the chest X-ray or computed tomography (CT) scan, as well as the small number of organisms visible on the initial stains.

The patient who does not improve needs to have her/his compliance and potential for drug resistance reevaluated. Any results on drug-resistant isolates should be communicated as soon as possible by the reference laboratory conducting the susceptibility testing. The presence of red urine indicates the use of rifampicin. It is critical to recognize those who are more vulnerable to reactivated or acquired TB for clinical and infection control reasons (Figure 2.11). Ensuring patient safety, stopping the spread of infectious agents, and preserving the integrity of healthcare facilities all depend heavily on infection control. This field includes a variety of tactics and procedures intended to successfully detect, contain, and handle infections. Key components of clinical microbiology infection control are as follows:

1. **Sterilization and Disinfection:** To stop the spread of infectious agents, medical equipment must be thoroughly sterilized, and surfaces must be thoroughly cleaned. Making sure that all equipment and work areas are routinely cleaned in clinical microbiology labs reduces the possibility of cross-contamination.
2. **Personal Protective Equipment (PPE):** Wearing the proper PPE, such as gowns, gloves, masks, and eye protection, is essential for healthcare personnel working in clinical microbiology labs. By serving as a

barrier, PPE lessens the possibility of coming into contact with infectious materials.

3. **Aseptic Procedures:** When handling and processing clinical samples, clinical microbiologists follow stringent aseptic procedures. To reduce the risk of contamination, this entails using sterile equipment, washing your hands properly, and keeping your lab space clean.
4. **Isolation Precautions:** One of the most important ways to stop the spread of pathogens within healthcare facilities is to identify and isolate patients who have infectious diseases. The mode of transmission of sp. determines whether isolation precautions, such as airborne, droplet, or contact precautions, should be used.
5. **Monitoring and Surveillance:** Ongoing monitoring for infections linked to healthcare facilities aids in the detection of patterns, clusters, or outbreaks. Monitoring infection rates makes it possible to take targeted measures to control and stop further transmission and to act quickly.
6. **Education and Training:** To ensure that healthcare personnel are aware of infection control procedures, they must participate in ongoing education and training programs. Staff members are guaranteed to be knowledgeable about the most recent protocols and guidelines, adept at using PPE, and proficient in adhering to aseptic procedures through training.
7. **Antibiotic Stewardship:** A vital part of antibiotic stewardship initiatives is played by clinical microbiologists. They support the responsible use of antimicrobial agents, lowering the risk of antibiotic-resistant infections, by promptly and accurately disseminating information about microbial susceptibility, resistance patterns, and the best course of treatment.
8. **Environmental Control:** To stop the spread of infectious agents, clinical microbiology labs must have adequate ventilation and environmental hygiene. Ensuring the safety of laboratory personnel and preserving the integrity of diagnostic testing can be achieved through environmental control.
9. **Biosecurity Measures:** To prevent unintentional releases or deliberate misuse, laboratories that work with potentially dangerous pathogens put strict biosecurity measures in place. This covers following legal requirements, limiting access, and storing information securely.

In clinical microbiology, infection control is a multidimensional and all-encompassing approach that incorporates strict protocols, education, and ongoing monitoring. Clinical microbiologists make a substantial contribution to the general safety and efficacy of healthcare delivery by giving priority to these measures.

2.5. Public Health Issues

Public health issues are a wide range of problems that affect the general well-being of populations and communities. Global public health is constantly at risk from infectious diseases, which include the resurgence of previously eradicated viruses as well as the emergence of new ones. Non-communicable illnesses, such as mental health conditions, diabetes, and cardiovascular diseases, greatly increase the burden of illness. Health disparities are made worse by limited access to healthcare services, which is especially problematic for marginalized or underserved populations. The ongoing negative effects of substance abuse, particularly the opioid epidemic, on people and communities call for all-encompassing approaches to treatment and prevention. Pollution and climate change are two examples of environmental factors that have a significant impact on health. They also contribute to the spread of vector-borne diseases by affecting the quality of the air and water. Furthermore, health emergencies such as the COVID-19 pandemic highlight the significance of readiness, international cooperation, and efficient public health initiatives. To address these complex issues and advance health equity, disease prevention, and population resilience overall, a comprehensive strategy integrating public policy, healthcare systems, and community engagement is needed.

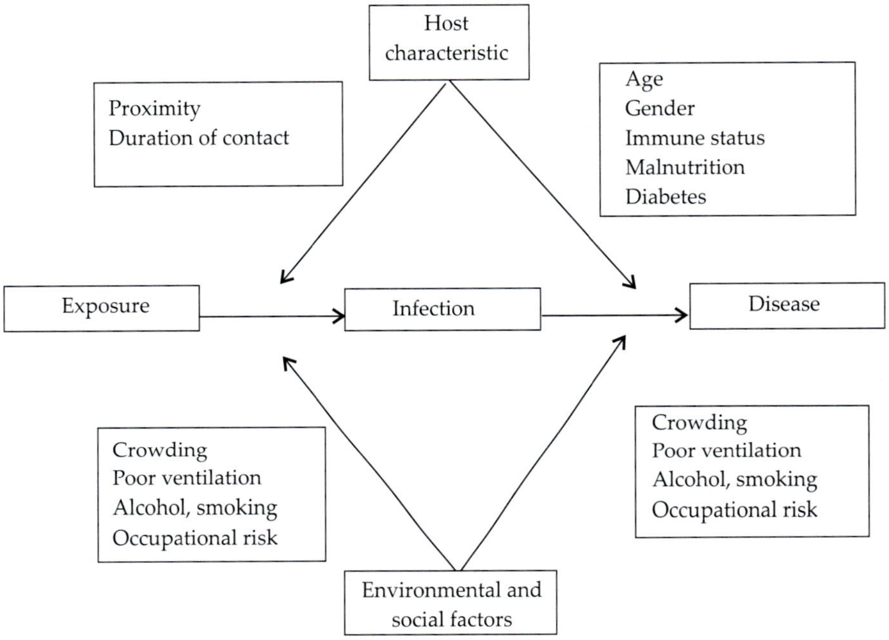

Figure 2.11. *Individuals in these categories are at increased risk of Mycobacterium tuberculosis infection, and these risk factors can be used in the clinical assessment of patients, and staff, as relevant.*

Source: Padmanesan, N., James, W., Chandini, R. M., & Dilip, M., (2013). "Risk factors for tuberculosis." Pulmonary Medicine (p. 11). Article ID: 828939, https://doi.org/10.1155/2013/828939.

There are a number of guidelines regarding the use of the IGT and tuberculin skin test (TST), including the use of the IGT test in patients who test positive for the disease after first testing with the TST. Screening programs that aim to ascertain the annual infection rate in a community employ PPD skin tests. They can be used to help with diagnosis or to find out the status of people who are a case's contacts. The decision regarding whether a contact requires BCG vaccination, chemoprophylaxis, or additional clinical investigation is based on the various responses to PPD. The use and effectiveness of the live attenuated strain of Mycobacterium bovis, or BCG vaccine, varies globally. Health care workers who work in high-risk clinical and laboratory settings, prison staff, people who have contact with someone who has an active pulmonary disease, and immigrants from regions of the world where TB is highly prevalent are among those who should be prescribed it in the UK if they do not have a positive TST. BCG administration cannot take place until an HIV-negative status has been verified.

PPD is injected into the anterior forearm dermis during the Mantoux test (Figure 2.12(a)). Examining the injection site 48–72 hours later allows one to gauge the level of hypersensitivity (Figure 2.12(b)). Patients who have not received a BCG vaccination benefit the most from the response to PPD, as it can yield a positive outcome. An individual who exhibits a reaction greater than 15 mm is considered to be infected and requires additional testing, which may involve a chest X-ray. Those who don't react to PPD may not have come into contact with the organism, or they may be in the early stages of primary exposure, before DTH manifests itself. These latter people may be offered prophylactic medication with indomethacin for a period of six months in the event that they are exposed to a TB case.

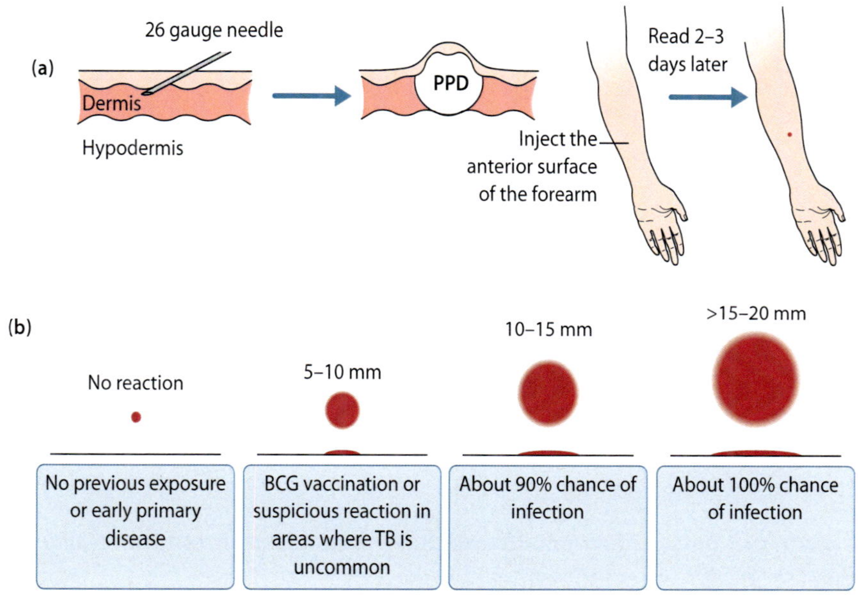

Figure 2.12. *(a) The Mantoux test involves injecting purified protein derivative (PPD) into the anterior forearm. The extent of induration is then recorded. (b) The size of the reaction to PPD is used in the management of contacts.*

Source: http://repository.stikesrspadgs.ac.id/25/1/Clinical%20Microbiology%20Struthers-299hlm.pdf.

Figure 2.13 provides a summary of public health measures that ought to be implemented in the event that the index case is found to have active pulmonary TB. For the sake of this illustration, none of the case's five contacts have received the BCG vaccination. The next step for each contact is decided by the TST results and additional tests, like a chest X-ray. Two of the cases in Figure 2.13 involve minors who are younger than 16 years old. Since the 1-year-old child did not respond to TST, INH prophylaxis is administered in light of the possibility of a serious primary disease at this age. When the TST is done again six weeks later, the results remain negative. Assuming that this child is not infected is reasonable. After the BCG vaccination, the INH can be stopped. The 12-year-old responds in a dubious manner. The possibility of pulmonary disease is ruled out by a normal chest X-ray, and INH prophylaxis is administered. The reasoning behind this is that at this point, the single agent will aid in the CMI response's ability to control infection. Over the course of six weeks, the 30-year-old adult's TST increases from 3 mm to 12 mm, suggesting a recent infection and developing CMI. In this case, INH prophylaxis is also appropriate. The adult, age 31, exhibits a florid hypersensitivity reaction. Additional interrogation produces tuberculosis symptoms, which are verified by a chest X-ray and sputum examination. The adult, age 40, has a normal chest X-ray and a positive Mantoux test result. She is advised to get a repeat chest X-ray 3 and 12 months later, as there is evidence of prior infection.

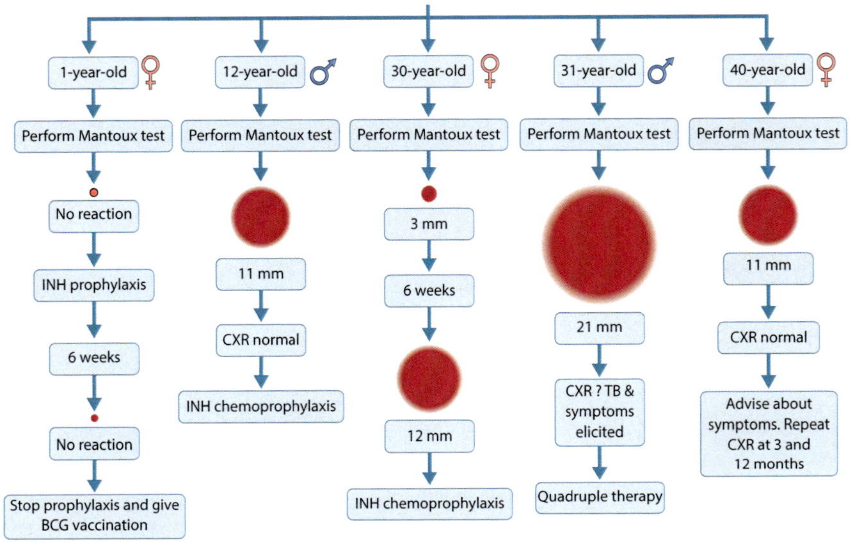

Figure 2.13. *A 45-year-old patient is identified as having active pulmonary tuberculosis, with profuse numbers of mycobacteria seen on the Ziehl–Neelsen stain.*

Source: http://repository.stikesrspadgs.ac.id/25/1/Clinical%20Microbiology%20Struthers-299hlm.pdf.

Notifying the public health authorities of any case, including patients who are empirically started on a "trial of treatment" before laboratory results are available, is crucial to the control of TB. It is appropriate to advise contacts to get tested for HIV.

A Closer Look

Rapid Diagnosis of TB

In India, TB is a major health issue. While most TB cases respond well to antibiotics, diagnosing the disease remains a significant challenge. One of the recommended diagnostic methods of the WHO involves fluorescence imaging of rod-shaped *M. tuberculosis* from Auramine O-stained sputum smears. Unfortunately, this method is largely inaccessible in rural and developing areas due to the high costs associated with equipment, maintenance, trained technicians, and laboratory infrastructure.

The newly created device is a user-friendly, small, and easily transportable fluorescence imaging tool designed for on-the-spot sputum microscopy to swiftly identify *M. tuberculosis* (the bacteria causing TB). It captures fluorescence images of *M. tuberculosis* bacteria (Mtb) from a patient's sputum spread on a microscope glass slide after staining with an appropriate fluorescent dye (Auramine O). The detection of Mtb fluorescence relies on the interaction of rod-shaped Mtb with Auramine O dye, resulting in green fluorescence when exposed to blue light.

A Graphic User Interface (GUI) software allows control of the device's hardware and automated counting of Mtb bacteria within the microscope's field of view. The device's notable advantage is its significantly lower cost (approximately 1 L) compared to the routinely used fluorescence microscope (costing over 50 L) for TB diagnosis. This, coupled with its compactness, portability, and automated counting capability, makes it suitable for use in resource-limited settings, especially in remote areas, facilitating prompt initiation of treatment and minimizing patient dropouts.

Summary

- The infectious disease TB is a potentially fatal illness that is caused by the *M.tuberculosis* bacteria. Although it can affect other organs in the body, the lungs are the primary organ affected by this airborne pathogen.
- Although TB can affect any area of the body, it most frequently affects the lungs (pulmonary TB). It can also affect other organs and parts of the body outside of the lungs and is termed extrapulmonary TB. Pulmonary and extrapulmonary TB can coexist.
- The fundamental units of life on Earth, organisms have a remarkable diversity that has developed over billions of years. Organisms vary greatly in size, structure, and function, from microscopic bacteria to enormous trees and intricate animals.
- It is challenging to diagnose active TB based solely on signs and symptoms, as well as to diagnose the illness in people with compromised immune systems...
- A complicated web of interactions involving the host, the infectious agent, and the environment is known as pathogenesis, and it describes how diseases start and spread within the body.

References

1. Clark, M., Riben, P., & Nowgesic, E., (2002). "The association of housing density, isolation, and tuberculosis in Canadian first nations communities. *International Journal of Epidemiology, 31*(5), 940–945.
2. Ferri, F. F., (2010). *Ferri's Differential Diagnosis: A Practical Guide to the Differential Diagnosis of Symptoms, Signs, and Clinical Disorders* (2nd edn.). Philadelphia, PA: Elsevier/Mosby. p. Chapter T.
3. Fitzgerald, D. W., Sterling, T. R., & Haas, D. W., (2020). Mycobacterium tuberculosis; Chap 249. In: Bennett, J. E., Dolin, R., Blaser, M. J., (eds.), *Mandell, Douglas, and Bennett's Principles and Practice of Infectious Diseases* (9th edn.) Philadelphia, PA: Elsevier.
4. Fraser, A., Paul, M., Attamna, A., Leibovici, L., et al., (2006). Drugs for preventing tuberculosis in people at risk of multiple-drug-resistant pulmonary tuberculosis. *The Cochrane Database of Systematic Reviews, 2006*(2), CD005435.
5. Harris, R. E., (2013). Epidemiology of tuberculosis. *Epidemiology of Chronic Disease: Global Perspectives* (p. 682). Burlington, MA: Jones & Bartlett Learning.
6. Hauk, L., (2018). Tuberculosis: Guidelines for diagnosis from the ATS, IDSA, and CDC. *Am. Fam. Physician., 97*(1), 56–58.
7. Hawn, T. R., Day, T. A., Scriba, T. J., Hatherill, M., Hanekom, W. A., Evans, T. G., et al., (2014). Tuberculosis vaccines and prevention of infection. *Microbiology and Molecular Biology Reviews, 78*(4), 650–671.
8. Wallace, W. A. H., (2019). Respiratory tract; Chap 14. In: Cross, S. S., (ed.), *Underwood's Pathology* (7th edn.). Philadelphia, PA: Elsevier.

Chapter 3

INFECTIONS OF THE BLOOD AND RESPIRATORY TRACT

Contents

Unit Introduction

Blood and respiratory tract infections are common health issues that can have serious consequences for both individuals and communities. As an essential component of the circulatory system, the blood transports nutrients, oxygen, and immune cells throughout the body. Pathogens, which include bacteria, viruses, and fungi, can enter the bloodstream, and induce sepsis or bacteremia, resulting in severe inflammation and even organ failure. Like septicemia, bacterial infections frequently arise from the introduction of bacteria into the bloodstream from a localized infection site. This can set off a systemic reaction that, if left untreated, can be fatal.

Simultaneously, the respiratory tract is a sophisticated system of tissues and organs that facilitates the exchange of carbon dioxide and oxygen. Either the lower respiratory tract (bronchi and lungs) or the upper respiratory tract (nose, throat, and sinuses) can be impacted by respiratory infections. Common culprits include bacteria like *Streptococcus pneumoniae*, *Haemophilus influenzae*, and *Mycoplasma pneumoniae*, as well as viruses like influenza and respiratory syncytial virus (RSV). Respiratory tract infections commonly present with symptoms such as cough, dyspnea, and chest pain. Severe cases may result in pneumonia, a dangerous illness marked by lung tissue inflammation.

The complex relationship between these two essential systems is highlighted by the interaction between blood and respiratory tract infections. Respiratory infections have the potential to spread into the bloodstream in certain situations, which could lead to sepsis and complicate the clinical picture. Furthermore, people with weakened immune systems—such as those receiving immunosuppressive treatments or living with chronic illnesses—may be more vulnerable to both kinds of infections.

Orientation and Directional Terms

Term	Definition	Illustration
Septicemia	Septicemia, also known as sepsis, is a life-threatening medical condition characterized by the presence of pathogenic microorganisms, such as bacteria, viruses, fungi, or their toxins, in the bloodstream.	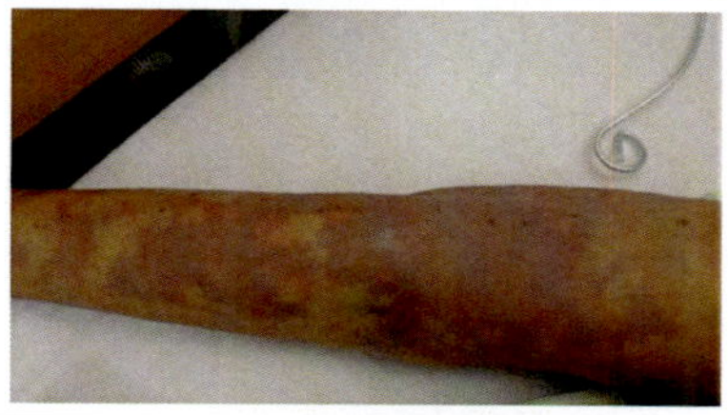
Red blood cells	Red blood cells, or erythrocytes, are one of the components of blood. They are continuously produced in our bone marrow. Just two or three drops of blood can contain about 1 billion red blood cells – in fact, that's what gives our blood that distinctive red color.	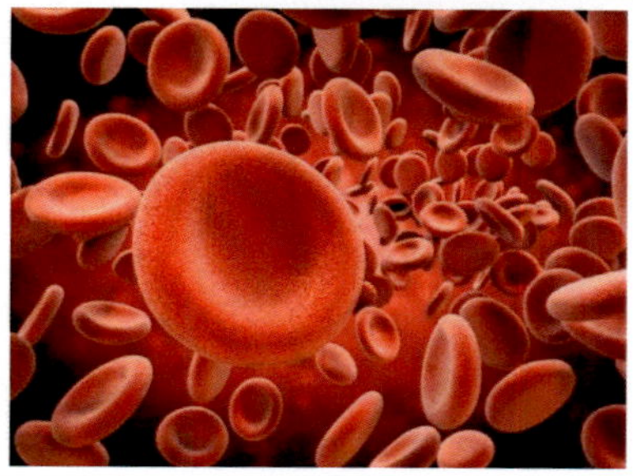
Blood culture	Blood culture is a medical laboratory test used to detect bacteria or fungi in a person's blood.	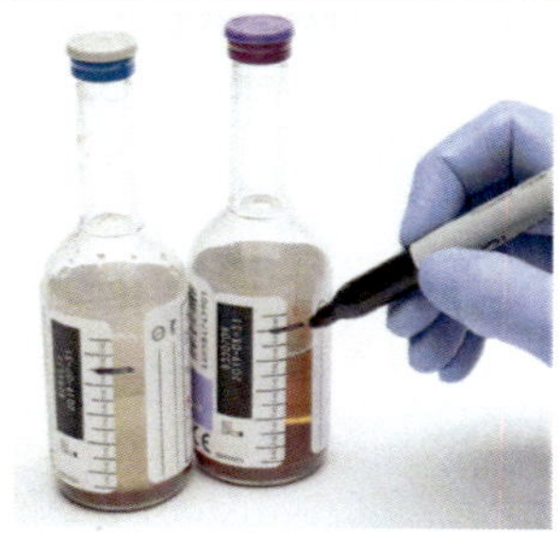
C-reactive protein	C-reactive protein is an annular pentameric protein found in blood plasma, where its circulating concentrations rise in response to inflammation.	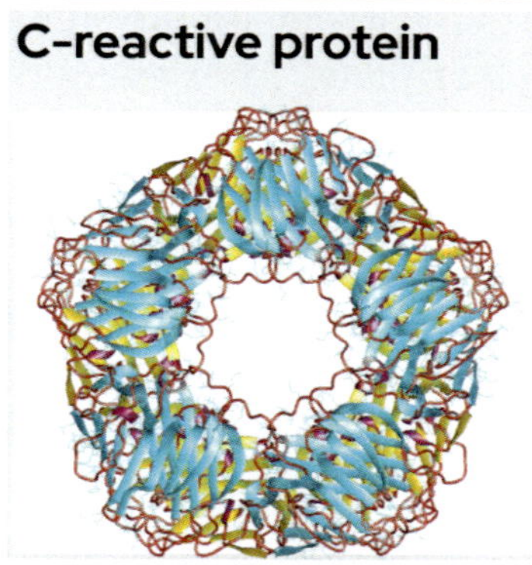
Otitis media	Otitis media is inflammation or infection located in the middle ear. Otitis media can occur as a result of a cold, sore throat, or respiratory infection.	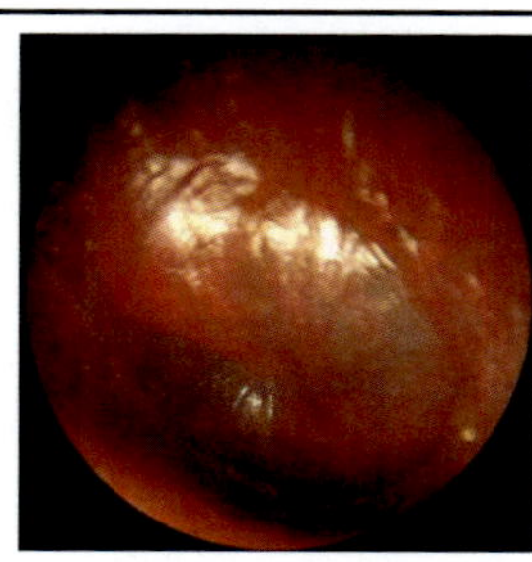

3.1. Blood Infections

Environmental microorganisms have the ability to attack humans at any time, contaminate blood, and cause infections. Blood infections are caused by a variety of microbial infections that are carried in the blood, which are potentially fatal and can result in sepsis.

Many other organisms can cause illness by entering the bloodstream. These include diseases spread by a variety of arthropod vectors, including the tsetse fly *Glossina morsitans* (African trypanosomiasis/sleeping sickness) and mosquitoes belonging to the genera Anopheles (malaria), Aedes (dengue fever, yellow fever), Culex (West Nile virus), and Anopheles (yellow fever). Ixodes ticks carry *Borrelia burgdorferi* that causes Lyme disease, whereas Dermacentor (which causes Rocky Mountain spotted fever) and Amblyomma (which causes African tick-bite fever) ticks carry rickettsial illnesses. Tissue nematodes like *Wucheria bancroi* are found in some regions of the tropics and subtropics. The microfilaria of adult worms, which live in the lymphatics, are ingested by blood-feeding female mosquitoes belonging to the genera Aedes, Anophyles, and Culex. After going through the midgut of the insect, they emerge as larvae that infect humans when the mosquito feeds again in the thoracic muscles.

There are several ways for organisms to enter the bloodstream. When you sleep, the bacteria that is colonizing your upper respiratory tract may aspirate into your lungs, where it may cause lobar pneumonia and further spread to your bloodstream. These organisms can also travel through the alimentary canal. The pork tapeworm's (*Taenia solium*) sole host is the human, and any person who consumes contaminated food is susceptible to cysticercosis if the food is contaminated by eggs found in the feces of an infected person. After emerging from the egg, larvae pass through the intestinal wall and enter the bloodstream, where they can travel to different organs with the cysticerci. Seizures may be the initial sign of neurocysticercosis. Figure 3.1 illustrates a few sources of exogenous organisms that can infiltrate the blood.

Finding the most likely source of the bacteria in the blood is necessary. *Escherichia coli* in blood and an ascending urinary tract infection (UTI) are clearly related. For example, once native valve endocarditis has been diagnosed, identifying the organism's most likely source can be simple. The treatment plan for a patient with endocarditis brought on by a *streptococcus* of the mouth flora, like *Streptococcus sanguinis*, must take into account the patient's possible poor dentition. The maxilla-facial surgical team is typically involved with this process.

Often time, there can be strange occurrences, such as the discovery of *Streptococcus gallolyticus* in blood cultures, an organism which is a small part of the colon's typical flora. It is acknowledged, nevertheless, that a correlation may arise between it and a large bowel cancer, most likely as a result of a particular interaction between the organism and these cancerous cells. From there, the *streptococcus* obtains an advantage in selective growth and can enter the bloodstream. It can cause infectious endocarditis once it gets into the blood. *S. gallolyticus* is a blood culture bacterium that is frequently found in the context of endocarditis, and if this bacterium is detected, it should be removed prior to any valve surgery.

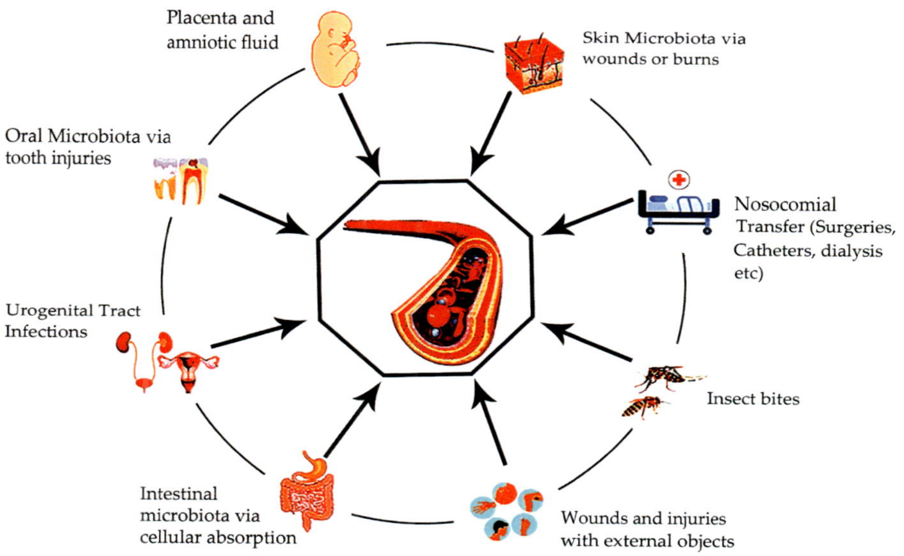

Figure 3.1. *Some examples of how exogenous organisms that reach the blood from various sources.*

Source: Goraya, M. U., Li, R., Mannan, A., Gu, L., Deng, H., & Wang, G., (2022). Human circulating bacteria and dysbiosis in non-infectious diseases. Front. Cell. Infect. Microbiol., 12, 932702. doi: 10.3389/fcimb.2022.932702.

3.1.1. Pathogenesis

Bacteremia is the term used to describe the presence of bacteria found in blood cultures. Although septicemia also refers to the presence of bacteria in the blood, it indicates a need for immediate patient care. Along with clinical parameters like fever, hypotension, tachycardia, multi-organ failure, and leucocytosis, the terms sepsis and septic shock are also used to inform the clinician of the severity of the situation and the urgency of taking immediate action in the patient's care.

Bacteremia can be classified as intermittent, continuous, or transient (one episode lasting less than half an hour). These definitions are significant ideas regarding the possible source of these terms. A brief bacteremia may result from pyelonephritis brought on by *E. coli* or from pneumococcal pneumonia. An extravascular site, like a *Staphylococcus aureus* abscess (Figure 3.2), where bacteria enter the lymphatics and then the blood at irregular intervals, is thought to be manipulated in intermittent bacteremia. Endocarditis is the most significant example of an intravascular source of bacteremia that is continuous.

It is most likely common to have a few bacteria in the blood for brief periods of time. For instance, it is known that brushing and other dental manipulations allow a tiny amount of oral bacteria to enter the bloodstream. These few organisms are usually harmless because the body's defenses quickly eliminate them. Even when known pathogens get into the bloodstream, the host may not always suffer a significant consequence. Occasionally, the microbiologist will call the clinician with the results of a positive blood culture and discover that the patient was sent home without antibiotics the day before they were admitted.

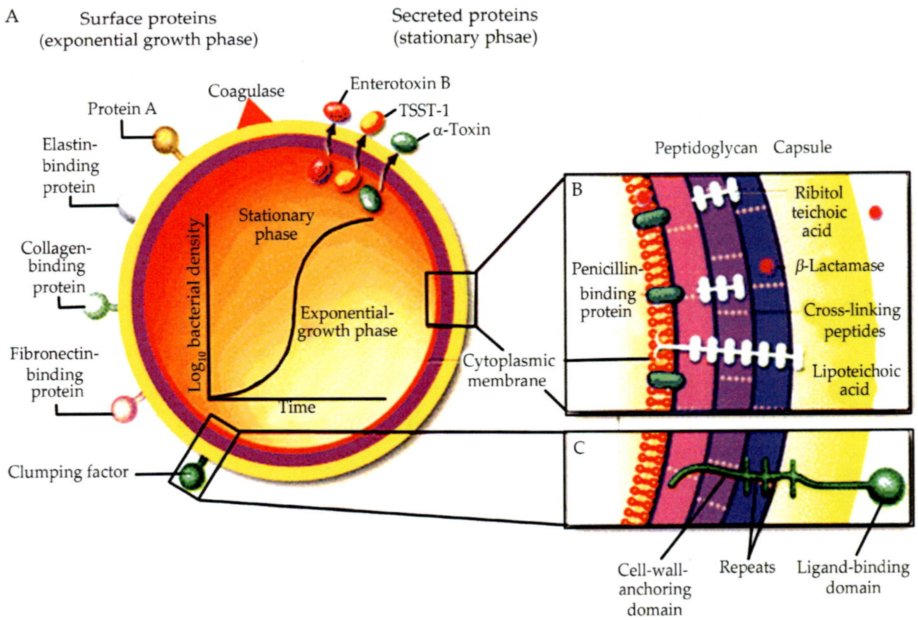

Figure 3.2. *Examples of virulence factors that cause bacteremia.*

Source: Youssef, D., & Molony, K., (2017). Staphylococcus aureus bacteremia in adults. InTech. doi: 10.5772/66225.

For instance, gram-positive diplococci that were later identified as pneumococcus were found in the blood culture obtained upon admission. In this instance, the issue was resolved quickly by the body's defenses by removing the organism from the blood. This finding obviously calls for a thorough evaluation of the patient and the appropriate administration of antibiotics. Although the body's natural defenses drive out pathogenic organisms, it is reasonable to assume that members of the community who become ill for brief periods of time may carry them in their blood. The person will therefore consult a doctor if their body's defenses are ineffective or weak.

Once bacteria enter the bloodstream, they may spread to other parts of the body and establish new infection foci. When an infected peripheral venous cannula (PVC) site harbors *S. aureus* bacteremia, the bacteria may attach to a heart valve and cause endocarditis, or they may settle in the spine and cause an abscess. The bacteria can cause septic arthritis by penetrating a joint's synovial membrane. These illustrations highlight how crucial it is to perform a thorough clinical assessment on a patient who is septic or bacteremic.

The spleen and liver's macrophage populations are crucial components of the blood's defense system. Pneumococcus, meningococcus, and *Haemophilus influenzae* type b (Hib) are among the encapsulated bacteria that can cause an overwhelming infection in people who have had a splenectomy. These people are also more vulnerable to malaria because they lack the spleen's ability to filter aberrant red blood cells (RBCs) from the bloodstream. Severe infection can occur from the related protozoal parasite Babesia, which is spread by Ixodes ticks in regions like Scotland and the eastern and upper mid-western states of the United States.

3.1.2. Infective Endocarditis

3.1.2.1. Native Valve Endocarditis

There may be a predisposing anatomical abnormality of the affected valve in native valve endocarditis. These abnormalities may be inherited or developed as a result of acquired illnesses like rheumatoid arthritis or, more frequently these days, age-related degenerative valve disease. Turbulence caused by the aberrant blood flow through the valve orifice harms the endothelium. On the damaged surface, platelets and fibrin are deposited, and these deposits are susceptible to colonization by bacteria that enter through the blood valve orifice. Figure 3.3 outlines the process. The valve endothelium of an injecting drug user (IDU) may be directly harmed by particulate contaminants in the injected material. Next, platelets and fibrin are deposited, which could provide a surface for bacteria to stick to.

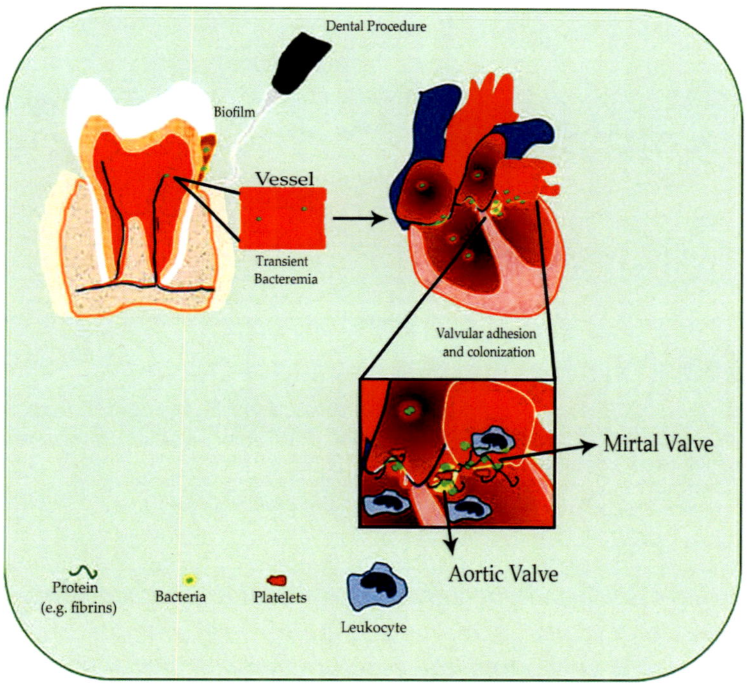

Figure 3.3. *An outline of the pathogenic changes that occur in the heart valves that predispose to infective endocarditis.*

Source: Del Giudice, C., Vaia, E., Liccardo, D., Marzano, F., Valletta, A., Spagnuolo, G., Ferrara, N., Rengo, C., Cannavo, A., & Rengo, G., (2021). Infective endocarditis: A focus on oral microbiota. Microorganisms, 9(6), 1218. https://doi.org/10.3390/microorganisms9061218.

Once the bacteria have taken up residence, they multiply and cause localized damage to the valves, which results in the growth of vegetation. Damage may worsen to the point where valve function is compromised, leading to heart failure. It is possible for the infection to spread into the myocardium and form an abscess in the valve root. The immune system is stimulated by the ongoing bacteremia caused by the infected valve. Weight loss and fever are symptoms of a chronic cytokine response, and glomerulonephritis can be brought on by immune complexes that accumulate in the kidney. Any organ's arterial system may become clogged with infected emboli that are emerging from a plant. For instance, as shown in Figure 3.4, septic emboli in the brain can result in the complication of a brain abscess.

Endocarditis can present as an acute life-threatening illness requiring urgent surgical intervention to remove the infected valve. A patient can present weeks into a vague illness with lethargy and low-grade fever being the only symptoms. An embolic event such as a stroke can be the first evidence of endocarditis caused by an oral *streptococcus*, such as *Streptococcus salivarius*. A heart murmur in such a setting must alert the clinician to the diagnosis of bacterial endocarditis and direct the collection of three sets of blood cultures before any antibiotics are given.

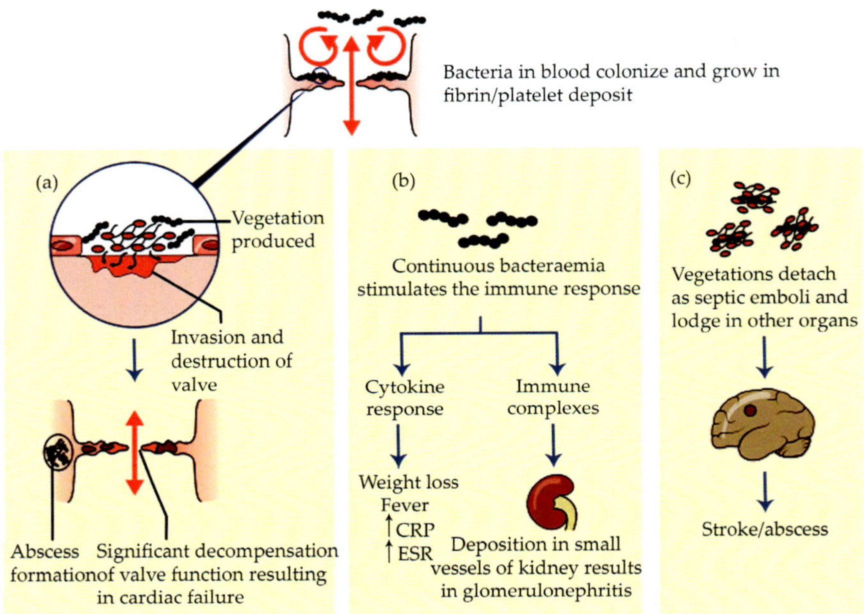

Figure 3.4. *Bacteria from an occult bacteremia can initiate endocarditis. (a) Destruction of the valve can occur; (b) the continuous bacteremia stimulates the immune system; and (c) vegetation can detach from the infected valve, and the resultant emboli can lodge in distant organs. (CRP: C-reactive protein; ESR: erythrocyte sedimentation rate.)*

Source: https://www.routledge.com/Clinical-Microbiology/Struthers/p/book/9781498786898.

3.1.2.2. Prosthetic Valve Endocarditis

Localized abnormalities in blood flow will result from a prosthetic heart valve, and turbulence could harm the endothelium next to the valve. Prosthetic valve endocarditis (PVE) can result from the colonization of a structure created by the deposition of fibrin and platelets (Figure 3.5). There are two types of PVE: early and late endocarditis. Early PVE develops within one year of valve replacement and is frequently brought on by staphylococci that are not coagulase-negative and were introduced during the procedure. The term "late PVE endocarditis" refers to endocarditis that develops more than one year following valve replacement. A variety of bacteria and fungi, most commonly Candida, can cause this condition. Any patient who is not feeling well and has a prosthetic valve should be evaluated for PVE right away. Before administering antibiotics, three sets of blood cultures should be obtained. This is crucial because a coagulase-negative *Staphylococcus* that grows in only one set of blood cultures presents a diagnostic challenge because the organism may be a skin contaminant. If the same coagulase-negative *Staphylococcus* grows in three sets of blood cultures spaced apart by time, this guarantees the appropriate antibiotic therapy. Antibiotic-based conservative therapy can be effective, but prosthetic valve replacement might be necessary.

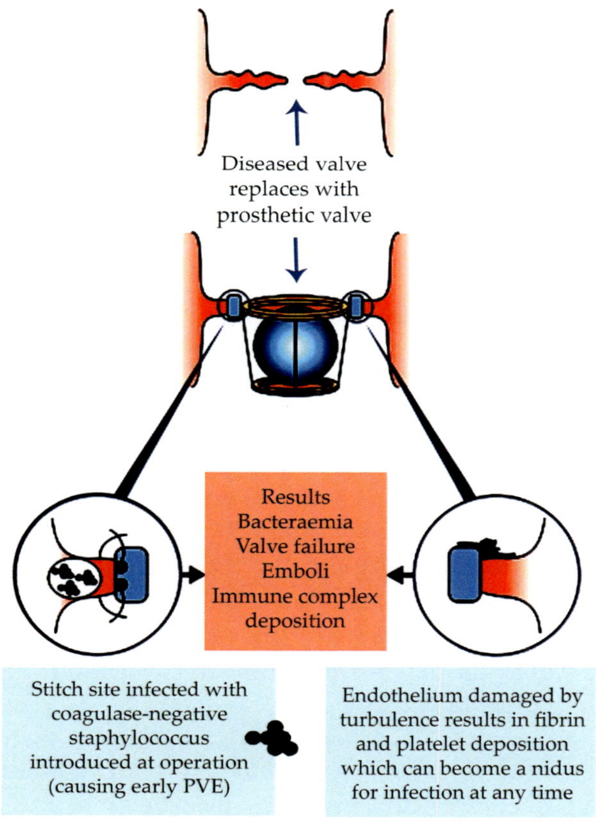

Figure 3.5. *Replacement of a native valve with a prosthetic valve can predispose to prosthetic valve endocarditis (PVE). Bacteria such as the coagulase-negative staphylococci are important.*

Source: http://repository.stikesrspadgs.ac.id/25/.

3.1.3. Infections of Implantable Cardiac Electronic Devices

When defibrillation and resynchronization are necessary to treat cardiac conduction disorders, implantable cardiac electronic devices, or ICEDs, are utilized. They are made up of a generator device or box that is inserted into the upper chest's subcutaneous tissue. The box leads enter the subclavian vein and proceed to the right heart, where they end at the base of the right ventricle and the medial side of the atrium (Figure 3.6).

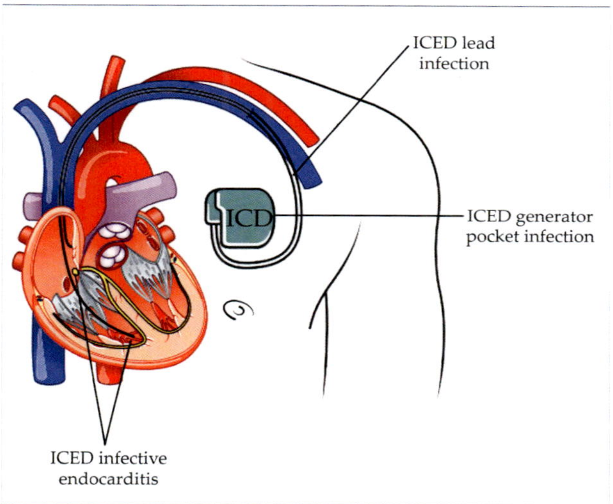

Figure 3.6. *An implantable cardiac electronic device in the subcutaneous tissue. Leads pass into the subclavian vein and terminate at the medial wall of the right atrium and ventricle. The sites where infection can occur are indicated.*

Source: http://repository.stikesrspadgs.ac.id/25/.

Following ICED insertion, infection is a major risk factor, and early infection typically develops around 6 months after insertion. Risk factors include the formation of haematomas, wound dehiscence, inadequate antibiotic prophylaxis during insertion, and prior temporary pacing.

Most organisms isolated from ICED infections are gram-positive bacteria, with *S. aureus* and coagulase-negative staphylococci being the most common types. Propionibacterium and other skin commensals may also be implicated. Up to 15% of infections are caused by gram-negative bacteria like *Pseudomonas aeruginosa* and "coliforms."

The obvious role of common skin commensals like Propionibacterium and coagulase-negative staphylococci highlights the necessity of meticulous skin decontamination and surgical technique during the device insertion procedure. For perioperative prophylaxis, the right antibiotic at the right dose needs to be administered. In the United Kingdom, guidelines suggest giving one dose of teicoplanin (e.g., 800 mg), which can be administered along with a single gentamicin dose of 160 mg.

3.2. Diagnosis and Management

The *Plasmodium* genus of malaria parasites is a significant parasitic infection to rule out in patients who have traveled to tropical and subtropical areas. This highlights the importance of finding out the patient's risk of vector exposure if they have a travel history and a fever.

3.2.1. Blood Cultures

3.2.1.1. When to Take Blood Cultures?

Hospitalized patients with fever (usually ≥ 38.2°C) and an infection focus should have blood cultures taken. Fever, however, is not always a reliable indicator in the elderly patient; confusion, or heightened confusion, is crucial.

It is necessary to obtain at least one set of carefully taken blood cultures. It can occasionally be challenging to obtain a specimen from the likely site of infection, especially in older patients. For example, it could be challenging to obtain a clean-catch midstream urine (MSU) sample from an elderly patient who is demented or incontinent. If endocarditis or infection of an ICED is suspected, three time-separated sets of blood cultures are needed. Central venous access devices are essential to the care of patients in a number of clinical domains, such as oncology and hematology patients, patients in need of continuous hemodialysate, and patients with total parenteral nutrition. These lines are susceptible to infection by a variety of bacteria, such as Candida and environmental mycobacteria. A set of blood cultures from each lumen of the central venous catheter (CVC) as well as a peripheral set should be promptly considered in the setting of sepsis, even if there are no overt signs of infection at the CVC insertion site. Every set's location needs to be properly labeled.

3.2.1.2. What Blood Cultures Do?

Less than 100 bacteria per milliliter (pc) are found in the blood obtained from the bacteremic patient. Blood cultures are intended to amplify these bacteria to quantities suitable for use in the laboratory; Figure 3.7 describes the procedure. The patient's blood and the commercial medium serve as a rich source of nutrients, and organisms multiply rapidly at 37°C. When they reach a critical concentration of about 105 organisms/mL, a metabolic signal triggers an alarm indicating that the bottle is "positive."

The chemical basis for detection in standard blood culture systems is the dissolved metabolic CO_2 of the reproducing organisms. When combined with water, this creates carbonic acid, which splits into carbonate and hydrogen ions. The sensor located at the base of the bottle initiates the electronic signal when a predetermined concentration of hydrogen ions is attained. Usually, organisms are visible when the fluid from the bottle is stained with the

Gram stain. The results of the Gram stain are examined along with the information on the request form, and the clinical team is consulted. This outcome also affects the range of agar plates that are tested for antibiotic susceptibility using a "direct" method.

Blood cultures are typically incubated for five days, but in situations where more fastidious organisms are being considered, such as infective endocarditis or a potential Brucella infection, this period is extended.

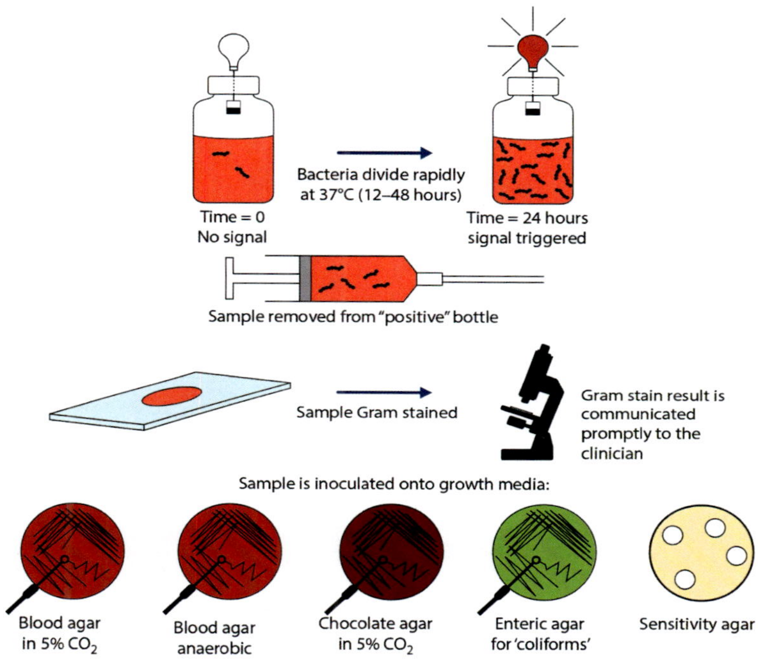

Figure 3.7. *Reproducing organisms in the blood culture bottle produce a metabolic signal that alerts it as positive. The example here shows the emission of gaseous CO_2 produced by respiration or fermentation of the organisms in the blood culture 'broth.'*

Source: http://repository.stikesrspadgs.ac.id/25/1/Clinical%20Microbiology%20Struthers-299hlm.pdf.

3.2.1.3. How to Take a Blood Culture?

Every hospital will have a blood culture collection training program, and it is crucial that this program be offered and followed. Figure 3.8 illustrates some of the tools needed to obtain a blood culture. Following instructions to guarantee that the blood is free of organisms from the patient's or the taker's skin is essential when collecting blood cultures. This is particularly important when drawing blood from a CVC, as it is crucial to avoid contaminating the lines in the process.

Place all the components together on a tray along with a sharps disposal container. It is important to verify that the bottles are in date and that the base of the bottle is green or blue in color. Following hand washing and drying, the plastic caps are taken off and the area is cleaned using an alcohol-chlorhexidine wipe. Once the collector has palpated the patient's vein, from which blood will be drawn, they put on disposable surgical gloves, followed by carefully cleaning the venepuncture site for 30 seconds with the disinfection applicator, and then wait another 30 seconds for it to dry.

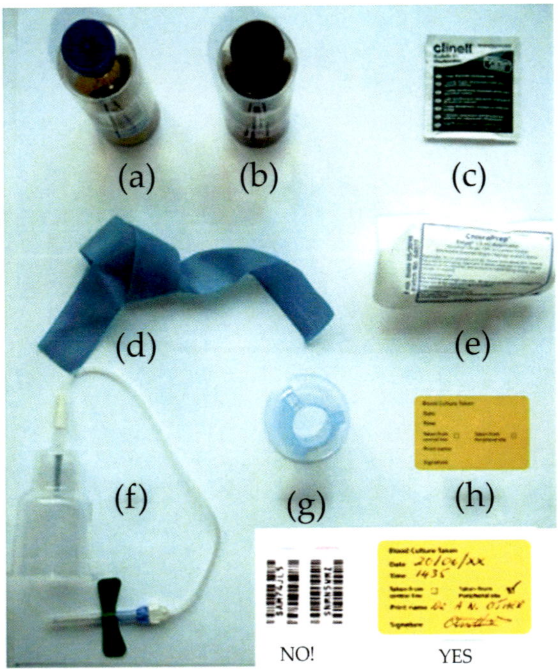

Figure 3.8. *Equipment needed to collect a blood culture set: (a) aerobic bottle; (b) anaerobic bottle; (c) alcohol wipe to decontaminate bottle septum after cap removal; (d) disposable tourniquet; (e) alcohol/chlorhexidine skin disinfector; (f) butterfly needle and connector; (g) insert to collect other blood samples; and (h) sticker to record collection time and date in the notes. The barcode copies go on the request form, and not in the notes.*

Source: https://www.routledge.com/Clinical-Microbiology/Struthers/p/book/9781498786898.

Venepuncture is accomplished without re-palpating the area, and the plastic sleeve/needle is clamped over the aerobic bottle. Blood flow draws air out of the collecting system and into this bottle, preventing oxygen from entering the anaerobic bottle during transfer. Each bottle holds about 10 mL of blood. The plastic adapter insert can then be used to take additional blood samples. Figure 3.9 illustrates several blood culture collection-related topics.

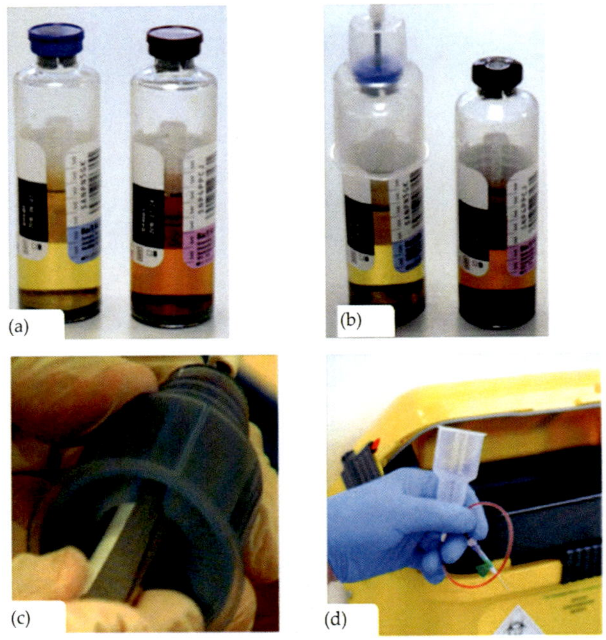

Figure 3.9. *The blood culture set. (a) The aerobic (left) and anaerobic bottle (right) before caps is removed; (b) collection starts with the aerobic bottle; (c) after the blood culture bottles are filled, tubes for other blood tests can be collected; and (d) dispose of the 'sharp' safely.*

Source: http://repository.stikesrspadgs.ac.id/25/.

Blood culture bottles need to be properly labeled, with a copy of the barcode placed on the form and the barcodes visible, and the request form needs to be filled out completely. Credible information is necessary, such as the clinical data and the fact that the set is peripheral or comes from the designated CVC lumen. The date, time, access site (peripheral or CVC), and reason for taking blood cultures must all be clearly documented in the patient's notes. Blood cultures must be received by the laboratory as soon as possible in order to be installed in the blood culture machine; four hours after collection is the acceptable time frame. This is because the sensor system keeps an eye out for organisms growing exponentially. When bacteria in bottles are kept at room temperature for extended periods of time, they will grow and the machine won't detect the signal.

3.2.1.4. What Happens in the Laboratory?

The biomedical scientist in the lab will use the barcode reader to compare the bottles with the request form.

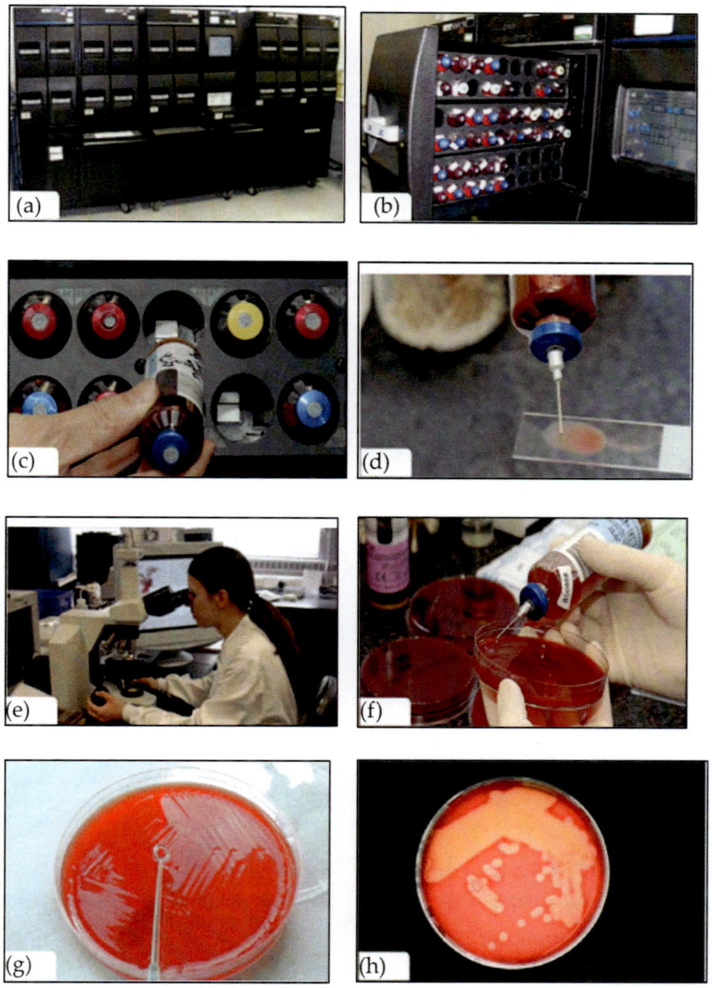

Figure 3.10. *(a) The BacT/Alert™ Biomerieux blood culture machine; (b) bottles in racks (yellow is a pediatric bottle); (c) removing the positive bottle; (d) a Gram stain is prepared; and (e) examined under the microscope; (f) a sample is inoculated onto appropriate culture media; (g) spreading the inoculum; and (h) after overnight incubation, plates are examined for growth and single colonies selected and 'picked off' for identification and, as required, additional antibiotic susceptibility testing (Streptococcus pyogenes here).*

Source: http://repository.stikesrspadgs.ac.id/25/.

In order to maintain a suspension of the organism and blood cells and provide a consistent growth medium, the bottles are subsequently put in the machine's trays, incubated at 37°C, and rocked. Following a 12- to 18-hour period in which the bottle signals as positive, it is taken out of the machine and a sample is placed on a glass slide, Gram stained, and examined under a microscope using a safety needle. Additionally, inoculating agar plates with fluid from the blood culture bottle is done. In addition to dictating which antibiotic susceptibility tests are performed using the fluid (direct testing), the Gram stain result also determines which plates are inoculated for identification and culture. Figure 3.10 depicts this process.

3.2.2. The Gram Stain – Aiding the Diagnosis and Treatment

Figure 3.11 shows examples of blood culture Gram stains in various clinical settings. Blood cultures from the patient with fever, lymphangitis, and painful induration at a recent PVC site on the hand are growing gram-positive cocci in clusters that resemble staphylococci (Figure 3.11(a)). This needs to provide an initial Methicillin Sensitive (MSSA) or Methicillin Resistant (MRSA) identification of *S. aureus*. Gram-positive cocci in chains growing in blood culture are present in the patient with spreading cellulitis after a right shin abrasion (Figure 3.11(b)). It is most likely *Streptococcus pyogenes*, a member of group A *streptococcus*. This organism can induce necrotizing fasciitis, which progresses quickly.

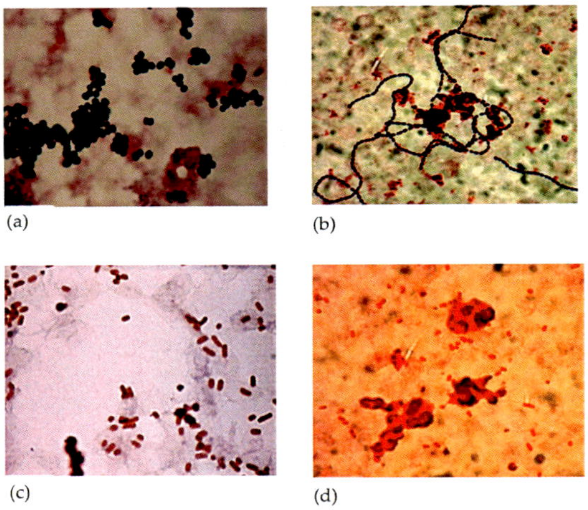

(a) (b) (c) (d)

Figure 3.11. *Examples of clinical situations and the Gram stain result of blood culture taken. (a) Infected antecubital fossa (peripheral venous cannula) site and gram-positive cocci in clusters, staphylococcal like; (b) cellulitis of the right shin and gram-positive cocci in chains, streptococcal like; (c) from a young woman with cystitis, pyelonephritis, sepsis, and gram-negative rods; (d) from a young man who returned from India 10 days ago with fever, malaise and gram-negative rods.*

Source: https://www.routledge.com/Clinical-Microbiology/Struthers/p/book/9781498786898.

The blood culture of a young woman with a history of cystitis and symptoms of pyelonephritis, fever, and hypotension (Figure 3.11(c)) reveals gram-negative rods, which are most likely *E. coli*. The young man in Figure 3.11(d), who has recently traveled to the Indian subcontinent, has a one-week-long fever and malaise. Gram-negative rods are strewn throughout the RBC debris; the patient has enteric fever; this organism is most likely Salmonella Typhi or Salmonella Paratyphi. It would have been imperative to incorporate this travel history information on the request form that came with the blood culture set. This not only gives clinical managers information, but it also serves as a critical warning to the laboratory staff, telling them to process the positive blood culture in the category 3 room for their own safety. Nine Examples of a blood culture's Gram stain along with the initial management procedure are shown in Table 3.1. Going over each of these examples is helpful because they illustrate crucial ideas for managing the bacteremic/candidemic patient.

Table 3.1. *Examples of Gram Stains of Blood Cultures Showing Bacteria and Yeasts**

Gram Stain	Gram Stain Description	Specimen and Patient Details	Other Specimen	Comment
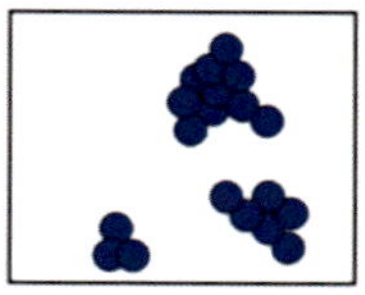	Gram-positive cocci in clusters; staphylococcal-like.	Peripheral blood culture collected from a 25-year-old female patient with first episode cystitis/ pyelonephritis.	Purulent MSU specimen collected on admission growing *Escherichia coli* $>10^8$ CFU/L.	Improving on co-amoxiclav 1.2 g q8h IV; await antibiotic sensitivity result of *E. coli*. Blood culture likely to be a contaminant (coagulase-negative *Staphylococcus*).
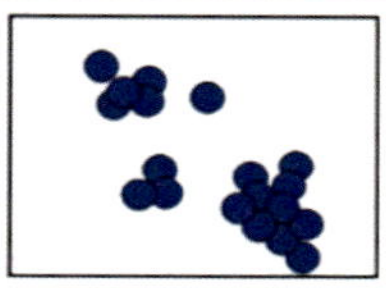	Gram-positive cocci in clusters; staphylococcal like	Peripheral blood culture collected from a 75-year-old male patient with infected PVC site. Line was in for 5 days.	None, the patient was MRSA negative on admission screening 7 days ago.	No improvement with flucloxacillin. Change to vancomycin 1 g q12h IV. Review infection control.
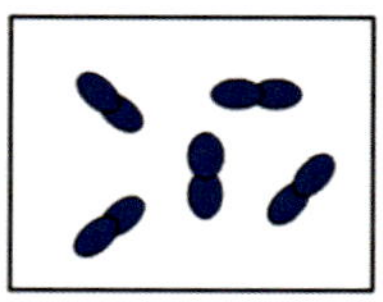	Gram-positive cocci in chains; streptococcal like.	Peripheral blood culture collected from a 35-year-old male patient with right shin cellulitis after trauma.	Swab of shin abrasion taken on admission growing mixed 'coliforms' and a *streptococcus*.	Good response to benzyl penicillin 1.2 g q6h IV. Review infection control, nurse in a single room.
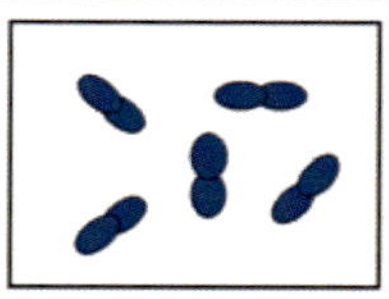	Gram-positive diplococci; pneumococcus	Peripheral blood culture collected from a previously well 55-year-old male patient (smoker) with right middle-lobe pneumonia.	Urine antigen test taken on admission positive for pneumococcus. Advise HIV test.	Good response to benzyl penicillin 1.2 g q6h IV. Consider change to oral amoxicillin once culture and sensitivity result is available.
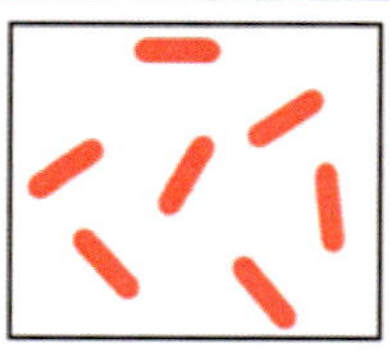	Gram-negative rods	Peripheral blood culture collected from a 23-year-old male patient with ongoing fever. Returned from India 10 days ago.	Purulent MSU specimen collected on admission growing *Escherichia coli* $> 10^8$ CFU/L. Sensitivities awaited.	No significant improvement on co-amoxiclav 1.2 g q8h IV. Change to ertapenem 1 g q24h IV. Review infection control.

	Gram-negative rods	Peripheral blood culture collected from a 23-year-old male patient with ongoing fever. Returned from India 10 days ago.	None. No signs or symptoms of a UTI, thus no MSU sent.	With travel history, likely enteric fever. Start ceftriaxone 2 g q24h IV. Review infection control. Lab staff alerted as to likely category 3 organism. Inform Public Health now; the patient works in a local restaurant kitchen.
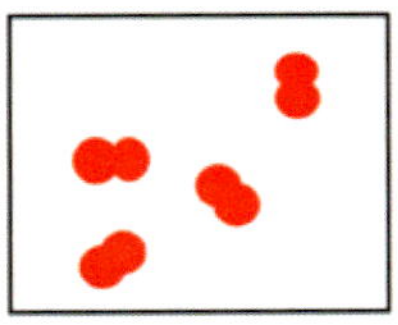	Gram-negative diplococci; meningococcus.	Peripheral blood culture collected from a 25-year-old female patient with pyrexia, hypotension and non-blanching rash.	EDTA blood collected for meningococcal PCR.	No evidence of meningitis or 'seeding' elsewhere. Good response to benzyl penicillin 1.2 g q6h IV. Consider change to oral ciprofloxacin once culture and sensitivity result is available. Review infection control and inform Public Health.
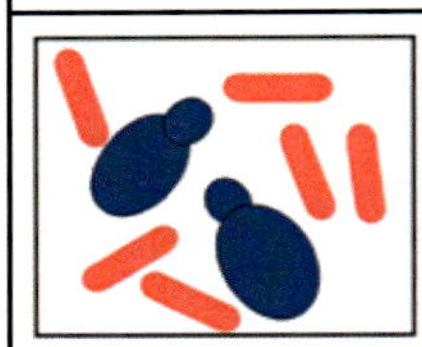	Gram-negative rods, and yeasts, candida-like.	Peripheral blood culture collected from a 45-year-old male patient with AML, and currently neutropenic.	Hickman line blood cultures (red and white lumens) also gram-negative rods and yeasts. *Candida glabrata* grown from previous HL site swab.	Still pyrexial with rigors after 48 hours of piperacillin/tazobactam 4.5 g q8h IV. Change to meropenem 1 g q8h IV. Stop prophylactic fluconazole and give caspofungin. Discuss prompt line removal.
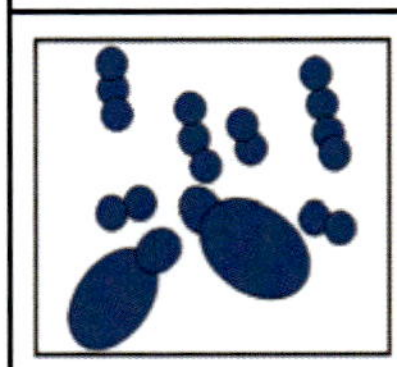	Gram-positive cocci in pairs and short chains, and yeasts, candida-like.	Peripheral blood culture collected from a 65-year-old male patient following biliary tract surgery, on ITU and HDU before return to the ward. Broad spectrum antibiotics given for 10 days.	*Candida albicans* grown from ET aspirate and CSU on ITU. No central line present now.	Spiking temperature, rising WCC; abdominal source. On vancomycin and meropenem since blood culture collected. Change vancomycin to linezolid 600 mg q12h IV and add fluconazole 400 mg q24h PO.

*Each is a scenario that outlines several management steps relevant to the organism(s) identified in the gram stain.

Source: http://repository.stikesrspadgs.ac.id/25/.

The prompt removal of the line must be considered when blood cultures confirm a CVC infection and the line and peripheral sets are growing the same organism. Numerous organisms possess the ability to relocate within the body. All patients with candidemia require an ophthalmology review because the candida yeasts have the potential to cause endophthalmitis. *Necrotrophomonas maltophilia*, an environmental bacterium, is one example of a relatively benign bacterium that can colonize the CVC of a patient suffering from neutropenia. In cases where blood cultures are positive, the "benign" nature of the organism shouldn't permit a "wait and see" approach. An extremely dangerous consequence is the subsequent development of embolic skin lesions that harbor the organism, especially if co-trimoxazole resistance is documented, the only antibiotic that effectively treats the organism.

3.2.3. Infective Endocarditis

Infectious endocarditis affects people without a known history of valve disease in about half of cases in developed nations. The majority of the remaining patients have ICED, prosthetic valves, unrepaired cyanotic congenital heart disease, or a history of infective endocarditis. Other conditions that increase the risk include diabetes, HIV infection, hemodialysis, and IDU. In at least 80% of cases, a fever is a common presentation. Moreover, there may be presenting symptoms such as renal failure, weight loss, splinter hemorrhages, haematuria, and unexplained heart failure. Raised white cell count and anemia are observed in approximately 50% of cases, while elevated C-reactive protein (CRP) is elevated in approximately two-thirds of cases.

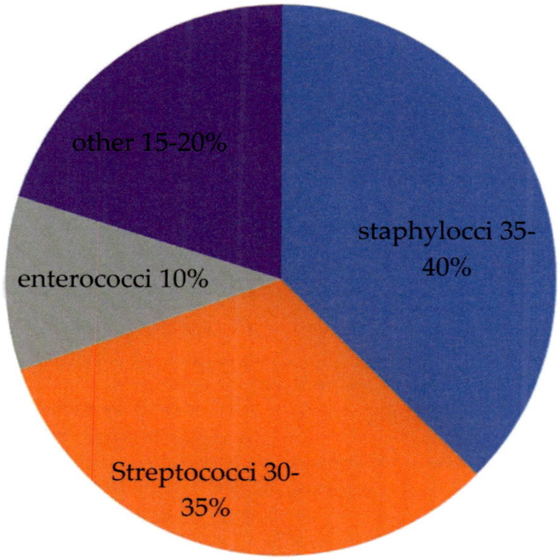

Figure 3.12. *A list of common organisms that cause infective endocarditis. The coagulase-negative staphylococci are usually associated with prosthetic valve endocarditis, but can cause natural valve endocarditis on occasion, e.g., Staphylococcus lugduniensis.*

Source: Cimmino, G., Bottino, R., Formisano, T., Orlandi, M., Molinari, D., Sperlongano, S., Castaldo, P., D'Elia, S., Carbone, A., Palladino, A., et al., (2023). Current views on infective endocarditis: Changing epidemiology, improving diagnostic tools, and centering the patient for up-to-date management. Life, 13(2), 377. https://doi.org/10.3390/life13020377.

Figure 3.12 lists the common organisms that are associated with infective endocarditis, which indicates that staphylococci and streptococci make up the majority. Though it is becoming more widely known that *Staphylococcus epidermidis* and *Staphylococcus lugduniensis* can occasionally cause native valve endocarditis, coagulase-negative staphylococci play a significant role in prosthetic valve endocarditis.

The acquisition of three sets of blood cultures, spaced apart in time and prior to the administration of antibiotics, is essential for the microbiological diagnosis of infective endocarditis and ICED infection. Under most conditions, it takes a few hours to gather all three sets. Antibiotics can be given over the course of minutes from various locations in the acute setting, when it is deemed necessary to administer them. Additional microbiological testing is carried out to make sure that a variety of antibiotic options are available for treatment once an organism has been identified in serial blood cultures. Tests for the minimum inhibitory concentration (MIC) of suitable antibiotics are conducted. These include penicillin, vancomycin, daptomycin, and gentamicin, which can be used in combination (synergy) with one of these antibiotics to treat streptococci and enterococci. MICs for daptomycin and vancomycin are established in the case of staphylococci. Additional medications like rifampicin and linezolid may also be employed. For native valve endocarditis caused by a sensitive *streptococcus*, the course of treatment varies from two weeks to six weeks.

When evaluating any patient who has endocarditis suspicion, the cardiology team must be involved. Transoesophageal echocardiography (TOE) and transthoracic echocardiography (TTE) have to be performed as soon as possible to confirm the diagnosis, evaluate the extent of valve failure, and look for local complications like the development of an aortic root abscess. Since quick surgery might be judged necessary, the cardiology team would collaborate closely with the cardiothoracic surgeons as well.

3.3. Respiratory Tract

Infections that impact the airways, encompassing the nose, throat, bronchi, and lungs, are known as respiratory tract infections (RTIs). These infections can be triggered by different pathogens, including viruses, bacteria, and sometimes fungi. RTIs are prevalent and vary in severity, ranging from mild, self-restricting illnesses to more serious conditions.

3.3.1. Pathogenesis

The respiratory tract's primary purpose is gas exchange. As a result, it is continuously exposed to gaseous pollutants, including organic particulate matter like bacteria, viruses, and spores. Even though the respiratory tract is continuously exposed to air, most particles are filtered out by inertial impaction with mucus-covered surfaces in the posterior nasopharynx and nasal hairs (Figure 3.13).

The lower respiratory tract is less likely to become contaminated by microorganisms thanks to the epiglottis, its closure reflex, and the cough reflex. The "mucociliary escalator" is the action of cilia that propel particles small enough to enter the trachea and bronchi towards the oropharynx by sticking to the respiratory mucus lining their walls. Respiratory secretions contain antimicrobial agents, such as secretory IgA, lactoferrin, and lysozyme, that further inhibit the growth of inhaled microorganisms.

Particles with a diameter of 5–10 µm have the potential to enter the lungs and even make it to the alveolar air spaces. Potential pathogens can be phagocytosed by alveolar macrophages in this situation, and if they are overpowered, the inflammatory response can draw in neutrophils. The respiratory tract's defenses mirror its susceptibility to microbial invasion. Microbial pathogens are mostly acquired by inhalation, although aspiration, mucosal contact, and hemorrhagic dissemination are also possible. Rarely do people with healthy lungs contain any bacteria outside of the carina.

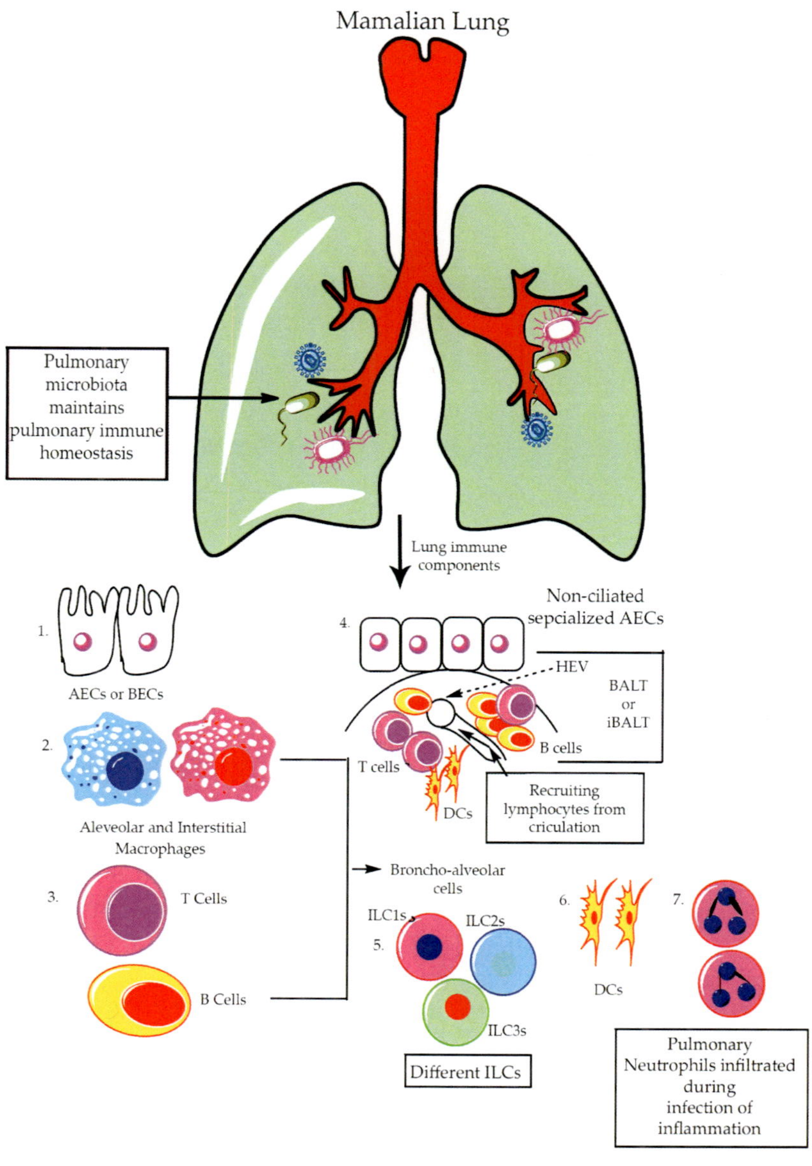

Figure 3.13. *Defenses of the respiratory tract.*

Source: Kumar, V., (2020). Pulmonary innate immune response determines the outcome of inflammation during pneumonia and sepsis-associated acute lung injury. Front. Immunol., 11, 1722. doi: 10.3389/fimmu.2020.01722.

Respiratory pathogens have evolved a variety of tactics to get past host defenses. For instance, the influenza virus clings to mucosal epithelial cells with its unique surface antigens. Periodically, the virus also changes genetically, expressing new adhesins against which the general public is not effectively immune. There are two bacteria, *Streptococcus pneumoniae* and *Haemophilus influenzae*, are known to produce and disable mucosal IgA is called IgA protease. They are not susceptible to phagocytosis, nor are other capsulated bacteria or mycobacteria. Although viruses that cause colds seem to be an exception, damage usually requires penetration of local tissues before damage even occurs. The host response is primarily responsible for damage in certain cases of lower RTIs.

Respiratory infections can also be a result of unhealthy habits and lifestyle. Smoking tobacco is such an example and can increase the production of viscous respiratory secretions and decrease the effectiveness of cilial function. When tracheal intubation is used for extended periods of time in critically ill patients, it avoids the upper respiratory tract and creates a pathway for microbes to enter the lungs.

3.3.2. Diagnosis

3.3.2.1. Clinical Features

The structures where inflammation is localized and the degree to which function is compromised determine the characteristics of many RTIs. Therefore, a nasopharyngeal infection will cause a nasal discharge, while cough and sputum production are seen in bronchitis, cough and sputum from pneumonia, as well as changes to the chest radiograph and an increased respiratory rate.

The majority of viral infections of the upper respiratory tract are self-limiting. A precise etiological diagnosis would be expensive and have no effect on the course of treatment. The doctor's duties are restricted to comforting the patient and identifying more serious bacterial infections that call for more intensive supportive care or specialized antimicrobial chemotherapy. Since lower RTIs are more likely to result in significant morbidity or even death, they should always be treated seriously.

3.3.2.2. Laboratory Tests

The degree of respiratory compromise and the identification of the causative pathogen are the two main concerns that are addressed by the history, physical examination, X-rays, and laboratory tests.

It may be necessary to take into account a large variety of candidate pathogens, so it is best to narrow down the pool of potential candidates as much as possible by looking for hints in the history, examination, and preliminary findings. One should look for a history of tobacco use, recent travel, occupation, pets, and contacts who have experienced similar symptoms.

It is surprisingly simple to obtain diagnostic specimens from the respiratory tract; however, their usefulness is frequently restricted due to contamination from the oral cavity's native flora. The upper respiratory tract needs to be avoided in order to avoid contaminating specimens from the lower respiratory tract.

A vital component of diagnosing lower RTIs include chest X-rays which more accurately show the location and severity of the illness than auscultation-elicited symptoms. Although lateral views can yield important extra information, postero-anterior views are the most frequently utilized.

A blood gas analysis ought to be carried out if acute respiratory compromise is suspected. Raised respiratory rate (> 30 beats/min), hypoxia, hypercapnia, bilateral or recently enlarging radiographic opacities, shock, renal failure, and confusion are the main markers of pneumonia disease severity.

3.4. Diseases and Syndromes

The main infectious diseases of the respiratory tract are listed in Table 3.2.

Table 3.2. *Infectious Diseases of the Respiratory Tract*

Pharyngitis	Acute inflammation of the throat, resulting in pain on swallowing and swollen, red pharyngeal mucosa.
Common Cold	Self-limiting rhinitis, causing nasal discharge, nasal obstruction, discomfort, and sneezing.
Influenza	Acute, usually self-limiting, viral infection with respiratory and systemic features.
Otitis Media	Acute inflammation of the middle ear.
Otitis Externa	Inflammation of the external auditory meatus.
Acute Sinusitis	Inflammation of the maxillary, frontal, ethmoid or sphenoidal sinuses.
Laryngitis	Inflammation of the larynx, with hoarseness and loss of voice.
Bronchitis	Cough and sputum production; can be acute or chronic.
Pneumonia **Acute, Community-Acquired** **Acute, Hospital-Acquired**	Occurs prior to or immediately after hospital admission; cough, chest signs and fever. Occurs in vulnerable patients in hospital; onset gradual and symptoms unreliable for diagnosis.
Chronic	Insiduous onset, prolonged course; usually diagnosed by radiological findings.
Pulmonary Tuberculosis	Coughing and sneezing occur, fever, night sweats, weight loss and coughing blood; chest X-ray demonstrates lung changes.
Empyema	Accumulation of purulent fluid in the pleural space.

Source: https://www.uib.cat/depart/dba/microbiologia/ADSenfcomI/material_archivos/infeccion%20respiratoria.pdf.

3.4.1. Pharyngitis

Pharyngitis causes swelling and redness of the pharyngeal mucosa in addition to pain when swallowing. The most common causes are respiratory viruses, such as coxsackievirus, Epstein-Barr virus, rhinovirus, coronavirus, adenovirus, influenza virus, and parainfluenza viruses.

Aetiological clues include:

- Conjunctivitis: adenovirus.
- Constitutional symptoms (lethargy and malaise) and tonsillar exudate: Epstein–Barr virus.
- Posterior palatal ulcers: coxsackievirus.
- Abrupt onset, 'doughnut' pharyngeal lesions and beefy uvula: *Streptococcus pyogenes* (*S. pyogenes*-group A *streptococcus*).
- Grey pharyngeal pseudomembrane in unvaccinated subject: *Corynebacterium diphtheriae*.

3.4.1.1. Bacterial Pharyngitis

S. pyogenes is the most common cause of bacterial pharyngitis, although it is not as common. Some uncommon bacterial sources are *Mycoplasma pneumoniae*, *Clostridium difficile*, and *Neisseria gonorrhoeae*, *Arcanobacterium hemolyticum* and *Corynebacterium diphtheriae*. In temperate regions, peak incidence occurs in the fall and spring; in tropical regions, it occurs during the rainy season. Transmission occurs either directly through droplet spread or more quickly amongst groups living in close quarters.

3.4.1.2. Viral Pharyngitis

Viral pharyngitis is a self-limiting condition that does not usually require a specific etiological diagnosis.

- **Diagnosis:** It is recommended to obtain a full blood count, blood film, and Paul-Bunnell test for heterophile antibodies when an Epstein-Barr virus infection (infectious mononucleosis) is suspected. Since people of Asian descent are not sensitive to the tests; it is recommended to look for IgM in the viral capsid antigen in this population. Finding *S. pyogenes* is the most commonly requested investigation for pharyngitis. Either direct antigen detection or culture on blood agar followed by a latex agglutination reaction for group-specific polysaccharide are used to identify this species.

  Antibiotic susceptibility testing is only possible through culture; neither technique can differentiate between oropharyngeal colonization and actual infection. Suspicion of Aspergillus, *Mycoplasma* spp. Arcanobacterium species, or Corynebacterium varieties should be shared with the lab in order to utilize specialized, non-standard culture media.

- **Treatment:** Treatment for streptococcal pharyngitis involves the use of an oral penicillin or erythromycin. Treatment should lower the risk of major non-infective sequelae like Sydenham's chorea, poststreptococcal glomerulonephritis, and rheumatic heart disease, but it may not change the course of the initial pharyngeal infection. Since there are few non-infectious consequences of streptococcal infection, the necessity for antibiotic treatment of streptococcal pharyngitis has been questioned in developed nations; however, the recent rise in streptococcal infection in North America and Europe may alter this opinion.

  Other complications of streptococcal pharyngitis include quinsy (paratonsillar abscess), streptococcal toxic shock syndrome (both caused by toxin), and scarlet fever (less common than in the past in developed countries). Although oral anaerobic bacteria can cause secondary infections in quinsy, these bacteria are frequently penicillin-sensitive. Purulent foci need to be drained.

3.4.2. Common Cold

Common colds are frequent during the autumn-spring season, especially in young children and their parents. The primary cause of the illness is rhinoviruses. The development of a successful vaccine has been hampered by the size of the rhinoviral group and the causative role of other respiratory viruses in a small percentage of common colds. Sneezing, nasal discharge, and nasal blockage are present. Myalgia and fever are uncommon symptoms; pharyngitis and cough are possible. Antimicrobial agents should not be used, and the goal of treatment should be limited to symptom relief.

3.4.3. Influenza

Influenza virus groups A–C are the cause of both endemic and epidemic influenza, and is an RNA virus with a segmented genome. While systemic and respiratory symptoms are more prominent, some of the characteristics of a common cold may still be present. Common symptoms typically include fever, fatigue, and myalgia. Haemagglutinin and neuraminidase are the two main surface antigens used to type epidemic strains. Genetic reassortment results in an antigenic shift, which is responsible for the various influenza virus types observed in subsequent epidemics. Between epidemics, the antigenic composition varies slightly. We call these things antigenic drift. Epidemics caused by antigenic shift occur when pre-existing specific immunity to influenza virus antigens is rendered obsolete. Due to cardiorespiratory failure or secondary bacterial pneumonia (caused by *St. aureus* or *S. pneumoniae*), high death rates have been observed during influenza epidemics.

- **Diagnosis:** It is usually clinical, with serology reserved for epidemiological studies and pandemic surveillance.
- **Treatment:** The goal of treatment is to relieve symptoms and address any complications that may arise. On the other hand, if amantidine treatment is started early in an epidemic type A strain infection, it might be beneficial. For some patients, new therapies for influenza infection, like the neuraminidase inhibitor oseltamivir, may shorten the duration of symptoms.

Although a vaccine is available, it is only effective against strains that have been previously isolated. Therefore, those who are most likely to experience complications are offered the vaccine, i.e., individuals who are elderly, suffer from heart or respiratory conditions, have renal failure, live in residential institutions, work in high-risk occupations (e.g., health care).

3.4.4. Otitis Media

Acute middle ear inflammation is known as otitis media. Due to their shorter and more horizontal eustachian tubes, younger children experience it more frequently. Due to a previous respiratory tract infection, it is also more vulnerable to blockage at the proximal end by hypertrophic lymphoid tissue.

A tense, red tympanic membrane collects purulent fluid, which may leak out of the membrane when it ruptures. The most common causes of infection are *H. influenzae* or *S. pneumoniae*. Localized pain and fever are typical symptoms, and hearing loss and secretory otitis media are frequent side effects. Meningitis and mastoiditis are far less common complications.

- **Diagnosis:** Primarily, diagnosis is clinical. It is necessary to do an aural examination of both tympanic membranes. Only after purulent exudate from the middle ear is cultured—either after tympanocentesis or after discharge via the eardrum—is an etiological diagnosis possible.
- **Treatment:** Antimicrobial treatment is with an antibacterial agent (e.g., oral ampicillin or erythromycin for 7–10 days). Some authorities recommend decongestant therapy as an alternative in uncomplicated acute otitis media.

3.4.5. Otitis Externa

The most common cause of external auditory meatus inflammation is Aspergillus niger, a hyphae-forming fungus. By cultivating fungus from exudate, a diagnosis is made. It might be enough to use an aluminum acetate topical agent and aural toilet. Antibiotic preparations for topical use ought to be avoided. *P. aeruginosa* is the cause of malignant otitis externa, a rare and occasionally fatal variant that affects diabetes treatment using drugs that work against *Pseudomonas* spp. should be applied.

3.4.6. Acute Sinusitis

Bacteria from the nasopharynx infect the axillary, frontal, ethmoid, or sphenoidal sinuses when there is insufficient sinus secretion drainage due to an upper respiratory tract infection or other similar cause. The bacteria most commonly implicated are *S. pneumoniae* and *H. influenzae*. Infection causes the sinus to fill up with mucopus, which alters the resonance of the voice and causes a feeling of local discomfort.

- **Diagnosis:** The main diagnostic criteria are the symptoms; however, special radiographic views may reveal maxillary sinus filling. Obtaining representative bacteriological specimens is a challenging task.
- **Treatment:** To improve drainage, decongestants are used as a treatment. In more serious or persistent cases, surgery might be necessary. According to certain authorities, oral antibiotics (e.g., erythromycin or ampicillin) ought to be taken in addition.
- **Laryngitis:** One of the "respiratory" viruses causes laryngitis, a self-limiting illness characterized by hoarseness and voice loss. It might also be a symptom of the flu or a common cold. Specialized therapy is not necessary.

3.4.7. Bronchitis

Acute exacerbation of chronic bronchitis, tracheobronchitis, and acute bronchitis (strictly defined) are three related conditions. Acute Bronchitis manifests as a cough and sputum production (typically white to cream in color), but an X-ray of the chest shows no radiographic abnormalities. *M. pneumoniae* is the cause of infection.

With tracheobronchitis, acute bouts of coughing are not accompanied by significant sputum production. Infection is caused by influenza virus, and features of systemic infection such as fever and myalgia may be present.

Acute exacerbation of chronic bronchitis is a chronic productive cough that changes to become productive of larger quantities of newly purulent sputum. This illness may be the result of infection with one of the respiratory viruses, *S. pneumoniae* or *H. influenzae*.

- **Diagnosis:** These three conditions overlap significantly in real-world situations. Sputum cultures are not very useful for diagnosis. According to some authorities, culture should only be considered if treatment is not working after 48 hours.
- **Treatment:** Some patients will benefit from receiving an antibacterial agent treatment for a few days (e.g., oral erythromycin or ampicillin), but many patients won't see any improvement with treatment. Pneumococcal infection and influenza vaccinations should be administered to patients who are at risk of heart or lung failure.

3.4.8. Pneumonia: Acute, Community-Acquired

Acute pneumonia can start before or right after being admitted to the hospital. Across the globe, it is among the most frequent infectious causes of mortality. A cough, chest pains, and fever are typical symptoms in patients with acute pneumonia. There's no guarantee that the cough will produce purulent sputum. The interpretation of chest signs can be subjective and varies widely. They could point to areas of consolidation, fluid in the voids, or even an effusion or cavity. Impaired respiratory function is the main effect of acute pneumonia, and it needs to be evaluated right away. The selection of antimicrobial therapy will depend on the identity of the most likely infectious agent. A careful history, a comprehensive examination, and the relevant chest X-rays should provide some indications as to the most likely cause of the illness.

Four main clinico-pathological patterns of acute pneumonia are recognized:

- Lobar pneumonia:
  - demarcated by border of segment or lobe;
  - Most often caused by *S. pneumoniae*;
  - Also caused by *S. aureus*, *S. pyogenes* (group A *streptococcus*) and *Legionella pneumophila*.
- Bronchopneumonia:
  - Patchy consolidation around the larger airways;
  - Caused by *S. pneumoniae*, *H. influenzae*, *S. aureus* and *L. pneumophila*.
- Interstitial pneumonia:
  - Fine areas of interstitial infiltration in lung fields;
  - Usually no sputum production at presentation;
  - Caused by *Legionella* sp., *Mycoplasma* spp. or virus;
  - Initial treatment is with erythromycin.
- Aspiration pneumonia:
  - Follows aspiration of oral or gastric contents;
  - Damage usually caused by chemical or mechanical insult;
  - Chest X-ray changes either in the lower right lobe or, if supine, the apex of the right lower lobe;
  - Bacterial damage caused by oral streptococci or anaerobes.

3.4.8.1. Aetiological Clues

The causative organism can be suggested by the type of symptom observed (Table 3.3).

Table 3.3. *Features of Pneumonia Caused by Different Bacteria*

Organism	Symptoms
Streptococcus pneumoniae	Sudden onset pleuritic pain, fever, rusty sputum, cold sores
Klebsiella pneumoniae	Thick, viscous red sputum, alcoholic patient
Staphylococcus aureus	Pneumonia following influenza
Streptococcus pneumoniae	Pneumonia in the chronic bronchitic
Haemophilus influenzae	Pneumonia in the chronic bronchitic
Mycoplasma pneumoniae	Non-productive cough, pharyngitis in young adult with family contacts; ambulant despite positive chest X-ray
Legionella pneumophila	Non-productive cough, confusion, diarrhoea, middle-aged male, smoker, exposure to air conditioning or hotel shower
Mycobacterium tuberculosis	Upper lobe consolidation, hilar lymphadenopathy, vagrant or alcoholic
Chlamydia psittaci	Close contact with parrot or similar type of bird

Source: https://www.uib.cat/depart/dba/microbiologia/ADSenfcomI/material_archivos/infeccion%20respiratoria.pdf.

- **Diagnosis:** The results of the sputum Gram stain may help narrow down the options for presumptive therapy. Results from culture and antibiotic susceptibility tests take too long to influence the first treatment decision, but they can be important in a later change, especially if the first therapy did not work well. It is best to collect sputum samples with as little oral flora contamination as possible. The ideal specimen is a deep cough that is obtained first thing in the morning. Before doing this, you should gargle with sterile water. If the patient is having trouble producing a specimen, a physiotherapist could be able to help. The patient should be instructed on how to prevent contamination of the outer surface of the screw-top container, which should be rigid.

  More invasive techniques that avoid the mouth can completely prevent specimen contamination by oral flora. These consist of transtracheal aspiration, transbronchial or transthoracic biopsy, and bronchoscopy with a protected specimen collection device. Each of these methods has potential negative effects and calls for patience, expertise, and specialized tools. A blood culture ought to be carried out if the patient is feverish.

  In a matter of minutes, after the laboratory receives the specimen, a preliminary Gram stain result is available. Should the smear be populated by neutrophil polymorphs and a solitary organism type (e.g., Gram-positive diplococcus), and the outcome might help prompt clinical judgment. The smear is not suitable for additional bacteriological analysis if there are significant amounts of saliva present or if there are buccal epithelial cells in it. Notifying the diagnostic laboratory of any potential Mycoplasma, Legionella, or Mycobacterium species is crucial since all of these organisms need unusual methods to be detected. Some labs provide *Chlamydia* spp. and Legionella direct or indirect immunofluorescent detection. Although mycoplasmas and legionella can be grown, the rate of detection is lower than when using serological techniques. However, the information gathered is less useful for patient management due to the time required for a second serum titer.

- **Treatment:** Presumptive therapy for acute pneumonia is currently based on a syndrome-based approach rather than a "best guess" method, which eliminates the need to identify the microbial cause of infection in order to select the best antimicrobial agents. Covering every potential pathogen with an assumed chemotherapy regimen is rarely feasible. The antimicrobial agents ought to be administered via the route, typically intravenous, and dosage that ensure optimal antimicrobial efficacy, after having been selected based on their ability to combat the most probable pathogens. It is important to closely monitor the response to presumed therapy. Even with the best antimicrobial therapy, some patients may not experience an immediate response and may pass away from acute pneumonia. Therefore, determining whether or not a specific antibiotic has had the desired effect may be challenging. Improvement on radiography may take several days to manifest in clinical response.
- **Prevention:** Pneumococcal pneumonia can be prevented by vaccinating with a polyvalent vaccine to capsular polysaccharides. Protection is only partial because of changes that occur in the relative prevalence of particular pneumococcal capsular types (around 84 at present). Vaccination is, therefore, limited to those at greatest risk: the elderly, those with chest or heart disease, chronic renal failure and prior to splenectomy.

Legionella infection can be prevented by public health measures to reduce the risk of exposure by bprogram biociding or heating water sources likely to act as a source of contaminated aerosols, e.g., evaporative condensers and air-conditioning cooling towers.

3.4.9. Pneumonia: Acute, Hospital-Acquired

Although pneumonia is the most common nosocomial infection to cause death, it is also the third most common infection acquired in hospitals. It affects smokers, patients who have had chest surgery, patients with a history of chest disease, and critically ill patients on ventilators who present with the highest relative risk.

Nosocomial pneumonia is most often caused by *P. aeruginosa*, *S. aureus* and the Enterobacteriaceae. Rarely Legionellas or respiratory viruses are implicated. There is a particular association between *S. aureus* pneumonia and traumatic head injury. The mechanically ventilated patient is prone to the colonization of the lungs by bacteria from the stomach and mouth. These organisms enter the trachea along the outside of the tracheal tube. Occasionally, bacteria from the mechanical ventilator and other respiratory support devices get into the lungs via the lumen of the tracheal tube.

- **Diagnosis:** Nosocomial pneumonia usually develops more slowly than infections obtained in the community. The typical symptoms of pneumonia in the critically ill, such as purulent sputum, fever, elevated leucocyte count, and radiographic infiltrates, may also indicate the presence of non-infective processes. As a result, bacteriological analysis of tracheal secretions will only show the expansion of upper respiratory tract bacterial flora into the trachea, making clinical diagnosis unreliable. Techniques for protected collection (e.g., In untreated patients, bronchoalveolar lavage using a protected bronchoscopy catheter) are recommended for obtaining adequate bacteriological specimens.

- **Management:** Antimicrobial chemotherapy needs to be customized to the hospital or unit in question's needs and susceptibility patterns. To plan presumptive therapy, laboratory results should be regularly reviewed epidemiologically. Numerous nosocomial pneumonia patients are already severely ill and may not benefit from the best antimicrobial treatment. As a result, several preventive techniques have been created. Currently, there is no preventive method that provides total immunity against nosocomial pneumonia; of these, antibiotic prophylaxis has proven to be the least effective.

3.4.10. Pneumonia: Chronic

Compared to acute pneumonia, chronic pneumonia develops more slowly and has a longer duration. Since there isn't just one set of symptoms, radiological findings are frequently used to make the diagnosis. While fever is unpredictable, it can occasionally be accompanied by rigors (shaking fits) and night sweats. Anorexia and weight loss are characteristics of chronic sepsis that may also exist. Sputum from a cough may occasionally be purulent and bloodstained (hemoptysis). Neoplasms and connective tissue diseases are additional causes, while not every cause of persistent pneumonia is communicable . The most frequent infectious cause is tuberculosis in the lungs. Other bacteria, fungi, and atypical mycobacteria are examples of infectious causes.

- **Diagnosis:** It is crucial to conduct a thorough history and clinical examination. A thorough workup for acute pneumonia ought to be part of the investigation. Requests for cytology, silver stain, and acid-fast stain (Ziehl-Neelsen or auramine-phenol) should be made in addition to the sputum examination. This will assist in ruling out fungi, mycobacteria, and neoplasms. Because the illness is chronic, diagnostic testing should be finished before starting a particular antimicrobial chemotherapy. Before committing a patient to a lengthy course of treatment, it is crucial to make every effort to obtain a precise diagnosis, as certain conditions may necessitate months of chemotherapy.

3.4.11. Pulmonary Tuberculosis

While chronic pneumonia is a common presentation of *M. tuberculosis*, there are several other presentations of pulmonary tuberculosis:

- Acute bronchopneumonia;
- Pulmonary cavitation;
- Miliary tuberculosis;
- Primary complex of focal, peripheral lung disease and hilar lymphadenopathy may be noticed as an incidental finding on a chest radiograph.

Due to a combination of urban poverty and acquired immunodeficiency syndrome (AIDS), the incidence of pulmonary tuberculosis has reversed in more developed nations during the

20th century, where it is more prevalent. Primary infection develops after airborne transmission from a pulmonary tuberculosis patient, and exposure causes the formation of a primary complex if the host has sufficient defenses. Mycobacteria are resistant to phagocytosis because of their thick, lipid-containing cell walls. The result is a granuloma with central caseating necrosis that is walled off by fibrosis from the inhaled bacteria. The immune system that is found in cells mediates immunity. Primary tuberculosis only arises when the initial infective challenge is too strong for cell-mediated immunity to withstand. Reactivation of the primary focus, usually at the left or right apex, may be followed by secondary pneumonia.

- **Diagnosis:** Haemoptysis, weight loss, fever, and night sweats are all indications of pulmonary tuberculosis. The radiographic appearance corresponds with one of the previously mentioned clinical presentations. Sputum should be stained with an acid-fast stain (either Ziehl-Neelsen or auramine-phenol) in addition to the standard Gram stain. This is the recommended staining process with three consecutive early-morning specimens. Sputum specimens should be handled with caution and warned to laboratory ward and portering staff that they may pose an infection risk.

  While results from the acid-fast stain can be obtained the same day, due to the slow growth of mycobacteria grow slowly, results from culture, identification, and susceptibility testing take several weeks. To obtain diagnostic specimens, either a gastric aspiration or bronchoscopy is necessary for children and patients who produce little to no sputum. In cases of sputum smear-positive disease, *M. tuberculosis* infection can be confirmed considerably faster with nucleic acid amplification (PCR) testing. The creation of susceptibility testing, and culture-based confirmation have been expedited by quick and automated analyzers. To show the presence of multidrug-resistant *M. tuberculosis*, however, may still take a few weeks. It is common practice to confirm the identity of suspected *M. tuberculosis* isolates using bacterial gene sequencing at the 16S ribosomal locus.

- **Treatment:** Existing treatment protocols use multiple antimycobacterial agents to ensure adequate antibacterial activity in various cellular and extracellular locations, such as granulomata, collections of respiratory secretions, and inside phagocytic cells. There have been numerous regimens examined. Currently available most effective regimens use up to four agents during an intense two- to four-week induction period; fewer agents are used during a five- to nine-month maintenance period. In cases where sputum contains acid-fast bacilli at the time of diagnosis, patients may be a source of secondary infection. It takes several days for them to become noninfectious due to the effectiveness of current treatment protocols, however relapse can occur by noncompliance with advised maintenance treatment. Rifampicin, isoniazid, ethambutol, pyrazinamide, and streptomycin are antituberculous drugs that are frequently used.

- **Prevention:** Intradermal inoculation of a live, attenuated strain of mycobacterium (BCG) is a prevention method once the tuberculin skin test has shown no reactivity. Contact tracing and treatment can stop the secondary spread of tuberculosis since adults with untreated pulmonary tuberculosis are the main reservoir of the disease in developed countries. Cattle represent a substantial additional reservoir in certain nations. Important strategies for preventing zoonotic tuberculosis include pasteurization of milk, meat inspection, and the creation of a national stock of cattle free of tuberculosis.

3.4.12. Empyema

The buildup of purulent fluid in the pleural space is known as an empyema. It is brought on by either haematogenous spread from a distant focus, infection as a result of penetrating thoracic trauma, or direct extension from underlying pneumonia. Numerous bacteria, such as *S. aureus*, Enterobacteriaceae, streptococci, and obligate anaerobes, can cause an infection.

- **Diagnosis:** On a chest radiograph, pleural effusion and a gas-fluid interface may be visible (a lateral view is a more sensitive method of detection), and the affected area will also be dull to percussion. Drainage is necessary for the collection of purulent fluid to facilitate diagnosis and treatment. Before starting the drainage process, it is best to request an anaerobic culture, preferably by contacting the laboratory. It is additionally best to consult a thoracic surgeon as soon as possible.
- **Treatment:** Presumptive antibiotic therapy depends on the results of Gram stain but should include an agent active against obligate anaerobes, e.g., metronidazole.

A Closer Look

Illuminating the Blood and Respiratory Tract

The intricate network of the blood and respiratory tract plays a vital role in maintaining the body's equilibrium, but it is also susceptible to various infections that can disrupt this delicate balance. Infections of the blood, known as bacteremia or sepsis, pose a serious threat as they involve the systemic dissemination of pathogens. These invaders may originate from wounds, surgical sites, or other infections within the body. The bloodstream serves as a conduit for these microorganisms, allowing them to spread rapidly and trigger a systemic inflammatory response. Sepsis, if left untreated, can lead to organ failure and, in severe cases, be fatal.

Conversely, the respiratory tract, encompassing the upper and lower regions, is constantly exposed to external elements. Infections in this intricate system manifest as a spectrum of illnesses, ranging from the common cold to more severe conditions like pneumonia. Respiratory infections are primarily caused by viruses such as influenza and rhinoviruses, but bacterial culprits like Streptococcus pneumoniae and Haemophilus influenzae are also significant contributors. The transmission of these infections often occurs through respiratory droplets, making them highly contagious and capable of spreading rapidly within communities.

Diagnosis and treatment for both blood and respiratory tract infections are critical in preventing complications. Symptoms like fever, cough, and fatigue are common indicators, but accurate identification of the causative agent is essential for targeted therapy. Antibiotics are frequently prescribed for bacterial infections, while antiviral medications are employed for viral respiratory illnesses. In severe cases, hospitalization may be necessary, especially for individuals with compromised immune systems.

Preventive strategies play a pivotal role in managing these infections. Vaccination campaigns, hygiene practices, and prompt treatment of underlying conditions are crucial components of public health efforts. By shedding light on the intricacies of blood and respiratory tract infections, healthcare professionals and communities can work together to enhance awareness, implement effective preventive measures, and ultimately reduce the burden of these infections on global health.

Summary

- Bacteraemia defines the presence of bacteria as detected by the culture of blood. Septicaemia also defines the presence of bacteria in blood, but it signals a sense of urgency in the management of the patient. The terms sepsis and septic shock are also used and, with clinical parameters such as fever, hypotension, tachycardia, multi-organ failure and leucocytosis, alert the clinician to the severity of the situation, and the need for immediate action in the management of the patient.
- A prosthetic heart valve will create local abnormalities in blood flow, and turbulence may damage the endothelium adjacent to the valve. Deposition of fibrin and platelets will give rise to a structure that can be colonized by bacteria, and cause prosthetic valve endocarditis (PVE).
- Implantable cardiac electronic devices (ICEDs) are used to manage cardiac conduction disorders that require defibrillation and resynchronization. They consist of the generator device or box, inserted into the subcutaneous tissue of the upper chest.
- Blood cultures should be collected from the hospitalized patient who has a fever (usually ≥38.2°C) and there is a focus of infection. However, fever is not always a reliable sign in the older patient, and confusion, or increased confusion, is important.
- Blood culture bottles must be correctly labelled, ensuring that the barcodes are not obscured, and the request form fully completed and a barcode copy placed on the form too. Legible details are essential, including the clinical information, and whether the set is peripheral or from the named lumen of a CVC.
- Fever is a common presentation occurring in at least 80% of cases. In addition, weight loss, haematuria, splinter haemorrhages, unexplained heart failure and renal failure may also be presenting manifestations. The C-reactive protein (CRP) is raised in about two-thirds of cases and raised white cell count and anaemia are seen in about 50% of cases.
- Respiratory tract infections (RTIs) are infections that affect the airways, including the nose, throat, bronchi, and lungs. They can be caused by various pathogens such as viruses, bacteria, and occasionally fungi. RTIs are common and can range from mild, self-limiting illnesses to more severe conditions.
- Blood gas analysis should be performed if there is any suspicion of acute respiratory compromise. The key indicators of disease severity in pneumonia are raised respiratory rate (> 30 beats/min), hypoxia, hypercapnia, bilateral or recently enlarging radiographic opacities, shock, renal failure and confusion.
- Pharyngitis is an inflammation of the throat, resulting in pain on swallowing and swollen, red pharyngeal mucosa. It is most often caused by a respiratory virus (rhinovirus, coronavirus, adenovirus, influenza virus, parainfluenza viruses, respiratory syncytial virus), Epstein–Barr virus or coxsackievirus.

References

1. Gotts, J. E., & Matthay, M. A., (2016). Sepsis: Pathophysiology and clinical management. *BMJ., 353*, i1585.
2. Gupta, S., Sakhuja, A., Kumar, G., et al., (2016). Culture-negative severe sepsis: Nationwide trends and outcomes. *Chest, 150*(6), 1251–1259.
3. Keeley, A., Hine, P., & Nsutebu, E., (2017). The recognition and management of sepsis and septic shock: A guide for non-intensivists. *Postgrad Med. J., 93*(1104), 626–634.
4. Kumar, A., Roberts, D., Wood, K. E., et al., (2006). Duration of hypotension before initiation of effective antimicrobial therapy is the critical determinant of survival in human septic shock. *Crit. Care Med., 34*, 1589–1596.
5. Levy, M. M., Artigas, A., Phillips, G. S., et al., (2012). Outcomes of the surviving sepsis campaign in intensive care units in the USA and Europe: A prospective cohort study. *Lancet Infect Dis., 12*, 919–924.
6. Lewis, S. R., Pritchard, M. W., Evans, D. J., et al., (2018). Colloids versus crystalloids for fluid resuscitation in critically ill people. *Cochrane Database Syst. Rev., 8*, CD000567.
7. Minasyan, H., (2017). Sepsis and septic shock: Pathogenesis and treatment perspectives. *J. Crit. Care, 40*, 229–242.
8. Rhee, C., Dantes, R., Epstein, L., et al., (2017). CDC prevention epicenter program. Incidence and trends of sepsis in US hospitals using clinical vs claims data, 2009–2014. *JAMA, 318*(13), 1241–1249.
9. Rhodes, A., Evans, L. E., Alhazzani, W., et al., (2017). Surviving sepsis campaign: International guidelines for management of sepsis and septic shock: 2016. *Crit. Care Med., 45*(3), 486–552.
10. Seymour, C. W., Liu, V. X., Iwashyna, T. J., et al., (2016). Assessment of clinical criteria for sepsis: For the third international consensus definitions for sepsis and septic shock (Sepsis-3) [published correction appears in *JAMA, 315*(20), 2237]. *JAMA, 315*(8), 762–774.
11. Seymour, C. W., Liu, V. X., Iwashyna, T. J., et al., (2016). Assessment of clinical criteria for sepsis: For the Third international consensus definitions for sepsis and septic shock (Sepsis-3). *JAMA, 315*, 762–774.
12. Singer, M., Deutschman, C. S., Seymour, C. W., et al., (2016). The third international consensus definitions for sepsis and septic shock (Sepsis-3). *JAMA, 315*, 801–810.
13. Yende, S., Austin, S., Rhodes, A., et al., (2016). Long-term quality of life among survivors of severe sepsis: Analyses of two international trials. *Crit. Care Med., 44*(8), 1461–1467.

Chapter

INFECTIONS OF THE URINARY TRACT AND ALIMENTARY CANAL

4

Contents

Unit Introduction

Every infection in any area of the urinary system, which is made up of the bladder, urethra, ureters, and kidneys, is referred to as a UTI. The latter occurs when bacteria get past the body's defenses in the urinary system and most infections affect the bladder and urethra, which are parts of the lower urinary tract. Although they can be uncomfortable and cause issues with urination, there are treatments that can help. While UTIs are mostly caused by bacteria, gastrointestinal (GI) infections can be the result of viruses, bacteria, and parasites. While bloody stool, vomiting, or a high fever require medical attention, the majority of cases resolve in a few days.

Orientation and Directional Terms

Term	Definition	Illustration
Bladder	The bladder is a hollow organ in your lower abdomen that stores urine.	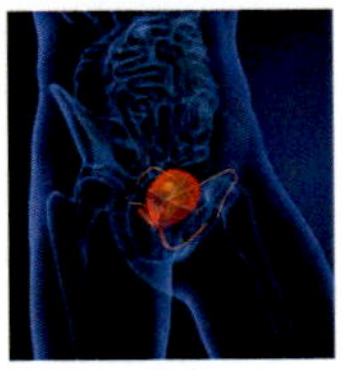
Clostridium difficile	*Clostridium difficile* is a type of bacteria that can cause colitis, a serious inflammation of the colon.	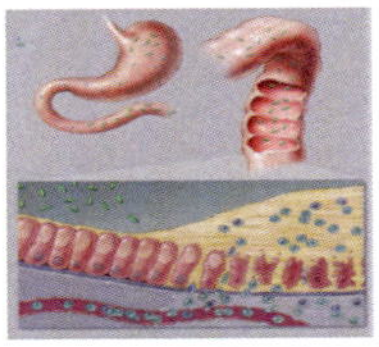
Cystitis	Cystitis is inflammation of the bladder. Most often it is caused by a bacterial infection known as a urinary tract infection (UTI).	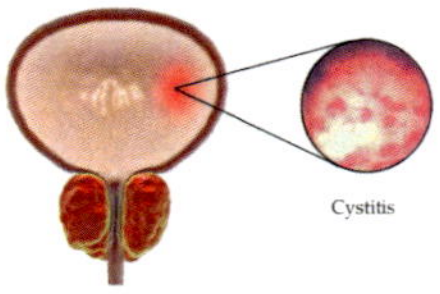
Dysuria	Dysuria means you feel pain or a burning sensation when you pee (urinate).	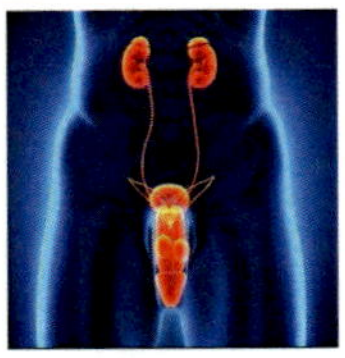
Hematuria	Hematuria is the presence of blood in the urine.	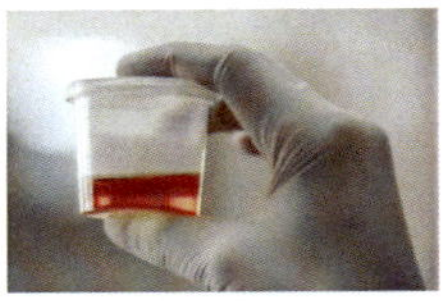
Polyuria	Polyuria is excessive or an abnormally large production or passage of urine Increased production and passage of urine may also be termed diuresis.	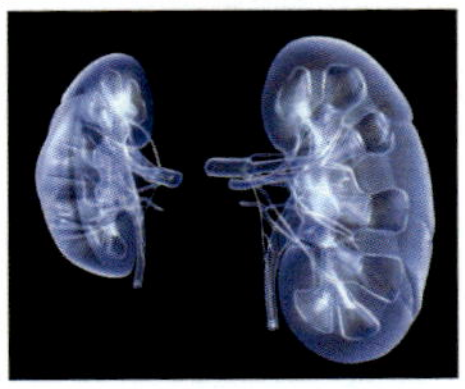
Pyelonephritis	Pyelonephritis is a type of urinary tract infection where one or both kidneys become infected.	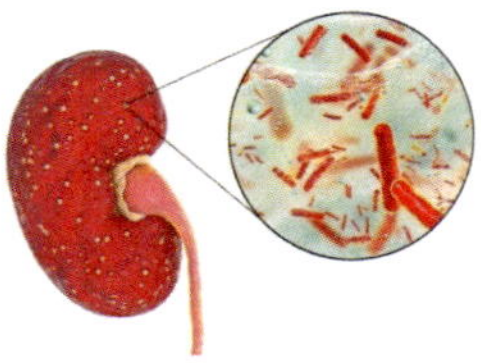
Ureter	Ureter is a tube that carries urine from the kidney to the urinary bladder.	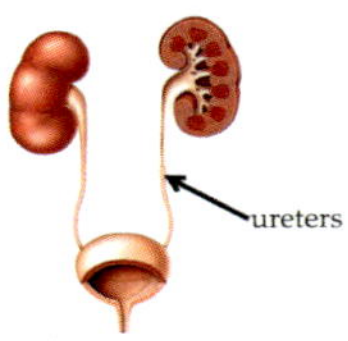

4.1. Urinary Tract Infections

Around 150 million people worldwide suffer from urinary tract infections (UTIs), which are among the most prevalent bacterial infections. An estimated 3–5 million office visits and 2–3 million ER visits for UTI symptoms were made in the United States alone in 2007. This accounts for 0–9% of all ambulatory visits. In the United States alone, the societal costs of these infections, including medical expenses and lost productivity, are currently estimated to be $30.5 billion annually. In older men, women, and infant boys, urinary tract infections (UTIs) are a major cause of morbidity. Prolonged recurrences, pyelonephritis with sepsis, renal damage in young children, preterm birth, and complications from repeated use of antibiotics, such as high-level antibiotic resistance and Clostridium difficile colitis, are among the grave aftereffects.

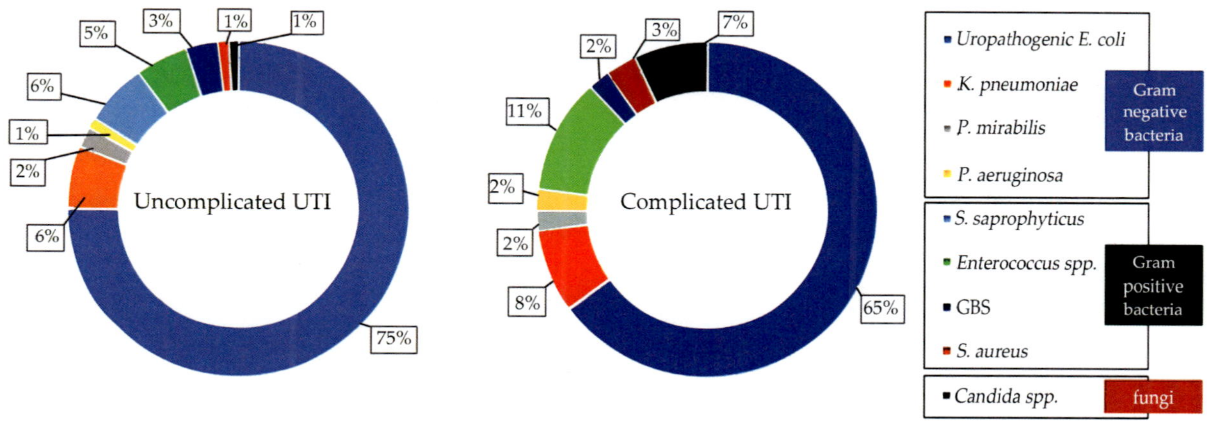

Figure 4.1. *Epidemiology of urinary tract infections.*

Source: Zhou, Y., Zhou, Z., Zheng, L., Gong, Z., Li, Y., Jin, Y., Huang, Y., & Chi, M., (2023). Urinary tract infections caused by uropathogenic Escherichia coli: Mechanisms of infection and treatment options. International Journal of Molecular Sciences, 24(13), 10537. https://doi.org/10.3390/ijms241310537.

Clinically, there are two types of UTIs: simple and complicated. Lower UTIs (cystitis) and upper UTIs (pyelonephritis) are two different types of uncomplicated UTIs that typically affect people who are otherwise healthy and do not have any structural or neurological abnormalities of the urinary tract. Risk factors including being female, a history of UTI, sexual activity, vaginal infections, diabetes, obesity, and genetic susceptibility, are linked to cystitis.

Urinary obstruction, retention due to neurological diseases, immunosuppression, renal failure, renal transplantation, pregnancy, and the presence of foreign bodies like calculi, indwelling catheters, or other drainage devices are all considered causes of complicated UTIs, which are defined as UTIs associated with factors that compromise the urinary tract or host defense. Around 1 million complicated UTIs occur annually in the US, with 70–80% of cases being related to indwelling catheters. As the most frequent cause of secondary bloodstream infections, catheter-associated UTIs (CAUTIs) are linked to higher rates of morbidity and mortality. Extended catheterization is one risk factor for CAUTI development.

Gram-positive and Gram-negative bacteria, as well as some fungi, can cause UTIs (Figure 4.1). *Proteus mirabilis*, *P. aeruginosa*, *S. aureus*, *Candida* spp., *Klebsiella pneumoniae*, *Staphylococcus saprophyticus*, *Enterococcus faecalis*, group B *streptococcus* (GBS), and uropathogenic *E. coli* (UPEC) are bacteriathat cause uncomplicated UTIs in order of prevalence (Figure 4.1). After UPEC, which is the most common causative agent for complicated UTIs, enterococci species are the most common (Figure 4.1).

Antibiotic treatment is a common practice for patients with symptomatic UTIs; however, this approach may alter the normal microbiota of the GI tract and vagina over time and lead to the emergence of multidrug-resistant microorganisms. Multidrug-resistant uropathogen colonization may be more likely in situations where there are available niches that the altered microbiota has replaced. Crucially, the "golden era" of antibiotics is coming to an end, which means that more carefully thought-out alternative therapies are required. In recent research, uropathogens from the urine of women with symptomatic UTIs have been directly analyzed using RNA sequencing. The molecular details of how uropathogens adhere, colonize, and adapt to the nutritionally limited bladder environment; elude immune surveillance; and persist and disseminate in the urinary tract have become clearer to us thanks to these studies, basic science, and improved animal models. Therefore, these studies have identified important virulence factors that can be targeted to prevent and counteract the pathogenic mechanisms associated with UTIs. We talk about the mol in this review.

4.1.1. Adherence and Colonization

A crucial factor that starts each stage of the pathogenesis of UTIs is adherence. A UTI usually begins with periurethral contamination by a gut-dwelling uropathogen, which is followed by colonization of the urethra and the pathogen's subsequent migration to the bladder, an action that necessitates appendages like flagella and pili (Figure 4.2). The ability of uropathogens to colonize or be eradicated in the bladder is ultimately determined by the outcomes of intricate host-pathogen interactions.

The uroepithelium, or bladder epithelium, has receptors that are recognized by several bacterial adhesins, which then facilitate colonization (Table 4.1). Toxins and proteases are produced by uropathogens like UPEC to liberate nutrients from the host cells, and siderophores are synthesized to obtain iron (Figure 4.2 and Table 4.1). Following bacterial attachment via adhesins or pili to colonize the renal epithelium, the uropathogens can reach the kidneys and produce tissue-damaging toxins by multiplying and evading host immune surveillance (Figure 4.2 and Table 4.1). As a result, the uropathogens can enter the bloodstream and breach the tubular epithelial barrier, which causes bacteremia (Figure 4.3).

The uropathogens, that cause simple UTIs include UPEC, *K. pneumoniae*, and *S. saprophyticus*, and have the capacity to attach directly to the bladder epithelium, which are made up of basal cells, intermediate cells, and umbrella cells—also referred to as superficial facet cells (Table 4.1). Uroplakins, the main protein components of the umbrella cell apical membrane, bind to pneumoniae and form a crystalline array that shields the tissue of the mammalian bladder from harmful substances found in urine. Apart from uroplakins, $\alpha3\beta1$ integrins, which are surface-expressed on uroepithelial cells, can also function as UPEC receptors.

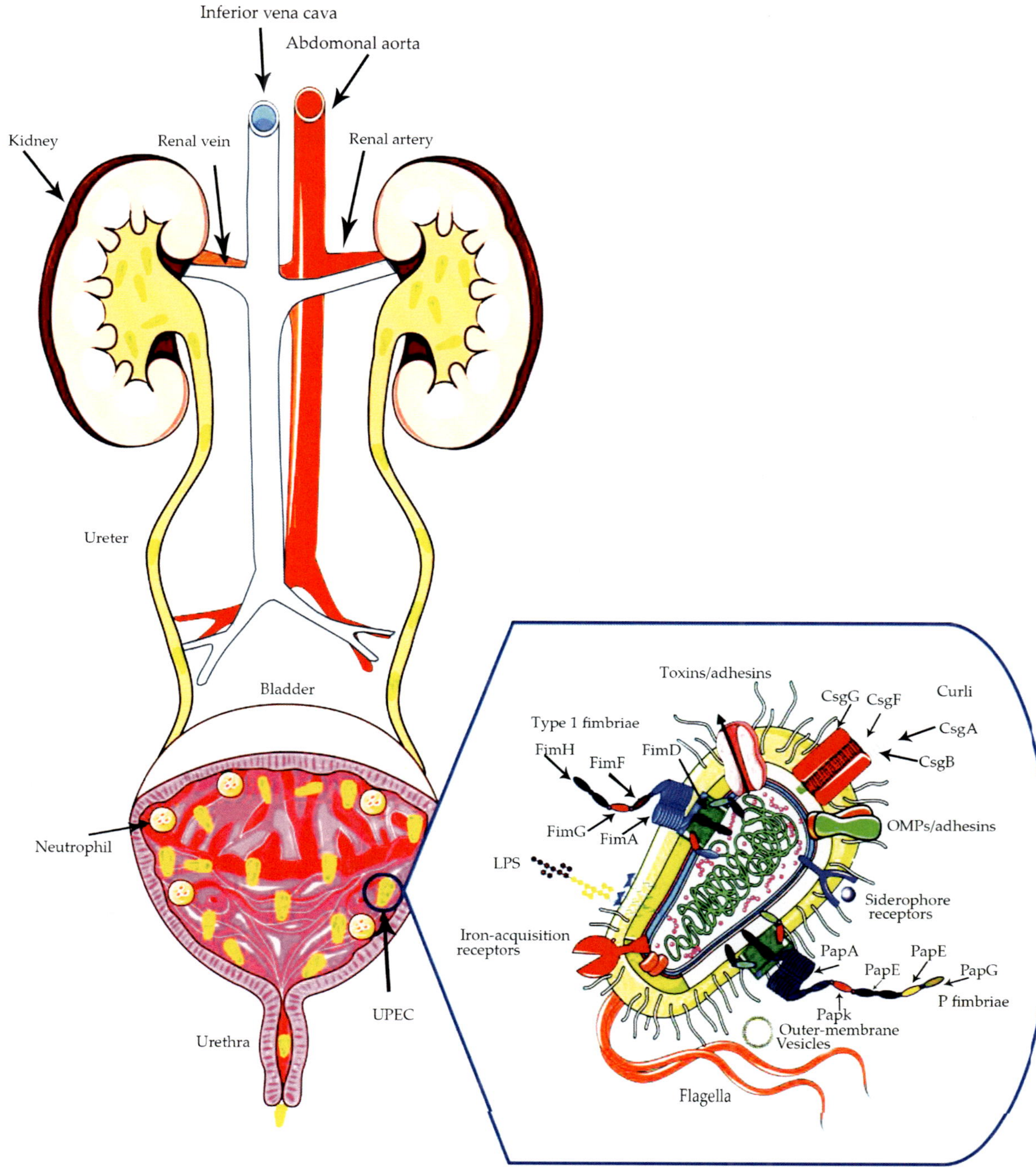

Figure 4.2. *Pathogenesis of urinary tract infections.*

Source: Zhou, Y., Zhou, Z., Zheng, L., Gong, Z., Li, Y., Jin, Y., Huang, Y., & Chi, M., (2023). Urinary tract infections caused by uropathogenic Escherichia coli: Mechanisms of infection and treatment options. International Journal of Molecular Sciences, 24(13), 10537. https://doi.org/10.3390/ijms241310537.

Table 4.1. *Virulence Factors Used by the Main Uropathogens*

Uropathogen	Virulence Factors				
	Adherence	Toxin	Immune Evasion	Iron Acquisition	Other
UPEC	·F1C pili ·P pili ·S pili ·Type 1 pili ·Dr adhesins	·HlyA ·CNF1	·HlyA ·Capsular antigens ·CNF1 ·Yersiniabactin	·Aerobactin ·Enterobactin ·Salmochelin ·Yersiniabactin	·Antigen43 ·Flagella
Klebsiella pneumoniae	·Type 1 pili ·Type 3 pili	ND	Capsule	·Aerobactin ·Enterobactin	ND
Proteus mirabilis	·MR/P pili ·NAFs ·PMFs ·AipA adhesin ·TaaP adhesin	·Haemolysins (HpmA and HlyA) ·Pta	·Capsule ·ZapA	·Proteobactin ·Yersiniabactin-related	·Flagella ·Urease
Pseudomonas aeruginosa	·Extracellular DNA ·Exopolysaccharides (alginate, PEL and PSL)	ND	·Capsule ·Elastase ·ExoS ·Phospholipase ·Rhamnolipids	·Pyochelin ·Pyoverdin	Quorum sensing
Staphylococcus saprophyticus	·Aas adhesin ·SdrI adhesin ·Uaf adhesin	Aas	ND	ND	Urease
Enterococcus faecalis	·Ebp pili ·Ace adhesin ·Esp adhesin	ND	Epa	ND	·Sortase A ·SigV ·MsrA and MsrB
Enterococcus faecium	·Ebp pili ·Esp adhesin	ND	ND	ND	ND

On the other hand, complex UTIs begin when the bacteria attach themselves to a urinary catheter, a kidney stone, a bladder stone, or a physical obstruction that keeps them inside the urinary tract. Certain pathogens, like UPEC, can cause both simple and complex urinary tract infections, while others, like *P. mirabilis*, *P. aeruginosa* and species of *Enterococci* mostly result in complex

UTIs. These uropathogens then frequently create biofilms, which are in charge of colonization and persistence.

4.1.2. Chaperone–Usher Pathway Pili

Pili are a common tool used by uropathogens to cause UTIs. They mediate adherence to host and environmental surfaces, facilitate invasion into host tissues, and encourage interbacterial interactions to form biofilms. As an illustration, many Gram-negative pathogenic bacteria, such as *E. coli*, *Klebsiella* spp. *Propeus* spp., *Pseudomona* spp., *Haemophilus* species, *Salmonella* spp. and *Yersinia* species. The chaperone-usher pathway (CUP) pili are a large, highly conserved family of adhesive fibers. Comprising of pilin subunits with incomplete immunoglobulin-like folds and without the usual carboxy-terminal seventh β-strand, CUP pili are assembled by the chaperone-usher molecular machinery. A specific periplasmic chaperone "donates" an β-strand to finish the immunoglobulin fold of the subunits, forming a complex with each subunit and guaranteeing their correct folding and stabilization. This process is known as donor-strand complementation. After that, the chaperone-subunit complex is directed toward the usher assembly protein located in the outer membrane. Through a process known as do, the usher selectively separates chaperone-subunit complexes and catalyzes the ordered assembly of pili on the cell surface.

4.1.3. Uropathogenic E. coli

It has been determined that this pathogen contains 38 unique CUP pilus operons. More than 12 distinct CUP pili can be encoded by a single UPEC strain, and *E. coli* genomes. CUP operon distribution, however, varies amongst distinct UPEC isolates; certain operons are only present in a small number of strains, while others are found in UPEC everywhere. Many adhesins are present on the numerous CUP pili encoded by UPEC, some of which are known to mediate distinct tropisms in the upper and lower urinary tract by identifying receptors with stereochemical specificity, particularly in the kidney or bladder epithelium.

The better characterized CUP pili are type 1 pili and pyelonephritis-associated (P) pili. For UPEC to colonize, invade, and persist in the mouse bladder, type 1 pili are necessary. The adhesin FimH, which has stereochemical specificity in identifying mannosylated uroplakins and α1β3 integrins, tips type 1 pili and initiates invasion and colonization of umbrella cells. When type 1 pili attach to these cells, a signal transduction cascade is set off, which in turn activates Rho GTPases, including those in the Rac family. This results in actin rearrangement and the internalization of UPEC through a zippering mechanism that encloses the bacterium in a sheath of plasma membrane. Through invasion, UPEC can weaken some host defenses and resist antibiotic therapy. Nonetheless, the uroepithelium is protected from UPEC invasion by an innate defense expulsion mechanism that is dependent on the expression of Toll-like receptor 4 (TLR4) by uroepithelial cells. The activation of TLR4 by lipopolysaccharide (LPS) triggers the production of cyclic AMP by adenylyl cyclase 3 (AC3), which in turn triggers the exocytosis of vesicular UPEC into apical plasma membrane of the umbrella cells.

The adhesin of type P pili, PapG, binds glycolipids that are present in globosides and is different from the mannose-binding adhesin FimH of type 1 pili. Furthermore, by interacting with TLR4 to decrease polymeric immunoglobulin receptor (PIGR) expression and impede immunoglobulin A transport through the lamina propria and epithelial cells to the kidney lumen, PapG modifies the local secretory-antibody immune response. UPEC circumvents a crucial host defense mechanism by preventing immunoglobulin A from entering the urinary space, which permits the development of ascending infection.

Crucially, the initial innate host response to UPEC colonization and invasion is critical for determining host susceptibility to subsequent infections as well as dictating the outcome of the initial infection. Not as commonly believed, but rather as a result of an unchecked lymphocyte-dependent innate inflammatory response to acute infection, which can cause severe acute injury to the mucosal uroepithelium and magnify subsequent infections, an increased susceptibility to recurrent UTIs can arise.

4.1.4. Klebsiella pneumoniae

In line with UPEC, *K. pneumoniae* forms biofilms and colonizes bladders using type 1 pili (Table 4.1). Remarkably, even though the K. Although UPEC FimH and *K. pneumoniae* adhesin FimH have distinct binding specificities, they are substantially similar. Unlike methyl mannose, which inhibits UPEC FimH, heptyl mannose inhibits *K. pneumoniae* FimH-mediated biofilm formation. Additionally, compared to UPEC FimH, *K. pneumoniae* FimH adheres to the bladder less firmly, which results in noticeably lower IBCs than those observed for UPEC and *K. pneumoniae* titers in the mouse bladder. Despite its comparatively weak adhesive qualities, FimH in the urinary tract, it continues to be a significant factor in its virulence. Pneumoniae throughout the colonization, development of biofilms, and persistence in CAUTIs and UTIs. Furthermore, numerous additional CUP pili, such as type 3 pili, which are also essential for colonization, persistence, and biofilm formation during UTIs and CAUTIs, are encoded by *K. pneumoniae*.

4.1.5. Proteus mirabilis

P. mirabilis is a Gram-negative, rod-shaped bacterium commonly found in soil, water, and the intestinal tract of humans and animals. It is known for its remarkable motility, attributed to peritrichous flagella, allowing it to rapidly move and colonize various environments.

While often considered a harmless commensal organism, *P. mirabilis* can cause opportunistic infections, particularly in individuals with compromised immune systems or underlying health conditions. It is a common cause of UTIs, especially in patients with urinary catheters, due to its ability to ascend the urinary tract and form biofilms on catheter surfaces.

P. mirabilis infections can lead to symptoms such as dysuria (painful urination), frequency, urgency, and suprapubic discomfort. Additionally, it is associated with the formation of urinary tract stones or calculi, often composed of struvite (magnesium ammonium phosphate), which can lead to further complications if left untreated.

Treatment of *P. mirabilis* infections typically involves antibiotic therapy, although the organism's propensity to develop resistance poses challenges in clinical management. Proper hygiene practices, urinary catheter care, and infection control measures are essential in preventing and managing infections caused by this bacterium.

4.1.6. Enterococci

The collagen adhesin Ace, enterococcal surface protein (Esp), enterococcal polysaccharide antigen (Epa), and endocarditis- and biofilm-associated (Ebp) pili are among the adhesion factors that are encoded by enterococci (Table 4.1). Of these, Ebp pili are necessary for infection persistence and play a role in CAUTIs. Clinical research has demonstrated that the mechanical stress brought on by urinary catheterization alters the bladder's histology and immune system, causing exfoliation, edema, a strong inflammatory response, and mucosal lesions in the kidney and uroepithelium. Significantly, a mouse model of CAUTI exhibits catheter-induced inflammation, severe uroepithelial damage, exfoliation, and the beginning of bladder wall edema, which is made worse by prolonged catheterization. This model appears to recapitulate these immunological changes brought on by urinary catheterization. Urinary catheters provide a surface for *Enterococcus faecalis* to instigate biofilm formation and attachment, which encourages the growth and spreading of *E. faecalis* in the bladder and the kidneys, respectively. However *E. faecalis* cannot grow in urine and bind to catheter material *in vitro*, which is a paradox.

4.2. Types of UTIs

Germs or microorganisms, primarily bacteria, are the cause of UTIs, and the various UTI kinds include the following:

i. **Cystitis:** A bladder infection is called cystitis. The most typical lower UTI is cystitis.
ii. **Urethritis:** Urinary tract infection, or urethritis.
iii. **Pyelonephritis:** kidney infection, or pyelonephritis.
iii. **Vaginitis:** A vaginal infection is called vaginitis.

4.2.1. Cystitis

UTIs caused by bacteria nearly always result in cystitis, an infection of the bladder. In women especially, it is the most prevalent kind of UTI.

The muscular sac that houses the bladder is where the kidneys store urine. The urethra is the tube that allows urine to exit the body. When bacteria enter the urine and cause inflammation in the lining of the bladder, it can lead to cystitis.

At some point in their lives, the majority of women will develop cystitis. It is uncomfortable and painful, but it is not dangerous or contagious, and you cannot infect your partner while having sex.

If treatment is not received, the infection may "backtrack" from the bladder further into the urinary system, eventually reaching the kidneys. Since kidney damage or even renal failure can result from a kidney infection, it is extremely serious and requires immediate medical attention.

1. **Symptoms of Cystitis:** Cystitis varies in severity. The symptoms include:
   - Often feeling the need to urinate, even just a little bit.
   - Burning discomfort or a "scalding" feeling when urinating.
   - Strong-smelling urine.
   - Murky or bleeding urine.
   - Discomfort in your lower abdomen.
   - Urine containing blood.
2. **Treatment for Cystitis:** The faint prickling sensation experienced when urinating is typically the first sign of cystitis. If treatment is started right away, mild cystitis can be cured. Some preventive measures are as follows:
   - Drink a lot of water.
   - Utilize a commercial urinary alkalizer (consult your pharmacist for recommendations) or mix one teaspoon baking soda (bicarbonate of soda) with one cup of water.
   - Steer clear of acidic foods and beverages since they counteract the effects of urinary alkalizers and may make the burning sensation when urinating worse.
   - Immediately seek medical

advice if self-help remedies aren't working. To determine which microorganism is present in your urine, your doctor will likely do a test. An antibiotic course, or courses of courses, can be used to treat cystitis.

- A general practitioner should look into any episodes of cystitis that are severe or frequent as they may be caused by an underlying condition like kidney stones or a kidney infection.

3. **Cause of Cystitis:** *E. coli* is the most frequent bacteria or bug that causes UTIs. The bacterium is frequently discovered when the urine is examined under a microscope, a test known as a microscopy and culture (M and C) test.

   E. coli is frequently discovered in the colon and digestive system, and in typical circumstances, it poses no harm. However, the acidic environment of the bladder is ideal for the growth of bacteria, which causes inflammation of the bladder lining.

4. Cystitis in Women: The majority of women who develop cystitis are those in their late teens and older, and particularly those who engage in sexual activity. Since the female urethra is so short—only 4 cm—bacteria can easily enter the bladder.

   The secretions secreted by the vagina and the ability of bacteria to survive are influenced by female sex hormones. Women are therefore more prone to infection under the following conditions:

   - During certain stages of the menstrual cycle;
   - During pregnancy;
   - During menopause;
   - After a total hysterectomy.

5. **Cystitis in Men and Older People:** Men typically develop cystitis later in life. If an individual experiences difficulty with urine flow, it could be a sign that there is an underlying prostate gland issue.

   Elderly people are more likely to get cystitis, especially if they are ill. Cystitis risk may also be raised by some urinary tract procedures and bladder catheters.

6. **Cystitis in Children:** When a child has cystitis, it should always be looked into as it could be a sign of something more serious, like vesicoureteric reflux, or urinary reflux. Urine can flow back towards the kidneys due to a bladder-valve issue.

7. **Long-Term Prevention of Cystitis:** Some women's urinary systems develop a kind of immunity after only one episode of cystitis, making subsequent episodes rare. Other women may get cystitis regularly.

   Although not always backed up by research, some women have found that useful suggestions include:

   - As soon as you feel the urge to urinate, go to the bathroom and do so instead of holding it in.
   - Each day, make sure to flush your urinary system by drinking a lot of water.
   - After using the restroom, wipe yourself from front to back (urethra to anus).
   - Before having sex, wash your genitalia, and advise your partner to do the same.

- Urinate after having sex.
- Put on cotton underwear instead of nylon.
- Steer clear of tight jeans, tight pants, and nylon pantyhose.
- Avoid using any kind of deodorant, talc, or scented soap near your genitalia.
- Steer clear of bubble baths.
- Thrush and trichomonas should be treated as soon as possible because they can cause cystitis.

UTIs have been avoided by using cranberries, usually in the form of cranberry juice. There is a component in cranberries that can prevent *E. coli* from adhering to the cells lining the urinary tract. However, new studies have revealed that cranberry juice does not significantly help prevent UTIs, and most users are unable to stick with the juice over an extended time.

4.2.2. Kidney Infection (Pyelonephritis)

UTIs can include kidney infections. The majority of kidney infections stem from bacteria or viruses that initially infect your lower urinary tract, typically your bladder. The infection then travels upstream to either or both of your kidneys, which are a component of the urinary tract's upper segment. After surgery, there's a chance that bacteria will enter your body during the process and make their way to your kidneys through your blood.

UTIs can be prevented by your body in a few different ways. For instance, urine normally travels from your kidneys to your bladder in a single direction, and urinating helps to flush out bacteria or viruses that enter the body. Urine flowing in only one direction typically keeps your urinary tract from becoming infected. Bacteria or viruses can occasionally overcome your body's defenses and lead to a bladder UTI. Visit a medical practitioner if you experience any of the signs of a bladder infection. To stop the infection from spreading to your kidneys, you might need medical attention. Infections of the kidneys can lead to major health issues and are frequently extremely painful.

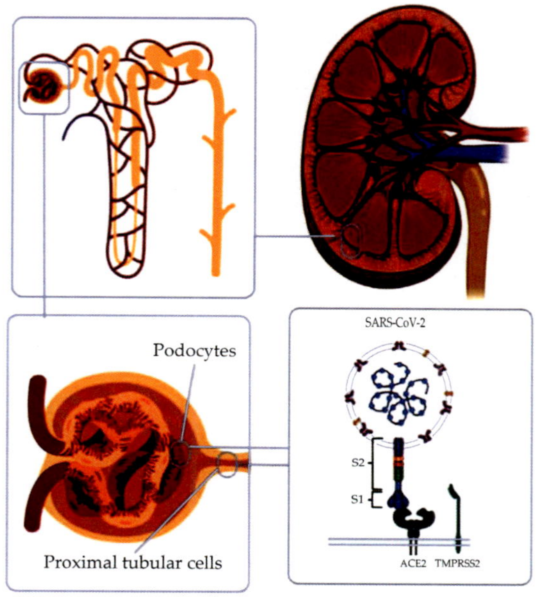

Figure 4.3. *Kidney infections often begin in the bladder, and then move up through the ureters to infect one or both kidneys.*

Source: Chávez-Valencia, V., Orizaga-de-la-Cruz, C., & Lagunas-Rangel, F. A., (2022). Acute kidney injury in COVID-19 patients: Pathogenesis, clinical characteristics, therapy, and mortality. Diseases, 10(3), 53. https://doi.org/10.3390/diseases10030053.

4.2.2.1. Who Is More Likely to Develop a Kidney Infection?

A kidney infection is more likely to occur if you:

- are a female.
- suffer from a bladder UTI.
- experienced a UTI in the previous 12 months.

- are expecting a child. Researchers believe that during pregnancy, hormonal changes and changes in the urinary tract's location facilitate the spread of bacteria that can lead to kidney infections.
- possess an issue with your urinary tract that prevents or alters the regular flow of pee. If you have a structural flaw in your urinary tract, such as a narrowed urethra, an enlarged prostate, or a kidney stone, the flow of urine may be obstructed.
- possess vesicoureteral reflux (VUR), a condition in which one or both kidneys may experience a reflux of urine. The majority of VUR diagnoses made by medical professionals involves children.
- possess diabetes or issues with your immune system, which is your body's natural defense.
- possess a nerve injury surrounding the bladder or a spinal cord injury.
- have urinary retention, which is the inability to completely empty your bladder.

4.2.2.2. Complications of Kidney Infections

Kidney infections may cause in rare instances.

- Elevated blood pressure;
- Renal bozulma;
- Chronic kidney disease can result from permanent kidney scars, also known as renal scarring.

If you have, your risk of experiencing a complication is marginally higher.

- Other causes of kidney disease;
- An issue with your urinary tract's structural integrity;
- Recurring kidney infection episodes.

If an antibiotic is prescribed by a medical professional to treat your infection, complications from a kidney infection are rare.

4.2.2.3. Symptoms and Causes of Kidney Infection (Pyelonephritis)

Kidney infection symptoms change with age. Some possible symptoms are (Figure 4.4):

- Chills;
- Fever;
- Pain in your back, side, or groin;
- Nausea;
- Vomiting;
- Cloudy, dark, bloody, or foul-smelling urine;
- Frequent, painful urination.

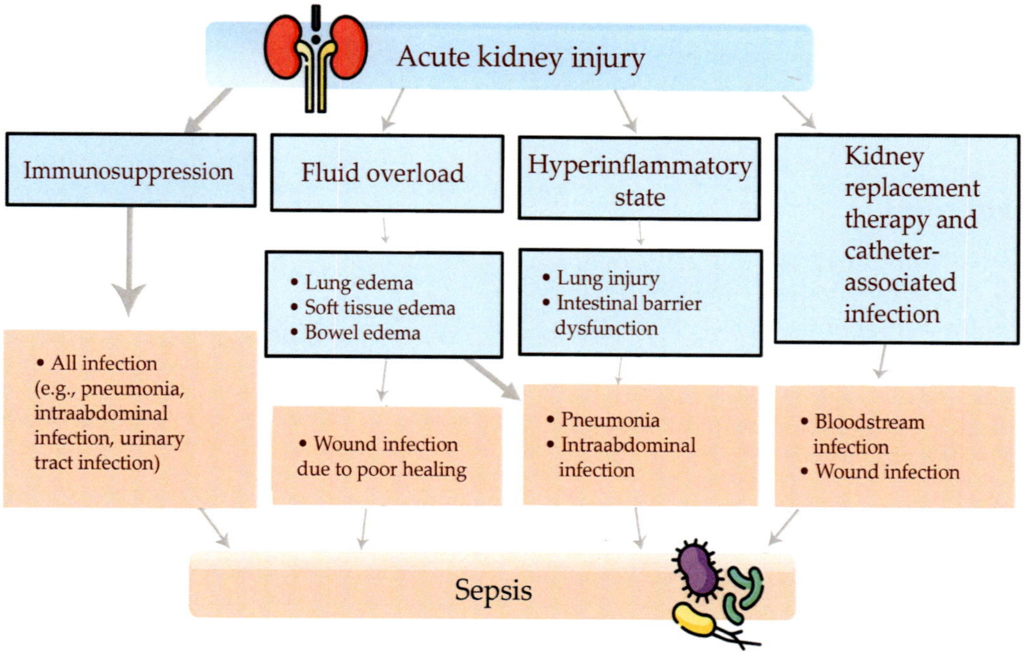

Figure 4.4. *A kidney infection is a cause for concern.*

Source: Chang, Y. M., Chou, Y. T., Kan, W. C., & Shiao, C. C., (2022). Sepsis and acute kidney injury: A review focusing on the bidirectional interplay. International Journal of Molecular Sciences, 23(16), 9159. https://doi.org/10.3390/ijms23169159 https://www.niddk.nih.gov/-/media/Images/Health-Information/Urologic/woman_thermometer_300x451.jpg.

A kidney infection in a child under two years old may only cause a high fever. If an adult over 65 has a kidney infection, they might not experience any of the common symptoms. An elderly person might only experience cognitive issues, such as:

- Confusion;
- Hallucinations;
- Jumbled speech.

4.2.2.4. Seek Care Right Away

If you have symptoms of a kidney infection, get medical attention right away. Occasionally, a kidney infection can result in sepsis NIH external link, a potentially fatal illness. Sepsis is characterized by fever, chills, fast heartbeat and breathing, rash, and confusion. If a kidney infection persists for a long time, it can lead to irreversible kidney damage.

4.2.2.5. Causes of a Kidney Infection

Viral or bacterial infections can contribute to kidney infections. According to scientists, most kidney infections begin as bladder infections and spread upstream to affect one or both kidneys. Most frequently, bacteria that ordinarily reside in your intestines are the source of the infection. The urinary tract can stop an infection from spreading further up its length in a few different ways. As an illustration, urinating typically eliminates bacteria before it enters the bladder. A UTI can occasionally be caused by bacteria that your body is unable to combat, and your kidneys could become infected with the bacteria if you don't receive medical attention to treat the infection. Your blood may also occasionally contain viruses or bacteria that are transferred from another area of your body to your kidneys.

4.2.2.6. Diagnosis of Kidney Infection (Pyelonephritis)

A physical examination, tests, and your medical history are used by medical professionals to diagnose kidney infections.

A medical professional will inquire about any past medical issues that could increase your risk of kidney infection. The medical practitioner will question you about your symptoms during a physical examination.

The medical professional may do a digital rectal examination (DRE) if you are a man and they believe you have a kidney infection. The medical professional will have you lie on your side or bend over a table and hold your knees close to your chest during a DRE. The medical practitioner puts on a glove and inserts a lubricated finger into your anus to examine the bladder neck for obstructions caused by an enlarged or swollen prostate.

4.2.2.7. Tests Doctors Use to Diagnose a Kidney Infection

To diagnose a kidney infection, doctors may employ imaging or laboratory testing:

1. Lab Tests:

   i. **Urinalysis:** To obtain a urine sample for a urinalysis, you will need to go to a lab or your doctor's office and fill out a special container. A medical expert will examine the sample under a microscope to check for white blood cells, which the body makes to fight infection and bacteria. The diagnosis of a kidney infection is made using a combination of laboratory testing and your symptoms since healthy individuals can also have bacteria in their urine.

   ii. **Urine Culture:** The type of bacteria causing the infection may be identified by a health care professional from a culture of your urine. The best course of action can be determined by a medical professional after they have observed how the bacteria have multiplied, which typically takes 1 to 3 days.

   To have your kidney infection tested, you can give a urine sample in a designated container.

2. **Imaging Tests:** A kidney infection may be diagnosed with the aid of imaging tests such as an ultrasound, magnetic resonance imaging (MRI), or computed tomography (CT) scan. In a hospital or outpatient center, a technician conducts these tests. An ultrasound can also be done by a technician in a doctor's office. The images are read by and reported on by a radiologist. For these tests, anesthesia is not required NIH external link.

4.2.2.8. Treatment for Kidney Infection (Pyelonephritis)

An antibiotic prescription will be given by a medical professional if you have a kidney infection. The doctor may recommend an antibiotic that targets the most prevalent kinds of bacteria even before you receive the results of your test. Even though your symptoms might subside, follow your doctor's instructions, and take the antibiotic for the full recommended duration.

The doctor may replace the antibiotic with one that more effectively addresses the kind of infection you have after receiving the results of your lab work. You can take these antibiotics orally, intravenously (IV), or by both methods.

If your kidney infection is making you very sick, you might need to stay in bed at a hospital. A medical practitioner might use an IV to administer fluids to you.

A doctor may occasionally perform surgery or another procedure to treat a condition that is obstructing your urinary tract, such as a kidney stone or an enlarged prostate.

In order to ensure that your kidney infection has fully healed and hasn't returned, the medical professional performing your treatment will frequently perform additional urine cultures if you recently had one. Antibiotics are recommended and prescribed for a longer duration if a retest reveal a continuous infection.

If an antibiotic is prescribed by your healthcare provider, take them all as directed and heed their recommendations. It's important to take all of your medication even if you start to feel better.

4.2.2.9. Prevent a Kidney Infection

Preventing bladder infections may aid in the prevention of kidney infections, as many kidney infections originate from bladder infections. Although the best ways to prevent bladder infections are still being researched, you may find that making these little daily habit changes can help:

1. **Drink Lots of Liquid, Especially Water:** Drinking liquids, especially water, can help the urinary system rid itself of bacteria. The majority of healthy individuals should aim to consume six to eight eight-ounce glasses of liquid every day. Ask your healthcare professional how much liquid is healthy for you if you have other health conditions that require you to drink less water, such as kidney failure, heart disease, or issues with bladder control NIH external link.
2. **Wipe from Front to Back After Using the Toilet:** To prevent bacteria from entering the urethra, women should wipe from the front to the back. The importance of this step increases after a bowel movement.
3. **Urinate Often and When the Urge Arises:** Make an effort to go potty once every three to four hours. Urine that remains in the bladder for an extended period of time is more likely to harbor bacteria.
4. **Urinate After Sex:** Men and women should both urinate soon after sexual activity \to remove any bacteria that might have entered the urethra.

4.2.3. Non-Specific Urethritis (NSU)

Any inflammation of a man's urethra, the tube that transports urine from the bladder to the outside, that is not brought on by gonorrhea—a sexually transmitted infection—is referred to as non-specific urethritis (NSU). It is also referred to as NGU, or non-gonococcal urethritis. Numerous organisms have the potential to cause NSU, but it is frequently impossible to pinpoint the exact culprit.

Vaginal sex is an easy way to contract the infection, and although less common, it can also be acquired through oral or anal sex. NSU can occasionally happen without sexual transmission.

4.2.3.1. Symptoms of Non-Specific Urethritis (NSU)

The symptoms may go unnoticed if they are extremely mild. They include the following and happen two to four weeks after infection:

- A discharge from the penis that is clear or white.
- A feeling of burning when urinating. Sometimes there is no discharge along with the pain.

- Swollen testicles and pain. This could indicate a more serious infection.

4.2.3.2. Complications of Untreated NSU

NSU can result in the following if it is not identified and treated:

- Infection spreading to the testicles or prostate.
- Infertility – In severe situations, this may happen.
- Transmission of the infection to a female partner who may experience infertility due to pelvic inflammatory disease (PID).

4.2.3.3. Treatment for NSU

Antibiotics are used in NSU treatment. It is important to keep in mind that even if your symptoms have subsided, you still need to take all of the prescribed antibiotics.

4.2.3.4. Recurrences of NSU

Even though NSU is generally treatable, there are situations when the illness is hard to eradicate, and symptoms can recur. If you get the right treatment, it will eventually go away.

4.2.3.5. Condom Use Effectively Prevents NSU

Using condoms during sexual activity is the best way to avoid nonsexual sex initiation. Following these guidelines will help you use condoms correctly.

- Take great care when opening the packet to avoid tearing the condom.
- Before gently rolling the condom down the entire shaft of the erect penis, pinch its tip.
- Spit, Vaseline, baby oil, or other lubricants containing oil should not be used.
- Make use of water-based lubricants like Wet Stuff, Muko, or KY.
- In order to prevent the condom from falling off, retract the penis before the erection ends. To stop spills, grasp the condom's base.
- Examine the expiration date and keep condoms in a cool, dry location.

4.2.4. Risk Factors

As stated previously, UTIs are more common in women, and they encounter multiple UTIs in their lifetime. Risk factors for UTIs that are specific to women include:

1. **Female Anatomy:** The urethra is shorter in women than in men. Because of this, germs have a shorter path to take to reach the bladder.
2. **Sexual Activity:** UTIs are more common in those who engage in sexual activity. Risk is further increased by having a new sexual partner.
3. **Certain Types of Birth Control:** The risk of UTIs may rise when using diaphragms for birth control. Risk may also rise from the use of spermicidal drugs.
4. **Menopause:** Urinary tract changes are brought on by a decrease in estrogen levels in the bloodstream after menopause. UTI risk may rise as a result of the modifications.

Other risk factors for UTIs include:

1. **Urinary Tract Problems:** Urination difficulties may be experienced by newborns who are born with urinary tract issues. UTIs can result from urine backing up in the urethra.

2. **Blockages in the Urinary Tract:** Urine can become stuck in the bladder due to kidney stones or an enlarged prostate. The risk of UTIs is increased as a result.
3. **A Suppressed Immune System:** The body's defense against pathogens, the immune system, can be weakened by diabetes and other illnesses. This may make UTIs more likely.
4. **Catheter Use:** A catheter is a tube that is used to urinate by people who are unable to urinate on their own. The risk of UTIs is increased when using a catheter. People who are hospitalized may use catheters. They may also be used by those who are paralyzed or have neurological issues that make it difficult to control their urination.
5. **A Recent Urinary Procedure:** A UTI can be more likely to occur after urinary surgery or a medically assisted urinary tract exam.

4.3. Treatment of UTIs

UTIs have a significant negative impact on the quality of life for those who get them, as well as significant financial and public health costs. Antibiotics, including ampicillin, ciprofloxacin, trimethoprim sulfamethoxazole, and others, are currently the most often prescribed treatments for UTIs. However, the burden that these common infections place on society could be significantly increased due to rising rates of antibiotic resistance and high recurrence rates. The goal is to develop substitute treatments that won't give in to the emergence of resistance. Numerous intriguing strategies are being developed, such as precisely targeting virulence pathways by applying our understanding of the fundamental biology of UTI pathogenesis. Since antivirulence therapeutics target processes that are essential for UTI pathogenesis but not for the vital processes of growth and cell division (which are the targets of conventional antibiotics), they should theoretically enable us to effectively neutralize, or "disarm," the capacity of UTI pathogens to cause disease without changing the gut commensal microbiota.

Here, we'll talk about the difficulties that have recently emerged as a result of the emergence of bacterial strains that are resistant to drugs, and we'll also highlight the advancements that have been made in the creation of antivirulence treatments for UTIs. We also go over how new methods for enhancing and modifying existing treatment options are being made possible by our growing understanding of the mechanisms underlying the evolution of bacterial resistance and how they spread.

4.3.1. Multidrug Resistance

Treatment for UTIs is getting harder and harder because a variety of antibiotic resistance mechanisms are spreading. Enterobacteriaceae members, such as *E. coli* and *K. pneumoniae* are especially concerning, as they both have plasmids encoding extended-spectrum β-lactamases (ESBLs). These plasmids spread resistance to other antibiotics and third-generation cephalosporins very quickly. Other members of the Enterobacteriaceae family generate class C β-lactamases (AmpC enzymes), which are resistant to β-lactamase inhibitors and active against cephamycin and third-generation cephalosporins. Carbapenem resistance in *K. pneumoniae* is also linked to the expression of AmpC enzymes, devoid of an outer membrane protein measuring 42 kDa.

Enterococci are naturally resistant to trimethoprim, clindamycin, cephalosporins, and penicillins, which makes them prone to multidrug resistance as well. More recently, vancomycin, which is thought to be one of the last lines of defense against organisms that are resistant to multiple drugs, is among the glycopeptides to which *Enterococcus* spp. have developed deep resistance. Enterococci specifically developed resistance to glycopeptides by expressing the genes for teicoplanin A-type resistance (van) and vancomycin, which encode the penicillin-binding proteins (PBPs) VanA, VanB, VanD, VanE, VanG, and VanL. VanA, the predominant penicillin-binding protein expressed by enterococci, binds less efficiently to vancomycin by substituting D-alanine-D-lactose for the cell wall precursor D-alanine-D-alanine. Alternative control strategies and treatment options have been prompted by the concerning trend of multi-drug-resistant uropathogens becoming more common.

4.3.2. Combination Therapies

New classes of β-lactamase inhibitors, which target both β-lactamases and KPCs, or *K. pneumoniae* carbapenemases are being developed to be used in conjunction with new antimicrobials that are resistant to being inactivated by ESBLs. *In vitro* studies have demonstrated the efficacy of these combination therapies against Enterobacteriaceae members that are resistant to carbapenem. Furthermore, when combined with the β-lactamase inhibitor avibactam, ceftazidime, a third-generation cephalosporin that is active against both Gram-positive and Gram-negative organisms, is effective against Gram-negative bacteria that produce ESBL and carbapenemase. These findings were made in clinical trials involving complex UTIs. Ceftazidime-avibactam has the potential to be effective against a wide range of cephalosporin-resistant Enterobacteriaceae family members; however, further research is required to test the drug combination's effectiveness against ESBL-, KPC-, and AmpC-producing Gram-negative pathogens during infection. The development of resistance to β-lactamase inhibitors is poorly understood, despite the promise of these antibiotic-inhibitor combinations. Additionally, the efficacy of some antibiotic-inhibitor treatments varies.

4.3.3. Vaccines Targeting Bacterial Adhesion

Targeting CUP pili has proven to be an appealing approach for the development of antivirulence therapies, including vaccines since adherence plays a crucial role at almost every stage of UTI pathogenesis. Generally speaking, whole pili vaccination has not been successful in producing an antibody response that can guard against UTIs. Adhesin-based vaccinations, on the other hand, have demonstrated efficacy in preventing host-pathogen interactions and thereby the development of disease. Studies with UTI models in mice and cynomolgus monkeys showed that immunization against UTIs with PapD–PapG or FimC–FimH chaperone–adhesin complexes provided protection. It has been established that antibodies that inhibit FimH's role in bladder colonization account for a significant portion of the FimC–FimH vaccine's efficacy. Moreover, it did not appear that the anti-FimH antibodies changed the *E. coli* niche in the microbiome of the gut. Currently, efforts are being made to modify this vaccine to stimulate the immune system. To elicit a more significant acute inflammatory response, for instance, one method has been to fuse FimH to the flagellin FliC, which operates through TLR4 signaling via the MYD.

Adhesins from P in addition to the UPEC adhesins. Mirabilis and *E. faecalis* have also been targeted by vaccines. A UTI-prone mouse model was vaccinated with the P. Similar to the outcomes of UPEC in the FimH vaccine trials, mirabilis MR/P pilus adhesin, MrpH, decreased bacterial burdens when compared with those of unvaccinated controls. Furthermore, a vaccination approach that works well against *E. faecalis* based on immunization with the Ebp pilus adhesin, EbpA, CAUTIs is being developed. In a CAUTI-affected mouse model, this tactic decreased bacterial burdens and increased antibody titers. To sum up, adhesin-based vaccinations are a promising field for the production of anti-uropathogen medications. Thus, for the development of vaccine strategies, an understanding of the molecular basis of host-pathogen interactions is essential.

4.3.4. Vaccines Targeting Bacterial Toxins and Proteases

In order to determine protection against renal damage, the UPEC pore-forming toxin HlyA was tested in a mouse model of pyelonephritis. It has also drawn interest as a possible target for a vaccine. When compared to controls, the HlyA vaccination decreased the incidence of renal scarring, but it offered no defense against kidney colonization by UPEC. Furthermore, in a UTI mouse model, vaccination with the *P. mirabilis* HpmA, or hemolysin, did not offer any defense against bacterial colonization. Pta, an alkaline protease that is toxic to epithelial cells, can prevent upper UTIs in mice, but it has no effect on bladder bacterial burdens. This is a promising finding from a UTI model. Thus, more research is required to ascertain the efficacy of hemolysins and proteases as vaccine targets, even though they may offer useful targets for preventing upper UTIs.

4.3.5. Vaccines Targeting Siderophores

The need for an iron supply for uropathogens to survive during colonization and persistence has made iron acquisition systems extremely promising as targets for vaccine development. In addition, studies have demonstrated that siderophores and hemoglobin acquisition systems are activated both in the urine of UTI-afflicted women and during experimental infection. A vaccine based on the ferric yersiniabactin uptake receptor (FyuA), hemoglobin acquisition protein (Hma), iron uptake transport aerobactin receptor (IutA), and siderophore receptor iron-responsive element A (IreA) was developed in response to these parameters. Immunization with IutA and IreA decreased bladder colonization in mice, while vaccination with FyuA and Hma protected mice against pyelonephritis, demonstrating the significance of these proteins during infection. Fascinatingly, the distinct tissue-specific protection observed with these four proteins implies that these systems function differently or have distinct expression profiles in various niches, such as the kidneys or bladder.

Other siderophore systems, such as the iron receptors FitA and ChuA, were not immune-stimulating vaccines in mouse models of UTI and were largely associated with decreased humoral responses specific to the antigen during experimental UTI. This is an exciting area of therapeutic development against UTIs because these studies suggest that effective siderophore-based vaccines work in part by preventing cognate siderophore uptake, as is the case with FyuA, Hma, IutA, and IreA.

4.3.6. Small Molecules Targeting Urease

With differing degrees of success, a number of urease inhibitors have been explored as possible UTI treatments. Numerous early inhibitors had considerable promise due to their low binding and inhibitory concentrations. These inhibitors were effective against ureases from a variety of bacterial species, including *Helicobacter pylori*, *P. mirabilis*, and *S. saprophyticus*.

In fact, urease-producing organism-related UTIs have been successfully treated with acetohydroxamic acid (AHA), the most well-characterized urease inhibitor. FDA-approved in 1983, AHA prevents urine from becoming alkaline. Unfortunately, there were a lot of these inhibitors that had harmful side effects. In addition to musculo-integumentary and psychoneurological effects, AHA, for instance, caused teratogenicity. Research conducted later revealed that AHA derivatives possessed significant inhibitory qualities as well, but once more, these substances were mutagenic, making them unsuitable for use as medicines. Phosphoramidites, an additional class of urease inhibitors, demonstrated strong efficacy against *P. mirabilis* were successful in an infection model using the urease. However, this class of compounds displayed low.

4.3.7. Small Molecules Targeting Bacterial Adhesion

The creation of two classes of tiny, logically constructed synthetic compounds to inhibit pili—mannosides, which inhibit pilus function, and pilicides, which inhibit pilus assembly—has been made possible by an understanding of pilus assembly and pilus–receptor binding. It may be therapeutic to target CUP pilus function or assembly since it should inhibit UPEC colonization, invasion, and biofilm formation, thereby averting disease.

The original purpose of pilicide development was to specifically prevent UPEC type 1 pili from assembling. They work by specifically targeting and disrupting important chaperone–usher interactions. They have a 2-pyridone scaffold. To find out more about their wide range of activity against other CUP pili, more research has been done. An examination of 35 *Escherichia* spp. Based on usher phylogeny, 458 CUP operons representing 38 different CUP pilus types were found using 132 plasmids and genomes. Only one *Escherichia* sp. genome can contain up to 16 different, intact CUP operons, indicating the possibility of broad-spectrum activity for drugs that target CUP pili by interfering with their assembly. For instance, it was discovered that the pilicide ec240 interfered with flagellar motility and several virulence-associated pili, such as type 1 pili, P pili, and S pili. The type 1 pilus genes were found to be the most downregulated genes in on the proteome and transcriptome of the cystitis isolate *E. coli* UTI89 following growth in the presence of ec240. The type 1 fimbriae promoter element (fimS), which has oscillation potential, is responsible for controlling the expression of type 1 pilus.

The development of mannosylated receptor analogs, or mannosides, allowed for the high affinity binding of FimH and the blocking of FimH binding. Mannosides are strong antagonists of FimH that present a promising therapeutic option for the management and avoidance of UTIs by severing important host-pathogen relationships. Research conducted on mouse models has indicated that mannosides have the potential to be a novel therapeutic approach against UTIs. Mannosides are orally bioavailable, fast-acting, potent, and prevent bladder colonization and invasion. They also work by preventing bladder invasion and colonization, are effective against multidrug-resistant UPEC, enhance the effectiveness of antibiotics, and are effective against both established UTIs and CAUTIs.

Fascinatingly, during transit through the usher pore, the receptor-binding lectin domain of adhesin FimH experiences a significant structural change, causing it to bend by roughly 37° in relation to the pilin domain. As a result, FimH takes on an extended conformation prior to passing through the usher pore, but following transport, the lectin domain swings closer to the pilin domain. The elongated conformation of the lectin domain binds mannose with a significantly higher affinity than the compact form, which has important implications for binding and pathogenesis. It has been demonstrated that the residues governing these conformational transitions are subject to positive selection, leading to the identification of pathoadaptive alleles of FimH. As a result, we now comprehend how ligand binding and protein–protein interactions can control a dynamic conformational equilibrium in the receptor-binding domain of FimH, which enhances the development of mannosides and provides previously unanticipated insights into UTI pathogenesis. The dynamics of how allostery controls CUP pilus assembly and function are being uncovered, and this knowledge is crucial for understanding macromolecular protein assembly and Gram-nega virulence.

4.4. Alimentary Canal

The alimentary canal is a lengthy, muscular tube that runs from the mouth to the anus. It is also referred to as the digestive tract or GI tract. With the anus at the end and the mouth at the front, it is approximately 8 to 10 meters long with openings at both ends (posterior). The mouth, throat, esophagus, stomach, small intestine, and large intestine are all included. Digestion, nutrient absorption, and waste removal fall under its purview. The tongue and teeth are examples of accessory structures that help with digestion. Maintaining appropriate nutrition and general health depends on the alimentary canal, which is crucial to the digestive process.

The GI tract is an essential organ system in the human body and is also known as the alimentary canal. The alimentary canal, which runs from the mouth to the anus, can measure between 5 and 7 meters (16 and 23 feet) in an average adult human. It oversees nutrient absorption and digestion. Mastication is the first step in the process, during which saliva starts to break down the carbohydrates, followed by the passing of food down the esophagus and into the stomach, where protein digestion occurs. The majority of digestion and nutrient absorption takes place in the small intestine, whereas the main functions of the large intestine include water absorption and feces production. Feces are held in the rectum until they are expelled through the anus, and this procedure is necessary to disintegrate food into its constituent parts, facilitating the absorption of nutrients for bodily functions and energy (Figure 4.5).

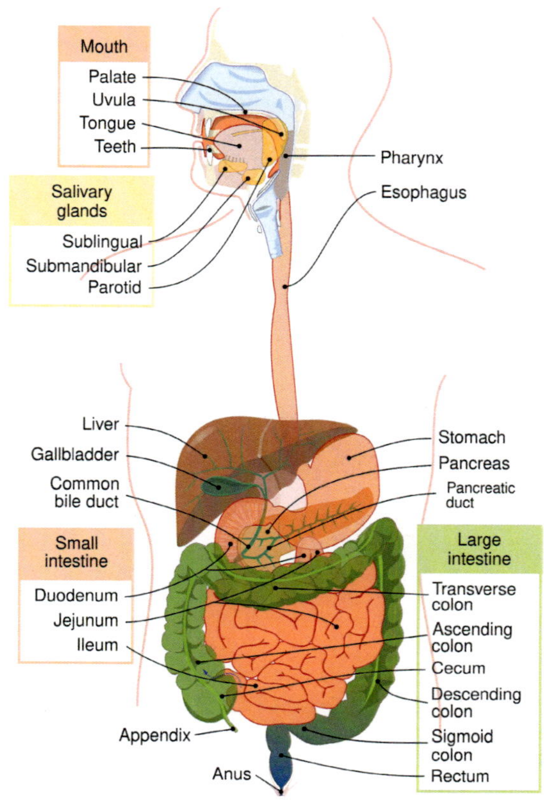

Figure 4.5. *Human digestive system.*

Source: By Mariana Ruiz, Jmarchn – Own work, Public Domain, https://commons.wikimedia.org/w/index.php?curid=2898771.

4.4.1. Organs of the Alimentary Canal

The organs that make up the alimentary canal include the rectum, anus, stomach, esophagus, small intestine, and large intestine. Together, these organs reduce food into smaller molecules and particles that the bloodstream can absorb.

1. **Mouth:** Food is first broken down in the mouth, where saliva and chewing action combine to break it down chemically and mechanically. Saliva contains enzymes that begin to break down carbohydrates, such as amylase. The oral cavity and vestibule are the two sections that make up the mouth.

2. **Oral Cavity:** Food and air enter the body through the mouth, also referred to as the oral cavity. The tongue, lips, teeth, and hard and soft palates are all parts of the oral cavity. The oral cavity has the following parts and purposes (Figure 4.6):

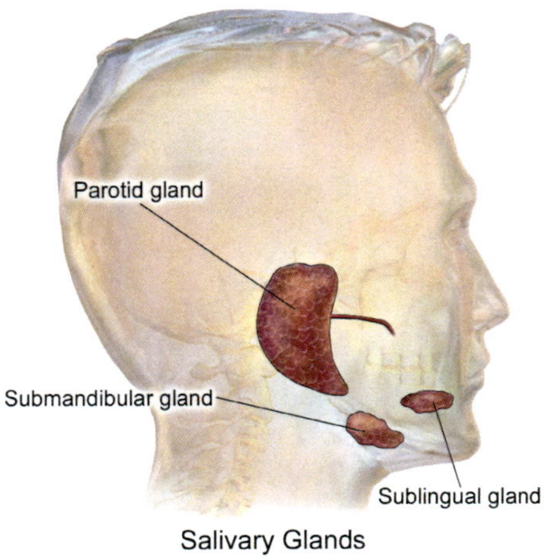

Figure 4.6. *The salivary glands.*

Source: Blausen.com staff (2014). "Medical gallery of Blausen Medical 2014." WikiJournal of Medicine, 1(2). doi: 10.15347/wjm/2014.010. ISSN: 2002-4436. Own work, CC BY 3.0, https://commons.wikimedia.org/w/index.php?curid=29294590.

i. **Lips and Cheeks:** The walls of the oral cavity are made up of the cheeks and lips. In addition to helping to produce speech sounds, it supports and confines food and saliva.

ii. **Tongue:** Food enters the mouth with the assistance of tongue movement. The process of digestion begins in the mouth. The base of the oral cavity is where the tongue is attached. The papillae's taste buds are sensory organs. There are three different kinds of lingual papillae: fungiform, filiform, and cerciculIate.

iii. **Palate:** The front (hard palate) and rear (soft palate) of the palate are separated. The soft palate seals off the nasal passages during swallowing to keep food and liquid from entering the nose, while the hard palate aids in chewing.

iv. **Salivary Glands:** Saliva is produced by salivary glands in the oral cavity and surrounding tissues. Saliva contains amylase, an enzyme that starts the breakdown of carbohydrates. Food is lubricated by saliva, which facilitates swallowing. Salivary glands can be broadly classified into three pairs: parotid, submandibular (submaxillary), and sublingual).

3. **Teeth:** The hardest tissue in the body, enamel, covers dentin, a material resembling bone, which makes up teeth. The oral cavity contains several types of teeth, which are used in different mastication processes to break food into tiny pieces. These types of teeth are as follows:

Type	Function
Incisor	Used for biting
Canines	Used for tearing
Premolars	Tearing and grinding food
Molars	Chewing and grinding food

When food is chewed with the help of saliva and mucus, a soft bolus is formed that can be swallowed to enable it to travel through the upper GI tract and into the stomach. The digestive enzymes in saliva dissolve any food particles that may have become stuck in teeth, helping to keep teeth clean.

4. **Esophagus:** It is a muscular tube with a length of about 10 to 13 inches. It joins the stomach and the throat, or pharynx. Its main purpose is to facilitate the passage of liquids and food from the mouth to the stomach for digestion. Food is propelled downward

by the coordinated contraction of the esophageal muscles, a process known as peristalsis. The throat's flap-like structure called the epiglottis makes sure that liquids and food go down the esophagus rather than the windpipe during swallowing.

5. **Stomach:** It is situated immediately below the diaphragm in the upper abdomen. A J-shaped bag describes an empty stomach. The stomach's gastric glands secrete gastric juice, which promotes digestion and eliminates microbes. There are four distinct parts to the stomach.

a. **Cardiac:** It is located close to the heart and forms the first segment where the stomach begins. It takes food from the esophagus and permits it to pass into the stomach.

b. **Fundus:** The fundus, or the top part of the stomach, is primarily used to hold and gather the gases released during digestion. As food and gas fill the stomach, this region swells.

c. **Body:** Most of the body's digestive functions take place in the center. Digestive enzymes and hydrochloric acid are among the gastric juices secreted by its gastric glands, which are necessary for the digestion of food.

d. **Pyloric:** The pylorus, which makes up the lower portion of the stomach, controls how much partially digested food (chyme) enters the small intestine.

6. **Small Intestine:** Pyloric, the lowest portion of the stomach, opens into the duodenum. Within the alimentary canal, the small intestine is the longest segment. The intestine has a larger surface area because of the villi covering its inner surface. The three additional sections that make up the small intestine are as follows.

i. **Duodenum:** It is the S-shaped joint that joins the stomach to the intestine. It is located where bile from the liver (via the common bile duct) and pancreatic digestive enzymes are combined with partially digested food, or chyme. Better nutrient absorption is made possible by the breakdown of proteins, fats, and carbohydrates aided by these enzymes and bile.

ii. **Jejunum:** The jejunum is the middle section of the small intestine, and it comes after the duodenum. It serves as the main site of nutrient absorption, especially for proteins and carbohydrates. Villi and microvilli, finger-like projections that line the walls of the jejunum, increase the surface area available for the bloodstream to absorb nutrients.

iii. **Ileum:** The ileum, which joins the large intestine at the ileocecal valve, is the last segment of the small intestines. Bile salts, vitamin B12, and any leftover nutrients are the main targets as it proceeds with the absorption process.

7. **Large Intestine:** The colon, sometimes referred to as the large intestine, is principally in charge of the last phases of digestion, the absorption of water, and the removal of waste. It is located in the digestive tract after the small intestine and is made up of the cecum, sigmoid colon, ascending colon, transverse colon, descending colon, and rectum. The three sections that make up the large intestine are as follows:

i. **Caecum:** A pouch-like structure at the start of the large intestine, receives material from the ileum, the last segment of the small intestine. It has the vermiform appendix, a tiny projection that resembles a finger and may play various roles in the immune system, though these are yet unknown. The residing microorganisms exhibit a symbiotic relationship. The caecum is the area where the vestigial organ is connected.

ii. **Colon:** As the longest segment of the large intestine, the colon is further subdivided into the ascending, transverse, descending, and sigmoid colons. Feces formation and water absorption are the functions of the colon.

iii. **Rectum:** The last section of the large intestine before the anus is called the rectum. It holds on to waste products until the body can get rid of them.

4.4.2. Function of Alimentary Canal

The alimentary canal, sometimes referred to as the digestive tract or GI tract, is in charge of several vital bodily processes. These are some of these roles:

1. **Ingestion:** The act of receiving food and liquids through the mouth to process them further.
2. **Mastication:** Food should be chewed in the mouth and broken up into smaller pieces for easier digestion.
3. **Digestion:** It uses a combination of chemical and mechanical processes to break down food into smaller, more absorbable molecules.
4. **Absorption:** Nutrition uptake (e.g., glucose, fatty acids, amino acids, vitamins, and minerals) into the bloodstream after digestion. It disperses the same throughout the tissues and cells of the body. The small intestine is the site of this process.
5. **Secretion:** The secretion of digestive acids, enzymes, and other materials from the pancreas (enzyme production), salivary glands, stomach, liver, and other accessory organs.
6. **Mixing and Churning:** Food is mechanically mixed with digestive juices in the intestines and stomach. It facilitates digestion by breaking down food particles even more.
7. **Excretion:** The rectum and anus are the organs that remove undigested waste, indigestible food items, and other metabolic byproducts from the body.

4.5. Alimentary Canal or GI Infection

The digestive tract, or alimentary canal, is a lengthy tube that runs from the mouth to the anus and is in charge of breaking down and absorbing food. The presence of numerous pathogens, such as bacteria, viruses, parasites, and fungi, can cause alimentary canal infections.

The digestive system allows these infectious agents to enter the human body, which may result from eating food tainted with infectious agents, leading to food poisoning. Gastroenteritis, which is usually accompanied by vomiting, diarrhea, and cramping in the abdomen, is caused by these infections. When an infectious agent is contracted, these symptoms typically appear 12–72 hours later and, if viral in nature, they last less than a week. Fever, exhaustion, headaches, and muscle aches are also possible side effects of certain viral infections. A bacterial infection is more likely to be the cause of bloody stool than a viral one. When left untreated, certain bacterial infections can cause excruciating stomach pain and persist for weeks. These gastrointestinal (GI) infections impact the abdominal region, and stomach infection types include those brought on by bacteria and those contracted both inside and outside of a hospital. Diarrhea, nausea, cramps, loss of appetite, and fever are some of the symptoms associated with gastrointestinal infections. The majority of these infections resolve on their own in a few days, but depending on the precise cause, those that persist may need to be treated with antibiotics or antiparasitic drugs. If necessary, a lab test can be used by a healthcare professional to determine which organism is causing your symptoms.

4.6. Types of Gastrointestinal Infections

Based on where the infection occurs in the body, what kind of germs cause it, and how it was obtained, there are various classifications for GI infections.

4.6.1. Body Area-Based Infections

While lower GI tract infections impact the intestines, upper GI tract infections typically happen in the mouth, esophagus, or stomach.

Additionally, the specific organ and body part affected determine how serious the infection is. "Complicated" infections are those that spread beyond the initial site and have the potential to cause life-threatening sepsis or even septic shock.

4.6.2. Germ-Based Infections

Gastritis can be caused by a variety of microorganisms, including viruses, parasites, and bacteria. Abdominal infection-causing bacteria may vary depending on:

- Degree of economic development;
- Geographic region;
- Hygienic standards;
- Sanitation level.

4.6.3. Location-Based Infections

The separation of one's abdominal infection from another can also be based on the initial site of infection. Additionally community-acquired infections can spread outside of medical facilities like hospitals. Healthcare environments are the source of nosocomial infections, or infections acquired in hospitals, and they can involve hard-to-treat, antibiotic-resistant bacteria, which makes them usually more serious.

4.6.4. GI Infection Symptoms

GI infections can cause the following main symptoms:

- Abdominal pain;
- Diarrhea;
- Fever;
- Nausea and vomiting;
- Stomach cramps.

In most cases, the symptoms of a GI infection are transient. Seeking medical attention is necessary if they continue for more than a few weeks.

4.6.5. Causes of GI Infections

GI infections are most frequently caused by viruses and bacteria. Most infections in adults are caused by norovirus, whereas rotavirus is more common in children, as well as adenovirus.

The most frequent bacteria that causes gastroenteritis is salmonella. It conceals itself in tainted poultry, eggs, produce, and meat products. These are some additional typical bacterial sources of GI infections:

- *St. aureus* is abacteriuma that can be found on your skin and in foods such as dairy products, meat, poultry, and eggs.
- Shigella, discovered in water contaminated with excrement.
- Fried rice is associated with *Bacillus cereus*.

- Meat, poultry, produce, dairy products, and meat all contain campylobacter.
- *E. coli* that can be foung in water tainted with produce, raw beef, eggs, and excrement.
- *C. difficile* is frequently acquired in hospital environments, which means that individuals who are already medically vulnerable are frequently affected.
- Listeria can be found in undercooked meats, deli meats, and produce.
- *Hyprobacterium pylori* from contaminated food or drink, contaminated eating utensils, or bodily fluids from another person, such as saliva. This kind of infection is connected to stomach cancer and ulcers.

Another source of GI infections is parasites. *Giardia lamblia*, which is found in water, intestinal worms like hookworms and tapeworms, Cryptosporidium, and *Toxoplasma gondii* are examples of parasites.

Infections frequently spread from person to person in communities or through tainted food or water. They can also spread through contaminated surgical instruments or catheters in healthcare settings.

4.6.6. GI Tract Infections Diagnosed

Most GI or abdominal infections clear up on their own in a few days, so there's usually no need for a diagnosis. If you need to see a doctor, they will probably start by taking your medical history and doing a physical examination in the office. Often, laboratory testing can pinpoint the exact cause of the infection. Some possible test examples are:

1. **Breath Tests:** A healthcare professional can perform a breath test on a patient to check for bacteria like *H. pylori*.
2. **Imaging Tests:** These imaging-based tests, like CT scans, can provide additional details about the state of the internal organs.
3. **Molecular Tests:** This test can be used by a provider to search for organism traces, and the results can be obtained rapidly—sometimes within a few hours.
4. **Stool Sample:** A stool sample enables a healthcare professional to check a patient's feces for parasitic and bacterial infections.

4.6.7. Treatment for GI Infections

Treating oneself is usually the best course of action. Viral or parasitic GI infections are not treatable with antibiotics. Antibiotics may actually worsen the condition and raise the chance of relapse in less complicated cases of bacterial infection, even though they can be helpful in more complex cases. Furthermore, antibiotics have the potential to cause harmful side effects in some infections. If you or your child need antibiotics, your doctor can help. It is possible that high-fiber foods can exacerbate diarrhea, so your doctor may advise against them. Also, they may suggest over-the-counter drugs to relieve diarrhea, nausea, and stomach discomfort as well as medications to neutralize stomach acid. Staying hydrated is the most crucial self-care intervention for GI infections in adults and children.

A Closer Look

The Anatomy of the Urethra

For the purpose of eliminating bodily fluids, the urethra is a tube that joins the genitalia and the bladder. The striated muscle known as the external urethral sphincter regulates the flow of urine from the bladder into the urethra, enabling voluntary control over urination.Urine travels through the urethra, a duct, from the bladder to the outside of the body when urinating. The urethral sphincter, a muscular structure that aids in holding urine in the bladder until it is time to void, keeps the urethra closed.

Male and female urethra characteristics differ greatly because of their anatomical connection to the reproductive structures. The urethra of a male is approximately 18 to 20 cm (7 to 8 inches) in length and travels the entire length of the penis before emptying. The urethra is the passageway for both the discharge of urine and the transmission of semen. It exits the bladder through the prostate gland and is entered on both sides by seminal ducts from the testes. Three sections make up the male urethra: the spongy urethra, which is the longest and lowest section within the penis, the membranous urethra, which is the segment within the urethral sphincter, and the prostatic urethra, which is the uppermost segment within the prostate. Other sections that may be identified are the fossa navicularis, pendulous urethra, bulbous urethra, and preprostatic urethra (at the neck of the bladder). These are all subdivisions of the spongy urethra. Furthermore, it is possible to characterize the male urethra as having two regions: the anterior (spongy urethra) and posterior (membranous and prostate urethras).

The female urethra is located between the labia and is embedded in the vaginal wall. The female urethra is only 4 cm (1.5 inches) long, significantly shorter than the male urethra. It starts at the neck of the bladder and immediately opens to the exterior after emerging from the urethral sphincter.

A number of different conditions can affect the urethra. A congenital condition known as hypospadias causes the urethra to open on the underside of the penis. Urethritis is an inflammatory disease that affects both the male and female urethra and is frequently caused by infection. In addition to inflammation, infection, or injury, developmental conditions can also result in urethral stricture, or narrowing of the urethra. In addition to conditions linked to chronic inflammation of the urethra, such as bladder cancer, urethral cancer is an uncommon condition that affects women more frequently than men, e.g., frequent infections of the urinary tract). Difficulty urinating, frequent urination, dysuria (pain during urination), and bleeding or discharge from the urethral opening are common signs of inflammation or infection. When there are symptoms that point to a urethral infection but no visible infection, a condition known as urethral syndrome may be identified.

The Female Urethra:

The urethra is shorter in females than in males, and it protrudes above the vaginal opening. Non-keratinized stratified squamous epithelium, which becomes transitional close to the bladder, makes up the majority of its lining. There are three layers of tissues that make up the urethra.

- The smooth muscle of the bladder continues into the muscular layer.
- Specialized tissue known as the erectile urethral tissue has the potential to swell with blood when a person is sexually aroused.
- The mucous membranes lining the inside of the urethra are known as the mucous urethral tissue. Particularly crucial for shielding the urethral tissues from urine's caustic effects are the mucous membranes.

The bladder and urethra are kept apart by the urethral sphincter. The pudendal nerve supplies the external urethral sphincter with somatic (conscious) innervation, enabling the sphincter to open and close. Due to their shorter urethras than males, females are more susceptible to urinary tract infections caused by bacteria.

The Male Urethra

The urethra in males passes through the penis and transports both urine and semen. Semen is a fluid composed of sperm cells and other fluids that travels through a few different glands, including the vas deferens, from the testes to the urethra. It does not pass through the bladder or the rest of the urinary tract. The male urethra is structurally similar to the female urethra, except for semen and its longer length.

The male urethra is a small, fibromuscular tube that travels outside the body to carry urine and semen from the bladder and ejaculatory ducts, respectively (see illustration below). The male urethra is a single structure, but it is made up of a variety of segments, including prostatic, membranous, and spongy sections.

The prostatic urethra is the most common site of bladder outlet obstruction in the Western world, and it is also the source of involuntary continence and semen transmission into the common genitourinary tract. The membranous urethra is extremely vulnerable to damage in cases of pelvic trauma due to its rigid attachments, which makes it essential for voluntary continence. The corpus spongiosum encircles the spongy urethra, which serves as the terminal conduit for communication with the external body.

Because urethral catheterization is one of the most often performed procedures in healthcare, understanding the male urethral anatomy is essential for all health professionals. A multitude of pathologic conditions, including traumatic, infectious, and neoplastic ones, can affect the male urethra. Reproductive failure and infertility are two terrible outcomes that can result from pathophysiologic variations of the urethra.

Summary

- UTIs and alimentary canal infections are common microbial infections affecting millions globally.
- UTIs are primarily caused by bacteria like Escherichia coli, while alimentary canal infections can be triggered by bacteria, viruses, parasites, or fungi.
- UTIs can occur due to ascending infection from the urethra, while alimentary canal infections often result from ingesting contaminated food or water.
- Common symptoms of UTIs include frequent urination, burning sensation during urination, and abdominal discomfort. Alimentary canal infections may manifest as diarrhea, vomiting, abdominal pain, and fever.
- Risk factors for UTIs include female anatomy, urinary catheterization, sexual activity, and underlying medical conditions. Alimentary canal infections can be influenced by poor hygiene, contaminated food or water, and compromised immune systems.
- Diagnosis of UTIs involves urinalysis, urine culture, and imaging tests. Alimentary canal infections are diagnosed through stool cultures, blood tests, and imaging studies.
- Antibiotics are commonly prescribed for UTIs, with specific agents chosen based on bacterial susceptibility. Alimentary canal infections may require supportive care, oral rehydration therapy, and, in some cases, antimicrobial treatment.
- Untreated UTIs can lead to kidney infections (pyelonephritis), sepsis, and long-term urinary tract damage. Alimentary canal infections can result in dehydration, electrolyte imbalances, and, in severe cases, systemic infection.
- Preventive measures for UTIs include staying hydrated, practicing good hygiene, urinating after sexual intercourse, and avoiding irritating substances. Alimentary canal infections can be prevented by practicing proper food safety measures, including washing hands and cooking food thoroughly.
- UTIs and alimentary canal infections pose significant burdens on healthcare systems and public health, emphasizing the importance of prevention strategies, early diagnosis, and appropriate treatment interventions.

References

1. Czaja, C. A., Scholes, D., Hooton, T. M., & Stamm, W. E., (2007). Population-based epidemiologic analysis of acute pyelonephritis. *Clinical Infectious Diseases, 45*(3), 273–280.
2. Fisher, J. F., Kavanagh, K., Sobel, J. D., Kauffman, C. A., & Newman, C., (2011). A Candida urinary tract infection: Pathogenesis. *Clin. Infect. Dis., 52*(Suppl 6), S437–S451.
3. Foxman, B., (2010). The epidemiology of urinary tract infection. *Nature Rev. Urol., 7*, 653–660.
4. Grabe, M., Bartoletti, R., Bjerklund, J. T. E., & Cai, T., (2015). *Guidelines on Urological Infections*. European Association of Urology; The Netherlands.
5. Guarino, N., Casamassima, M. G., Tadini, B., Marras, E., Lace, R., & Bianchi, M., (2005). Natural history of vesicoureteral reflux associated with kidney anomalies. *Urology, 65*(6), 1208–1211.

6. Hooton, T. M., (2012). Uncomplicated urinary tract infection. *New Engl. J. Med., 366*, 1028–1037.
7. Jepson, R. G., Williams, G., & Craig, J. C., (2012). Cranberries for preventing urinary tract infections (review). *Cochrane Database of Systematic Reviews,* (10), article no. CD001321.
8. Lichtenberger, P., & Hooton, T. M., (2008). Complicated urinary tract infections. *Curr. Infect. Dis. Rep., 10*, 499–504.
9. Lo, E., et al., (2014). Strategies to prevent catheter-associated urinary tract infections in acute care hospitals: 2014 update. *Infect. Control Hosp. Epidemiol., 35*, 464–479.
10. Prakash, K., Kuruvilla, K., & Lekha, V., (2001). Primary tuberculous stricture of the oesophagus mimicking carcinoma. *Trop. Gastroenterol., 22*, 143, 144.
11. Stamm, W. E., & Norrby, S. R., (2001). Urinary tract infections: Disease panorama and challenges. *J. Infect. Dis., 183.*
12. Staroverov, V. V., Kisel, A. T., Sumarokov, U. A., & Kachanova, T. N., (2001). A case of phlegmonous gastritis diagnosed by echography. *Eur. J. Ultrasound., 13*, 197–200.
13. *Urinary Tract Infection (UTI),* (2018). Kids Health Info, Royal Children's Hospital, Melbourne.
14. Vieth, M., Dirshmid, K., & Oehler, U., (2001). Acute measles gastric infection. *Am. J. Surg. Pathol., 25*, 259–262.
15. Xiao, S. Y., & Hart, J., (2001). Marked gastric foveolar hyperplasia associated with active cytomegalovirus infection. *Am. J. Gastroenterol., 96*, 223–226.

Chapter

INFECTIONS OF THE LIVER AND BILIARY TRACT

5

Contents

Unit Introduction

Hepatitis, commonly referred to as a liver infection, is a chronic illness that can have many causes. For its successful treatment and early detection, it is essential to comprehend the signs and typical causes of liver infections. Cholangitis and cholecystitis are examples of biliary tract infections. In older patients with comorbid disease, they are linked to increased morbidity and mortality rates. The most frequent pathogens are Gram-positive pathogens such as *Enterococci* spp. and Enterobacteriaceae, which ascend from the GI tract. Fungi, viruses, and parasites are not often the cause of the infections. A blood-borne infection or an infection that spreads through the portal-venous channels is the main cause of biliary tract infections, as is the ascending infection brought on by the reflux of duodenal contents. Additional risk factors for biliary tract infections include immunosuppressive disorders, diabetes, non-biliary surgery, trauma, burns, sepsis, HIV infection, and immunological suppression.

Antibiotics such as fluoroquinolones, carbapenems, cephalosporins, and derivatives of β-lactams, among others, decrease the infection. For moderate and severe acute cholecystitis, empirical treatment with piperacillin/tazobactam or a cephalosporin with or without metronidazole is advised, regardless of the presence of growth on culture. Unfortunately, because clinical symptoms are often unexpected and imaging investigations are often unclear, it is challenging to correctly identify patients with severe cholecystitis, both clinically and radiologically. However, the morbidity and mortality rates of people with mild cholecystitis and those with severe cholecystitis differ significantly. Early detection and successful treatment of those at risk of developing severe cholecystitis are necessary to avoid the associated consequences.

Orientation and Directional Terms

Term	Definition	Illustration
Ascites	Ascites is the buildup of fluid in the abdomen that can occur with liver failure, cirrhosis, and liver cancer.	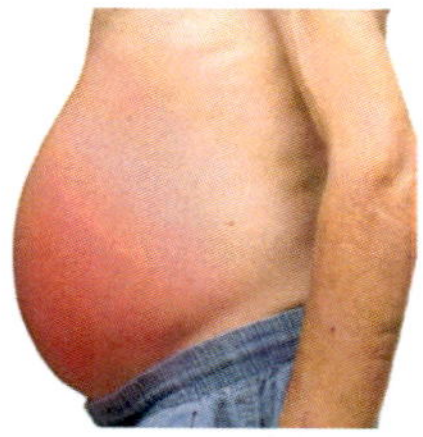
Bile ducts	Bile ducts are tubes that drain the bile from the liver into the intestine.	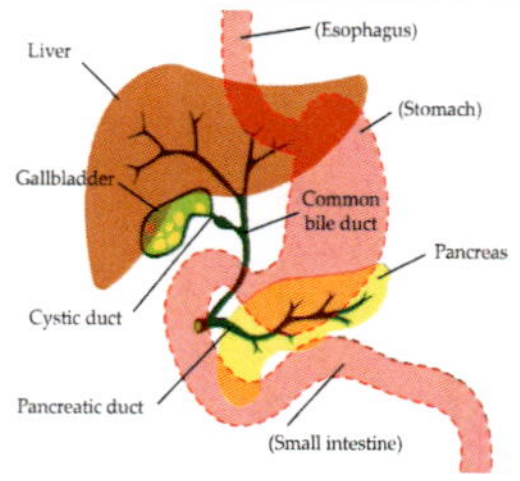
Cholestasis	Cholestasis is a liver disease. It occurs when the flow of bile from your liver is reduced or blocked.	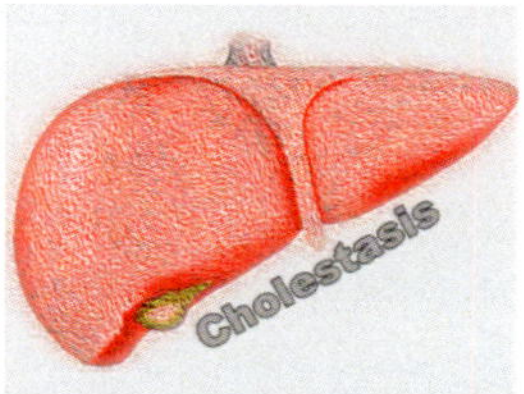
Fibrosis	Fibrosis is the initial scarring of the liver.	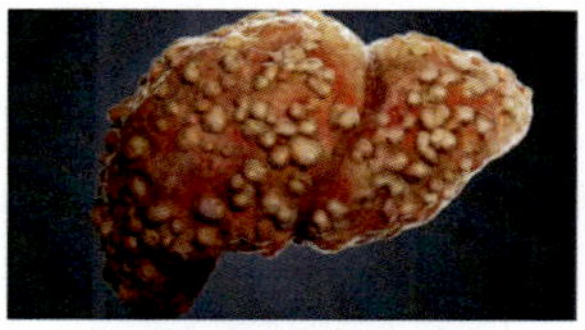
Hepatitis A	The hepatitis A virus (HAV) causes the liver to swell and prevents it from working well. HAV is passed from person to person through fecal matter.	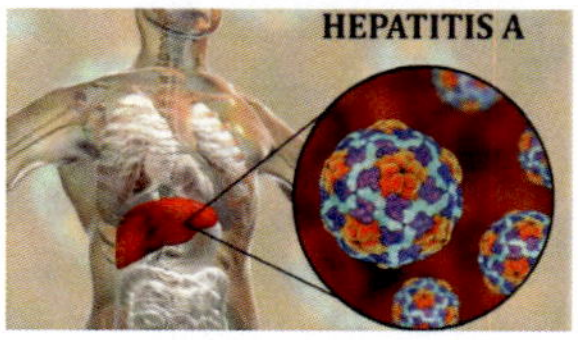
Hepatitis B	Hepatitis B is a liver disease caused by the hepatitis B virus (HBV). HBV causes the liver to swell and prevents it from working well. HBV is passed from person to person through bodily fluids such as blood, semen, or vaginal secretions.	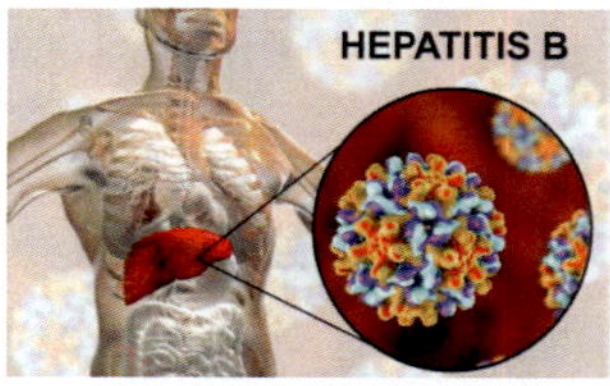
Hepatitis C	Hepatitis C is a liver disease caused by the hepatitis C virus (HCV). HCV causes the liver to swell and prevents it from working well. HCV is passed from person to person by blood.	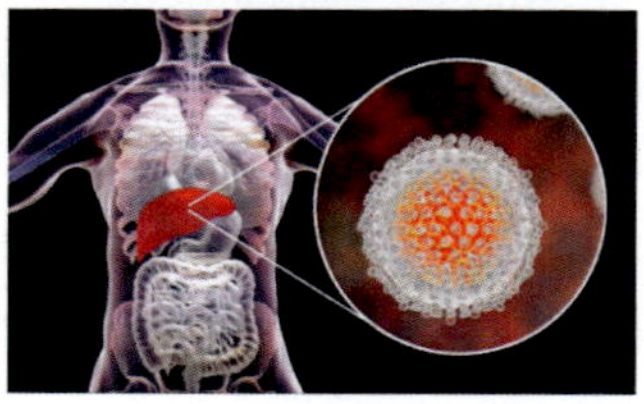

5.1. Infections of the Liver

Microbes are transported with blood by the portal vein, which carries blood from the GI tract to the liver. It follows that a wide range of microbial infections may affect the liver. Although immunocompromised hosts are frequently the target of certain infections, it also impact others with immune competence. Primary or secondary hepatic infections can occur as a component of a contagious or systemic illness.

5.1.1. Bacterial Infection Involving the Liver

5.1.1.1. Gram-Positive and Gram-Negative Infections

Hepatic compromise can result from various bacterial infections, both gram-positive and gram-negative. This includes streptococcal species belonging to group A and infections caused by *S. aureus*. Surgical wounds and teenage tampon use are two common risk factors for *S. aureus* infections. Hypotensive shock is also one possible consequence. Jaundice and elevated serum transaminases are examples of hepatic disease manifestations. Liver failure and widespread hepatic necrosis are possible outcomes of the disease's progression. Histology may reveal granuloma formation and microabscesses punctuating the liver. Clindamycin treatment is advised for infections; methicillin-resistant infections may need to be treated with antibiotics like vancomycin or linezolid.

In a study in cirrhotic patients from Spain, extended-spectrum β-lactamase-producing *Enterobacteriaceae* were the main organism identified in sepsis, followed by bacteria such as *P. aeruginosa*, methicillin-resistant *S. aureus*, and *Enterococcus faecium*. Septic shock (26% vs. 10%; $P < 0.0001$) and mortality rate (25% vs. 12%; $P = 0.001$) were significantly higher in infections caused by multi-resistant strains. Third-generation cephalosporins were found to be clinically ineffective for treatment in these patients.

Additionally, hepatic disease has been linked to *Clostridium perfringens*. Children with clostridial infections can develop during the neonatal stage of necrotizing enterocolitis, during chemotherapy, or after puncture wound infections. There is a high death rate linked to the development of gas gangrene. About 20% of these patients may develop jaundice, and hepatic disease can cause gas to appear in the portal vein and abscesses to form. Penicillin and clindamycin therapy, along with surgical debridement of the afflicted tissue, are necessary.

5.1.1.2. Listeria Monocytogenes

Infections occurring with Listeria during the neonatal period are characterized as severe, uncommon, and frequently linked with the formation of hepatic abscesses. Contributing factors include premature birth, while in older children, susceptibility increases with conditions such as immunosuppression, diabetes mellitus, and cirrhosis. The recommended treatment for the infection involves the use of ampicillin and gentamicin, and efforts are underway to develop a vaccine for use in individuals with compromised immune systems.

5.1.1.3. Salmonella and Shigella

In less developed regions, Salmonella and Shigella infections are prevalent. Typhoid fever, in particular, results in systemic illness often affecting the liver. *Salmonella typhi* infection is contracted through contaminated food or water, presenting symptoms like high fever and abdominal pain. While serum transaminase levels increase, bilirubin elevation is minimal. Cholecystitis and liver abscesses may develop. Hepatic compromise mediated by bacterial endotoxins is addressed with ciprofloxacin and ceftriaxone as primary interventions. Diagnosis involves blood cultures, enzyme immunoassays, and bone marrow cultures. Hepatitis may also accompany *Salmonella paratyphi* A and B infections, known as paratyphoid fever, with recommended treatments involving cephalosporins or fluoroquinolones. Shigella infections lead to dysentery or acute diarrheal illnesses, primarily contracted through contaminated food and water. Hepatic manifestations include cholestatic hepatitis, which are particularly common in developing countries.

5.1.1.4. Yersinia

In children, *Yersinia enterocolitica* infection typically manifests as diarrhea, abdominal discomfort, and often terminal ileitis mimicking Crohn's disease. Hepatic involvement may occur in immunocompromised individuals, such as those with cirrhosis or diabetes, leading to multiple hepatic abscesses. Mortality in such cases can be as high as 50%, with fluoroquinolones recommended for treatment.

5.1.1.5. Actinomyces

Pediatric infections with *Actinomyces israelii* affect immunocompromised hosts, involving cranial, thoracic, and abdominal regions. This gram-positive anaerobic bacterium causes hepatic infection in 15% of abdominal actinomycosis cases, often spreading from contiguous abdominal sites. The disease progresses indolently, with nonspecific elevation of inflammatory markers and leukocytosis. Multiple liver abscesses may form, and treatment includes intravenous penicillin or oral tetracycline. Surgical resection may be necessary for large abscesses.

5.1.1.6. Legionella

Legionnaire disease, resulting from infections with *Legionella pneumophila*, manifests as pneumonia and hepatitis. Jaundice is minimal, and hepatic steatosis and necrosis may be evident on biopsy. Treatment involves fluoroquinolones or azithromycin.

5.1.1.7. Gonococci

Gonococcal infections, as seen in the Fitz-Hugh–Curtis syndrome, present with perihepatitis, right upper quadrant pain, and fever. Patients often have a history of pelvic inflammatory disease with gonococci demonstrated on vaginal culture. Ceftriaxone is the treatment of choice, leading to the resolution of perihepatitis.

5.1.1.8. Brucellosis

Various species of Brucella can cause human disease, acquired from contaminated sheep, pigs, cattle, and goats. Clinical manifestations include an acute onset of fever, abdominal discomfort, and jaundice. Noncaseating hepatic granulomas are identified on biopsy. Surgical drainage of abscesses may be necessary, and a combination of streptomycin and doxycycline is used for treatment.

5.1.1.9. Coxiella burnetii

Infections with this organism lead to Q fever, characterized by relapsing fevers, pneumonitis, endocarditis, and hepatitis. Alkaline phosphatase elevation is disproportionate to the mild rise in serum bilirubin and transaminases. Liver biopsy reveals fibrin ring granulomas, and treatment involves doxycycline.

5.1.1.10. Bartonella

Bartonella henselae infection, known as "cat scratch disease," is associated with hepatosplenic necrotizing granulomas. Peliosis hepatis or blood-filled cysts may occur in infections in patients with concomitant AIDS. Symptoms may also include papular dermatitis, pulmonary, and neurological symptoms. Bacillary angiomatosis is treated with erythromycin, while doxycycline may be considered for the treatment of visceral disease.

5.1.2. Other Gram-Negative Infections

Chlamydia trachomatis infections can lead to perihepatitis, known as Fitz-Hugh–Curtis syndrome, resembling the presentation observed in gonococcal disease. Typically, liver function tests remain within the normal range. The recommended treatment for this infection involves the use of azithromycin or doxycycline.

Rocky Mountain spotted fever, a tick-borne rickettsial infection, is characterized by the development of a maculopapular rash, fever, and hepatic disease. The hepatic manifestation involves portal inflammation and vasculitis, accompanied by jaundice and increased liver enzymes. Hemolysis may result in hyperbilirubinemia and biliary obstruction. In contrast, *Ehrlichia* infections, caused by another tick-borne intracellular bacteria, are associated with liver injury due to hepatocyte proliferation and an immune response. Focal necrosis, fibrin ring granulomas, and cholestasis are observed, and the recommended treatment is with doxycycline.

5.1.3. Spirochetes

5.1.3.1. Leptospirosis

Leptospirosis, transmitted by exposure to urine or contaminated soil and water from various animals, often manifests as anicteric leptospirosis in over 90% of cases. The illness follows a biphasic pattern, with the initial phase marked by fever and conjunctival injection. The second phase is associated with myalgias, nausea, vomiting, abdominal pain, aseptic meningitis, increased serum liver enzymes, and jaundice. Weil disease, the icteric form, occurs in 5–10% of patients, presenting with jaundice in the earlier phase and high fever, renal manifestations, and acute tubular necrosis in the second phase. Hemorrhagic complications are common, and doxycycline is the recommended treatment.

5.1.3.2. Lyme Disease

Lyme disease, caused by the tick-borne spirochete Borrelia burgdorferi, manifests with hepatic symptoms including anorexia, nausea, vomiting, weight loss, and right upper quadrant pain. Increased liver enzymes and the appearance of erythema migrans rash are also observed. Diagnosis involves serology and clinical history confirmation, and treatment is with oral doxycycline or azithromycin.

5.1.3.3. Tuberculosis

In developing countries where tuberculosis is endemic, hepatic disease is often observed. Liver biopsy may reveal granulomas with central caseation necrosis in 25% of patients with pulmonary tuberculosis and approximately 80% of those with extrapulmonary disease. Similar granulomas may be found in immunocompromised individuals vaccinated with the Bacillus Calmette–Guérin vaccine. Diagnosis involves identifying acid-fast bacilli, and treatment consists of 4-drug therapy. Jaundice and an increase in serum alkaline phosphatase may occur in cases of miliary disease.

5.1.3.4. Syphilis

Hepatic involvement in secondary syphilis is infrequent in children, leading to cholestatic hepatitis. Symptoms include anorexia, weight loss, a characteristic maculopapular rash on the palms and soles, jaundice, hepatomegaly, and right upper quadrant pain. Liver histology reveals hepatitis with spirochetes demonstrated on silver stain, and treatment involves penicillin.

5.1.3.5. Liver Abscess

Liver abscess formation typically follows underlying issues such as immunocompromise, diabetes, surgery, or malignancy. Pyogenic abscesses may result from appendicitis, perforated bowel, or inflammatory bowel disease, and may also be the initial manifestation of hepatic malignancy. Most abscesses are due to infections with *E. coli*, *Klebsiella*, *Proteus*, *Pseudomonas*, and *Streptococcus*. Anaerobic infections with Bacteroides may also occur, as well as infections with *Clostridium*, *Actinomyces*, *Yersinia*, *Haemophilus influenzae*, *Listeria*, and *Staphylococcus*. Disseminated fungal infections may lead to micro- or macro-abscess formation in an immunocompromised host. The patient typically presents with abdominal discomfort, severe right upper abdominal pain, and high fever, along with tender hepatomegaly.

Ultrasound and CT scans are the preferred initial imaging modalities, allowing identification of abscesses up to 1 cm in diameter. A CT scan identifies abscess localization and gas presence, facilitating aspiration or drain insertion when necessary. Treatment involves pus drainage and initiation of appropriate antibiotic therapy. For larger abscesses (>5 cm), an indwelling catheter may be placed, while intermittent needle aspiration may be attempted for smaller abscesses. Broad-spectrum antibiotic therapy is initiated before culture results are available, typically with amoxicillin, an aminoglycoside, and a third-generation cephalosporin. Anaerobic coverage may be required with metronidazole. Treatment is initially intravenous for at least 2 weeks, followed by oral therapy for up to 6 weeks. Streptococcal infections may necessitate high-dose oral antibiotics for 6 months. Despite treatment, the mortality rate is high, and complications of delayed diagnoses include shock, pleural effusion with sepsis, and multiorgan dysfunction.

5.1.4. Parasitic Infections of the Liver

Parasitic infections of the liver encompass both protozoan and helminthic infections, exhibiting variable distribution and epidemiology across different geographic regions.

5.1.4.1. Protozoa

1. **Malaria:** Caused by the protozoan species Plasmodia, malaria affects an estimated 300–500 million people globally annually. The hepatic phase presence varies among Plasmodium species, with *Plasmodium falciparum* and *Plasmodium malariae* lacking a hepatic cycle, while *Plasmodium vivax* and *Plasmodium ovale* have a persistent exoerythrocytic phase in the liver. Hepatic injury severity is species-dependent, leading to active hemolysis and an increase in unconjugated bilirubin. Liver failure results in impaired synthetic function, decreased serum albumin, prolonged prothrombin time, hyperglycemia, and lactic acidosis. Congenital malaria may cause severe liver disease in newborns. Diagnosis involves history, physical examination, and parasite identification on blood smears. Treatment varies by Plasmodium species, with chloroquine, mefloquine, quinine, pyrimethamine-sulfadoxine, and proguanil being common choices.
2. **Babesiosis:** Transmitted by the deer tick *Ixodes scapularis*, babesiosis manifests as fever, anemia, and hepatosplenomegaly. Anemia, hemoglobinuria, and hemophagocytosis characterize the infection, treated with azithromycin and atovaquone or clindamycin and quinine. Exchange transfusions may be necessary in complicated cases.
3. **Leishmaniasis:** Caused by *Leishmania donovani* and transmitted by sand flies, leishmaniasis is endemic in various regions. Initial papular or ulcerative lesions progress to fever, weight loss, diarrhea, and massive hepatosplenomegaly. Hepatocyte necrosis leads to cirrhosis and complications. Diagnosis involves

clinical features, history, and parasite identification on various stains. Pancytopenia, bacterial infections, and cutaneous pigmentation may occur. Treatment includes pentavalent antimonials, liposomal amphotericin B, paromomycin, and miltefosine.

4. **Toxoplasmosis:** *Toxoplasma gondii* infection, acquired congenitally or through contaminated sources, may lead to severe disseminated infection with hepatosplenomegaly. Symptoms include fever, headache, lymphadenopathy, myocarditis, and encephalitis. Diagnosis relies on specific antibody identification, and treatment involves pyrimethamine, sulfadiazine, and folinic acid.

5.1.4.2. Entamoeba

- Ø **Amoebic Liver Abscess:** Common in the developing world, amoebic liver abscess presents with abdominal pain and hepatomegaly, often preceded by diarrhea. Pulmonary, pericardial, and peritoneal involvement is rare. Diagnosis involves patient history, clinical examination, imaging, and serological analysis, and caution is needed in interpreting serological tests, as antibodies may remain elevated post-treatment. Aspiration may be performed, revealing a characteristic reddish-brown anchovy paste. Treatment includes metronidazole, with intravenous administration if necessary, and additional use of tinidazole or chloroquine. An oral luminal amebacide follows the metronidazole course for 7–10 days.

5.1.5. Helminthic Infections of the Liver

Helminthic infestations in humans are highly prevalent worldwide, impacting approximately 1.5 to 2 billion people. Parasitic worms, known as helminths, infecting the liver and hepatobiliary system consist of nematodes (roundworms), cestodes (tapeworms), and trematodes (flatworms or flukes). The primary cause of morbidity and mortality in these infestations is the immune response of the host to the larvae or adult worms. The manifestations of helminthic diseases range from asymptomatic carriage to severe conditions like cirrhosis and decompensated liver disease. Ongoing research focuses on enhancing medical therapy, mass screening, chemoprophylaxis, and the development of preventive vaccine strategies.

While liver infections by helminths are rare in developed countries, nematode-related hepatic diseases are more common in the developing world.

5.1.6. Nematodes

1. **Toxocariasis:** Infection with *Toxocara canis* and *Toxocara cati*, affecting dogs and cats respectively, can lead to human disease. Visceral larva migrans commonly occurs in children with a history of pica ingestion, presenting with symptoms such as fever, hepatomegaly, urticaria, and increased eosinophil count. Cholestatic hepatitis and liver abscess formation may result. Treatment involves mebendazole or albendazole.
2. **Ascariasis:** Caused by *Ascaris lumbricoides*, this infection affects over a million people in the developing world through the ingestion of contaminated fruits and vegetables. Symptoms may include respiratory issues, hepatomegaly, and complications such as obstructive jaundice and liver abscesses. Mebendazole, albendazole, or pyrantel pamoate are used for treatment, and interventions like endoscopy or surgery may be necessary for obstruction.

3. **Strongyloidiasis:** Prevalent in tropical regions, *Strongyloides stercoralis* infection involves skin penetration by larvae, leading to symptoms like pruritus, abdominal discomfort, and diarrhea. Hepatic infection can cause jaundice and cholestasis. Diagnosis is achieved through serological tests or identifying larvae in stool or intestinal biopsy specimens. Ivermectin or albendazole is used for treatment.
4. **Trichinosis:** Acquired through the consumption of contaminated raw pork, *Trichinella spiralis* infection manifests as diarrhea, fever, marked eosinophilia, and obstructive jaundice. Diagnosis involves a characteristic history and serological analysis. Treatment includes anti-helminthics like albendazole or mebendazole.

5.1.7. Trematodes

1. **Schistosomiasis:** Schistosoma infection, prevalent in various regions, particularly in Africa and the Middle East, causes liver disease. Clinical features include headache, fever, cough, tender liver, and diarrhea. Chronic infection may lead to liver complications and an increased risk of hepatocellular carcinoma. Diagnosis involves stool tests and serological analysis, and praziquantel is used for treatment.
2. **Fascioliasis:** Caused by *Fasciola hepatica*, this liver fluke infection leads to acute, chronic, or obstructive hepatic disease. Clinical features include fever, right upper quadrant pain, and eosinophilia. Diagnosis is made through antibody detection or identifying eggs in stool, duodenal aspirate, or bile. Treatment involves triclabendazole.
3. **Clonorchiasis:** *Clonorchis sinensis* infection, acquired through contaminated seafood, presents with fever, abdominal pain, and diarrhea. Diagnosis involves detecting eggs in the stool or identifying flukes in the bile ducts or gallbladder. Treatment includes praziquantel.

5.1.8. Cestodes

- Ø **Echinococcosis:** Infection with *Echinococcus granulosus* occurs through contaminated food ingestion. The liver is commonly involved, leading to the formation of hydatid cysts. Diagnosis includes identifying hepatic calcifications on X-ray and confirming with ultrasound or CT scan. Treatment may involve surgical interventions, cystectomy, or albendazole administration.

5.2. Liver Infections Caused by Fungal Organisms

The occurrence of liver infections caused by fungi, primarily *Candida* spp., is frequently observed in individuals undergoing chemotherapy for hematologic malignancies. The primary source of *Candida* dissemination is believed to be the colonization of the GI tract, and mucositis and neutropenia contribute to the easy spread of *Candida* from the GI tract to the liver. In this context, hepatic involvement due to other types of fungi is a less common complication. Fungal infections are a relatively rare cause of hepatic abscesses in individuals without hematologic malignancies, and there seems to be a decreasing trend in recent years.

In oncohematologic patients and recipients of hematopoietic stem cell transplantation (HSCT), invasive fungal infections (IFIs) have emerged as a significant cause of both morbidity and mortality. *Candida* spp. are generally the predominant causative agents of fungal liver infections in oncohematologic patients. Although less common, the involvement of the liver by yeasts other than *Candida* spp., molds, and dimorphic fungi represents a severe infectious complication in this specific population. Fungal infections account for less than 2% of the total isolates in pus from hepatic abscesses in patients without hematologic malignancies.

5.2.1. Candidiasis

Invasive candidiasis is a severe fungal infection with life-threatening potential if not appropriately diagnosed and managed. It occurs when *Candida* spp. enters the bloodstream, spreading to various parts of the body, including:

- Bones;
- Brain and central nervous system;
- Eyes;
- Heart valves;
- Kidneys;
- Liver;
- Spleen.

This condition can lead to prolonged hospital stays and, in some cases, fatalities. *Candida* is a prevalent type of yeast found ubiquitously, and resides on the skin and within specific body regions. Occasionally, the yeast can proliferate uncontrollably, causing minor infections in localized areas, such as thrush (in the mouth) and vaginal yeast infections. However, if *Candida* infiltrates the bloodstream, it triggers candidemia, one of the most common healthcare-associated infections. If left untreated, severe candidemia can progress to invasive candidiasis, affecting internal organs. Certain individuals face a higher risk of developing candidemia and invasive candidiasis, including:

- Those who have undergone surgery, particularly abdominal surgery.
- Individuals hospitalized for an extended period, especially in the intensive care unit (ICU).
- Premature infants.
- Individuals with a central venous catheter (central line) or a similar device inserted into a vein.
- People with compromised immune systems (e.g., organ transplant recipients, chemotherapy recipients), diabetes, or kidney failure.
- Users of illicit drugs.

5.2.1.1. Causes of Invasive Candidiasis

Invasive candidiasis arises when *Candida* enters the bloodstream and spreads to internal organs. This typically occurs during the insertion of a medical device into the skin or GI tract, such as a catheter draining bodily fluids or an intravenous (IV) line providing nutrition or medication. *Candida* can be transferred from the skin to the bloodstream via a medical device, and in some cases, the hands healthcare staff may transmit the fungus to contaminate the device.

5.2.1.2. Symptoms of Invasive Candidiasis

Symptoms of candidemia and invasive candidiasis can be challenging to discern, as individuals developing the condition are often already unwell or recuperating from surgery. Moreover, these signs resemble those of other infections, such as bacterial infections.

Common symptoms of invasive candidiasis may include:

- Abdominal pain;
- Chills or fever;
- Low blood pressure;
- Muscle aches;

- Skin rash;
- Weakness or fatigue.

Specific symptoms may be related to the location of the infection. For instance, invasive candidiasis affecting the eyes can manifest as:

- Blurred vision;
- Light sensitivity;
- Changes in vision.

Meanwhile, an infection in the brain may result in:

- Confusion;
- Headaches;
- Memory loss.

5.2.2. Histoplasmosis

Histoplasmosis is an infection resulting from the inhalation of spores released by a fungus commonly found in the droppings of birds and bats. Individuals typically contract the infection when exposed to airborne spores during activities like demolition or cleanup projects.

Contaminated soil, particularly from bird or bat droppings, can also contribute to the spread of histoplasmosis, posing a higher risk for farmers and landscapers. While the infection is prevalent in the Mississippi and Ohio River valleys in the United States, it can also occur in other regions, including Africa, Asia, Australia, and parts of Central and South America.

While many individuals infected with histoplasmosis remain asymptomatic and unaware of their condition, infants and individuals with weakened immune systems may experience severe symptoms. However effective treatments exist for even the most critical forms of histoplasmosis.

5.2.2.1. Symptoms

Histoplasmosis may manifest as mild or severe, with the mildest forms showing no noticeable signs. Severe infections can be life-threatening, and symptoms typically appear 3 to 17 days after exposure. Common symptoms include fever, chills, headache, muscle aches, dry cough, chest pain, and fatigue. Joint pain and a rash may also accompany histoplasmosis. Individuals with pre-existing lung conditions, like emphysema, may develop chronic histoplasmosis, characterized by symptoms such as weight loss and a bloody cough, which may mimic tuberculosis.

5.2.2.2. Severe Histoplasmosis

The most critical form, known as disseminated histoplasmosis, primarily affects infants and individuals with compromised immune systems. This severe variant can impact various parts of the body, including the mouth, liver, central nervous system, skin, and adrenal glands. Without treatment, disseminated histoplasmosis is often fatal.

5.3. Viral Infections of the Liver

The liver performs a variety of vital tasks, including creating hormones, storing vitamins, and eliminating toxins from the blood. These crucial procedures can be interfered with by viral hepatitis, leading to a number of health issues. Viral hepatitis is caused by five main viruses, which are referred to as A, B, C, D, and E. These kinds are the most dangerous as they can lead to disease and sometimes even fatal consequences.

5.3.1. Hepatitis A

The Hepatitis A virus (HAV) belongs to the Picornaviridae family, specifically as an enterovirus. It is characterized by its icosahedral shape and lack of an envelope, and the virion measures 27–28 nm in diameter and has a single known serotype. HAV's genome is a 7.48 kb-long positive-sense RNA, single-stranded, and linear, with a lengthy open reading frame of

6,681 nucleotides. Various strains of the virus exhibit significant sequence variability. Human HAV is categorized into genotypes 1, 2, 3, and 7, while simian strains fall under genotypes 4, 5, and 6. The antigenic structure of human HAV remains highly conserved, with potential genomic differences contributing to fulminant hepatic failure.

While the incidence of HAV infection has decreased in the USA since 1995, underreporting persists due to asymptomatic cases. Predominantly affecting children aged 5–14 years, the epidemiology in the USA shows diverse transmission routes, including international travel, contact with infected individuals, sexual activities, contaminated food/water, and daycare-related exposure. In regions with poor hygiene, children acquire immunity early in life, and symptomatic infection is more common in older children.

Primarily transmitted through the fecal–oral route, person-to-person contact, or ingestion of contaminated food/water, HAV infection rarely occurs through parenteral transmission. Perinatal and neonatal transmission is minimal but has been observed in specific settings. The virus targets the liver, and immunologically mediated hepatocyte injury is the presumed mechanism.

HAV hepatitis manifests as an acute infection without chronic progression. Some cases exhibit a prolonged or relapsing course, with about 10% of patients experiencing relapse over 6–10 weeks. Acute hepatic failure is rare but more likely in older children and adults, with higher mortality in the elderly and those with chronic liver disease and HIV.

In contrast to hepatitis B virus infection, acute hepatitis A seldom presents with arthralgias, rashes, vasculitis, or glomerular nephritis. Extrahepatic manifestations include myocarditis, renal failure, optic neuritis, transverse myelitis, polyneuritis, and cholecystitis. Aplastic anemia and red cell aplasia may also occur, and autoimmune hepatitis has been reported post-infection.

5.3.1.1. Diagnosis

Diagnosing HAV infection involves detecting specific antibodies in serum. Anti-HAV IgM elevation indicates acute infection, persisting for about 4 months, while IgG remains for life, signifying past infection or vaccination. RNA testing is limited to research, with detectable RNA in body fluids such as serum, stool, and liver tissue.

Vaccination, licensed for use after 12 months of age, aims to eliminate transmission. Universal childhood vaccination, implemented in 2006 in the USA, reduced incidence rates, particularly in high-risk populations. While there are no specific medications treat acute hepatitis A, serum immunoglobulins were historically used for prevention, although with the vaccine's availability, their use has diminished. The vaccine serves for post-exposure prophylaxis, recommended within 2 weeks of exposure.

5.3.2. Hepatitis E

The Hepatitis E virus (HEV) is a small RNA virus belonging to the Hepeviridae family, presenting as a non-enveloped, icosahedral particle measuring 32–34 nm in diameter. HEV has four genotypes, with different regions of prevalence worldwide. Epidemics have occurred in the Indian subcontinent, Central Asia, the Middle East, and Africa, with varying attack rates among age groups.

Transmission occurs through contaminated food and water, often following the monsoon season. HEV antibodies develop less universally than Hepatitis A in endemic areas. The incubation period is approximately 4–5 weeks, with viral shedding occurring before symptom onset.

Hepatitis E symptoms include fever, abdominal pain, nausea, vomiting, cholestasis, and jaundice. HEV infection is usually self-limiting, with case fatality rates ranging from 0.5–4%. Pregnant women, especially in the second and third trimesters, face higher mortality rates. Diagnosis involves detecting the virus in stool and serum through PCR and enzyme immune assays for IgM and IgG antibodies.

Supportive care is the mainstay of treatment, and prevention in endemic areas focuses on improved hygiene. Candidate vaccines are being studied, showing promise for travelers to endemic regions.

5.3.3. Hepatitis B

Hepatitis B virus (HBV) is a global health concern, causing acute and chronic liver conditions, cirrhosis, and liver cancer. Prevalent in Asia, Africa, southern Europe, and Latin America, 2 billion people have been infected, with over 350 million chronic carriers. Mother-to-infant transmission contributes to half of chronic infections, leading to long-term complications like liver cirrhosis and hepatocellular carcinoma.

Table 5.1. *Phases of Chronic Hepatitis B Infection*

Phase	Laboratory Results and Histology	Note
Immune tolerant	HBsAg and HBeAg detectable.	Biopsy not indicated.
	HBV DNA >20,000 IU/mL (>105 copies/mL).	Antiviral therapies generally ineffective.
	ALT normal.	Risk of drug resistance if treated with nucleos(t)ide analogs.
	Absent or minimal liver inflammation and fibrosis.	Continued monitoring.
HBeAg + immune active	HBsAg and HBeAg remain detectable.	Most asymptomatic.
	HBV DNA >20,000 IU/mL (>105 copies/mL).	Biopsy
	ALT persistently elevated.	Rule out other liver diseases.
Inactive HBsAg	HBsAg present.	Age at serconversion influenced by HBV genotype.
	HBeAg undetectable, anti-HBe present.	Risk of developing cirrhosis declines.
	HBV DNA <2,000 IU/mL (>104 copies/mL) or undetectable.	Risk of developing HCC.
	ALT normal.	Biopsy generally not indicated.
	Absent or minimal liver inflammation, fibrosis regresses over time.	Continued monitoring.

Reactivation of HBeAg-negative, immune active.	HAsAg present.	Occurs in 20–30% of patients.
	HBeAg remains negative and anti-HBe positive.	"e-antigen-negative" hepatitis B.
	HBV DNA levels >2,000 IU/mL (>104 copies/mL).	Liver biopsy indicated, especially if ALT raised.
	ALT normal or elevated.	Treatment should be considered if moderate/ severe inflammation of fibrosis present.
	Active liver inflammation ± fibrosis.	–

Source: Karen, F. M., & Simon, H. Infections of the Liver. Springer Nature. doi: 10.1007/978-1-4614-9005-0_15.

HBV is an enveloped DNA virus in the Hepadnaviridae family, featuring structures like surface antigen, core antigen, and e antigen. Transmission occurs predominantly through the parenteral route, sexual contact, and perinatal exposure. Acute HBV infection may result in chronic disease, particularly in infants, with a higher risk of persistent infection and serious sequelae. Chronic HBV infection evolves through immune-tolerant, immune-active, and inactive phases, with varying risks of cirrhosis and HCC. Diagnosis involves testing for HBsAg and HBV DNA, with infant immunization recommended to prevent mother-to-child transmission. Antiviral therapy aims to reduce viral replication, minimize liver injury, and decrease infectivity, as complete eradication is challenging (Table 5.1).

The guidelines for treatment are represented in Figure 5.1.

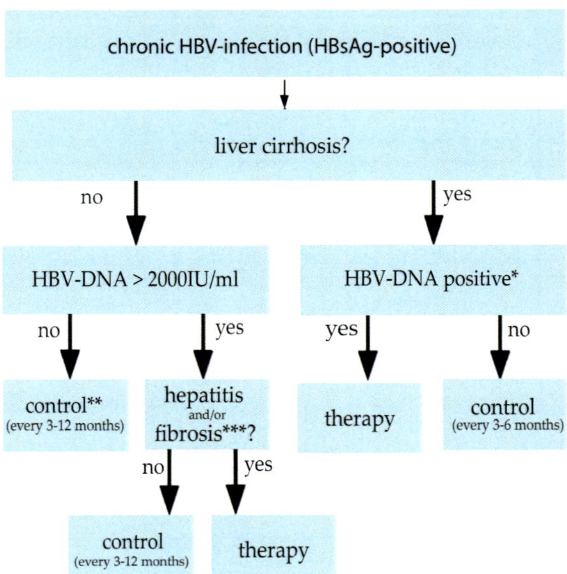

Figure 5.1. *HBV antiviral treatment in flowchart.*

Source: Schlaak, J. F., (2023). Current therapy of chronic viral hepatitis B, C, and D. Journal of Personalized Medicine, 13(6), 964. https://doi.org/10.3390/jpm13060964.

5.3.3.1. Treatment Options

1. **Interferon-Alpha:** IFN-alpha, administered through subcutaneous injection, was the pioneer among approved therapies for HBV. Predictors of responsiveness include active hepatitis, low HBV DNA levels, elevated serum alanine aminotransferase (ALT), short disease duration, non-Asian ethnicity, and horizontal transmission. Treatment goals focus on accelerating HBeAg clearance in children aged 2 years or older with specific criteria. IFN therapy's duration and response rates vary, and side effects include flu-like symptoms, behavioral disorders, GI issues, and temporary growth impact. Pegylated interferon-alpha (PegIFN) is not yet approved for children.
2. **Lamivudine:** Lamivudine, an orally administered nucleoside analog, inhibits HBV replication. Response rates in children vary, with increased efficacy in those with elevated ALT levels. Resistance rates rise over time, prompting consideration of alternative therapy after 6 months if complete viral suppression is lacking or resistant mutations emerge.
3. **Combination:** This therapy with lamivudine/IFN-alpha has shown effectiveness in adults, and some studies in children suggest increased seroconversion rates with combination therapy. The advantages over monotherapy in children remain unclear due to the absence of large clinical trials.
4. **Adefovir:** Adefovir dipivoxil, a purine analog, is approved for children aged 12 and older with chronic hepatitis B. Viral response rates are higher in older patients, with proximal renal tubular toxicity as a rare side effect. Treatment duration should extend at least 6 months after seroconversion, with discontinuation if incomplete viral suppression persists after 24 weeks.
5. **Entecavir:** A carbocyclic analog, has proven efficacy in adult patients, with rare resistance even after 5 years. FDA approval extends to adolescents aged 16 years and older. Ongoing clinical trials explore its effectiveness in children as young as 2 years.
6. **New Drugs:** Telbivudine, an L-nucleoside analog, exhibits potent antiviral activity with a safety profile akin to lamivudine. Resistance rates are lower than lamivudine but higher than adefovir, prompting combination use. Clinical trials are underway for children aged 2–18. Tenofovir disoproxil fumarate, initially licensed for HIV treatment, demonstrates higher antiviral activity than adefovir. Ongoing phase III trials are currently exploring its use in 12–17-year-old patients with HBV (Table 5.2).

Table 5.2. *Available Treatments for Chronic Hepatitis B in Children*

Treatment	Licensing	Dose	Duration	Advantages	Disadvantages
IFNa	≥12 months	5–10 M units/ m^2 SC 3×/week.	6 months	No resistance	Side effects
				Usable in young children.	Parenteral administration.
					Not for use in decompensated cirrhosis or transplantation.
Lamivudine	≥3 years	3 mg/kg po once daily (max 100 mg/day).	≥1 year	Few side effects	High resistance rate.
				Usable in young children.	
				Oral administration.	
Adefovir	≥12 years	10 mg po once daily	≥1 year (+6 months after HBeAG seroconversion).	Partially effective in lamivudine resistant patients.	–
				Oral administration.	
Entecavir	≥16 years + Phase III (2–17 years).	0.5 mg/day once Daily (1 mg/day for Lamivudine-resistant pts).	≥1 year (+6 months after HBeAG seroconversion).	Partially effective in lamivudine resistant patients.	Not approved for children < 12 years resistant mutations.
				Oral administration	
PegIFN	Phase III (2–18 years)	180 ug/week	6 months	No resistance	Side effects
				Once weekly administration.	Parenteral administration.
Telbivudine	Phase 1 (2–18 years)	600 mg/day once daily	≥1 year	Few side effects	High resistance
				Oral administration	
Tenofovir	Phase III (12–17 years)	300 mg/day once daily	≥1 year	High response rate.	No available preparation for young children.
				No resistance identified.	Reduced mineral density.
				Few side effects	
				Oral administration	

Source: Karen, F. M., & Simon, H. Infections of the Liver. Springer Nature. doi: 10.1007/978-1-4614-9005-0_15.

5.3.4. Hepatitis D

Hepatitis delta virus (HDV) is closely associated with HBV infection, requiring simultaneous presence for complete virion assembly. Most HDV-infected individuals experience suppressed HBV replication. The HDV genome is a small RNA molecule expressing the HDV antigen.

Coinfection of HBV and HDV leads to transient, self-limited acute hepatitis, with a higher risk of liver failure among drug users. HDV superinfection of chronic HBsAg carriers can present as severe acute hepatitis or exacerbate preexisting chronic hepatitis B, progressing to chronic HDV infection with suppressed HBV replication.

In the Western world, acute hepatitis D with genotype 1 HDV carries an increased risk of fulminant disease. Chronic HDV exacerbates existing liver disease, leading to rapidly progressive cirrhosis. In the Far East, where genotype 2 prevails, acute HDV infection has less frequent fulminant hepatitis, but chronic HDV results in rapidly progressive liver disease. South America, with genotype 3, has reported severe outbreaks of acute hepatitis D with a high incidence of liver failure.

5.3.4.1. Treatment

1. **Interferon:** IFNα is the only approved drug for chronic hepatitis D treatment. A multicenter trial in Italy showed promising results with improved serum transaminases in treated patients compared to controls. However, relapse occurred after treatment discontinuation.
2. **Pegylated Interferon:** Limited data exists for pegylated interferon in chronic hepatitis D treatment. Studies indicate comparable response rates between monotherapy and combination therapy with ribavirin, suggesting no significant impact on viral clearance. Another study with 12 months of pegylated IFN reported a higher virologic response rate.

Combination therapies with nucleoside and nucleotide analogs lack effectiveness, and there are no standard recommendations for pediatric HDV infection treatment. Vaccination against the helper virus, HBV, remains the primary prevention method for HDV infection.

5.3.5. Hepatitis C

Hepatitis C virus (HCV), an RNA virus, affects over 180 million people globally, with an estimated 28,000 new infections in the USA annually. Chronic HCV infection is estimated to impact 0.1–2% of children in the USA. Perinatal transmission is a common source of infection, and adolescents may be exposed through drug use and shared needles.

Six major HCV genotypes with over 50 subtypes exist. Genotype 1 predominates in the USA and Europe, impacting 60–70% of cases. Genotype 3 is common in India, the Far East, and Australia. Genotype 4 is prevalent in Africa and the Middle East, while genotype 5 is common in South Africa, and genotype 6 is found in Hong Kong, Vietnam, and Australia. Genotypes influence interferon therapy response, with higher rates for genotypes 2 and 3.

Infant-acquired infections often resolve spontaneously, with clearance rates of 20–45%. Progression to advanced liver disease during childhood is uncommon, but advanced fibrosis and cirrhosis have been reported.

5.3.6. Screening

Individuals suspected of chronic HCV infection or with risk factors should undergo HCV antibody testing. HCV RNA testing confirms infection, especially in cases of unexplained liver disease with negative anti-HCV tests, particularly in immunocompromised individuals. HCV RNA quantitation is crucial for treatment consideration, with genotyping determining therapy duration, ribavirin dosage, and response likelihood (Table 5.3).

Table 5.3. *Screening for HCV Infection*

Group	Screening
Injected illicit drug use.	Antibody
Persons with conditions associated with a high prevalence of HCV infection including:	Antibody or RNA
HIV infection.	
On hemodialysis.	
Unexplained abnormal aminotransferases.	
Earlier recipients of transfusions or organ transplants before July 1992 including:	Antibody or RNA
Children born to HCV-infected mothers.	Antibody after 18 months of age. RNA for younger ages.
Health care, emergency medical, and public safety workers after a needle stick injury or mucosal exposure to HCV-positive blood.	Antibody or RNA
Present sexual partners of HCV-infected persons.	Antibody
Children from a region with high prevalence of HCV infection.	Antibody

Source: Karen, F. M., & Simon, H. Infections of the Liver. Springer Nature. doi: 10.1007/978-1-4614-9005-0_15.

The NASPGHAN guidelines propose testing for anti-HCV antibodies in infants at or after 18 months of age, with confirmation through PCR in case of a positive result. If parents express the desire, HCV RNA testing may be conducted within the first year, provided the infant is over 2 months old at the time of testing. Chronic HCV infection is linked to hepatocellular carcinoma (HCC), particularly in individuals with cirrhosis. While HCC is rare in HCV-infected children, its occurrence seems higher in those who acquired HCV post-treatment for childhood leukemia.

5.3.6.1. Treatment

Children diagnosed with hepatitis C, exhibiting persistently elevated serum aminotransferases or showing liver fibrosis on histology, should be considered for treatment. Currently, available treatments include IFNα or PEG-IFNα combined with ribavirin. Both AASLD and NASPGHAN recommend the FDA-approved combination of PEG-IFNα with ribavirin as the primary treatment for children aged 3–17 years.

5.3.6.2. *Triple Therapy*

As of May 2011, two protease inhibitors, boceprevir and telaprevir, are approved in the USA for use alongside pegylated interferon and ribavirin in adults with chronic HCV genotype 1. This combination therapy demonstrates a significantly higher sustained virologic response compared to pegylated interferon and ribavirin alone. Pediatric trials with boceprevir are ongoing, and plans for a telaprevir trial are in progress.

Table 5.4. *Investigational Therapy for Hepatitis C Infection*

Direct Acting Antiviral Therapy
Ns3/4a protease inhibitors
· Boceprevir/Telaprevir
· BI201335
· Danoprevir
· TMC 435
· Asunaprevir
NS5B polymerase inhibitors
· GS7977
NS5A inhibitors
· Daclatasvir
Combinations without peginterferon
Treatment targeting host encoded factors
HCV vaccine
Complementary medicine

Source: Karen, F. M., & Simon, H. Infections of the Liver. Springer Nature. doi: 10.1007/978-1-4614-9005-0_15.

Practice recommendations for children with chronic HCV align with those for adults. However, due to limited pediatric data, treatment decisions may vary based on the child's age and individual disease characteristics. Combination treatment with pegylated interferon plus ribavirin is considered for children over 3 years old with progressive disease or advanced histological features, the specific course determined by the HCV genotype. Emerging treatments include direct-acting antivirals, potentially offering alternatives to injectable therapies (Table 5.4).

5.3.7. Hepatitis G

The Hepatitis G virus (HGV), named after a jaundiced surgeon, was discovered incidentally. Initially identified as GBV-A, GBV-B, and GBV-C, subsequent studies questioned the association with acute hepatitis, leading to doubts about the term "hepatitis G virus." HGV is a positive-strand RNA virus in the Flaviviridae family, sharing 27% homology with HCV. It has five genotypes worldwide.

Antibody development indicates past exposure and clearance, with about 16% of healthy blood donors showing antibodies. The natural clearance rate exceeds that of hepatitis C, and though detected in chronic hepatitis patients, HGV does not seem to cause liver disease. Infection duration depends on immune status and age. No links to malignancy or aplastic anemia have been established, and antibodies can confirm past infection, while PCR analysis may be conducted.

5.3.8. Transfusion-transmitted (TT) Virus

Identified in 1977, the TT virus is a non-enveloped single-stranded DNA virus considered hepatotropic. It has been found worldwide, is present in 1–40% of healthy blood donors and transmitted through parenteral routes. Despite an initial association with hepatitis, subsequent studies have not supported a link between the virus and liver disease. Similar viruses like Sanban, Yonban, and Sen Viruses exist, with their clinical significance remaining controversial.

5.3.9. Epstein–Barr Virus

Epstein–Barr Virus (EBV) infections present with varied clinical manifestations. While infants and young children are often asymptomatic, adolescents may display fever, lymphadenopathy, pharyngitis, and subclinical liver disease. Laboratory abnormalities include elevated lactic dehydrogenase, alkaline phosphatase, and hyperbilirubinemia.

Cholestatic jaundice may occur in women with EBV hepatitis using oral contraceptives. Fatal fulminant hepatitis can affect both immunocompromised and immunocompetent individuals. EBV infection can lead to the hemophagocytic syndrome, causing fever, hepatosplenomegaly, liver failure, and bone marrow suppression.

Diagnosis involves clinical features, lymphocytosis, monocytosis, thrombocytopenia, positive monospot test, and IgM/IgG antibodies.

Abdominal ultrasound may reveal hepatosplenomegaly, and liver biopsy is rarely necessary. No specific therapy exists, although acyclovir inhibits replication. Ganciclovir has shown promise, and liver transplantation is performed for fulminant hepatitis.

5.3.10. Cytomegalovirus

Cytomegalovirus (CMV), a member of the herpes family, persists in a non-replicative state for life. Clinically, it may cause primary infection or reactivate in immunocompromised patients. In immunocompetent individuals, primary infection is usually mild, mimicking EBV. Hepatic disease presents with elevated liver enzymes, alkaline phosphatase, and organomegaly. CMV can cause severe manifestations in congenital infections, AIDS-associated cholangiopathy, and primary sclerosing cholangitis. Diagnosis involves serological analysis and liver biopsy, with treatment options including ganciclovir, foscarnet, and cidofovir.

5.3.11. Herpes Simplex Virus

Herpes Simplex Virus (HSV) hepatitis occurs in immunocompromised individuals and neonates, with rapid progression and high mortality. Neonates may contract the infection during delivery, leading to fulminant hepatitis. Diagnosis requires a liver biopsy, revealing extensive hemorrhagic necrosis with intranuclear inclusions. Treatment involves acyclovir, and severe cases may require liver transplantation.

5.3.12. Varicella-Zoster Virus

Varicella-Zoster Virus may cause hepatitis in children, presenting as elevated liver enzymes. Dissemination in immunocompromised patients may lead to visceral involvement, requiring high-dose intravenous acyclovir if suspected.

5.4. Infections of Biliary Tract

Infections affecting the biliary tract, including conditions like biliary colic, cholangitis, cholecystitis, and cholelithiasis, are prevalent worldwide due to obstructions in the bile duct. Gallstones, common in the United States and other developed nations, often go unnoticed. However, when bacterial infections occur in the bile, they can lead to severe health issues and even death. Factors such as bile stasis, inflammation, and the loss of protective mechanisms contribute to these infections. Obstructions are thought to cause increased pressure, compromised blood supply, impaired lymphatic drainage, and acute inflammation in the presence of supersaturated bile. This section explores the development of biliary tract infections, the responsible microbial pathogens, and available antibiotic treatment options.

5.4.1. Current Scenario

Gallstone disease poses a significant health challenge in developed countries, affecting 10–

15% of the general population with variations across nations. Complications related to gallstones impact 20–40% of individuals with gallstones, resulting in an annual incidence of 1–3%. Acute calculus cholecystitis (ACC) is the initial clinical manifestation in 10–15% of cases.

5.4.2. Anatomy of Biliary Tract

The gallbladder, a component of the digestive system, consists of three parts: the fundus, corpus, and infundibulum. Positioned between hepatic lobes, the gallbladder empties into the cystic duct, and is a passive conduit with a mucosa containing spiral valves and a diameter of approximately 7 mm in humans (Valves of Heister). This duct lacks a sphincteric structure and connects to the common bile duct. Passing through the head of the pancreas and forming the ampulla of Vater as it enters the duodenal wall, the common bile duct concludes at the sphincter of Oddi. Figure 5.2 for the gallbladder's location in the human body and Figure 5.3 for its anatomy.

This duct empties into the common bile duct and lacks a sphincteric structure. The common bile duct travels through the head of the pancreas before entering the duodenum and forming the ampulla of Vater before ending in the sphincter of Oddi.

Roughly 10% of people are thought to have abnormalities in their biliary ducts, but not all of these issues are easily detectable during surgery. One common abnormality is known as the triple confluence, where the right posterior duct, right anterior duct, and left hepatic duct all empty into the common hepatic duct at the same time. This variation often results in the almost non-existent right hepatic duct. Another common variation involves the connection of the right posterior duct with the right anterior or left hepatic duct, leading to the formation of the right hepatic duct, which then joins with the left hepatic duct to create the common hepatic duct.

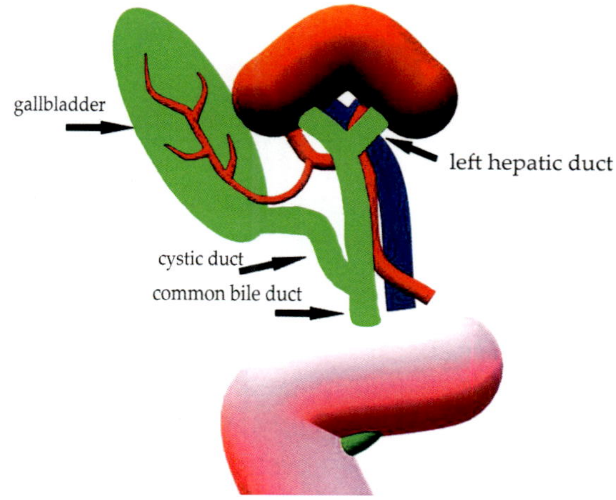

Figure 5.2. *The gallbladder lies beneath the lower liver edge at the bottom of the rib cage.*

Source: Dubovan, P., Aziri, R., & Tomáš, M., (2022). Routine and Innovation in Surgical Therapy of Gallstones. IntechOpen. doi: 10.5772/intechopen.100570.

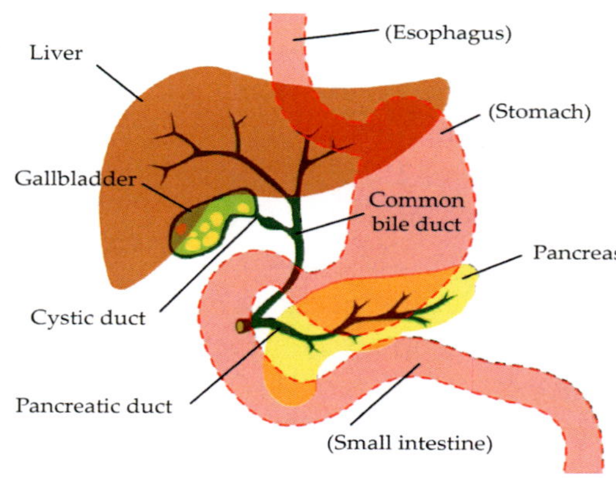

Figure 5.3. *Gallbladder parts and bile ducts.*

Source: Based on Pueblo.gsa.gov, Public Domain, https://commons.wikimedia.org/w/index.php?curid=98637242.

In simpler terms, the drainage of the right posterior duct into the left hepatic duct before merging with the right anterior duct is the most common configuration. Additionally, there are less frequent and more complex variations in the bile ducts, such as aberrant and accessory bile ducts. It's crucial in a clinical setting to distinguish between an aberrant bile duct, which is the sole duct draining a specific hepatic segment, and an accessory bile duct, which drains the same portion of the liver. Failure to identify these irregularities can result in bile leakage and irritation of the peritoneal membrane, leading to bile peritonitis.

To address these issues, a procedure called endoscopic retrograde cholangiopancreatography (ERCP) is employed. During ERCP, stents are inserted to treat leaks from the common bile or cystic ducts, preventing complications arising from bile leakage.

5.4.3. The Sphincter of Oddi: Anatomy and Physiology

The sphincter of Oddi in humans is about 10 mm long and possesses a distinct and robust musculature. It is separate from the duodenum both physically and functionally. The myoelectrical and contractile patterns of the sphincter of Oddi differ from those of the duodenum in terms of character and timing. While the contractions of the sphincter of Oddi happen simultaneously, there may be slight variations in configuration, resembling peristaltic movements at times. Its primary function, as a resistor to bile flow, aligns with the synchronous contractions. Due to the resistance of the sphincter of Oddi, the continuous production of bile by the liver is mainly directed into the cystic duct and gallbladder during fasting, where it is stored and concentrated. During the digestive process, the gallbladder contracts, releasing the majority of its contents, and bile flows into the duodenum through the relaxed sphincter of Oddi and duodenum. Bile salts aid in the digestion and absorption of fats in the duodenum and jejunum, and they are transported to the terminal ileum for recycling through the enterohepatic circulation.

5.4.4. Sphincter of Oddi Dyskinesia

Individuals with sphincter of Oddi (SO) dyskinesia experience symptoms resembling those of biliary issues, often observed after gallbladder removal (cholecystectomy). The symptoms and signs of dysfunction in the bile duct sphincter mimic temporary bile duct blockage, while dysfunction in the pancreatic sphincter of Oddi is associated with elevated pancreatic enzymes and even pancreatitis. Diagnosis of sphincter of Oddi dysfunction involves quantitative choledochoscintigraphy and/or sphincter of Oddi manometry tests to confirm the condition, especially when the initial investigation points towards this functional disorder.

5.4.5. Chronic and Acute Cholecystitis

5.4.5.1. Pathogenesis

The commonly proposed hypothesis for the development of chronic and acute cholecystitis is the migration of gallstones from the gallbladder, obstructing the cystic duct. This obstruction may lead to acute cholecystitis, evidenced by the inability to visualize the gallbladder in such cases, attributed to cystic duct occlusion. However, other explanations for this failure are more likely, such as acute inflammation and edema spreading to the cystic duct or an atonic gallbladder obstructing the entry of the isotope-labeled agent due to inflammatory fluids. The presence of cholecystitis without gallstones (acalculous gallbladder) or a single large stone challenges the idea of cystic duct obstruction. Additionally, acute inflammation on top of a chronically inflamed or atrophic fibrotic gallbladder suggests a long-term process rather than recurring obstruction events. Chronic cholecystitis, often histopathologically found without gallstones, is common in morbidly obese individuals with lithogenic bile. The pathogenesis involves impaired gallbladder motility and cytoprotective functions due to lithogenic hepatic bile with excess cholesterol, leading to chronic cholecystitis (Figure 5.4).

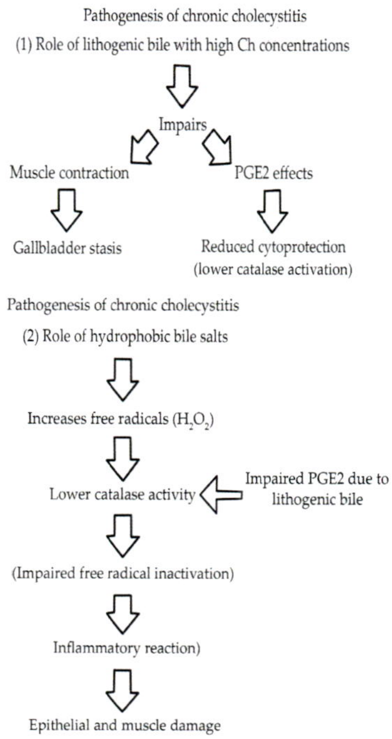

Figure 5.4. *Pathogenesis of chronic cholecystitis.*

Source: Prakash, K. P. H., & Payala, V., (2022). Infections of Biliary Tract. IntechOpen. doi: 10.5772/intechopen.100063.

Ultimately, the outcomes of the previously mentioned research on humans and animals strongly imply that lithogenic bile with elevated cholesterol concentrations causes cholecystitis by fostering an environment that is favorable for hydrophobic bile salts to raise oxidative stress levels and start the inflammatory process. This inflammatory process requires hydrophobic bile salts to continuously enter the sick gallbladder.

5.4.6. Clinical Presentation of Chronic Cholecystitis

Individuals with chronic cholecystitis may exhibit no symptoms or may suffer from recurring episodes of discomfort in the epigastric and right upper quadrant (RUQ) regions. This pain often radiates around the waist and toward the scapula. The intensity of the pain ranges from moderate to severe, and it typically occurs during the night rather than after meals. These episodes are not daily occurrences but manifest every two to three weeks. Diagnosis is commonly made using ultrasonography, which reveals the presence of gallstones and thickening of the gallbladder wall. Laboratory tests generally show normal results. While gallstones are frequently asymptomatic, they are often detected during imaging studies of gallbladders and are erroneously linked to various upper gastrointestinal issues. Gallstones are sometimes associated with nonspecific GI symptoms such as persistent dyspepsia, gastroparesis, and irritable bowel syndrome. Patients with functional disorders of the GI system often report daily symptoms, which are typically triggered by fatty foods or large meals and are postprandial in nature. Common complaints include epigastric pain, nausea, and bloating. Interestingly, even after surgical removal of the gallbladder (cholecystectomy), symptoms may persist despite the presence of gallstones.

5.4.7. Clinical Features of Acute Cholecystitis

Acute cholecystitis, which is characterized by an acute inflammation of the gall bladder, is most commonly associated with a history of chronic cholecystitis. Patients with acute cholecystitis experience a sudden onset of severe pain, often accompanied by nausea (90% of cases) and vomiting (50% of cases). Physical examination reveals pain in the epigastric and right upper quadrant areas, along with a positive Murphy sign and rebound tenderness in severe cases. Healthcare providers must rule out other acute abdominal conditions, such as acute appendicitis, acute pancreatitis, localized perforated peptic ulcer, intestinal perforation, or ischemia, before confirming the diagnosis of acute cholecystitis. These conditions share similarities in demographics and risk factors. Abdominal pain, which can be either localized or widespread, is a common feature in patients complaining of severe stomach pain, nausea, and vomiting.

5.4.8. Microbial Involvement in Biliary Tract Infections

In cases of acute cholecystitis, the leading cause is often an impacted gallstone obstructing the gallbladder outlet. This obstruction leads to increased intraluminal pressure, gallbladder distension, wall edema, and eventual gallbladder necrosis.

During the initial stages of acute cholecystitis, bile is typically sterile, and infection occurs as a secondary event. Biliary tract infections, frequently caused by the family Enterobacteriaceae from the GI system, are associated with high morbidity and mortality, especially in elderly individuals with comorbid conditions or when diagnosis and treatment are delayed.

5.4.8.1. Bacterial Etiology of Biliary Tract Infections

Gram-negative microorganisms, including *E. coli*, *Salmonella enteritidis*, *Acinetobacter baumannii*, *Citrobacter freundii*, *Enterobacter cloacae*, and various *Klebsiella* species, are the most commonly identified pathogens in biliary tract infections. Among Gram-positive microorganisms, *Clostridium perfringens* is frequently observed. Biliary infections have been linked to gallstone formation, suggesting a role for bacteria as nucleating factors for both pigment and cholesterol gallstones. Various studies have identified the presence of biofilm-forming bacteria in bile and gallbladder/gallstones, including *P. aeruginosa*, *E. coli*, *K. pneumoniae*, *Enterococcus* spp., and *Acinetobacter* spp. Molecular tools like NGS have shown that traditional culture methods may only identify a fraction of the bacteria present.

5.4.8.2. ESKAPE Pathogens and Bile in Drug Resistance

While bile possesses bactericidal activity, many pathogens resist its effects and use it as a signaling molecule to regulate virulence gene expression and enhance infection. The resistance strategies employed by pathogens align with antibiotic resistance mechanisms, with efflux pump genes such as acrAB in *E. coli*, Salmonella, Shigella, Klebsiella, and other pathogens playing a crucial role. The ESKAPE group of pathogens, including *Enterococcus*, *Staphylococcus*, *Klebsiella*, *Acinetobacter*, *Pseudomonas*, and *Enterobacter*, poses a significant public health threat due to rising antibiotic resistance rates. These pathogens have been isolated from bile, gallbladder, pancreatic or biliary stent biofilms, and bile duct infections, often exhibiting antibiotic resistance.

5.4.8.3. Rare Microbial Causes of Acute Cholecystitis

Uncommon cases of acute cholecystitis have been reported, including instances caused by *Kosakonia cowanii*, *Streptococcus bovis* biotypes, and isolated Serogroup O1 *Vibrio cholerae*. These cases highlight the diversity of microorganisms that can contribute to acute cholecystitis.

5.4.8.4. Viral Contributors to Biliary Tract Infections

Viral infections of the biliary tract are less frequent than bacterial infections and often result from liver infections or systemic viral illnesses. Hepatotropic viruses (A, B, C, and E) are commonly associated with hepatocellular pathology, but they can also manifest cholangitic symptoms. Systemic viruses, particularly those in the herpes virus family, can induce hepatic illnesses, including cholangitis.

5.4.8.5. Parasitic Causes of Biliary Tract Infections

Biliary parasitoses are prevalent in many nations and can be caused by various factors, including biliary calculi, strictures, parasites, post-endoscopic retrograde cholangiopancreatography (ERCP), and postoperative complications. Common parasites affecting the biliary system include *Ascaris lumbricoides*, liver flukes, and Echinococcus.

These parasites can lead to mechanical obstruction, inflammatory reactions, adenomatous hyperplasia, and periductal fibrosis, often detected through radiological findings of CT and MRI.

5.4.8.6. Diagnosis of Cholecystitis

The diagnostic criteria for cholecystitis involve assessing local inflammation signs, such as Murphy's sign, the presence of a mass, and pain or tenderness in the upper right quadrant of the abdomen.

Systemic inflammation is also considered, indicated by fever, elevated white blood cell counts, and increased levels of C-reactive protein. The severity of acute cholecystitis varies, and accurate diagnosis often relies on imaging techniques such as ultrasonography, MRI, and CT. Recent research has explored the use of biomarkers, such as high mobility group box protein 1 (HMGB1), for diagnosing acute cholecystitis.

5.4.8.6.1. Consensus Guidelines for Cholecystitis Diagnosis

To establish consensus guidelines for cholecystitis diagnosis, the Tokyo guidelines for the management of acute cholangitis and cholecystitis were formed in 2007 (TG07), and an updated version (TG13) was released in 2013. These guidelines help in grading the severity of acute cholecystitis (Table 5.5).

Table 5.5. *TG13 Diagnostic Criteria for Acute Cholecystitis*

Local signs of inflammation, etc. Murphy's sign RUQ Mass/pain/tenderness
Systemic signs of inflammation, etc. Fever Elevated CRP Elevated WBC count
Imaging findings Imaging findings characteristic of acute cholecystitis
Suspected diagnosis: One item in A + one item in B Definitive diagnosis: One item in A + one item in B + C
Acute hepatitis, other acute abdominal diseases, and chronic cholecystitis should be excluded. RUQ-right upper abdominal quadrant, CRP-C-reactive protein, WBC-white blood cell.

Source: Hema, P. K. P., & Vijayalakshmi, P. Infections of Biliary Tract. IntechOpen. doi: 10.5772/intechopen.100063.

5.4.8.6.2. TG07 Criteria for Assessing Severity of Acute Cholecystitis

The criteria for assessing the severity of acute cholecystitis were introduced globally in TG07 by Hirota and Takada. In this classification, acute cholecystitis severity is graded into three categories: "mild (Grade I)," "moderate (Grade II)," and "severe (Grade III)." Mild (Grade I) acute cholecystitis is observed in patients without signs of organ failure and with mild gallbladder illness. This allows for the safe performance of cholecystectomy with minimal risk. The severity score for individuals with mild acute cholecystitis in TG07 does not meet the criteria for the categories of "moderate (Grade II)" and "severe (Grade III)" acute cholecystitis.

Table 5.6. *TG 13 Severity Grading for Acute Cholecystitis*

Associated with Dysfunction of Any One of the Following Organ/Systems	
Cardiovascular Dysfunction	**Hypotension Requiring Treatment with Dopamine >5 ub/kg per min, or Any Dose of Norepinephrine**
Neurologic dysfunction	Decreased level of consciousness
Respiratory dysfunction	Pa2O/FiO2 ratio < 300
Renal dysfunction	Oluguria, creatinine >2.0 mg/dl
Hepatic dysfunction	PT – INR > 1.5
Hematological dysfunction	Platelet count <100,000/mm^3
Grade II (Moderate) Acute Cholecystitis	
Associated with any one of the following conditions: ·Elevated white blood cell count (18,000/mm^3). ·Palpable tender mass in the right upper abdominal quadrant. ·Duration of complaints (72 h). ·Marked local inflammation (gangrenous cholecystitis, pericholecystic abscess, hepatic abscess, biliary peritonitis, and emphysematous cholecystitis).	
Grade I (mild) Acute Cholecystitis	
Does not meet the criteria of "Grade III" or "Grade II" acute cholecystitis. Grade I can also be defined as acute cholecystitis in a healthy patient with no organ dysfunction and mild inflammatory changes in the gallbladder, making cholecystectomy a safe and low-risk operative procedure.	

Source: Hema, P. K. P., & Vijayalakshmi, P. Infections of Biliary Tract. IntechOpen. doi: 10.5772/intechopen.100063.

Moderate (Grade II) acute cholecystitis is characterized by a degree of acute inflammation that is expected to pose greater operating challenges during cholecystectomy.

Severe (Grade III) acute cholecystitis is defined as acute cholecystitis accompanied by organ dysfunction (Table 5.6).

5.4.8.7. Treatment Approaches for Acute Cholecystitis

Acute cholecystitis is typically managed promptly through interventions such as cholecystectomy or percutaneous cholecystostomy, coupled with antibiotic therapy for high-risk patients. The role of antimicrobial treatment varies based on the severity and etiology of the illness.

For mild (Grade I) acute cholecystitis, where there are no signs of organ failure and the gallbladder illness is mild, antimicrobial treatment is employed to prevent infection before cholecystectomy. The use of antimicrobials is both therapeutic and necessary for moderate (Grade II) acute cholecystitis until the gallbladder is removed. Patients with bacteremia may exhibit clinical deterioration and are categorized as severe (Grade III) acute cholecystitis, rendering them unsuitable for immediate surgery. Recent research highlights cholecystography as the most accurate diagnostic method for acute cholecystitis.

Studies have indicated that bile infections occur in 9–42% of patients undergoing elective laparoscopic cholecystectomy, with the incidence increasing to 35–65% in acute cholecystitis cases. Antimicrobial treatment is crucial for reducing systemic septic responses and local inflammation following cholecystectomy in individuals with moderate-to-severe acute cholecystitis. Timely and appropriate antibiotic treatment is imperative, particularly for patients in septic shock.

Bile culture results, however, cannot be obtained immediately upon admission, and percutaneous gallbladder puncture is required for bile culture. Empiric antibiotics, based on successful outcomes reported in the literature, form the basis for initial antimicrobial treatment. Given that most infections in acute cholecystitis are localized to the gallbladder, direct sampling from the infection site is essential to identify the true causative pathogen.

Bacterial infections are commonly reported in 50 to 90% of cases, with polymicrobial infections often treated using antibiotic regimens comprising two or more antibiotics. Commonly prescribed antibiotics for acute cholecystitis include ceftriaxone, piperacillin/tazobactam, and cefoperazone/sulbactam for 7 to 10 days. Second-line or alternative antibiotics, such as imipenem or meropenem, may be considered for similar durations. *Enterococci* species, non-faecium *enterococci*, *E. coli*, and *Klebsiella* spp. are frequently isolated microorganisms in positive bile cultures.

Antimicrobial susceptibility tests, information on likely infecting microorganisms, pharmacokinetics/pharmacodynamics, adverse reactions/effects of available medicines, local antibiograms, severity of illness, and prior antimicrobial exposure are essential factors in making antimicrobial therapy decisions. Empiric treatment for moderate and severe acute cholecystitis often involves piperacillin/tazobactam or a cephalosporin with or without metronidazole. Gram-negative bacteria are commonly targeted with broad-spectrum β-lactam and β-lactamase inhibitors, while first-line antibiotics for Gram-positive bacteria include ampicillin-sulbactam.

Recent findings reported the emergence of vancomycin-resistant Enterococcus faecium (VREFM) in patients with Grade II acute cholecystitis. Recommendations for alternative antibiotics, such as linezolid and tigecycline, have been suggested for advanced infections. Tigecycline, due to its broad spectrum of effectiveness against Gram-negative microorganisms, may be used in various cases.

5.4.8.7.1. Empiric Antibiotic Treatment of Community-Acquired Biliary Tract Infections (CA-BTI)

Managing Community-Acquired Biliary Tract Infections (CA-BTI) relies significantly on primary source controls, including procedures like biliary drainage, elimination of biliary stones, and cholecystectomy. These measures facilitate the penetration of antibiotics into the biliary tract, enhancing their bactericidal efficacy, especially in the presence of biliary obstruction. When considering medical intervention, the selection of empiric antibiotics hinges on two critical factors. Antibiotic administration is crucial for BTI treatment, complementing primary source control. Given that BTI is typically caused by endogenous agents from the gastrointestinal tract flora (e.g., *E. coli*, *Klebsiella* spp., *Enterococci* spp., *Bacteroides* spp.), empirical antibiotic choices should target these organisms rather than opting for definitive therapy. However, the use of inappropriate empiric antibiotics poses potential risks, including fatal consequences. Achieving positive treatment responses requires that over 80% of the presumed causative microorganisms exhibit sensitivity to the antibiotics. In cases of septic shock, susceptibility rates should ideally surpass 100%. Furthermore, the antibiotics must attain adequate concentrations at the infection sites to exert the desired antimicrobial effects.

Therefore, when selecting empirical antibiotics for the treatment of BTI, it is essential to consider both the susceptibility rates and the potential for biliary penetration. Table 5.7 provides a compilation of commonly used antibiotics for BTI along with their ability to penetrate the biliary system, measured as the ratio of bile-to-serum concentrations. Only individuals with a favorable ratio (>1), as indicated in Table 5.7, should be considered suitable candidates for empirical antibiotic treatment of BTI, based on the previously outlined criteria. Additionally, prescribing appropriate empirical antibiotics should take into account the local antimicrobial susceptibility patterns of the typical causative agents for BTI. To ensure a positive outcome, only those antibiotics demonstrating a 20% resistance rate should be utilized empirically.

Table 5.7. *Antibiotics Frequently Used to Treat Biliary Tract Infections and Their Biliary Penetration Ability (Indicated as the Ratio of Bile to Serum Concentrations)*

Good Penetration Efficiency (>1)		Low-Penetration Efficiency (<1)	
Antibiotics	**Bile/ Serum**	**Antibiotics**	**Bile/ Serum**
Tazocin	60	Cefotaxime	0.75
Tigecycline	38	Meropenem	0.75
Augmentin	30	Ceftazidime	0.5
Ciprofloxacin	30	Vancomycin	0.5
Unasyn	9	Amikacin	0.3
Ceftriaxone	5	Gentamycin	0.3
Levofloxacin	5	Cefipime	0.1
Penicillin G	5	Imepenem	0.01
Cefazolin	3	–	–
Clindamycin	3	–	–
Doripenem	1.17	–	–
Cefuroxime	1	–	–
Metronidazole	1	–	–

Source: Hema, P. K. P., & Vijayalakshmi, P. Infections of Biliary Tract. IntechOpen. doi: 10.5772/intechopen.100063.

Key-Augmentin = amoxicillin + clavulanate; Bile/serum = bile concentration/ serum concentration; Tazocin: Piperacillin + tazobactum; Unasyn = ampicillin + sulbactum.

Unfortunately, identifying patients with severe cholecystitis proves challenging, both clinically and radiologically, due to unpredictable clinical presentations and frequently ambiguous imaging findings. However, there exist significant disparities in morbidity and fatality rates between patients with uncomplicated cholecystitis and those with severe cholecystitis. Timely detection and meticulous management of patients at risk of severe cholecystitis are imperative to prevent adverse outcomes.

A Closer Look

Infectious Complications in Liver Transplantation

In transplant recipients, the ongoing challenge of morbidity and mortality due to infections persists. These infections encompass bacterial, viral, or fungal pathogens. It is crucial to acknowledge that immune suppression in solid organ transplant recipients often masks the typical signs and symptoms of infection. Additionally, the use of antibiotics or antimicrobials may interact with immunosuppressive medications. The presence of latent infections in either the transplant recipient or donor is a significant risk factor.

Screening potential transplant donors for infections such as cytomegalovirus, herpes virus, tuberculosis, hepatitis B and C, syphilis, and human immunodeficiency virus is standard practice. Pretransplant infections with methicillin-resistant *Staphylococcus aureus* (MRSA) or vancomycin-resistant enterococcus (VRE) may lead to posttransplant infections. However, colonization with these pathogens doesn't necessarily preclude transplantation.

Surgical complications during transplant surgery are another risk factor. For instance, individuals undergoing Roux-en-Y biliary anastomosis or multiple abdominal surgeries face an increased risk of bacterial infections. Patients experiencing rejection or poor graft function are also at higher risk due to the aggressive immunosuppression required.

Efforts to minimize infections involve strategies such as appropriate vaccination before transplantation. Given that immunosuppressive medications hinder optimal vaccine responses, certain vaccines like pneumococcal and influenza vaccines may need repeating after transplantation. Live vaccines are generally avoided due to the potential risk of disseminated disease.

Liver transplant recipients, compared to recipients of other solid organs, have a higher likelihood of developing surgical site infections. Treatment with trimethoprim-sulfamethoxazole is commonly employed for 3–12 months post-liver transplantation to reduce the risk of Pneumocystis and prevent infections with Listeria, Nocardia, Toxoplasma, and other common pathogens.

While cytomegalovirus remains a significant viral infection posttransplant, other viruses like HSV I and 2 and VZV are also noteworthy. Ganciclovir and valganciclovir are used for posttransplant viral prophylaxis. CMV-negative recipients receiving organs from CMV seropositive donors are at increased risk of CMV reactivation. CMV infection raises the risk of bacterial and fungal infections, contributing to almost a fourfold increased risk of death within a year posttransplant.

Fungal infections pose challenges posttransplant, with *Candida albicans* being the most common pathogen. Antifungal prophylaxis, especially for high-risk liver transplant recipients, involves fluconazole or liposomal amphotericin B for 14–27 days. Liver transplant recipients maintain an elevated risk for active Mycobacterium tuberculosis infection. Treating latent TB prior to transplantation is optimal but can be challenging due to the hepatotoxicity of isoniazid. Attempts at treatment may be made posttransplantation.

In the initial three months following transplantation, bacterial infections dominate, often originating nosocomially from indwelling catheters, drains, or prolonged intubation. Common infections include abdominal abscesses, cholangitis, wound infections, and nosocomial pneumonias, with the possibility of *Clostridium difficile* colitis (Figure 5.5).

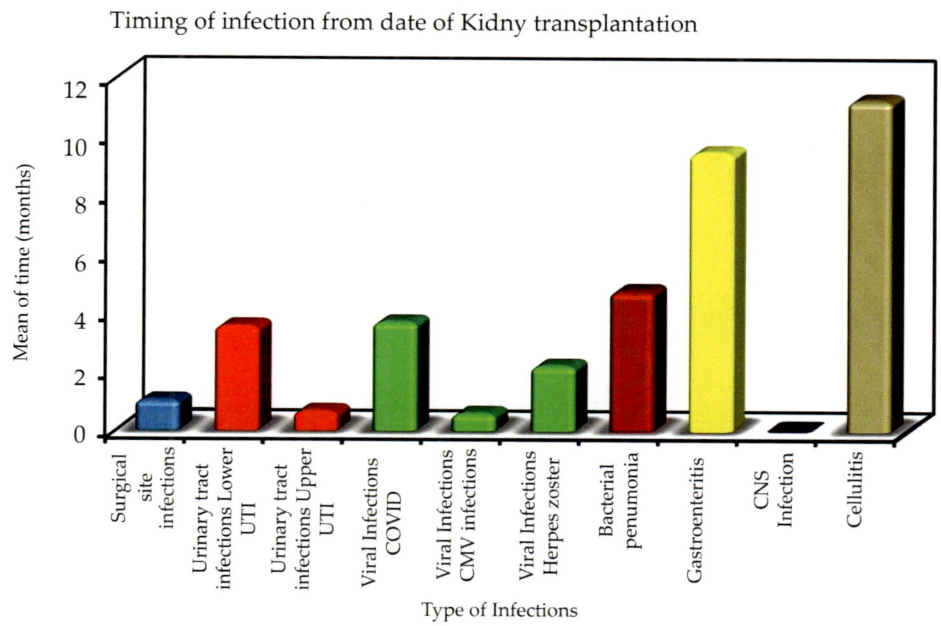

Figure 5.5. *Common patterns of opportunistic infection.*

Source: Khedr, L., Teama, N., & El Sharkawy, M., (2023). Infections in the first year of living related kidney transplantation in a young transplant cohort. BMC Nephrol, 24, 328. https://doi.org/10.1186/s12882-023-03379-9.

Summary

- Hepatitis, a severe condition with diverse causes, is commonly known as liver infection. Recognizing the symptoms and typical causes of liver infections is essential for early identification and effective treatment.
- The portal vein, responsible for transporting blood from the gastrointestinal tract to the liver, can carry various microbes. Consequently, the liver may become susceptible to infections caused by a multitude of microbial organisms.
- Parasitic liver infections encompass both protozoan and helminthic infections, with distribution and epidemiology varying across different geographic regions globally.
- Global human helminthic infestation is highly prevalent, affecting 1.5 to 2 billion people worldwide. Helminths, including nematodes, cestodes, and trematodes, can infect the liver and hepatobiliary system.
- The liver plays a vital role in detoxifying the blood, storing vitamins, and producing hormones. Viral hepatitis can disrupt these crucial functions, leading to various health issues.
- Hepatitis A virus (HAV) belongs to the *Picornaviridae* family, is non-enveloped, and has an icosahedral shape. It has a diameter of 27–28 nm and exists as a single serotype.
- Hepatitis E virus (HEV) is a small RNA virus, 32–34 nm in diameter, belonging to the family Hepeviridae, with three open reading frames (ORF).
- Hepatitis B virus (HBV) is a global health concern, causing acute and chronic hepatitis, cirrhosis, and liver cancer. Complete virion assembly and secretion of hepatitis delta virus (HDV) require the simultaneous presence of HBV.
- Cytomegalovirus (CMV), a member of the herpes family, persists in a non-replicative state for life. It may cause clinical disease as a primary infection or reactivation in immunocompromised patients.
- Biliary tract infections, such as biliary colic, cholangitis, cholecystitis, and cholelithiasis, are prevalent globally due to bile duct obstruction.
- Gallstone disease is a significant health issue in developed countries, affecting 10–15% of the general population. Gallstone-related problems impact 20–40% of individuals with gallstones, with an annual incidence of 1–3%. Acute calculus cholecystitis (ACC) is the initial clinical manifestation in 10–15% of cases.
- The gallbladder, an integral part of the digestive system, is a thin-walled sac with three anatomical parts: the fundus, corpus, and infundibulum. It is typically located between hepatic lobes.

References

1. Aggarwal, R., & Krawcyznski, K., (2013). *Sleisenger and Fordtran's Gastrointestinal and Liver Disease, Pathophysiology/Diagnosis/Management*, 1337–1342.
2. Behar, J., (2013). Physiology and pathophysiology of the biliary tract: The gallbladder and sphincter of Oddi: A review. *ISRN Physiology, 2013*, 1–15. doi: 10.1155/2013/837630.
3. Feld, J. J., & Heathcote, E. J., (2013). Hepatitis caused by other viruses. *Sleisenger and Fordtran's Gastrointestinal and Liver Disease, Pathophysiology/Diagnosis/Management*, 1343–1350.
4. Kim, A. Y., & Chung, R. T., (2013). Bacterial, parasitic, and fungal infections of the liver, including liver abscess. *Sleisenger and Fordtran's Gastrointestinal and Liver Disease, Pathophysiology/Diagnosis/Management*, 1351–1369.
5. Sjogren, M. H., Cheatham, J. G., & Hepatitis, A., (2013). *Sleisenger and Fordtran's Gastrointestinal and Liver Disease, Pathophysiology/Diagnosis/Management*, 1279–1285.
6. Wadhwa, V., Jobanputra, Y., Garg, S. K., Patwardhan, S., Mehta, D., & Sanaka, M. R., (2017). Nationwide trends of hospital admissions for acute cholecystitis in the United States. *Gastroenterology Report (Oxf), 5*(1), 36–42. doi: 10.1093/gastro/gow015.

Chapter

INFECTIONS OF THE SKIN, SOFT TISSUES, JOINTS, AND BONE

6

Contents

Unit Introduction

Skin and soft tissue infections can be caused by a variety of pathogens and clinical scenarios. This natural barrier is crucial because many infections start after the skin is broken. Organisms have the ability to penetrate deeper soft tissue once the skin is compromised. The barrier is breached by a surgical incision, and surgical site infection (SSI), and involves bacteria like *S. aureus* and MRSA which is a significant phenomenon. Dog and cat bites can result in serious local and systemic infections because they introduce members of their oral flora, such as *Pasteurella multocida* and *Capnocytophaga canimorsus*, into the tissues. A component of the human mouth flora called *Eikinella corrodens* plays a significant role in soft tissue and joint injuries sustained by the aggressor in cases of "clenched fist" injuries. These people frequently show up at the hospital a few days following the incident (HIV, HCV, and HBV must also be taken into account).

The more frequent causes of infections in the joints and bones are streptococci and staphylococci. In children under five, *Haemophilus influenzae* type B was frequently identified as the cause of osteomyelitis and arthritis. However, in nations where the Hib vaccination is used, cases of this invasive disease are currently uncommon. Mycobacteria is one of the many organisms that should always be taken into consideration when treating a chronic joint infection in a patient a few instances of the microorganisms that can infect bones and joints. Orthopaedic surgery frequently involves joint replacement, which can be particularly difficult to treat when an infection develops (Figure 6.1).

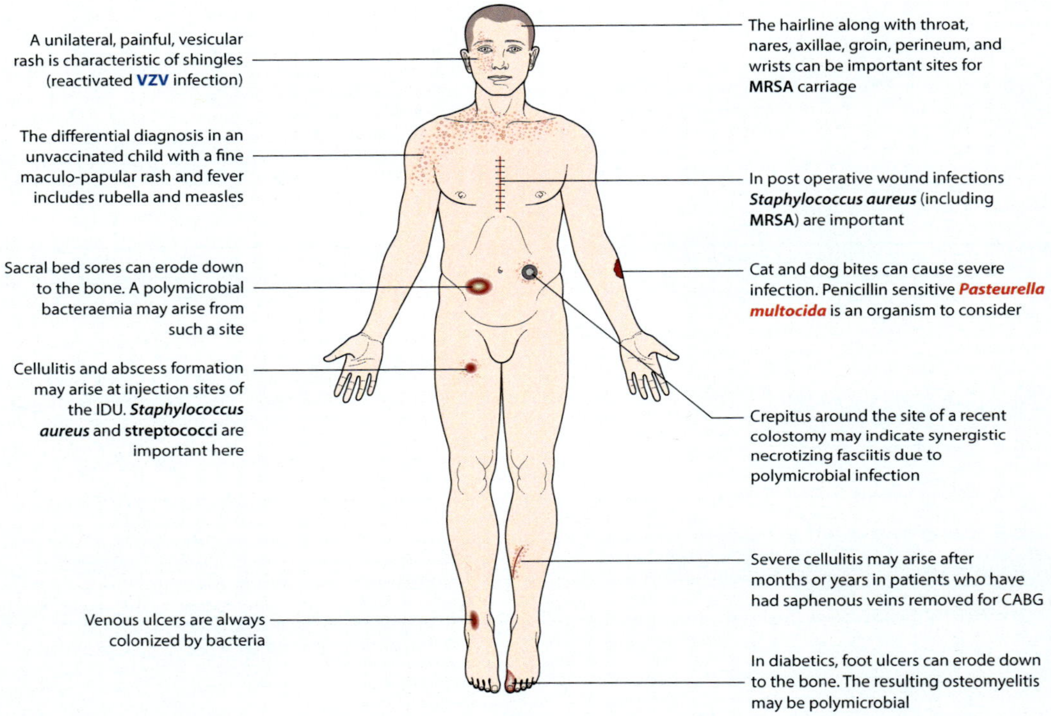

Figure 6.1. *Some of the important clinical situations involved in infection of the skin and soft tissue.*

Source: http://repository.stikesrspadgs.ac.id/25/1/Clinical%20Microbiology%20Struthers-299hlm.pdf.

The skin is a key location for the manifestation of systemic disease in addition to local infections. A few terminologies for grouping skin lesions. Meningococcal sepsis should be taken into consideration when small, non-blanching lesions grow to larger petechial and eventually ecchymotic lesions. New skin lesions in an immunosuppressed patient should be seen by a dermatologist and biopsied for histological and microbiological analysis. It is possible for organisms to enter the skin from a focus located elsewhere in the body. Examples include the environmental fungus Fusarium and *Cryptococcus neoformans.*

Orientation and Directional Terms

Terms	Description	Illustration
Cellulitis	Cellulitis is a common bacterial skin infection that causes redness, swelling, and pain in the infected area of the skin. If untreated, it can spread and cause serious health problems.	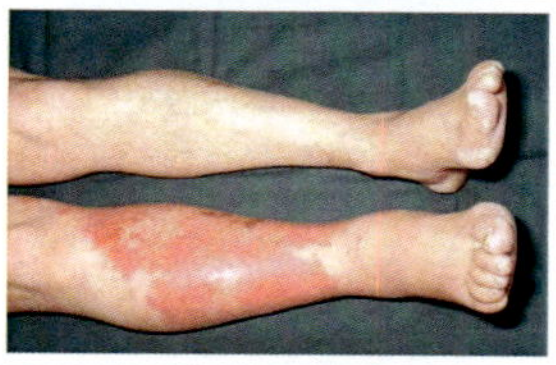
Hansen's disease	Hansen's disease (also known as leprosy) is an infection caused by slow-growing bacteria called *Mycobacterium leprae*. It can affect the nerves, skin, eyes, and lining of the nose (nasal mucosa). With early diagnosis and treatment, the disease can be cured.	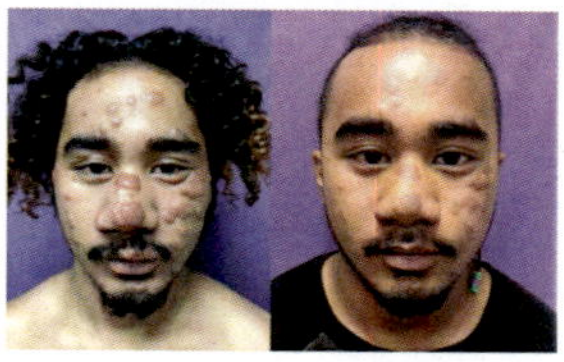
Blister	A blister is a pocket of fluid between the upper layers of skin. The most common causes are friction, freezing, burning, infection, and chemical burns. Blisters are also a symptom of some diseases. The blister bubble is formed from the epidermis, the uppermost layer of skin.	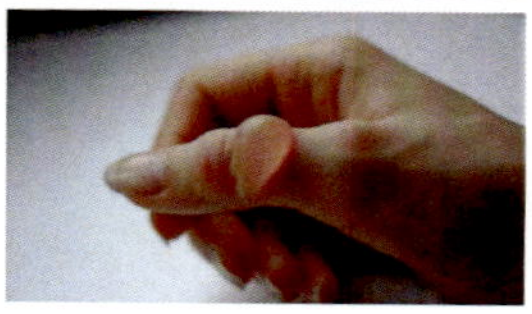
Varicella zoster virus (VZV)	VZV is a human alphaherpesvirus that causes varicella (chickenpox) as the primary infection and establishes latency in the sensory ganglia. Infectious virus is transmitted by aerosolized respiratory droplets or by contact with the virus in varicella or zoster skin lesions.	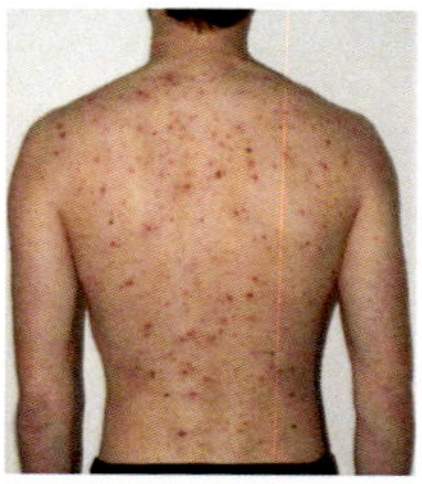
Folliculitis	Folliculitis is a common skin condition that happens when hair follicles become inflamed. It's often caused by an infection with bacteria. At first, it may look like small pimples around the tiny pockets from where each hair grows (hair follicles). The condition can be itchy, sore and embarrassing.	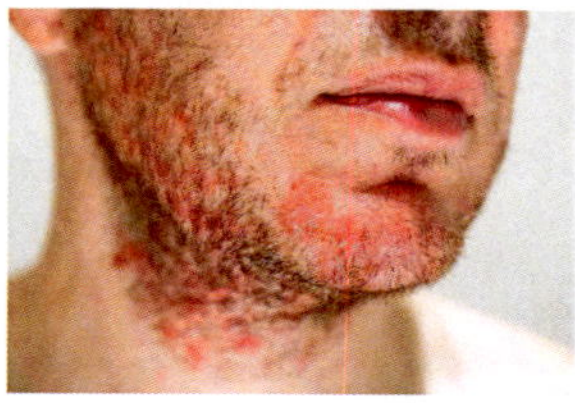
Osteomyelitis	Osteomyelitis is a serious infection of the bone that can be either acute or chronic. It is an inflammatory process involving the bone and its structures caused by pyogenic organisms that spread through the bloodstream, fractures, or surgery.	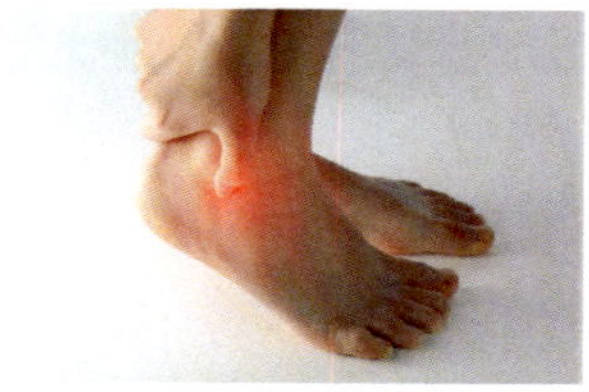
Methicillin resistant *S. aureus* (MRSA)	MRSA is a group of gram-positive bacteria that are genetically distinct from other strains of *S.s aureus*. It is responsible for several difficult-to-treat infections in humans.	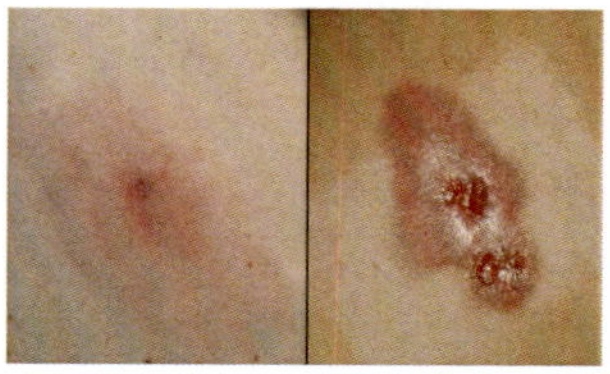

6.1. Skin Infections

Bacteria can infect not only the skin but also the deeper tissues beneath the surface, leading to skin infections. A common kind of skin infection called cellulitis results in pain, swelling, and redness in the affected area. A skin abscess, or collection of pus under the skin, is another kind of skin infection. The common offenders are *S. aureus* and *S. pyogenes*. Herpes simplex and varicella-zoster are examples of viral skin infections that appear as painful blister clusters. Fungal infections, such as candidiasis or dermatophytosis, can affect different parts of the skin. An additional factor in health problems pertaining to the skin are parasitic infestations, such as scabies or lice. Usually, a clinical examination, microbial cultures, or microscopic examination of skin scrapings are used to make the diagnosis. Depending on the underlying cause, different treatment modalities may be used, such as topical creams, antifungals, or antibiotics. Effectively treating skin infections is essential to avoiding consequences, like the development of an abscess or systemic spread, as well as to ease the discomfort experienced by those who are impacted (Figure 6.2).

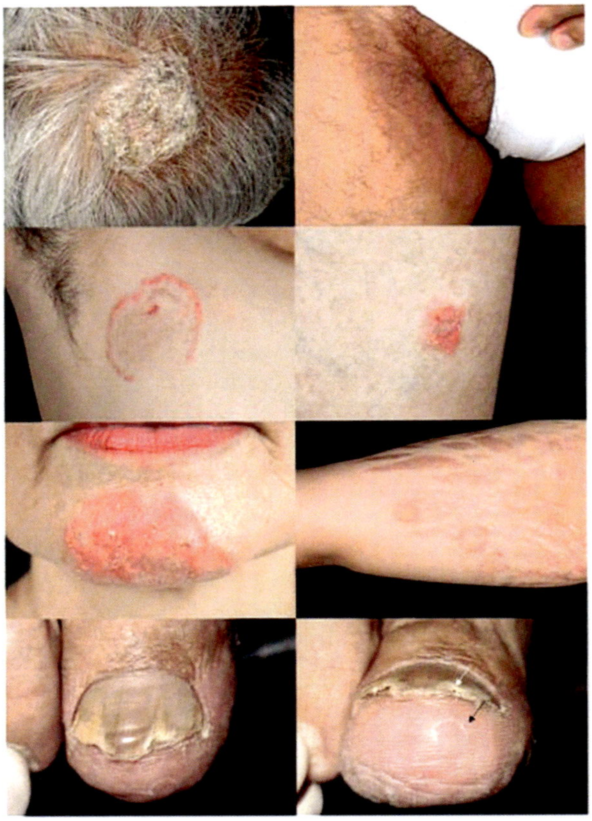

Figure 6.2. *Fungal infections of the skin.*

Source: Chanyachailert, P., Leeyaphan, C., & Bunyaratavej, S., (2023). Cutaneous fungal infections caused by dermatophytes and non-dermatophytes: An updated comprehensive review of epidemiology, clinical presentations, and diagnostic testing. Journal of Fungi, 9(6), 669. https://doi.org/10.3390/jof9060669.

6.1.1. Types of Skin Infections

The following are four different types of skin infections:

1. **Bacterial Skin Infections:** When bacteria penetrate the skin, either from the outside or because they are already there, bacterial skin infections result. They can get into the skin after a wound or through a hair follicle.

   Example include Anthrax, a kind of bacterium that can come in through the surroundings, and commonly found bacteria on the skin, such as *Staphylococcus* and *Streptococcus*, that only become problematic under specific conditions. Skin symptoms are a common symptom of Lyme disease, an infection spread by ticks.

   Infections with bacteria can be localized or systemic. A fever and other symptoms that affect the entire body are signs of a systemic infection, whereas local infections only affect a particular area. Certain bacterial infections can start in one place in the body and work their way throughout.

   Certain bacterial skin infections, like impetigo, can be transmitted from person to person by direct skin contact, bodily fluids, tainted food or water, or by coming into contact with surfaces that harbor bacteria. Some, like cellulitis, cannot be spread.

   Different types of bacterial skin infections include:

- Cellulitis;
- Impetigo;
- Boils;
- Hansen's disease (leprosy).

Systemic infections that can cause skin rashes include:

- Syphilis;
- Tuberculosis;
- Leptospirosis.

   Some bacterial infections are mild and easy to treat with topical antibiotics, but other infections require an oral antibiotic or other medical treatment.

2. **Viral Skin Infections:** Viruses can cause different types of infections that have skin symptoms, such as:

- Shingles (herpes zoster);
- Chickenpox;
- Molluscum contagiosum;
- Warts;
- Measles;
- hand, foot, and mouth disease.

These viruses are often contagious, and most are systemic.

3. **Fungal Skin Infections:** Fungal infections can also contribute to skin infections, which usually appear in moist areas of the body where surfaces meet, like the feet, underarms, or in seams in the skin.

   An allergy to the fungus may occasionally result in symptoms in non-affected areas. For example, someone may get a rash on their fingers if they have a fungal infection on their foot. However, it does not occur as a result of the person touching their foot (Figure 6.3).

Different types of fungal infections:

- Athlete's foot;
- Yeast infection;
- Ringworm;
- Nail fungus;
- Oral thrush;
- Diaper rash.

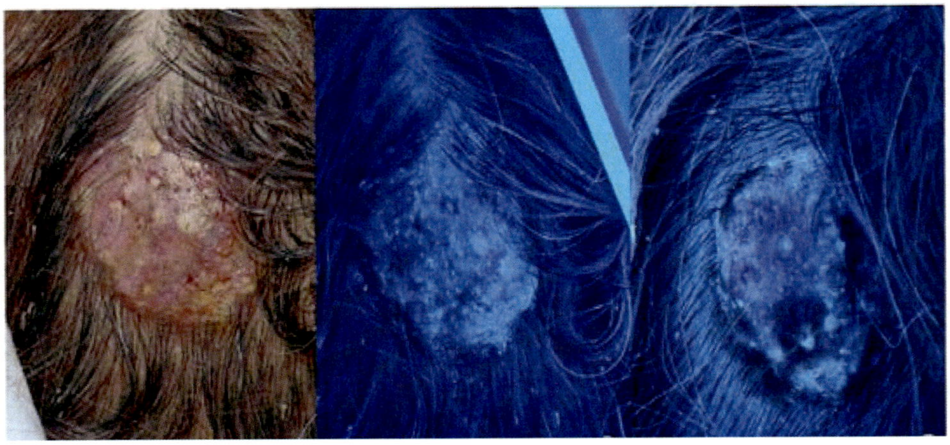

Figure 6.3. *Skin fungal infection.*

Source: Chanyachailert, P., Leeyaphan, C., & Bunyaratavej, S., (2023). Cutaneous fungal infections caused by dermatophytes and non-dermatophytes: An updated comprehensive review of epidemiology, clinical presentations, and diagnostic testing. Journal of Fungi, 9(6), 669. https://doi.org/10.3390/jof9060669.

6.1.1.1. Parasitic Skin Infection

There is a parasite responsible for these kinds of skin infections. These infections can travel to the bloodstream and organs in addition to the skin. Although not fatal, a parasite infection can cause discomfort.

Different types of parasitic skin infections include:

- Lice;
- Bedbugs;
- Scabies;
- Cutaneous larva migrans.

6.1.2. Symptoms of a Skin Infection

The symptoms of a skin infection will depend on:

- the type of infection;
- the cause;
- individual factors, such as whether the person has a weakened immune system.

Common symptoms of skin infections include:

- Redness on pale skin, or purple or darker areas of skin if you have a darker skin tone;
- Lesions that may be flat or raised, bumpy, wart-like, and so on;
- Itching;
- Pain and tenderness.

In some cases, a person may also have other symptoms, such as a fever.

Signs of a severe infection include:

- Pus;
- Blisters;
- Skin sloughing, breakdown;
- Dark areas that can indicate necrosis or tissue death;
- Pain and discoloration;
- Widespread swelling.

6.1.3. Risk Factors of Skin Infection

Skin and soft-tissue infections are common and can affect all age groups; however, certain (co-morbid) conditions such as immunosuppression, trauma, certain pre-existing skin conditions such as ambient skin fever, pre-existing inflammatory dermatoses, and other skin conditions such as reactions to insect's bites and scabies, as well as drug use may influence an individual's skin and soft-tissue infections or increase the risk of erysipelas and cellulitis. Infections of the skin and soft tissues rank among the most serious health issues that drug injectors face. Drug injectors are highly vulnerable to several health issues, such as bacterial and viral infections. When there is a high bacterial load on the skin, the availability of bacterial nutrients, excessive skin moisture, insufficient blood supply, immunosuppression, and corneal layer damage, the skin's integrity is compromised, and acute bacterial skin and skin structure infections arise. Contagious skin infections like furuncles, carbuncles, and impetigo are spread by filthy living conditions, sharing of personal items, physical contact, and poor hygiene. Diabetic foot infections are frequently the result of poorly managed diabetes (DFI). Injuries from traumatic events like bites, cuts, and injectable drug use raise the risk of infections in the skin and its supporting structures. Surgical site infections (SSIs) are categorized according to the type of operation; clean, low-risk procedures have the lowest risk of infections, while contaminated, high-risk procedures have the highest risk.

The high frequency and incidence of common skin infections in developing nations are generally attributed to poverty-related factors, such as poor hygiene, which includes trouble in accessing clean water, climatic conditions, and cramped living quarters. One of the primary prognostic factors is the timely diagnosis. However, as certain clinical features are absent in the early stages of the disease, the diagnosis is frequently incorrect. Several other variables, including advanced age, underlying pre-existing conditions, or bacterial virulence—such as invasive group A *Streptococcus*—have also been demonstrated to have an impact on mortality.

6.1.4. Epidemiology of Skin Infection

Even though they occur frequently, little is known about the frequency and trends of common bacterial skin infections like impetigo, erysipelas, and non-necrotizing cellulitis. A greater number of patients are being seen and treated in the emergency department (ED) and admitted to the hospital as a result of the rising incidence of skin and soft-tissue infections in the general population in recent years.

Numerous factors, such as geographic location, socioeconomic status, hygiene habits, and the prevalence of specific pathogens, have an impact on the epidemiology of skin infections. Bacterial skin infections, including cellulitis and impetigo, are common worldwide, with common causative agents being *S. aureus* and *S. pyogenes*. The prevalence of these infections can differ by location, with crowded housing or areas with poor access to healthcare being associated with higher rates of occurrence. Human papillomavirus (HPV) and herpes simplex are two examples of viral skin infections that frequently display a variety of epidemiological patterns and are influenced by immunization rates and sexual behavior. Worldwide, dermatophytosis and other fungal skin infections are common, and their occurrence is correlated with variables like weather and personal hygiene habits.

Parasitic infestations, like scabies and lice, are more prevalent in communities with close human-to-human contact. Certain populations, such as children in schools or individuals in communal living environments, may be more susceptible.

The prevalence of resistant strains in communities and healthcare settings is influenced by shifts in antibiotic resistance patterns, which are reflected in the epidemiology of skin infections. Global travel, environmental factors, and newly developing infectious diseases all add to the dynamic nature of epidemiology related to skin infections.

Comprehending the epidemiology of skin infections is essential for devising effective treatment strategies customized for specific populations and areas, putting preventive measures into place, and planning public health initiatives. To address the problems caused by skin infections and lessen their effects on people and communities, surveillance, research, and education are essential.

6.1.5. Role of Microorganisms in Skin Infection

The mode of entry can also affect the severity of infections in the skin and soft tissues. As a result, normal host flora from the environment or the instrument of entry may be the source of the skin and soft tissue infections. Acute bacterial skin and skin structure infections (ABSSSIs) make up most of the skin and soft-tissue infections that are caused by bacteria. Some cases are brought on by viruses, most notably the varicella zoster virus (VZV), which is the organism that causes shingles and chickenpox. Group A hemolytic streptococci, *S. aureus* and *S. pyogenes*) continued to be the most common Gram-positive coli that were isolated from every part of the body.

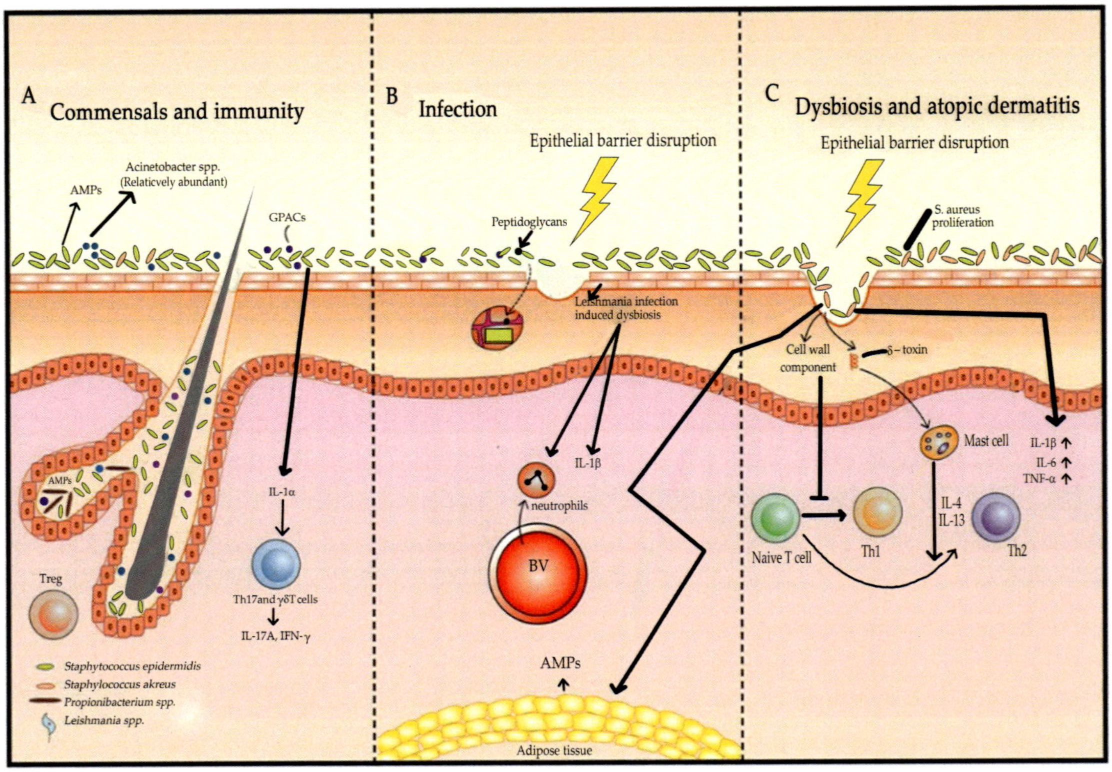

Figure 6.4. *Role of microorganisms in skin infection.*

Source: Park, Y. J., & Lee, H. K., (2018). The role of skin and orogenital microbiota in protective immunity and chronic immune-mediated inflammatory disease. Front. Immunol., 8, 1955. doi: 10.3389/fimmu.2017.01955.

On the other hand, organisms present in the mucous membranes close to the lesions were more common in infections that followed these membranes. This is how enteric Gram-negative bacteria and *Bacteroides* spp. were mostly discovered in lesions on the limbs and buttocks. The possible foundations of these organisms are vagina and the rectum, where they exist normally. Group α-hemolytic Streptococci, *Fusobacterium* spp., *Prevotella* spp., and *Porphyromonas* spp. were most normally found in lesions of the face, head, fingers, and neck. These microorganisms in all probability had reached these sites from the oral cavity, where they are a part of the normal flora. The most recurrent agents in ABSSSIs) are aerobic Gram-positive cocci pathogens including MRSA and methicillin-susceptible *S. aureus* (MSSA), and β-hemolytic *Streptococci*. MRSA is an infrequent pathogen in community-acquired (CA) infections and is rather more commonly found in hospital-acquired infections. Conversely, the prevalence of community-acquired MRSA (CA-MRSA) has critically increased in the past years, and is now a predominant cause of purulent acute bacterial skin and soft-tissue infections in the US.

In skin infections that have a more complex etiology, such as those resulting from necrotizing fasciitis, diabetic foot infection and ecthyma gangrenosum, the range of pathogens is abundant and is dependent on the clinical setting. Anaerobic Gram-positive bacilli containing *Clostridium* spp. and *Enterobacteriaceae* are also involved in skin infections. Furthermore, certain anaerobic Gram-negative bacteria, mostly with polymicrobial infections are involved in acute bacterial skin and soft-tissue infections like *Peptostreptococcus* spp., *Bacteriodes* spp., *Prevotella* spp., *Porphyromonas* spp. and *Fusobacterium* spp. Other organisms, such as *Staphylococcus epidermidis*, group B *Streptococci*, *E. coli*, *P. aeruginosa* and some Gram-negative bacteria, are rarely involved in skin infections (Figure 6.4).

6.1.6. Effects of Hygienic Condition on Skin Infection

For more than a century, good hand hygiene has been recognized as one of the main defenses against the transmission risk of infectious agents through contact and the fecal-oral pathways. It's crucial to practice basic hygiene to prevent infection, such as washing your hands frequently and keeping your fingernails trimmed to prevent scratching and dressing sores. Inadequate hygiene habits can ultimately lead to chronic consequences by encouraging the spread of infectious diseases, including skin infections.

6.1.7. Frequent Hands Washing Effect on Skin Infection

The skin is profoundly altered after every washing. Most of these alterations are temporary, but long-term skin changes can cause chronic damage, irritant contact dermatitis and eczema, and concurrent alterations in flora in people working in industries like healthcare, where frequent hand washing is necessary. Health care workers are at work risk for irritant contact dermatitis, which is linked to frequent hand washing and has a prevalence of 10% to 45%.

6.1.8. Diagnosis of Skin Infection

Most of the diagnosis of soft tissue and skin infections is based on clinical impression. Exams conducted in research laboratories aid in validating the diagnosis and elucidating the physical traits of specific etiologies. Depending on the clinical manifestations, bacterial investigations may involve tissue swabs with culture, blood cultures, needle aspiration, ultrasound, x-ray, CT scan, or MRI screening. Given that skin infections frequently mimic the symptoms of other clinical diseases, diagnosing them can be challenging. Identifying whether the infection has the potential to develop into a serious or life-threatening condition is crucial for accurate diagnosis.

The doctor must describe whether the infection is deep or superficial, localized or spreading, and if blistering, skin necrosis, or purple discoloration are present. Most infections are curable if detected early and treated appropriately; however, some infections have the potential to result in serious side effects, such as septicemia, nephritis, arthritis, and carditis, if detected later or if treatment is not adequate. Cellulitis, in particular, requires quick intermediation.

6.1.9. Treatment and Management of Skin Infection

Prior to the availability of a microbiological diagnosis, empirical antimicrobial therapy for bacterial skin and skin structure infections is typically begun with an agent that exhibits strong antimicrobial activity against the most likely pathogen or pathogens. As a result, the type, severity, and suspected pathogens all play a role in the initial antibiotic selection. The clinical presentation and infection severity determine how to treat infections of the skin and soft tissues. Broad-spectrum antibiotic therapy and quick surgical debridement are essential for managing skin infections. Generally, the infection is treated with a combination of surgical debridement or drainage and antibiotic therapy; however, simple boils or abscesses can usually be treated with incision and drainage alone, without the need for antibiotics. To choose the appropriate type of care and empirical therapy for skin and soft-tissue infections, assessing the severity of the disease is a crucial first step in the clinical management process. If this isn't performed, prescriptions may be written inappropriately, as well as treating minor infections of the skin and soft tissues too much while leaving severe infections untreated. For the treatment of skin infections, three methods are preferred: (a) surgical drainage and debridement; (b) wound culture combined with susceptibility testing; and (c) early and suitable empirical antibiotic therapy. Clinical manifestations were used to stratify therapeutic indications into three categories: mild, moderate, and severe. For non-necrotizing skin and soft-tissue infections, including those caused by MRSA, commonly used antibiotics include Penicillin G, Cloxacillin, Ceftriaxone and Clindamycin. Antibiotics are used empirically with consideration for resistance patterns. Current antibiotic recommendations include penicillinase-resistant penicillins, first-generation Cephalosporins, Azithromycin, Clarithromycin, Amoxicillin-clavulanic acid, or a second-generation fluoroquinolone in the skeletally mature patient. For suspected polymicrobial acute bacterial skin and soft tissue infection, treatment includes coverage of Gram-negative and anaerobic pathogens with a second-, third-, or fourth-generation Cephalosporin; and is usually indicated in children under three years and in patients with diabetes or who are immune compromised.

6.2. Soft Tissue Infections

Soft tissue infections comprise a range of ailments impacting the body's non-osseous structures, such as the skin, muscles, fascia, and subcutaneous tissues. Pathogens of all kinds, including bacteria, viruses, fungi, and parasites, can cause these infections. Cellulitis, an infection of the skin's deeper layers, and abscesses, which are small collections of pus frequently brought on by *S. aureus*, are common bacterial soft tissue infections.

Necrotizing fasciitis is a potentially fatal soft tissue infection that affects the deeper fascial layers and progresses quickly. It is frequently linked to polymicrobial infections, and anaerobic bacteria and streptococci are often the cause of necrotizing fasciitis.

Viral soft tissue infections, which manifest as excruciating vesicular lesions, can be caused by viruses such as varicella-zoster or herpes simplex. Even though they are less frequent, fungal soft tissue infections can happen to people with compromised immune systems or those who already have skin conditions.

Injection drug use, diabetes, trauma, surgery, and compromised immunity are risk factors for soft tissue infections. Clinical assessment, imaging studies, and occasionally laboratory tests like wound cultures are all part of the diagnosis process (Figure 6.5).

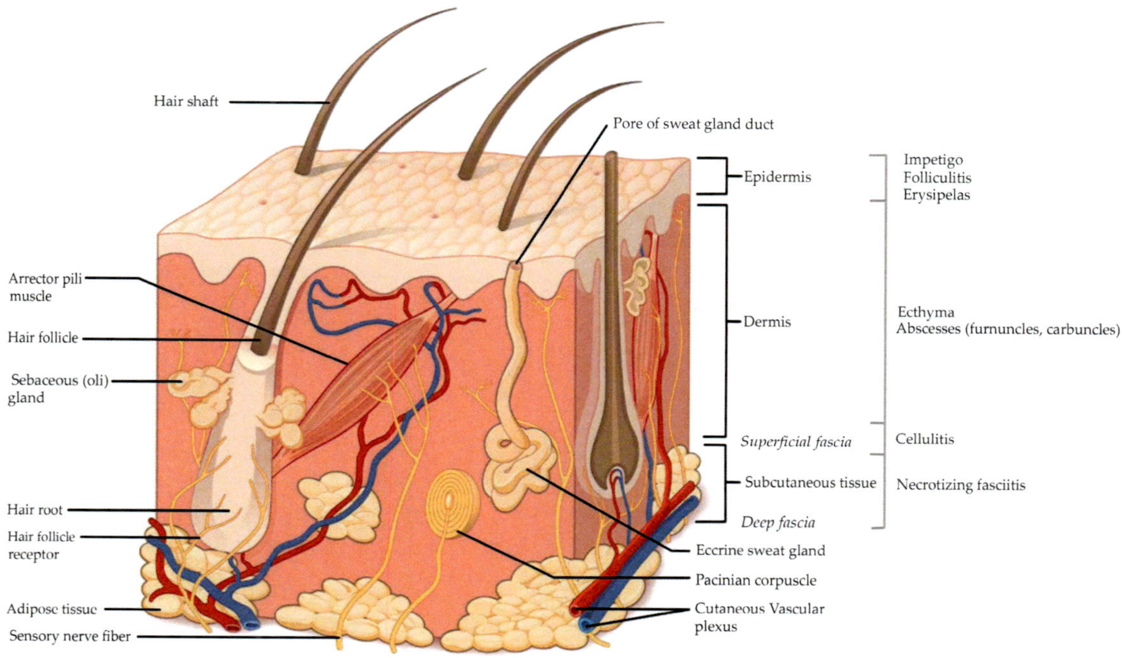

Figure 6.5. *A structured approach to skin and soft tissue infections.*

Source: Silverberg, B., (2021). A structured approach to skin and soft tissue infections (SSTIs) in an ambulatory setting. Clinics and Practice, 11(1), 65–74. https://doi.org/10.3390/clinpract11010011.

Treatment usually consists of wound care, antibiotic therapy targeted at the causing agent, and occasionally surgery, particularly for debridement or abscess drainage in necrotizing infections. Timely and appropriate management is essential to avoid complications like tissue loss, chronicity, or systemic spread. The prevention of soft tissue infections and their recurrence also requires education on appropriate wound care and hygiene practices.

6.2.1. Impetigo

Impetigo is most common in children and usually involves the skin of the face, often around the mouth and nose. It has two forms:

- Non-bullous, which is most commonly caused by *S. pyogenes* (group A streptococci) and is typified by "honey-crust" lesions; and
- Bullous, which is caused by *S. aureus*; rupture of the bullae leaves a thin "varnish-like" crust.

6.2.2. Folliculitis

The hair follicles may become infected spontaneously or following exfoliation, shaving, and the use of a loofah sponge. A particular type of folliculitis called "whirlpool", or "hot tub" folliculitis is brought on by *P. aeruginosa*.

6.2.3. Skin Abscesses and Furuncles

S. aureus is the most common pathogen in the community that causes furuncles and abscesses. Certain phage types can spread among family members and are linked to recurrent episodes of furunculosis. Staphylococcal bacteremia may result from a minor skin lesion or furuncle, with potentially severe complications, including osteomyelitis, septic arthritis and endocarditis. Recently, infections caused by CA-MRSA have been described in both adults and children in Australia. These bacteria are resistant to beta-lactam antibiotics, but retain susceptibility to agents such as clindamycin, in contrast to multi-resistant *S. aureus*, which is usually hospital-acquired.

This β-lactam resistance may delay effective therapy. In patients with recurrent *S. aureus* soft tissue infection, attempts can be made to eradicate the causative strain from long-term carriage in the nasal passages and on skin with nasal mupirocin and skin antiseptic solutions. Penicillins and cephalosporins are ineffective in eradicating nasal carriage.

6.2.4. Cellulitis

The inflammation that affects the dermis, epidermis, and subcutaneous fat is acute and spreads quickly in cellulitis. *S. aureus* and ß-hemolytic streptococci are the most frequent causes. If at all feasible, host factors that may predispose to cellulitis should be addressed. Some of these are non-infective (e.g., eczema, trauma, local ischemia, venous, arterial, or vasculitic ulceration, lymphatic impairment, surgery, and radiation) and infectious (e.g., varicella, tinea pedis, and scabies). Certain exposures are linked to less common causes of cellulitis. Infection with *S. pyogenes* may also be confined to the dermis, termed erysipelas.

1. **Clinical Features:** Localized pain in the affected limb is a common "wildfire" onset of streptococcal infections. Vigors may appear 24 hours before skin involvement or lymphangitis symptoms become apparent. It frequently results in tender regional lymphadenitis. Before there is any improvement at the cellulitis site, the fever frequently goes down and the leukocyte count and C-reactive protein level drop. In fact, even days after a systemic clinical response, the affected area may still experience blistering and local necrosis. Desquamation happens after healing.
2. **Diagnosis and Management:** In actuality, the precise causative organism is rarely isolated because skin swabs are rarely diagnostic and blood cultures are typically negative. However, an aspirate from an intact blister may be useful for culture, and an aspirate obtained by needling the leading edge of the cellulitis is useful in immunocompromised patients or after unusual exposures. Initial preference is for intravenous antibiotics, with the exception of minor infections. Consideration should be given to exposure to uncommon pathogens at work or in the environment if cellulitis does not improve with empirical beta-lactam therapy. These organism-related infections can also manifest as nodules, nodular lymphangitis, or solitary ulcers. A supply of antibiotics can be given to patients who have recurrent cellulitis so they can take them when their symptoms return. This, however, isn't always successful. Effective prophylactic measures could include twice-daily penicillin V, cephalexin, or erythromycin; however, monthly injections of benzathine penicillin are necessary for certain patients.

6.2.5. Toxic Shock Syndromes

These *S. aureus* or *S. pyogenes*-caused syndromes include hypotension, fever, a faint "sunburnlike" rash, and multiorgan failure. If *S. aureus* is present, there might only be a vaginal or wound infection, or there might be a noticeable skin infection. Eliminating the source of bacterial toxin production (such as by debriding the wound or getting rid of the vaginal tampon) is crucial. A better prognosis for streptococcal toxic shock has been linked to the initial antibiotic regimen including clindamycin, possibly because this antibiotic inhibits bacterial protein synthesis, which lowers the production of toxins.

6.2.6. Necrotizing Fasciitis

Necrotizing fasciitis is a surgical emergency needing prompt recognition and radical debridement of devitalized tissue. It can take two forms:

- **Type 1:** Caused by multiple organisms, often of gut origin (synergistic gangrene); and
- **Type 2:** Caused by group A streptococci.

Both forms cause severe systemic toxicity that leads to hypotension, respiratory distress and multiorgan failure. There is usually severe pain in the affected area, with only modest overlying skin changes in the early stages, progressing rapidly to fascial and skin necrosis and deep tissue infarction, particularly of the muscle layers.

6.2.7. Clostridial Myonecrosis (Gas Gangrene)

Clostridial myonecrosis can develop spontaneously (often in conjunction with underlying bowel malignancy) or as a result of trauma involving the penetration of contaminated material (e.g., injection of contaminated recreational drugs). Crepitus in the soft tissues may result from clostridium gas production.

6.3. Bone and Joint Infection

Osteomyelitis is the term for bone infections. Trauma (such as severing a finger with a knife), wounds like diabetic ulcers that penetrate to the bone, or bloodstream infections that lodge in the bone (which frequently occurs with osteomyelitis of the spine or vertebrae) can all be the cause of Osteomyelitis. Joints, whether natural or artificial (prosthetic), can also become infected. Other causes include direct trauma or infections from other sources that enter the bloodstream and lodge in the joint (Figure 6.6).

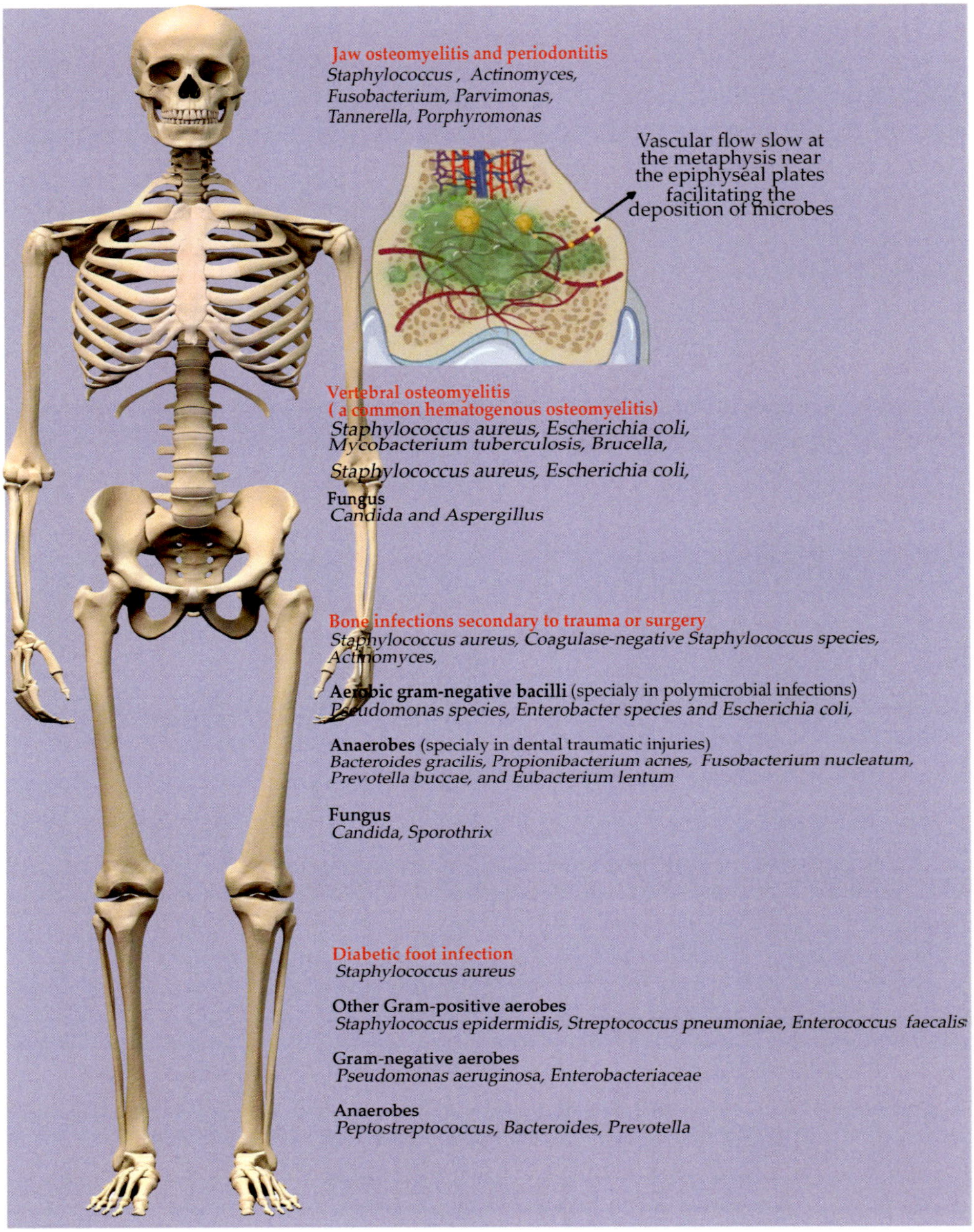

Figure 6.6. *Bone and joint infection.*

Source: Wu, S., Wu, B., Liu, Y., Deng, S., Lei, L., & Zhang, H., (2022). Mini review therapeutic strategies targeting for biofilm and bone infections. Front. Microbiol., 13:936285. doi: 10.3389/fmicb.2022.936285.

6.3.1. General Considerations

Pathogens can enter bones and joints directly through inoculation from a contiguous focus of infection or through hematogenous spread. Bone injuries make it easier for infections to spread, possibly because they reveal extracellular matrix proteins that many bacteria, particularly staphylococci, can attach to. Biomaterials, which in this case include acrylic bone cement, devascularized bone graft, synthetic bone substitutes, and the metal and plastic components of a prosthetic joint, also increase the risk of infection. All these inert substances weaken the local immune system and give nonpathogenic skin commensals like coagulase-negative staphylococci the opportunity to develop into serious pathogens. The microbiology, presentation, and symptoms of infections in the bones and joints are compiled in Table 6.1. Inflammatory reactions brought on by musculoskeletal infections cause bone resorption, cartilage degradation, and bone death (via thrombosis and disruption of the blood vessels supplying bone). Dead bone then acts like foreign material, giving bacteria a surface to attach to and a phenotype that is comparatively resistant to both phagocytosis and antibiotics. Because of this, even in the face of extended antibiotic therapy, a chronically established orthopedic infection may prove to be remarkably persistent or even develop.

Table 6.1. *Manifestations of Bone and Joint Infection*

History	Structure infected	Microbiology	Seen by:
Acute	Joint:		
	Native	SA, BHS, aGNR, Gc, Pn	P; O; M; R
	Prosthetic	SA, BHS CoNS, aGNR; E	O
	Bone:		
	Spine	SA, aGNR, PA	M; O; R
	Long bones	SA, BHS	O; P
	Any bone following insertion of metalware	SA, BHS, CoNS, aGNR	O
	Following open fracture	As above and aGPR, PA, anO_2	
Chronic	Joint:		
	Native	MTB, SS, SA	R; O; M
	Prosthetic	CoNS, SA, aGNR, E	O
	Bone:		
	All sites	Original organism when treatment for acute osteomyelitis fails	O
	Spine	SA, aGNR, PA, MTB, B	M; O; R
	Long bones	SA, CoNS, aGNR, PA	O
	Foot bones	SA, BHS, aGNR	M; O; D; N
		PA	O
	Sternum, ribs	SA, aGNR, PA	Ct; C; M
	Pelvis, trochanter, calcaneus	SA, aGNR, anO_2, PA, E	M
	Skull	SA, aGNR	ENT; NS

Source: https://www.rcpjournals.org/content/clinmedicine/4/6/510.full.pdf.

Since it takes at least 7–10 days for periosteal reaction or detectable bone loss to develop, acute infections typically do not present with radiographic changes, in contrast to subacute and chronic infections, which usually have abnormal plain radiology. However, scans are useful for identifying collections in soft tissue or bone edema; for native bone, MRI is the preferred scanning method. There is no standardized and thoroughly tested scanning methodology for infections linked to metalware. When feasible, antibiotic therapy ought to be determined by the outcomes of cultures from high-quality specimens removed from deep tissues. Cultures are still vulnerable to reduced sensitivity and contamination issues, particularly under long-term circumstances. While still in the experimental stage, molecular techniques on aspirates or biopsies show promise in specific centers. In cases of acute native joint and bone infections, it is generally advisable to start empirical treatment; however, this is much less frequently required in cases of chronic or implant-related infections, unless the patient's presentation indicates bacteremia or necrotizing soft tissue infection.

The regimen should contain a medication that is active against *S. aureus*, but the duration, choice, and mode of administration remain mainly non-evidence-based. If oral medication is preferred over intravenous therapy, the antibiotic(s) selected need to have a high bioavailability. Consulting with a microbiologist or infectious disease expert is advised.

In many cases, surgery is necessary in addition to antibiotics. Surgery is indicated in cases of acute infections when there is an abscess, necrosis, wound dehiscence, or when the patient does not improve with prescribed treatment. Surgery is always necessary for a radical infection cure in cases of chronic infections. In addition, it is recommended for chronic systemic illness, functional impairment, drainage, and unbearable pain (Table 6.1).

6.3.2. Specific Conditions

6.3.2.1. Acute Septic Arthritis and Osteomyelitis

Both osteomyelitis and acute septic arthritis are typically of hematogenous origin, however in rare instances, the former makes arthrocentesis or arthroscopy more difficult. The Northern Hemisphere is experiencing a decrease in hematogenous infections, while the Southern Hemisphere is experiencing higher rates, especially among ethnic groups that are less privileged in society.

In addition to a high fever and upset constitution, both conditions are accompanied by bacteremia in 50% of cases. Notable symptoms include joint irritability or bony tenderness, warmth, swelling, and loss of function. Although the absence of erythema does not rule out deep infection, it does suggest bursitis accompanying septic arthritis or tracking of a subperiosteal abscess from bone into the soft tissues.

6.3.2.2. Diagnosis

The findings of investigations should be utilized to confirm the diagnosis, which should be made based on clinical considerations. It is not appropriate to postpone treatment while awaiting confirmation test results. Acquiring blood, synovial fluid, or direct aspirate of bone cultures (which can be performed on newborns and infants) is a crucial component of optimal care; a positive result provides assurance when selecting antibiotics. Joint aspirates can identify conditions other than infection, such as gout, pseudogout, or hemoglobinopathy; however, gram-stain cannot rule out infection in a joint that has been impacted by gout or pseudogout due to its lower sensitivity when compared to culture. Only in subacute or acute-on-chronic osteomyelitis will bone destruction or periosteal reaction be visible on plain films. Soft tissue swelling or an effusion may also be seen. If you have acute osteomyelitis, MRI is the recommended confirmatory test. Ultrasonography can show periosteal elevation in children, as well as soft tissue edema, abscess, and joint effusion, and also be used to guide joint aspiration in all age groups.

6.3.2.3. Treatment

Once the diagnosis has been considered, time is of the essence. The likelihood of recovery from acute septic arthritis and osteomyelitis is high as long as there hasn't been any joint damage or bone death, but it drastically decreases if these things happen. Intravenous antibiotics that are effective against beta-hemolytic streptococci and staphylococci, including MRSA, should be used as the first line of treatment when the appropriate risk factors are present. These strains seem to be biologically successful and frequently cause serious soft tissue infections that can occasionally become worse due to musculoskeletal involvement. Gram-negative organisms are uncommon pathogens in this situation, but the grave consequences of not receiving proper treatment make it justified to include anti-gram-negative cover in the initial regimen.

6.3.2.4. Surgery

It is advisable to seek an orthopedic opinion if the diagnosis is suspected. It's not always necessary to perform surgery for acute osteomyelitis. "Medical" therapy is a well-researched treatment option for joints that can be aspirated on a daily basis in cases of acute septic arthritis in children. Arthrotomy is reserved for joints that do not settle after five days of treatment. The shoulder and hip, on the other hand, are exceptions and can store significant amounts of pus. Since high intra-articular pressure can damage the circulation to the femoral and humeral heads, arthrotomy or arthroscopic washout is the recommended course of treatment.

Unless the patient is not suitable for anesthesia, orthopedic surgeons typically recommend washouts for all acutely infected joints in adults. Unlike arthrotomy, arthroscopic washout is well tolerated and offers a way to examine the articular cartilage, get rid of debris, and take tissue samples for diagnostic purposes.

Clinical conditions, host biology, and microbiological factors all affect how long antibiotic therapy lasts, and in kids with simple illnesses, the length of their treatment plans is getting shorter. Re-evaluation for a surgical focus using appropriate scans should be considered for both conditions if response is not achieved 48–72 hours after initiation of appropriate antibiotic therapy. Potential secondary foci, such as a distant focus like endocarditis, need to be taken into account if the patient's overall health status is still poor. A high mortality rate, usually in compromised hosts, and polyarticular presentation characterize 5% of cases of septic arthritis.

6.3.2.5. Rehabilitation

Pain, decreased joint mobility, or surgical complications typically determine how quickly a patient recovers from surgery. Restraints on one's activities or mandatory rest periods are not beneficial. When presentation occurs quickly and empirical treatment is initiated early, the prognosis is usually favorable. Delays in recovery either increase the risk of bone or cartilage degradation, which in turn increases the risk of chronicity, long-term disruptions in growth or function, and the requirement for surgery.

6.3.2.6. Unusual Sites of Infection

Most of the infections affect the big joints as well as the metaphyses of the long bones that surround them. Unusual infection localizations that nearly always present with atypical chest pain are infections in the sterno-clavicular, costo-chondral, or manubrio-sternal joints. These infections are typically detected first by the general practitioner. As with any joint, these may need aspiration, biopsy, or drainage.

6.3.3. Chronic Osteomyelitis

Unlike acute osteomyelitis, chronic osteomyelitis does not have a formal, accepted definition. Most experts believe that the presence of dead bone is the defining characteristic because it changes the prognosis (Figure 6.7).

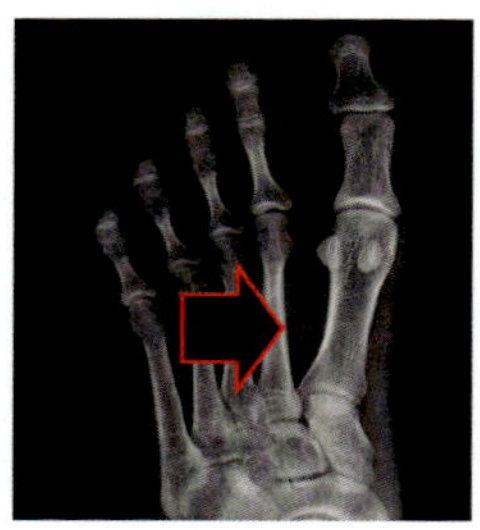

Figure 6.7. *X-ray (showing an area of osteomyelitis.*

Source: By James Heilman, MD – Own work, CC BY-SA 4.0, https://commons.wikimedia.org/w/index.php?curid=49086925.

6.3.3.1. Long-Bone Osteomyelitis

Usually, an infected fracture fixation or complex acute osteomyelitis precedes chronic long-bone osteomyelitis. The doctor is likely to become involved in such cases outside of highly specialized units only if there are medical complications from therapy or if comorbidities need to be managed. Osteomyelitis rarely results from venous ulceration unless there is exposed bone that can be felt or seen. We feel that plain films "to exclude osteomyelitis" are typically not indicated in the absence of these features.

Advanced techniques now exist in specialist centers for managing established chronic long-bone osteomyelitis.

These include the use of:

- External Ilizarov ring fixators and bone transplant or vascularized free fibular grafts for the management of large segmental bone defects; and
- Free muscle flaps for filling large soft tissue defects.

Both permits more aggressive resection of dead and infected bone and unhealthy soft tissue. The days of curettage of osteomyelitic bone blindly through a sinus or a minimal bone resection using an incision through an old scar should be over.

The physician may need to take the primary role, with surgical help, in three specific situations:

- Vertebral osteomyelitis;
- Osteomyelitis underlying decubitus ulcers (pressure sores); and
- Osteomyelitis in the diabetic foot.

6.3.3.2. Vertebral Osteomyelitis

Growing numbers of elderly patients with degenerate spinal pathology and bacteremia risk factors are likely to be associated with an increase in the incidence of vertebral osteomyelitis. Aerobic gram-negative rods, like *E. coli*, are thought to originate from GI or urinary sources and are the second most common pathogen after *S. aureus* (including MRSA). Severe back pain is the presentation, which is worse at night, when at rest, and when moving. Radicularly referred pain can present incoherently with thoracic or abdominal pain. Even though the condition may seem subtle and not cause a fever, it's important to keep in mind that severe acute back pain that develops into a fever and develops neurological symptoms and signs is a medical emergency. Urgent imaging and surgery are recommended for a spinal epidural abscess, which is strongly suggested by these symptoms.

While it is common for elderly hospitalized patients to experience back pain, which may initially be disregarded, chronic disease-related anemia and elevated erythrocyte sedimentation rate may only prompt a search for metastases or myeloma. Due to their low sensitivity, plain films are not advised for use in the evaluation of back pain, even though they can traditionally demonstrate erosion of the end plates and loss of disc space. The preferred investigation is MRI; if this is not possible, spiral CT can be used to evaluate the vertebral bodies, end plates, and disc space as well as detect swelling or abscess in the paraspinal soft tissues. In the early stages of the disease, blood cultures may be positive, but in chronic presentations, they are typically negative. A good way to get tissue for histology and microbiology is to biopsy an infected disc space or paraspinal tissue. When risk factors are present, cultures for Brucella species and TB should be sent.

Antibiotics are often the only treatment needed for spinal osteomyelitis. Post-adequate treatment recurrence, progressive deformity, persistent pain, spinal cord compression, and abscess formation are all indications for surgery. Back pain usually goes away in 2–4 weeks, with a generally good recovery rate. The likelihood of paralysis clearing up in tuberculosis is high. A spinal epidural abscess paralyzing a patient is particularly unlikely to recover due to spinal cord infarction, so the prognosis for pyogenic infections is uncertain (Figure 6.8).

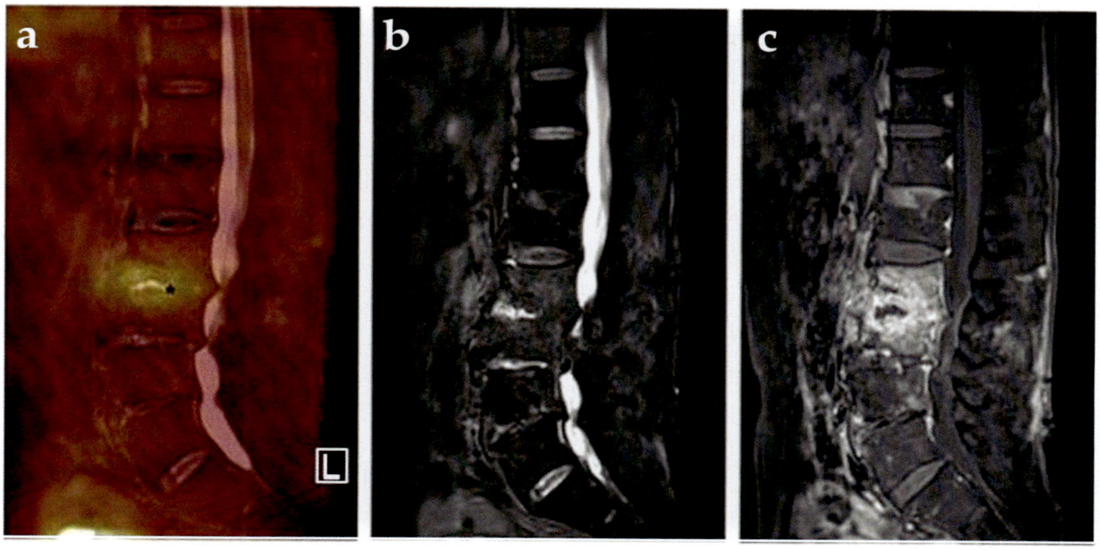

Figure 6.8. *Vertebral osteomyelitis.*

Source: Jeon, I., Kong, E., Yu, D., & Hong, C. P., (2020). Clinical and radiological analysis of pyogenic vertebral osteomyelitis immediately after successful antimicrobial therapy: considerations for assessing therapeutic response. Diagnostics, 10(11), 861. https://doi.org/10.3390/diagnostics10110861.

6.3.3.3. Associated with Decubitus Ulcers

The "contiguous focus" route of infection is best illustrated by osteomyelitis that exacerbates decubitus ulcers. Although polymicrobial infections originating from the mixed colonizing flora of the ulcer or wound covering the bone are more common, *S. aureus* still plays a significant role.

Osteomyelitis of this type also illustrates that, once underlying bone is infected, wound healing will not occur unless the deep infection is resolved. The result is a vicious circle of soft tissue loss, bone death, spreading infection and further soft tissue loss. It is essential to target the pathogens and the dead bone, address the soft tissue cover, reconstruct it where possible, and remove the factors that led to its initial breakdown. Recurrence is almost inevitable unless the following action is taken:

- Appropriate wound care;
- Pressure offloading;
- Avoidance of wound contamination with feces or urine; and
- Attention to metabolic, endocrine and nutritional derangements.

Presenting symptoms could include a pressure sore that won't go away, an acute soft tissue infection, or a systemic illness brought on by an increase in activity. Bone destruction is visible on plain films, but it can be challenging to interpret these in the common places (calcaneum, trochanter, ischium, and sacrum). While MRI provides more information about the extent of bone involvement, CT is more reliable in demonstrating bone destruction and will also show associated intra- or extrapelvic abscesses. To identify the causative organisms, a bone biopsy is advised as surface swabs are not a reliable indicator of the deep pathogens...

6.3.3.4. In the Diabetic Foot

Osteomyelitis in the diabetic foot is likely the most common cause of bone infection globally today, given the global epidemic of type 2 diabetes. Despite occasionally being categorized as "osteomyelitis associated with vascular insufficiency," neuropathy is typically the primary etiology. This degrades the protective function and has an impact on foot biomechanics. Ulceration results from repeated, excessive loading on high-pressure areas. Peripheral vascular disease worsens the prognosis in cases of infection, speeds up tissue loss, and sometimes hinders healing.

The distribution of diabetic foot ulceration and associated osteomyelitis is characteristic of the abnormal biomechanics:

- Hyperextension and subluxation at the metatarso-phalangeal joint, with clawing of the toes and exaggeration of the plantar arch, lead to ulcers under the metatarso-phalangeal heads, on the ends of the toes and over the proximal interphalangeal joints.
- Hallux rigidus causes ulcers on the medial side of the interphalangeal joint of the hallux.
- Ischemia leads to ulceration on the lateral border of the fifth metatarsal and over the calcaneus.
- End-stage mid-foot neuroosteoarthropathy results in the collapse of the plantar arch, causing a 'rocker bottom' foot prone to mid-plantar ulceration.

As with decubitus ulcers, the presentation can be indolent or triggered by an acute soft tissue infection. Bacteremia, abscess, necrotizing soft tissue infection or cellulitis can all complicate an ulcer that, if neglected long-term, may cause bone involvement.

Osteomyelitis in the diabetic foot should be suspected when a chronic ulcer:

- remains unhealed after 6–8 weeks of adequate debridement and offloading, provided that it is also adequately perfused.
- is large and deep.
- has bone visible or palpable in its base.
- has bone fragments being expelled from it, or
- has evidence of bone destruction beneath it on plain radiographs.

6.3.3.4.1. Clinical Guidelines

The International Consensus on the Diabetic Foot and the Infectious Diseases Society of America have released two clinical practice guidelines that address diabetic foot infections, including osteomyelitis.

Their advice is the following – when a diabetic patient presents with an infected foot ulcer, a standardized approach should be used to evaluate the patient's vascularity and involvement with infection of the limb and foot, the foot's biomechanics, the perfusion, extent, depth, degree of infection, and sensation related to the ulcer.

- Debridement of the ulcer early

in assessment, as it is not otherwise possible to determine the extent and depth of involvement. This can often be performed by a podiatrist or other trained specialist. The 'probe to bone' test, in which a sterile metal probe is inserted into the ulcer in search of stony-hard palpable bone, is moderately predictive of osteomyelitis if it is positive.

- Infection is categorized as 'mild,' 'moderate,' and 'severe.' The severity helps to determine who should be admitted to the hospital and how broad-spectrum empiric antibiotic therapy should be. For severe infections, do not delay antibiotic therapy and have a high index of suspicion for surgical complications.
- When osteomyelitis is suspected, obtain a bone biopsy if possible, for culture and histology. A biopsy can be performed percutaneously by a radiologist; if surgery is required, the surgeon should discuss the microbiological sampling technique with an infection specialist.
- The duration of antibiotic therapy can be fixed depending on the degree of bony resection or debridement. If residual infected bone remains, prolonged therapy is advised.
- The route of administration of antibiotics is less important than ensuring that high serum levels are obtained. Outpatient intravenous antibiotic therapy programs or the use of highly bioavailable oral antibiotics reduce the need for prolonged hospitalization purely for antimicrobial therapy.

Treatment for pressure sore-related osteomyelitis must include steps to maximize wound healing and reduce the chance of recurrence. Whether or not surgery is performed, this is crucial. Surgery may sometimes worsen the biomechanics of the foot, increasing the risk of recurrent ulcers. However, in a number of retrospective series, 60–80% of cases were eventually resolved with non-surgical wound care and antibiotics, so case selection may be crucial. Regarding diabetic foot osteomyelitis, there is a renewed lack of clarity regarding the relative benefits of surgery versus "conservative" therapy.

6.3.4. Chronic Septic Arthritis

Except in the case of prosthetic joints (see below), chronic septic arthritis is comparatively rare. Acute septic arthritis may be caused by environmental fungi like *Sporothrix schenkii*, *Brucella* spp., TB bacteria, or atypical mycobacteria, in addition to being overlooked or not fully treated (primarily due to *S. aureus* and beta-hemolytic streptococci). A plain X-ray with accelerated changes and extensive synovitis, pain, and crepitus are typically present in patients with chronic monoarthropathy. A long-term infection-related effusion, synovitis, bone alterations, and cartilage loss are all confirmed by MRI.

Some microbiological causes (such as TB) are amenable to prolonged antimicrobial treatment alone, although the joint will generally develop accelerated arthritis. In situations where extensive joint destruction has occurred, joint replacement will probably be required, depending upon progress over time. This can be performed either in a single operation with antibiotic-loaded cement or as a staged procedure, debriding the whole joint in the first stage and implanting the prosthesis in the second procedure once the infection has been treated. Involvement of a specialist in joint reconstruction with appropriate microbiological/infectious diseases support is advised.

6.3.5. Infections of Prosthetic Joints and Other Orthopedic Metalware

These issues can occasionally show up to the doctor as a bacteremia at any point in the joint's lifetime, though they are typically the exclusive domain of the surgeon. If the infection develops later in the implant's life, acute presentations may be accompanied by acute septic arthritis affecting the prosthetic joint or by localized symptoms of an acute wound infection. Most persistent infections manifest as progressive pain from mechanical loosening or sinus tract drainage from the prosthetic joint. Usually, a boil or granuloma in the old surgical incision or drain site is the first sign of sinus tract drainage. The suspicion of deep infection should be raised for any such lesion overlying the structure. Progressive pain that worsens with joint motion and has the feel of "start up" pain until there is a noticeable loosening. Patients frequently complain that the implant has "never felt right," which is a general but surprisingly common complaint.

Prosthesis loosening results in a painful loss of functionality. Loosening of these implants leads to instability and an increased risk of non-union or failed fusion procedures because other orthopedic metalware is used to stabilize fractures or fusion procedures.

6.3.5.1. Treatment

The implant's permanent or temporary function will determine the best course of action. The implant can be removed, and the bone debrided as for chronic osteomyelitis if the condition is transient and the function is fulfilled (for example, the fracture has united). The implant's mechanical condition determines the course of treatment if union or fusion has not yet taken place and the implant is temporary. Retention of the implant can be tried if it is still firmly embedded in the bone, an infection has appeared early, or the patient is not a good candidate for surgery. A microbiological diagnosis is made, the surrounding soft tissue is surgically debrided, and the administration of antibiotics is started. When treating acute infections, a combination of immediate surgery and long-term, culture-directed antibiotics can save the implant in more than half of the cases. Combinations of rifampicin and a fluoroquinolone drug (ciprofloxacin or ofloxacin) appear to be especially effective in treating sensitive staphylococci, the most prevalent pathogen.

These patients, who have been taking antibiotics for a long time, may present to doctors with drug side effects or, more frequently, unrelated medical issues. In this case, stopping the antibiotics without first speaking with a microbiology or infectious disease consultant is advised because stopping the antibiotics can cause recurrence even after a protracted course of treatment.

With or without surgery, implant salvage is rarely successful in cases of well-established infections. Aspiration or biopsy of the joint may provide a false-negative result, but it can also be useful in confirming the diagnosis. Usually, following antibiotic treatment, it is required to remove the infected hardware and replace it, either right away or in a second stage (operation). In certain series, cure rates of 95% have been attained using this method.

A Closer Look

X-Rays of the Extremities

Invisible electromagnetic energy beams are used in X-rays to create images of the surrounding soft tissues and bones. Common uses for standard X-rays include the diagnosis of infections, tumors, foreign bodies, and bone injuries. To create images of the extremity for diagnostic purposes, X-rays are created using external radiation. X-rays travel through bodily structures and land on specially prepared plates, much like film from a camera. It creates a "negative" type image, wherein structures appear whiter on film the more solid they are. Digital media and computers can also be used to create X-rays in place of film.

Different body parts allow different amounts of the X-ray beams to pass through during an X-ray. Depending on how much of the X-rays enter the tissues, different levels of lightness and darkness are produced in the images. The majority of the X-ray can pass through the body's soft tissues, which include blood, skin, fat, and muscle, appearing dark gray on the film. Because they are denser than soft tissues, a bone or tumor shows up as white on an X-ray and lets through less radiation. An X-ray beam appears as a dark line in the white bone when it passes through a break in a bone.

To check for injuries to the bones, X-rays of the arm, leg, hand, foot, ankle, shoulder, knee, hip, or hand may be taken. Broken or fractured bones are included in this. X-rays can also reveal signs of additional diseases or injuries, such as tumors, foreign bodies, tendinitis, arthritis, infection, and birth defects. X-rays can also be used to monitor a child's bone development and growth.

Your healthcare provider may request X-rays of joints to check for abnormalities of the joint such as bone spurs, narrowing of the joint, and changes in the structure of the joint.

There may be other reasons for your healthcare provider to recommend an X-ray of the arms and legs. It might be a good idea to inquire with your healthcare provider about the risks associated with the procedure and the amount of radiation used. To let your providers know, it's a good idea to maintain a record of your radiation exposure, including older scans and other X-ray kinds. Radiation exposure risks could be correlated with the total number of X-ray exams or treatments received over an extended period of time.

Inform your healthcare provider if you are expecting or suspect you may be pregnant. Pregnancy-related radiation exposure has been linked to birth abnormalities. You will receive extra care to reduce the radiation exposure to the fetus if you require an X-ray of your extremities.

There may be other risks depending on your specific medical condition. Be sure to discuss any concerns with your healthcare provider before the procedure.

An X-ray may be done on an outpatient basis or as part of your stay in a hospital. Procedures may vary depending on your condition and your provider's practices.

Generally, an X-ray procedure of the extremities follows this process:

1. You will be asked to remove any clothing, jewelry, hairpins, eyeglasses, hearing aids, or other metal objects that might interfere with the procedure.
2. If you are asked to remove clothing, you will be given a gown to wear.
3. The type of procedure being done will dictate your positioning, such as lying on a table, sitting, or standing, and the type of X-ray equipment used. You will be positioned on an X-ray table that carefully places the part of the body that is to be X-rayed between the X-ray machine and a cassette containing the X-ray film or digital media. Exams in the sitting or standing position are done similarly, with the body part being examined placed between the X-ray machine and the X-ray film or digital media.
4. Body parts not being imaged may be covered with a lead apron (shield) to avoid exposure to the X-rays.
5. The radiologic technologist will ask you to hold the extremity still in a certain position for a few moments while the X-ray exposure is made.
6. If an X-ray is being done to determine an injury, special care will be taken to prevent further injury. For example, a splint or brace may be applied to the leg or arm if a fracture is suspected.
7. Some X-ray studies may require several different positions of the extremity. It is extremely important to remain completely still while the exposure is made, as any movement may distort the image and even require another X-ray to be done to obtain a clear image of the body part in question.
8. The X-ray beam will be focused on the area to be photographed.
9. The radiologic technologist will step behind a protective window while the image is taken.

Even though getting an X-ray doesn't hurt, moving a body part that might be hurt could hurt or cause discomfort. To reduce any pain or discomfort, the radiologic technologist will take all reasonable comfort precautions and work quickly to finish the procedure.

Summary

- Infections of the skin and soft tissues include a wide range of clinical situations and organisms. Many infections arise following a breach of the skin, emphasizing the importance of this natural barrier. Once the skin is compromised, organisms can enter the deeper soft tissue.
- Staphylococci and streptococci are commoner causes of infections of the joints and bone. Haemophilus influenzae b was a common cause of arthritis and osteomyelitis in children under 5 years.
- Skin infections occur when bacteria infect the skin and sometimes the deeper tissues beneath the skin. Cellulitis is a common type of skin infection that causes redness, swelling, and pain in the infected area of skin.
- Regardless of their high frequency, there are limited data on the incidence and fluctuations of common bacterial skin infections such as impetigo, erysipelas or non-necrotizing cellulitis.
- The microbiology of skin and soft-tissue infections also may vary with the means of entrance. Thus, the skin and soft-tissue infections might be normal host flora transferred from the instrument of entry or transferred from the environment.
- Empiric antimicrobial therapy for bacterial skin and skin structure infections is usually initiated (before a microbiological diagnosis is available) with an agent that has excellent antimicrobial activity against the likely pathogen(s).
- Soft tissue infections encompass a spectrum of conditions affecting the non-bony structures of the body, including the skin, muscles, fascia, and subcutaneous tissues. These infections can result from various pathogens, such as bacteria, viruses, fungi, or parasites.
- Infections of the bone are called osteomyelitis. This can be caused by trauma (cutting a finger deeply with a knife), a wound such as a diabetic ulcer deepening down to the level of the bone, or infection from the blood stream lodging into the bone (often is the case with osteomyelitis of the spine or vertebrae).
- Acute septic arthritis and osteomyelitis are usually haematogenous in origin, but in rare cases the former complicates arthrocentesis or arthroscopy.
- Chronic long-bone osteomyelitis is usually preceded by an infected fracture fixation or a complicated acute osteomyelitis. Outside highly specialized units, the physician is likely to be involved in such cases only if medical complications of therapy or comorbidities require management.

References

1. Abrahamian, F. M., Talan, D. A., & Moran, G. J., (2008). Management of skin and soft-tissue infections in the emergency department. *Infectious Disease Clinics of North America, 22*, 89–116.
2. Baker, M., McNicholas, A., Garrett, N., Jones, N., Stewart, J., Koberstein, V., & Lennon, D., (2000). Household crowding a major risk factor for epidemic meningococcal disease in Auckland children. *The Paediatric Infectious Disease Journal, 19*, 983–990.

3. Baroux, N., D'Ortenzio, E., Amédéo, N., Baker, C., Ali Alsuwayyid, B., Dupont-Rouzeyrol, M., O'Connor, O., et al., (2014). The Emm-cluster typing system for group A *Streptococcus* identifies epidemiologic similarities across the Pacific region. *Clinical Infectious Diseases, 59*, 84–92.
4. Blume-Peytavi, U., Kottner, J., Sterry, W., Hodin, M. W., Griffiths, T. W., Watson, R. E., Hay, R. J., & Griffiths, C. E., (2016). Age-associated skin conditions and diseases: Current perspectives and future options. *The Gerontologist, 56*, 230–242.
5. Chang, A. L., Wong, J. W., Endo, J. O., & Norman, R. A., (2013). Geriatric dermatology review: Major changes in skin function in older patients and their contribution to common clinical challenges. *Journal of the American Medical Directors Association, 14*, 724–730. doi: 10.1016/j.jamda.2013.02.014.
6. Chen, W., Thiboutot, D., & Zouboulis, C. C., (2002). Cutaneous androgen metabolism: Basic research and clinical perspectives. *Journal of Investigative Dermatology, 119*, 992–1007.
7. Costerton, J. W., Stewart, P. S., & Greenberg, E. P., (1999). Bacterial biofilms: A common cause of persistent infections. *Review Science, 284*, 1318–1322.
8. Dao, Jr. H., & Kazin, R. A., (2007). Gender differences in skin: A review of the literature. *Gender Medicine, 4*, 308–328.
9. Emmerson, E., Rando, G., Meda, C., Campbell, L., Maggi, A., & Hardman, M. J., (2013). Estrogen receptor mediated signalling in female mice is locally activated in response to wounding. *Molecular and Cellular Endocrinology, 375*, 149–156.
10. Mandal, S., Berendt, A. R., & Peacock, S. J., (2002). *Staphylococcus aureus* bone and joint infection. *Review J. Infect., 44*, 143–151.
11. Stengel, D., Bauwens, K., Sehouli, J., Ekkernkamp, A., & Porzsolt, F., (2001). Systematic review and meta-analysis of antibiotic therapy for bone and joint infections. *Review Lancet Infect. Dis., 1*, 175–188.
12. Vandenesch, F., Naimi, T., Enright, M. C., Lina, G., et al., (2003). Community-acquired methicillin resistant *Staphylococcus aureus* carrying Panton-valentine leukocidin genes: Worldwide emergence. *Emerg. Infect. Dis., 9*, 978–984.
13. Ziran, B. H., Rao, N., & Hall, R. A., (2003). A dedicated team approach enhances outcomes of osteomyelitis treatment. *Clin. Orthop., 414*, 31–36.

Chapter 7

INFECTIONS OF THE CENTRAL NERVOUS SYSTEM

Contents

Unit Introduction

Acute infections of the central nervous system (CNS) are medical emergencies that, if left untreated, can have fatal consequences or cause severe long-term effects that severely impair the affected person's quality of life. A basic understanding of applied neuroanatomy is necessary to completely comprehend the pathogenesis, clinical implications, and management of CNS infections.

The cerebellum and cerebrum of the brain, spinal cord, and covering membranes of the optic nerves comprise the CNS. The inflexible walls of the skull and the spinal canal of the vertebral column shield these structures, and the three continuous layers of protective tissue, known as the meninges, cover the spinal cord and the cerebral cortex, which is the outermost gray tissue layer of the cerebrum. The pia mater is the name for the innermost meningeal layer that directly covers the cerebral cortex. The terms "arachnoid" and "dura mater," respectively, refer to the middle and outermost layers. The dura mater creates a number of intracranial cavities, such as the sinuses that drain veins. Arachnoid villi, which are segments of the arachnoid, protrude into these sinuses. The subarachnoid space is not connected to these two spaces, which carry piercing vessels from and to the brain parenchyma. The subdural space is found between the dura mater and the arachnoid, while the subarachnoid space is found between the pia mater and the arachnoid. The Virchow-Robin spaces, the subpial, the subdural and the subarachnoid spaces are all continuous. The epidural space separates the dura mater and the skull. The subpial and Virchow-Robin spaces are only accessible to some infections. When an infection spreads directly from one adjacent infection to another, it usually stays close to the source of the initial infection in the epidural spaces. Subdural infections can spread widely within the subdural compartment, far from the inciting source, although they are frequently linked to an extracerebral source. Germicidal meningitis frequently results in the development of serous subdural effusions. Most frequently, the hematogenous spread of bacteria or viruses is the cause of subarachnoid infections. The brain's choroid plexuses, located in each of the four ventricles, are constantly producing cerebrospinal fluid (CSF). En route to the fourth ventricle, situated amidst the cerebellum and midbrain, CSF fills the lateral and third ventricles. The CSF drains via the arachnoid villi into the superior sagittal sinus in the dura mater, where it is resorbed into the bloodstream. The CSF flows from the fourth ventricle into the subarachnoid space, where it bathes the WHOLE CNS.

It is also necessary to have a basic understanding of the blood supply to comprehend the pathogenesis of CNS infections. The brain and spinal cord have a special capillary supply because the outermost layers of the endothelium cells are fused together. The blood–brain barrier (BBB), which isolates the brain and meninges from the bloodstream and blocks the entry of germs, toxins, and most other substances, is made up of these specialized brain microvascular endothelial cells. It also controls the flow of vital nutrients and molecules required for normal brain function. Thus, CNS infections can be caused by pathogens that cross the BBB.

Among the reasons for these breaches are harm (e.g., microhemorrhage or necrosis of surrounding tissue) to the barrier; mechanical blockage of microvessels by parasitized red blood cells, leukocytes, or platelets; excessive cytokine production that breaks down tight junction proteins; or interactions between particular microbes and the BBB that enable the microorganism to pass through cells (e.g., mycobacteria, spirochaetes, and *E. coli*). Antimicrobials prescribed for CNS infections need to be able to cross the BBB in order to be effective, which has clear therapeutic implications.

Orientation and Directional Terms

Term	Definition	Illustration
Virchow-Robin spaces	Virchow-Robin spaces are perivascular fluid-filled cavities that surround perforating arteries and veins in the brain parenchyma. As a rule in healthy people, they are approximately 5 mm in diameter. Typical localizations are brainstem ganglia, mesencephalon, and the white matter of the brain.	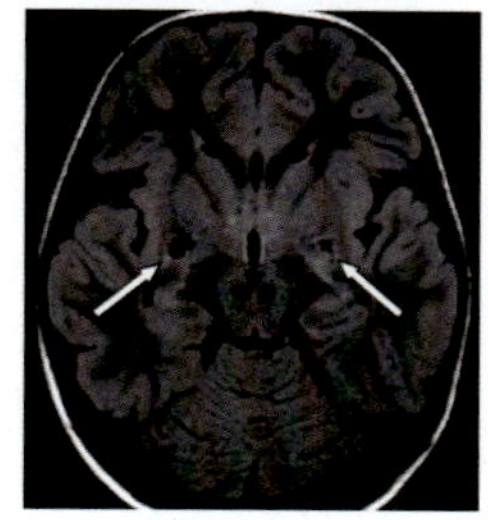
Meningitis	Meningitis is an inflammation (swelling) of the protective membranes covering the brain and spinal cord. A bacterial or viral infection of the fluid surrounding the brain and spinal cord usually causes the swelling.	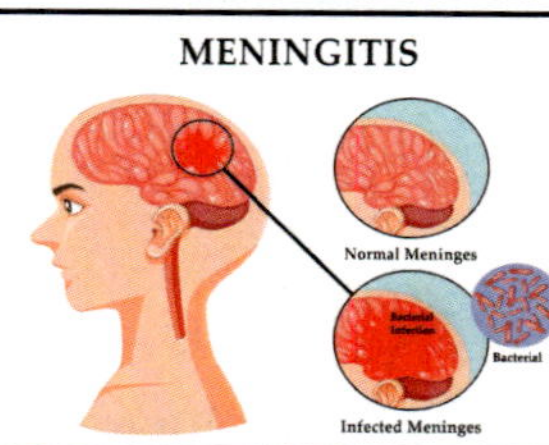
Encephalitis	Encephalitis is inflammation of the brain. Myelitis refers to inflammation of the spinal cord.	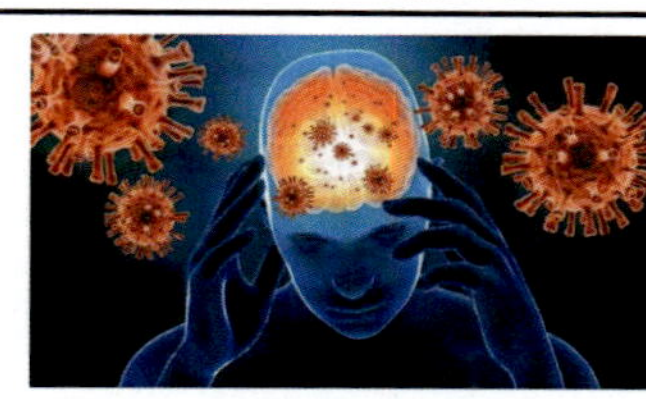
Herpes simplex virus (HSV)	Herpes simplex virus (HSV), known as herpes, is a common infection that can cause painful blisters or ulcers. It primarily spreads by skin-to-skin contact. It is treatable but not curable.	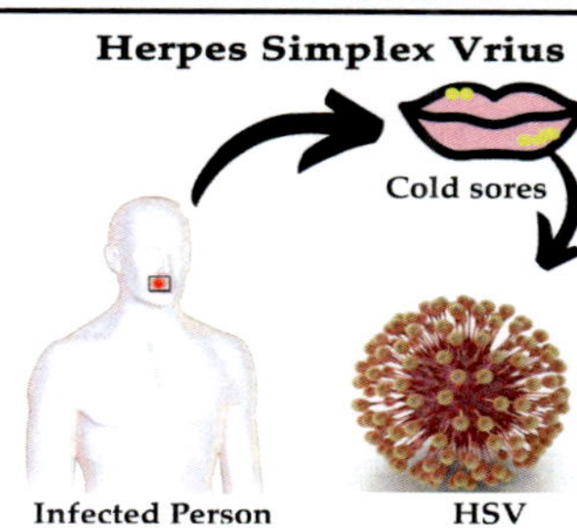
Cystic fibrosis	Cystic fibrosis is a disorder that damages your lungs, digestive tract, and other organs. It's an inherited disease caused by a defective gene that can be passed from generation to generation.	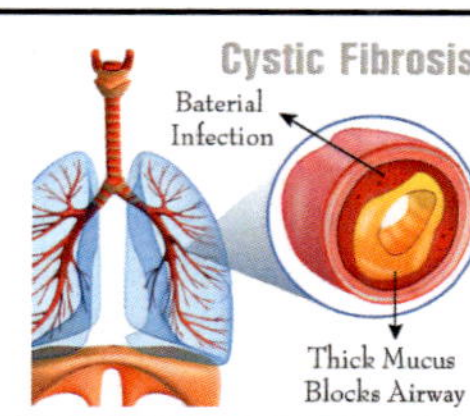
Cervical spondylosis	Cervical spondylosis is a general term for age-related wear and tear affecting the spinal disks in your neck. As the disks dehydrate and shrink, signs of osteoarthritis develop, including bony projections along the edges of bones (bone spurs).	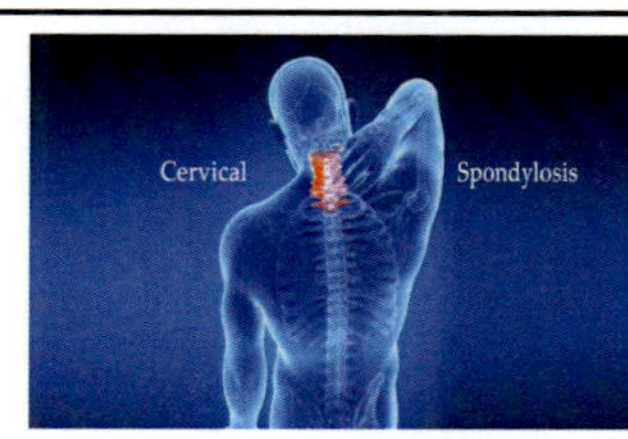

7.1. Routes of Infection

Meningitis, encephalitis, and abscesses are the three main kinds of acute CNS infections, which are typically caused by the blood-borne dissemination of the corresponding microbes. Bacteremia or viremia may arise from primary infections at more distant anatomic locations (e.g., lungs, heart, skin, GI tract, or kidney) or from infection at areas adjacent to or contiguous to the CNS, such as the mastoid, sinuses, or middle ear. The most frequent predisposing factors in children are middle ear or sinus infections, which can cause hematogenous seeding of the CNS and temporary bacteremia.

A common result of bacterial infections in the paranasal and otomastoid sinuses is phlebothrombosis of the nearby draining cortical (cerebral) veins. The dural sinuses in a given area may be affected by this thrombotic period. A direct pathway of transmission from the infected sinus to the surrounding extraaxial spaces or to the brain via cortical venous drainage pathways is provided by the thrombophlebitis that develops from the phlebothrombosis.

It is critical to identify the venous involvement because venous obstruction can cause intraaxial brain swelling, which can mask the extraaxial infection source and lead to inaccurate interpretations of brain and spinal imaging studies. The necessity for the clinician and radiologic imager to be well-versed in both head and neck and paraspinous anatomy is reinforced by the shared relationship between otomastoid and paranasal sinus causes of intracranial infection.

The organism can infect the CSF and spread throughout this anatomic space in patients with bacteremia or viremia if it enters the venous sinuses, crosses the BBB, penetrates the dura and arachnoid, and enters the subarachnoid space. The CNS may become open to the sinuses, mastoid, middle ear, or nasopharynx as a result of fractures at the base of the skull or the cribriform plate. The respiratory flora may be able to track back up into the subarachnoid space if there is a CSF leak at any of these sites because they are all adjacent to the upper respiratory tract.

Intraoperatively, during neurosurgical procedures, extrinsic contamination of the CNS may occur. The presence of additional hardware or implanted medical devices, such as shunts, ventriculostomies, or external drainage tubes, can instigate microbial colonization and act as infection foci. Sinus tracts and spina bifida are examples of congenital abnormalities that can harbor bacteria and act as infection sources. Encephalitis can be caused by viruses that travel through intraneural pathways to the CNS, such as polioviruses, HSV, or rabies.

An infection may occur directly, such as spreading directly into the CNS and causing brain abscesses in adjacent areas (e.g., middle ear or mastoid), or indirectly via venous drainage or the sheaths surrounding the cranial and spinal nerves. Abscesses can additionally localize in the epidural or subdural spaces, and if bacteria move from the abscess directly into the subarachnoid space, the development of meningitis may occyr. Pyogenic meningitis, septic emboli linked to endocarditis, lung abscesses, or other severe purulent infections, like those brought on by the *Streptococcus milleri* group, can all result in CNS abscesses.

7.2. Acute Bacterial Meningitis

Even in children or adults who have been healthy in the past, bacterial meningitis, a dangerous brain infection, can spread quickly and become fatal. Although the BBB acts as a protective barrier, it can be breached by bacteria which further reach the brain through the circulation and cause meningitis. The definition of bacterial meningitis is an inflammatory reaction to pyogenic bacterial invasion of the pia mater, arachnoid membranes, and the area around the CNS. Due to the continuity of the subarachnoid space, this infection usually affects the entire length of the neuraxis, including the brain (cerebrum, cerebellum), spinal cord, optic nerves, and the membranes that cover them. A noticeable, acute inflammatory exudate is connected to pyogenic meningitis; non-pyogenic microorganisms (e.g., such as Leptospira species of spirochetes or mycobacteria) are not frequently connected. Acute symptoms such as headache, fever, irritability, and stiff neck may appear within hours or days, along with or without focal neurological signs. Despite a declining overall yearly incidence in the US, untreated cases of pyogenic bacterial meningitis are always fatal.

7.2.1. Epidemiology

In the US, *Streptococcus pneumoniae*, *Neisseria meningitidis*, and group B *Streptococcus* spp. are the most common causes of bacterial meningitis, with a small percentage caused by microorganisms such as *Haemophilus influenzae*, and *Listeria monocytogenes*. These agents together account for more than 95% of cases. Table 7.1 and Figure 7.1 summarize the age distribution, predisposing conditions, and fatality rates for the most common agents.

Table 7.1. *Causes of Bacterial Meningitis and Overall Case Fatality Rate According to Organism*

Organism	Percentage of Total Cases	Incidence	Predisposing Conditions	Case Fatality Rate (%)
Streptococcus pneumoniae	47	1.1	Otitis media; sinusitis; alcoholism; cirrhosis; pneumococcal pneumonia; immunosuppression; skull fracture; CSF leak; myeloma; sickle cell disease.	21
Neisseria meningitidis	25	0.6	"Closed" institutional setting; lack of specific antibody; complement deficiencies.	3
Group B *Streptococcus*	12	0.3	Neonatal period; colonized mothers; preterm labor; prolonged rupture of membranes; intrapartum fever	7
Listeria monocytogenes	8	0.2	Neonatal period; immunosuppression; age; alcoholism/cirrhosis.	15
Haemophilus influenzae	7	0.2	Lack of antibody to polysaccharide capsule; preceding otitis media.	6

Source: https://www.ncbi.nlm.nih.gov/pmc/articles/PMC7122753/.

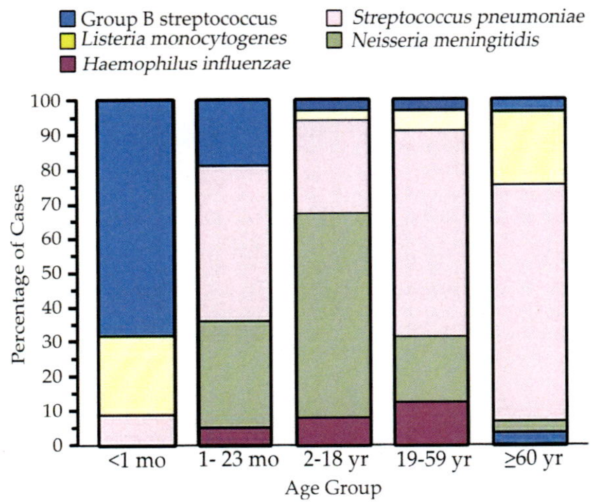

Figure 7.1. *Pathogenic agents of bacterial meningitis according to age group, Brazil, 2007–2019.*

Source: Parellada, C. I., Abreu, A. D. J. L. D, Birck, M. G., Dias, C. Z., Moreira, T. D. N. F., Julian, G. S., Batista, P. D. M., Orengo, J. C., & Bierrenbach, A. L., (2023). Trends in pneumococcal and bacterial meningitis in Brazil from 2007 to 2019. Vaccines, 11(8), 1279. https://doi.org/10.3390/vaccines11081279.

7.2.1.1. Streptococcus Pneumonia

The three main microbial species (*S. pneumoniae*, *N. meningitidis*, and *H. influenzae*) are the most frequent cause of community-associated meningitis in the US, and it affects people of all ages with the exception of newborns, who are still in the early stages of the neonatal period. Pneumococcal meningitis varies in risk with age, but it is much more common in infants than in adults and young children. The incidence increases once more to roughly double the average incidence for young and middle-aged adults over the age of 70.

Adults who have undergone splenectomy, alcoholism, HIV infection, other conditions related to acquired immunodeficiency, diabetes, and other underlying chronic conditions (e.g., a history of viral respiratory infection, chronic renal disease). Patients with CSF leaks are most frequently recurrently affected by pneumococcal meningitis. The nasopharynx becomes colonized by *S. pneumoniae*, which is typically found in 5–10% of healthy adults and is transmitted by respiratory contact in the general population. In certain populations, depending on age and other factors, carriage rates can increase to 20%–30% during the winter. In many cases, the transmission is linked to overcrowding in prisons, day care centers, and military barracks.

7.2.1.2. N. meningitidis

The mucosal surface of the nasopharynx is colonized by this gram-negative, and aerobic diplococcus. The primary method of transmission involves direct contact with respiratory secretions in the form of large droplets from patients or carriers who do not exhibit any symptoms with humans being the sole hosts. Three clinical manifestations of the invasive disease caused by this organism are meningitis (which accounts for 50% of cases), blood infections (30%), and pneumonia (10%). The remaining 10% of cases are caused by other factors. At least 10 times higher in less developed nations, *N. meningitidis* is estimated to cause 0–1 cases of bacterial meningitis per 100,000 people annually, making it the primary cause of bacterial meningitis in the United States. People who are at risk include those who live in the same home as infected patients, recruits for the armed forces, first-year college students living in dorms, and microbiologists who handle *N. meningitidis* isolates, people travelling to a nation where meningococcal disease is highly endemic or epidemic, individuals lacking a spleen, and those suffering from terminal complement component deficiencies. While infections can strike people of any age, including the elderly, the rates of disease are higher in infants under one year old and adolescents between the ages of 16 and 21.

Strains of *N. meningitidis* are characterized according to the serologic recognition of polysaccharide epitopes on their capsule and outer membrane and are classified into serogroups A, B, C, W135, and Y. In the US, strains from serogroups B, C, and Y cause the majority (45%) of infections, whereas in less-developed countries serogroups A and C predominate; serogroup A has also been implicated in epidemics in sub-Saharan Africa.

7.2.1.3. H. influenzae

Based on capsular polysaccharides a–f, six serologically distinct antigenic types are used to classify this small, pleomorphic, aerobic or facultative anaerobic gram-negative coccobacilli. Out of these, only *H. influenzae* type B (Hib) is pathogenic. In its nonencapsulated form, *H. influenzae* causes localized infection (e.g., fever) and is a common resident of healthy people's upper respiratory tract, e.g., without bacteremia, the more virulent encapsulated Hib serotype causes more invasive disease and is a major cause of meningitis or epiglottitis (conjunctivitis or otitis media in children).

The occurrence of passively transferred maternal antibodies is likely the reason why hepatitis B is comparatively rare in the first two months of life. Children, however, lose these antibodies by the fourth month of life and are then susceptible to Hib meningitis. The development of anticapsular antibodies specific to polyribosylribitol phosphate is directly linked to *H. influenzae* meningitis. Antibodies linked to protection against invasive H, whether generated by a vaccine or developing spontaneously, are positively correlated with their presence influenzae sickness.

Various clinical studies have shown these antibodies to be opsonic and bactericidal against *H. influenzae* in vitro and protective in vivo. In the pre-vaccine era, colonization with nontypable strains of *H. influenzae* led to the development of cross-reacting antibodies that were largely protective against infection caused by type b strains. Before the introduction of the Hib conjugate polysaccharide capsular vaccine in 1986, *H. influenzae* was the most common cause of acute bacterial meningitis in children under the age of 5, with as many as 1 in 200 children acquiring invasive *H. influenzae* infection, including epiglottitis, septicemia, arthritis, and soft tissue infections in addition to meningitis. However, by 1995, the prevalence of meningitis caused by Hib had fallen to 55%. Risk factors for Hib meningitis include malignancy, chronic renal disease, sickle cell disease, immunoglobulin dyscrasias, HIV infections, and cystic fibrosis.

7.2.1.4. Listeria Monocytogenes

This gram-positive, facultatively anaerobic, and intracellular bacillus is still a major cause of neonatal meningitis in the US. While fecal-oral transmission is the typical mode of transmission to humans, in mothers who had asymptomatic colonization of the GI tract or genitalia prior to delivery, the pathogen typically passes from mother to child at the time of birth.

The primary sources of *L. monocytogenes* are domestic and wild animals, although humans continue to be a tiny but important reservoir, the prevalence of this organism's stool carriage among asymptomatic adults is only around 1%.

Generally, healthy adults exposed to the organism do not become ill, unless exposed to high numbers of infectious organisms, such as during an outbreak. *L. monocytogenes* causes meningitis most often in adults with depressed cell-mediated immunity, patients on steroids or other immunosuppressive agents, HIV-infected individuals, transplant recipients, and other vulnerable populations, such as persons with diabetes, alcohol abuse, chronic liver disease, renal disease requiring hemodialysis, or persons greater than 60 years of age. Outbreaks of *L. monocytogenes* meningitis in the US and other places have been associated with unpasteurized milk products, such as Swiss or feta cheese, undercooked chicken or hot dogs, seafood, vegetables, or coleslaw.

7.2.1.5. Other Microorganisms

Gram-negative microorganisms play a significant role in the development of acute bacterial meningitis. Individuals with diabetes, a history of alcohol abuse, hepatic cirrhosis, or chronic UTIs are particularly vulnerable to this condition. In newborns, *E. coli* featuring the K1 capsular polysaccharide antigen is the primary culprit for gram-negative meningitis. The prevalence of *E. coli* K1 serotypes varies among different populations, ranging from 7 to 38% in women of childbearing age and possibly reaching 50% in nursing personnel.

In a study involving 231 children presenting with bacterial meningitis at the emergency department during the period of widespread heptavalent conjugate pneumococcal vaccination, *E. coli* was identified in 4% of cases, while other gram-negative bacilli were implicated in 3%. Additional gram-negative organisms, including *Klebsiella* spp., *Enterobacter* spp., *Pseudomonas* spp., *Citrobacter* spp., and *Salmonella* spp., can also cause meningitis in the neonatal period, sharing a similar epidemiology with *E. coli* K1 strains. Notably, gram-negative bacillary meningitis continues to have a poorer prognosis compared to meningitis caused by gram-positive organisms.

Beyond the neonatal period, most gram-negative meningitis cases occur in the inpatient setting, especially following neurosurgical procedures like craniotomy and during the placement of devices such as ventriculostomy tubes. Additionally, patients who have experienced head trauma are at an increased risk of developing gram-negative meningitis.

The most common cause of neonatal meningitis is Group B *streptococcus* (*Streptococcus agalactiae*). Around 30% to 40% of women's vaginal secretions before giving birth have been cultured and identified as this organism. The microbe can enter amniotic fluid during pregnancy, labor, and delivery, or for the newborn to get colonized as it goes through the birth canal.

Neonatal meningitis can develop during the first week of life if the baby contracts the virus during delivery. Alternatively, even though the baby may have looked healthy at delivery, the organism may be acquired from adult contacts—relatives or hospital staff—during the first few days after birth, and meningitis may manifest during the first 1–2 months following birth.

About 50% of neonates delivered vaginally have a chance of contracting invasive group B streptococcal disease from mothers who have colonized with *S. agalactiae*; however, only 2% of colonized neonates go on to develop this disease. Types Ia through VIII are the nine antigenic serotypes that are manifested in polysaccharide capsules produced by Group B streptococci. A large proportion of neonatal meningitis cases are caused by the type III group; virulence factors (e.g., an explanation for this has been proposed to be those that result in increased levels of neuraminidase production.

7.2.2. Pathogenesis of Meningeal Invasion

The colonization of the nasopharynx or respiratory tract is a crucial prelude to infection by any of the three microorganisms (*S. pneumoniae*, *N. meningitides* and *H. influenzae*) that are most frequently linked to meningitis contracted in the community. The nasopharyngeal mucosa is the biological medium through which these organisms facilitate colonization.

Microorganisms can replicate in the upper airway for extended periods of time owing to their attachment and adherence to cell surface receptors on nasopharyngeal epithelial cells, which facilitates colonization. Usually, none of the three microbial infections will cause symptoms when they colonize the upper respiratory tract. Host vulnerability and pathogen-specific elements (e.g., virulence and pathogenicity) are essential for the growth of invasive illnesses. Many of these factors are however still unclear, although though they have been recognized and described.

For instance, a splenectomy unquestionably puts the patient at risk for infection with *S. pneumoniae*, although it seems to have minimal impact on the incidence of invasive meningitidis disease even as an encapsulated organism. Adherence to nasopharyngeal mucosa is mediated by fimbriae or pili, in the case of gram-negative organisms. The pili of *N. meningitidis* are filamentous glycoproteins attached to the bacterial surface, traverse the polysaccharide capsule, and extend beyond the surface of the bacterium, where they can bind to specific receptors on nasopharyngeal cells, in this instance the CD4+ receptor. After receptor binding, further interaction with the host cell is established by certain outer membrane proteins on *N. meningitidis*, designated Opa and Opc. The binding of the outer membrane proteins to specific receptors promotes engulfment of the *N. meningitidis* by the epithelial cells followed by transportation of the bacteria across the cell in membrane-bound vacuoles to the intravascular space. Microorganisms also gain access to the intravascular space by creating separations in the tight junctions of columnar epithelial cells. *N. meningitidis* possess additional outer membrane proteins that function as IgA proteases, that can specifically degrade the surface IgA antibodies on epithelial cells, and further enhancing the probability of invasive disease. Once the mucosal barrier has been breached, the development of meningococcal disease is dependent upon the survival of the organism in the bloodstream.

Here, the polysaccharide capsule that shields the organism from complement-mediated phagocytosis by neutrophils in the reticular endothelium system is the most significant virulence factor for meningococci survival. The humoral antibodies that are currently present against specific polysaccharide capsular types and the innate immune system's cellular responses clearly dictate the host's defense. Protective IgG antibody for meningococcal disease is acquired through maternal transmission and is protective for the first few months after birth. The colonization by nonpathogenic Neisseria species and a possibly cross-reacting gram-negative organism such as *E. coli* K1 induces protective antibodies. Antibodies protect by promoting the optimization of phagocytosis through opsonization and specific lysis via complement activation. For this reason, patients who are deficient in complement factor C5 are particularly susceptible to repeated invasive infections by *N. meningitidis*. In fact, individuals with an inherited deficiency of any of the terminal components of complement C5, C6, C7, and C8 have a greater risk of invasive disease.

The type of capsular polysaccharide appears

to play a major role in virulence factors for *S. pneumoniae* invasion. It is known that *S. pneumoniae* has at least 93 capsular serotypes, and each serotype has a distinct tendency to cause illness or become resistant to antibiotics.

7.2.3. Clinical Manifestations

Although varied degrees of altered consciousness may be present, fever, headache, and stiff neck are the most common clinical presentations of meningitis in adults. Vomiting is a common symptom that is typically linked to elevated intracranial pressure (ICP), but it is also a well-known indication of the impact of the inflammatory process on the midbrain.

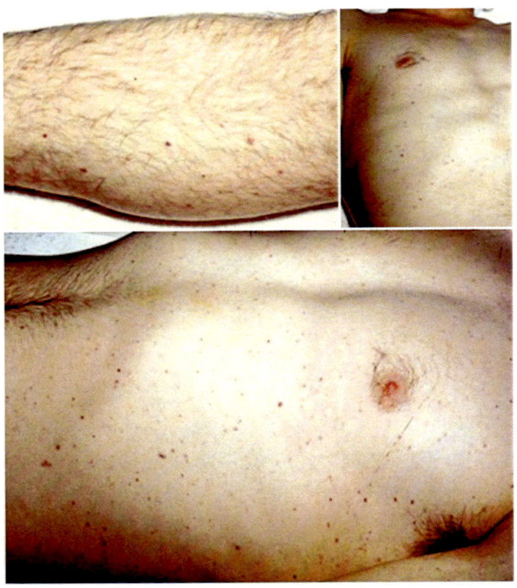

Figure 7.2. *Petechial rash associated with meningococcal meningitis.*

Source: https://www.ncbi.nlm.nih.gov/pmc/articles/PMC7122753/pdf/978-1-4471-5226-2_Chapter_22.pdf.

The underlying microorganism causing the infection determines how meningitis presents itself. For example, in pneumococcal meningitis (*S. pneumoniae* is the most common etiologic agent implicated in adult bacterial meningitis cases), the patient might have had pneumonia and bloodstream dissemination before progression to meningitis. Thus, the patient might have presented with chills and rigors or symptoms of upper respiratory tract infection, bronchitis, or pneumonia several days before the actual onset of meningitis symptoms.

Approximately 27% of patients in the cited series by Carpenter and Petersdorf experienced a sudden onset of headache, disorientation, fatigue, and altered consciousness in the 24 hours prior to hospital admission. In comparison, 53% of patients showed signs of a slower-moving course that persisted for one to seven days.

The patient may have a mild petechial rash early in meningococcemia, which is followed by fulminant disseminated intravascular coagulation (DIC) and a more severe, prodigious purpuric rash that eventually results in necrosis of the fingers and toes. Waterhouse-Friderichsen syndrome, or hemorrhagic necrosis of the adrenal gland, is traditionally linked to purpura fulminans in meningococcemia patients. Therefore, the severity of meningitis and the relative levels of meningococcemia and shock determine the clinical manifestation of meningococcal meningitis (Figure 7.2).

It is crucial to understand that, in contrast to young adults and children, meningitis may present more subtly or insidiously in the elderly and very young children. For instance, Gorse and colleagues reviewed 54 cases and discovered that, in comparison to the younger age group, the elderly presented with confusion more frequently as a symptom, and that the elderly also had a higher likelihood of pneumonia. The elderly are also less likely to report typical symptoms and signs because they frequently have cervical rigidity from osteoarthritis, cervical spondylosis, or pre-existing cerebrovascular disease. In addition, disorders such as Parkinson's disease may cause hypertonicity of the neck muscles. Compared to younger patient populations, meningitis in the elderly may progress more quickly and patients are more likely to present in a coma. The degree of nuchal rigidity may significantly decrease as the coma progresses. Therefore, a thorough physical examination is necessary to differentiate between true nuchal rigidity and meningitis in elderly patients. In the case of an elderly patient, meningitis diagnosis is not ruled out in the absence of fever.

Meningitis in children presents essentially the same as in young and middle-aged adults, except for nonspecific symptoms like irritability, nausea and vomiting, respiratory symptoms, and photophobia, which are more common in younger patients. Fevers and irritability are the most common symptoms of meningitis in newborns and infants; fever is typically higher in children than in adults. The physical indicators of meningeal inflammation or irritation that are commonly seen in medical textbooks are the Kernig's and Brudzinski's signs. The most well-known of these signs of meningeal inflammation is the so-called "nape of the neck" sign, also known as the classic Brudzinski's sign, though Brudzinski originally described several others. Flexing the neck forward produces this sign. The hips and knees flex involuntarily as a result of the meninges being stretched by this movement.

A supine position with the patient's thigh flexed on the abdomen and their knee bent at a 45° angle is required to elicit Kernig's sign. The patient complains of lower back and hamstring pain when the leg is passively extended when meningeal irritation is present. Of those with acute bacterial meningitis, only approximately 50% of children and 5% of adults may exhibit Kernig's and Brudzinski's signs, which are neither sensitive nor specific meningitis markers.

7.2.4. Diagnosis

Acute CNS infection is a medical emergency, and it may be necessary to distinguish between bacterial meningitis and other conditions that affect the CNS, such as encephalitis, brain abscess, subdural empyema, and aseptic meningitis. It can be challenging to distinguish from encephalitis, and the initial diagnosis is based on clinical factors. The traditional signs and symptoms of meningitis, such as headache, stiff neck, photophobia, fever, and vomiting, are frequently absent in elderly people, immunocompromised patients, or newborns.

The most common symptoms of encephalitis include altered consciousness, disorientation, convulsions, and obtundation. Differentiating between meningitis and encephalitis may become difficult as patients' consciousness decreases, and only laboratory and radiographic results may be able to make this determination. Acute bacterial meningitis should be treated on a clinical basis without waiting for laboratory or radiographic studies to confirm the diagnosis as it is a medical emergency.

In addition to non-infectious conditions, many systemic infections can cause fever and altered mental status, including meningismus. For instance, it's important to distinguish the petechial rash that accompanies early meningococcemia from the fever, shock, and other symptoms that can accompany Rocky Mountain spotted fever (RMSF).

At first, meningococcal disease may simply manifest as shock and skin rash associated with meningococcemia, with little to no meningeal signs. Infections such as brain abscess, influenza, leptospirosis, dengue, typhoid, parameningeal infections, or Q fever can also cause fever and headache.

Organic disorders that are not contagious, like subarachnoid hemorrhage, acute hemorrhagic or ischemic strokes, cerebral venous sinus thrombosis, and autoimmune disorders (e.g., abrupt presentation with severe headache, fever, or nuchal rigidity) can occur in some neuroleptic malignant syndromes, temporal arteritis, status epilepticus, and toxic encephalopathies of different causes.

7.2.5. Lumbar Puncture and CSF Analysis

Meningitis and other CNS-affecting conditions can be diagnosed more easily with a lumbar puncture and CSF analysis. However, the presence of elevated ICP precludes performing a lumbar puncture on a patient who presents with meningitis because it increases the risk of uncal, midbrain, medullary, or cerebellar tonsillar herniation following the procedure, which could result in irreversible brain damage or even death.

About 5% of patients with acute bacterial meningitis experience cerebral herniation, which accounts for 30% of the fatalities. It should be noted that a CT scan cannot rule out the presence of elevated ICP as its primary function is to determine if a space-occupying lesion is present. A very recent seizure, diminished consciousness, absence of oculocephalic reflexes, papilledema, and brainstem signs (such as pupillary changes, decorticate posturing, or irregular respirations) are among the clinical indicators that point to an imminent herniation.

Even in those with a normal CT scan, lumbar puncture should be postponed in these patients until interventions to lower ICP can be put in place. Some conditions that preclude an immediate lumbar puncture include hemodynamic or septic shock, cardiorespiratory failure, and the existence of factors that increase the risk of parameningeal abscesses (e.g., as suppurative lung disease, sinusitis, persistent ear discharge, hemorrhagic stroke, and skin loss or infection such as scorches) across the lower back.

Blood cultures should be taken as soon as possible, and intravenous antibiotic therapy should be started right away if the patient's clinical picture points to bacterial meningitis or another intracranial infection, and they are in critical condition—especially if they have a rash or altered mental status. Antimicrobial therapy can be delayed until radiographic studies and a lumbar puncture can be completed if the patient is not critically ill.

If elevated ICP is suspected and radiographic studies do not define focal lesions, an intravenous mannitol infusion (1 g/kg body weight) to reduce cerebral edema and a lumbar puncture after a 20-minute interval may be considered. Prior to the lumbar puncture procedure, the patient may also undergo elective intubation and mechanical ventilation in addition to mannitol infusion. A lumbar puncture can be done in these circumstances with a 22-gauge needle and if a noticeably lower risk of herniation is observed.

The patient should be measured while supine following needle insertion to determine the opening CSF pressure. Once a child reaches the age of 18, the normal opening pressure increases to 1 to 10 cm H_2O, and in obese patients, it can reach up to 25 cm H_2O. The Valsalva maneuver may be used to raise the level, which should change with breathing.

A complete CSF block should be taken into consideration if, at the conclusion of the procedure, the CSF pressure is measured once more after the appropriate volumes of CSF have been obtained and have dropped to zero. Similar to a fine gin, CSF is often colorless and crystal clear. To add turbidity to the fluid, the white blood cell or red blood cell count must be at least 200/mm^3. If there are more than 6,000 red blood cells/mm^3 in the CSF, it will appear reddish. Xanthochromia is a yellow, orange, or pink discoloration of the CSF and is caused by the lysis of red blood cells resulting in hemoglobin breakdown to oxyhemoglobin, methemoglobin, and bilirubin. Discoloration begins after RBCs have been in spinal fluid for about 2 h. In cases of subarachnoid hemorrhage, xanthochromia occurs within 2–4 h after the initial cerebral bleed; xanthochromia may develop *in vitro* if the CSF specimen contains increased numbers of red blood cells and is not centrifuged immediately upon arrival in the laboratory. Xanthochromia also occurs when CSF protein concentrations are greater than 150 mg/dL. The macroscopic appearance of CSF only enables a diagnostic path for purulent versus aseptic meningitis; however, appearance alone is not sufficient to make a specific diagnosis of bacterial or viral meningitis.

Typically, normal CSF has fewer than 5 white cells/mm^3 in adults and children older than the neonatal age group. These white cells are typically small lymphocytes. After a few days, the range of 8–9 white cells/mm^3 is observed in neonates, from up to 25–30 white cells/mm^3 and up to 60% neutrophils. It's crucial to monitor whether reddish or bloody CSF clears up as more specimen tubes of CSF are taken because red blood cells can end up in spinal fluid from traumatizing taps or subarachnoid hemorrhage. A traumatic tap may be suggested by such clearing, which can be verified in a lab setting by counting the red blood cells in successive tubes. Within one to two hours of collection, CSF cells should be counted in the lab. Any longer wait times could lead to a falsely low cell count due to cell lysis or adherence of the cells to the specimen tube walls.

Through the capillary endothelium in the subarachnoid space and the choroid plexus, glucose is transported into the CSF. Therefore, the rate at which glucose is consumed within the brain as well as the active transport of glucose into the brain determine the CSF glucose levels. In normal subjects, CSF glucose levels typically correspond to between 60% and 70% of blood glucose levels. However, a study by Skipper and Davis revealed that when the serum glucose level was between 89 and 115 mg/dL, the CSF to serum glucose ratio was accurate. The ratio was less than 60% for blood glucose levels over 125 mg/dL, and even in healthy individuals without meningitis symptoms, the ratio dropped to 50% for blood glucose levels over 192 mg/dL.

The BBB keeps larger proteins out, which is why CSF protein levels are typically less than 40 mg/dL. CSF protein levels tend to rise and increase with disease duration prior to starting therapy when the barrier breaks down during meningitis. The average protein level in a newborn baby is 90 mg/dL, with normal levels up to 170 mg/dL, significantly higher than in older children and adults. An indication of a CSF spinal block is very high CSF protein levels (greater than 1 g/dL). Nevertheless, an increase in CSF protein does not identify any particular kind of meningitis on its own.

7.2.6. Clinical Manifestations

In addition to varying degrees of nonspecific symptoms like malaise, myalgia, nausea, vomiting, abdominal pain, or diarrhea, viral meningitis is an acute illness marked by fever, headache, stiff neck, photophobia, and abdominal pain. Usually speaking, viral meningitis is not characterized by abnormal neurological symptoms or mental status disruption. A diagnosis of encephalitis or meningoencephalitis should be made if there are any localized neurologic symptoms, obtundation, disorientation, seizures, or other brain parenchymal involvement. If meningitis is caused by bacteria, neck stiffness is usually less severe.

Pneumonia, pleuropericarditis, viral exanthem, painful oropharyngeal ulcers, and peripheral vesicular lesions indicative of hand, foot, and mouth disease are among the clinical indicators of an enteroviral etiology. Within the first 24 to 48 hours, polymorphonuclear leukocytes may predominate in the CSF of patients with viral meningitis; however, this number rarely exceeds 80% of total CSF white cells. Patients with viral meningitis typically have clear CSF with an elevated white cell count. About 10%–15% of mumps patients and less frequently those with enterovirus or HSV infection have generally mildly elevated CSF protein, while glucose levels are typically normal.

When meningitis is caused by viruses, routine CSF cultures do not produce bacterial growth and the CSF gram stain will be negative. To ascertain whether there has been a shift towards a lymphocytic predominance, as one would expect in viral meningitis, clinicians frequently repeat lumbar punctures over the course of the next 12 to 24 hours after the initial CSF analysis reveals more than 50% polymorphonuclear leukocytes.

An infectious parameningeal condition (e.g., brain abscess) will typically show signs of normal glucose, normal CSF pleocytosis, and possibly elevated protein. Therefore, mild headache, fever, and a CSF picture identical to viral meningitis could be presented by a patient with an epidural abscess or a brain abscess. CSF pleocytosis may be present in certain frontal sinusitis or sphenoid cases. In general, the clinical course of fungal and tuberculous meningitis is longer than that of acute viral meningitis, though patients may also present with headache, fever, and stiff neck. Less than 40 mg/dL of glucose is typically present in the CSF of patients suffering from fungal or tuberculous meningitis.

Patients who have meningitis caused by cryptococcal bacteria may have completely normal CSF. Other infections like syphilis and ehrlichiosis, as well as non-infectious diseases like sarcoidosis, Behcet's disease, systemic lupus erythematosus, vasculitis, or uveoparotitis, can also cause fever, headaches, and nonspecific CSF findings.

Aseptic meningitis can also be caused by viruses other than enteroviruses. HSV type II, for instance, causes very typical aseptic meningitis as part of primary genital herpes infection, complete with low-grade fever, headache, stiff neck, and photophobia. It is crucial, therefore, to inquire about any history of genital herpes lesions from the sexually active patient and, if necessary, to perform a pelvic examination on female patients. Aseptic meningitis may also be considered a component of the primary HIV infection syndrome. Some leptospirosis strains usually cause aseptic meningitis as their initial symptom; however, most cases also show signs of systemic illness and severe involvement of other organs like the kidney, liver, and lung.

Globally distributed, the Lymphocytic Choriomeningitis Virus (LCMV) is a member of the Arenavirus family. Rodent exposure, including that of hamsters, guinea pigs, and common house mice (*Mus musculus* and *Mus domesticus*), is commonly linked to LCMV meningitis. Excreta or blood from infected rodents can be directly touched, inhaled (both aerosol and droplet), or transferred by fomites. The symptoms, which include fever, chills, myalgia, headache, photophobia, anorexia, pharyngitis, and cough, are non-specific and take 1–2 weeks to manifest. Few patients experience CNS invasion following an initial febrile illness.

Patients develop peripheral leukocytosis and aseptic meningitis during the neurologic phase. Low glucose levels and leukocyte counts exceeding 1,000 cells/μL are common in CSF. Transverse myelitis, encephalitis, and ascending paralysis are all possible co-occurring conditions with LCMV meningitis, while the overall case fatality rate is less than 1%. For viral meningitis, a laboratory diagnosis of exclusion is typically made, and diagnostic tests performed include CSF viral cultures that produce enterovirus growth. However, a positive result is obtained about 30% to 50% of the time. Enteroviral meningitis can now be diagnosed with PCR, and the results of viral culture closely match these PCR platforms. Unfortunately, there are many reasons why clinical microbiology laboratories might not regularly offer PCR testing, such as staff shortages and cost-cutting measures. Another option is to send specimens to highly specialized research laboratories or reference laboratories, but results are typically unavailable while the patient is still experiencing acute symptoms. If HSV is grown from CSF or found by PCR, the diagnosis of HSV meningitis is verified. Standard serologic testing routinely offered at state public health laboratories or reference laboratories can confirm the diagnosis of aseptic meningitis linked to systemic infections, such as leptospirosis, syphilis, or ehrlichiosis.

Testing is only feasible for a subset of the more than 75 distinct enterovirus serotypes. Moreover, there is significant overlap in the serologic response among the various serotypes, allowing for the possibility of seroconversion to one or more enterovirus serotypes. Furthermore, costly laboratory testing is unlikely to have an impact on the course of treatment because there is no specific treatment. For these reasons, serologic testing is typically not recommended for the diagnosis of enterovirus infections.

Acyclovir has been shown to be effective in improving patient outcomes, making the diagnosis of HSV encephalitis crucial. Spontaneous encephalitis is most frequently caused by HSV, and individuals diagnosed with HSV type I encephalitis typically arrive with a fever, headache, and focal symptoms, such as dysphasia and personality changes that could develop into obtundation and coma. The latter condition can happen suddenly and is linked to the start of seizures. From infancy to old age, HSV encephalitis can strike at any time of year in any age group—i.e., the occurrence does not follow a typical seasonal variation pattern. HSV encephalitis accounts for roughly 10–20% of viral encephalitides in the US, and the incidence is estimated at 1 in 250,000 to 1 in 500,000 persons annually.

MRI results demonstrating bilateral, usually asymmetrical involvement of the temporal lobes are consistent with an HSV encephalitis diagnosis. When HSV encephalitis occurs, frontotemporal changes may be seen on CT imaging. If left untreated, this can worsen and develop into hemorrhagic lesions. Swelling of the temporal lobe that is more severely affected could cause a mass effect resulting in the midline structures to shift and the development of a tentorial herniation. Even though the virus cannot be grown from CSF or patient specimens from other anatomic sites in 1–4% of cases, PCR for HSV in the spinal fluid is nearly always positive in patients with HSV encephalitis.

The gold standard for diagnosing and tracking the course of treatment for adult patients with HSV encephalitis is currently the use of PCR in conjunction with the identification of a particular intrathecal antibody response to HSV. Although all patients with HSV encephalitis will typically exhibit a marked increase in HSV titer in both the spinal fluid and serum, serologic diagnosis is not very helpful in the early stages; seroconversion can be determined in patients with primary HSV infection. Focused features may be found in EEG studies.

Disorders such as brain abscess, subdural empyema, and Listeria-related cerebritis can all resemble encephalitis. Mycoplasma, rickettsia, mucor, fungal infections, tuberculosis, cryptococcus, and toxoplasmosis are commonly linked to bacterial meningitis, like pneumococcus and meningococcus. During epidemics, the influenza A virus can cause encephalitis, and children are especially vulnerable. The symptoms and indicators of encephalitis can be mimicked by tumors, subdural hematomas, CNS lupus, adrenal leukodystrophy, acute strokes, neuroleptic malignant syndrome, or Reye's syndrome.

Encephalitis may manifest as a result of systemic infection caused by common viruses that typically do not lead to encephalitis. For instance, an Epstein-Barr virus (EBV) infection may occasionally exhibit symptoms such as seizures and even coma, with most patients fully recovering. In individuals with HIV, CNS complications from toxoplasmosis, lymphoma, varicella-zoster virus (VZV), and cytomegalovirus (CMV) can mimic encephalitis characteristics.

Even though it is uncommon, rabies should be taken into consideration in encephalitis cases that are unusual or when all tests come up negative. It is important to look for a history of close contact with potentially infected animals, such as bats, as affected patients frequently do not have a history of animal bites. Most infections result from an injection, though they can also sometimes be inhaled. Solid organ allografts and corneal transplants have been known to transmit rabies. Nerve trunks allow the virus to enter the CNS. Meningoencephalitis is inevitably fatal due to nerve cell proliferation in the brain and peripheral ganglia. The incubation time can range from two weeks to a year. Shorter incubation times are typically linked to close bites that contain a sizable virus inoculum. The symptoms come on quickly and include fever, headache, nausea, vomiting, sore throat, anorexia, anxiety, insomnia, headache, malaise, myalgia, and cough.

The patient may report symptoms indicative of paresthesia or fasciculation at the location of the initial animal bite, attributed to viral replication either at the inoculation site or in the dorsal ganglia of the sensory nerve supplying that specific area. The illness rapidly advances to an encephalitic stage marked by restlessness, heightened excitement, and increased motor activity. Individuals may encounter hallucinations, exhibit aggressive behavior, and develop muscle spasms, including opisthotonus, along with the engagement of respiratory muscles. Painful contractions of the throat muscles, triggered by attempts to swallow, may ensue—clarifying the inclination of patients to refrain from drinking or swallowing. Even slight air currents brushing against the face can induce spasms, and seizures are a common occurrence.

Periods of hallucinations and abnormal thinking may alternate with brief periods of clarity, diminishing in duration as the disease advances. Hyperesthesia, characterized by heightened reactivity to ordinary stimuli such as light, sound, and touch, is prevalent. Autonomic nervous system changes manifest, including dilated pupils, increased salivation, tearing, perspiration, and postural hypotension. As the disease progresses, brain stem function is compromised, leading to cranial nerve palsies, optic neuritis, and the distinctive hydrophobia. This hydrophobia results from painful and forceful involuntary muscle contractions in the respiratory, pharyngeal, and laryngeal muscles, triggered by attempts to swallow. Ultimately, the disease advances to cardiorespiratory depression, coma, and eventual fatality.

Sometimes rabies appears as a clinically similar ascending paralysis to Guillain-Barré syndrome; recipients of corneal transplants from two patients thought to have died from Guillain-Barré in reality died from receiving clinical rabies. Viral isolation, positive serology (if the patient has not received an immunization) or analyzing the presence of the distinctive

Negri bodies in brain tissue is necessary for the laboratory diagnosis of rabies. Serological testing and the identification of viral antigens by IFA in infected tissue, such as corneal scrapings, skin biopsies, or brain biopsies, as well as the examination of CSF or saliva specimens for the presence of rabies virus antigen or RNA, are all part of the laboratory diagnostic evaluation for rabies. Patients who have rabies rarely survive, whereas those who do survive typically received the vaccine prior to becoming ill.

Among individuals with a history of international travel, encephalitis can be attributed to a range of infectious diseases. These include Japanese B encephalitis, Murray Valley encephalitis, Omsk hemorrhagic fever, Kyasanur forest disease complex, Powassan virus, louping ill, Russian spring-summer encephalitis, Rift Valley fever, yellow fever, dengue, chikungunya, Hantaan virus, Puumala virus (a hantavirus species), and the extremely deadly hemorrhagic fevers induced by Marburg, Ebola, and Lassa fever viruses.

There is presently no designated drug or serologic treatment for enterovirus or arbovirus infections. Typically, enteroviral meningitis exhibits mild clinical symptoms, and most patients can be managed without hospitalization unless bacterial meningitis is a potential consideration in the diagnostic evaluation and requires exclusion. Individuals with enteroviral meningitis typically experience recovery within 7–10 days even without the use of antiviral therapy.

No specific drug or serologic therapy is currently available for enterovirus or arbovirus infections. In general, viral meningitis due to enteroviruses is clinically mild, and most patients can be treated without admission to the hospital unless bacterial meningitis is a possibility in the differential diagnosis and needs to be ruled out. Patients with enteroviral meningitis usually recover within 7–10 days without antiviral therapy.

Intravenous acyclovir is prescribed for patients diagnosed with HSV or VZV meningitis. For individuals displaying symptoms indicative of encephalitis or brain parenchymal involvement, and upon confirmation through appropriate radiologic imaging that alternative pathologies such as brain abscess or subdural empyema have been ruled out, the initiation of empiric intravenous acyclovir at doses suitable for treating HSV encephalitis is recommended. Complications arising from acyclovir are relatively rare, underscoring the critical importance of prompt diagnosis, as the likelihood of a favorable outcome is significantly associated with the early initiation of acyclovir therapy. It is not warranted to conduct a brain biopsy to confirm the presence of herpes encephalitis before commencing therapy. Prior to the availability of antiviral agents for treating HSV encephalitis, the condition resulted in a fatality rate of approximately 70%, with an additional 20–25% of survivors experiencing severe disabilities. The recommended dose of acyclovir is 10 mg/kg administered intravenously every 8 hours for 14–21 days.

7.3. Brain Abscess

The recognition of brain abscesses dates to the time of Hippocrates in 460 BC. By definition, a brain abscess is a localized suppurative infection of the brain parenchyma. The estimated incidence in the general population ranges from 1.3 to 100,000 person-years, with slightly higher rates observed in children aged 5 to 9 years and individuals over the age of 60. Most documented series indicate a male preponderance, typically ranging from 2:1 to 3:1 of males to females, and the age distribution is influenced by the associated underlying etiologies. While the etiology and distribution of associated diseases have remained essentially consistent over the years for pyogenic brain abscesses, the AIDS epidemic has introduced a significant population with brain abscesses due to toxoplasmosis. The advent of highly active antiretroviral therapy (HAART) has contributed to a reduction in morbidity and mortality associated with HIV-related cerebral opportunistic infections.

7.3.1. Pathogenesis

Brain abscesses begin as small-scale cerebral inflammation (i.e., poorly defined regions of encephalitis), which at first include inflammation, edema, and bacteria in the brain parenchyma. In the days that follow, a ring-enhancing capsule and necrosis in the center of the cerebritis area become more localized. In the end, a well-formed fibrous capsule develops as a result of host defenses. The most frequent risk factors for the development of a brain abscess are infections of the mastoids, paranasal sinuses, teeth (dental abscess), and middle ear. Bacteria are thought to enter the brain either retrogradely through the venous system or through valveless emissary veins, which pass through the cranium and enter the brain's venous drainage system. Alternately, access to the CNS can be gained by direct extension through an area of osteitis or osteomyelitis next to a sinus or middle ear infection; chronic otitis media is a common risk factor, and the temporal lobe or cerebellum are where abscesses most commonly form. The second main way that an extracranial infection focus spreads to the brain parenchyma is by metastatic transmission via the cerebral arteries. A contiguous focus accounts for about 20% of brain abscesses, whereas hematogenous spreading from a distant focus, such as a pyogenic lung abscess or bronchiectasis accounts for 25%, as well as trauma accounting for 25% of brain abscesses.

Hematogenous brain abscesses typically follow a vascular distribution within the brain, are multiple, and are found at the gray-white matter junction. It has also been reported that hematogenous dissemination can occur from an adjacent focus of infection. Numerous other distant foci, such as wound infections, osteomyelitis, pelvic infections, cholecystitis, and other intra-abdominal foci, have also been linked to brain abscesses. As a matter of fact, any procedure that causes a brief case of bacteremia may occasionally be linked to the subsequent development of a cerebral abscess. Only 3–5% of cases of brain abscess are caused by endocarditis, despite the condition's chronicity, relatively high bacteremia frequency, and brain involvement in 20–40% of cases. Brain abscesses are more common in patients with cyanotic congenital heart disease. A considerable proportion of brain abscesses are linked to penetrating trauma, including animal bites, depressed skull fractures that retain bone fragments, penetration of the brain by pencils, or even complications from cervical traction linked to pin-site infection. Reactivation of toxoplasmosis can result in brain abscesses in HIV-positive patients. Roughly 25% of cases have no discernible underlying cause.

7.3.2. Microbiology

The bacterial origin of brain abscess is heavily influenced by the abscess's location and predisposing factors. Consequently, aerobic, anaerobic, and microaerophilic streptococci are the most commonly identified bacterial species, and *S. aureus* accounts for 25% of brain abscesses, often linked to trauma, endocarditis, or post-neurosurgical procedures. Alongside streptococci, brain abscesses related to paranasal sinus or chronic otitis media infections may involve Haemophilus species, Bacteroides species, other anaerobes, and, in the case of chronic otitis media, *P. aeruginosa*. In instances of intra-abdominal bacteremia, Enterobacteriaceae, enterococci, and anaerobes are likely culprits. A urinary tract source is more likely associated with *Pseudomonas* spp.

or Enterobacteriaceae, excluding anaerobes. Brain abscesses caused by anaerobes, such as actinomyces, may result from the spread originating from a lung abscess.

Nocardia species serve as infrequent yet significant culprits behind brain abscesses, particularly in immunocompromised populations. The clinical presentation of Nocardia infections in the CNS remains consistent between normal and compromised hosts, albeit being more prevalent in the latter. In a study involving 11 cases and a review of 120 instances of nocardial brain abscess documented in the literature, 34% of cases displayed concomitant pulmonary disease. Most brain abscesses were solitary, with approximately one-third occurring as multiple abscesses. Overall, 38% of cases were observed in immunocompromised individuals due to factors such as HIV or other causes. On a rare note, *M. tuberculosis* may generate a space-occupying lesion known as a tuberculoma. Although uncommon in the US, tuberculomas are relatively frequent causes of brain abscesses in certain less-developed countries. Fungi and yeasts are significant contributors to brain abscesses. Though it can occasionally result in microabscesses when combined with disseminated candidiasis, *Candida albicans* rarely causes isolated brain abscesses. While patients with HIV infection are usually affected by cryptococcal infection of the CNS, cryptococcomas are uncommon. Brain abscesses have been linked to both phaeohyphomycosis agents (Cladosporium, Bipolaris, Curvularia, and Wangiella) and chromoblastomycosis agents.

Aspergillus species are known to cause brain abscesses, but they are almost exclusively found in immunocompromised patient populations—transplant patients especially. The most common species that affects humans is *Aspergillus fumigatus*, the primary *Aspergillus* spp. that frequently cause lung infections or maxillary sinusitis of dental origin infection. An infection can travel directly from the nasal sinuses to the brain via vascular pathways, or it can spread by blood from the lungs and GI system. In poorly managed diabetics, zygomycoses like Mucor, Rhizopus and Rhizomucor directly extend from the paranasal sinuses to cause brain infection. Parenteral drug abuse is the main cause of cerebral mucormycosis, an extremely rare condition without rhino-orbital or systemic involvement.

Brain abscesses are frequently caused by parasites, including protozoa. Less than 1% of CNS infections are caused by protozoa and helminths, but they are more common in young people, the elderly, and people with compromised immune systems. These infestations also often have a fatal course. *Toxoplasma gondii* is nearly exclusively linked to HIV infection and is likely the most common protozoal cause of brain abscess in the US. Particularly in less developed countries, reports of strongyloides, entamoeba, echinococcus, paragonimus, trichinosis, sparganosis, and angiostrongylus have been made, and in rare cases, naegleria and canthamoeba have been reported in causing brain abscesses in Americans.

7.3.3. Clinical Manifestations

The typical presentation of an intracranial mass lesion includes headache, focal neurological deficits, and subacute onset. Nuchal rigidity is not common in patients with brain abscesses; instead, the classic triad of focal neurological signs, fever, and headache is present in less than half of cases. Likewise, patients with subdural empyema appear to have a more focused headache, focal neurologic symptoms, and altered consciousness when they first arrive. Fever, chills, seizures, nausea, vomiting, and altered sensorium are some additional typical indications and symptoms, where the presence of a fever and a stiff neck are dependent on the location of the lesion. The most common symptom among patients with a brain abscess is headache, which can range in intensity. Usually poorly localized, the headache can be mild and hard to distinguish from regular headaches. Around 40% to 50% of cases have a fever, and one-third to half of cases may have focal neurologic symptoms and signs, such as hemiparesis, aphasia, ataxia, and sensory deficits. In a small percentage of cases, papilledema—a sign of elevated ICP—is evident.

Similarly, by the time a patient presents, 25–45% have already experienced seizures. Most frequently, frontal lobe lesions are linked to generalized seizures. Alterations in mental states, such as confusion, abnormal behavior, and somnolence, are also common CNS findings. The location of the abscess influences the presenting signs and symptoms to some degree. For instance, vomiting, dysmetria, nystagmus, and ataxia in the ipsilateral extremities are frequently observed in patients with cerebellar abscesses. Frontal lobe abscesses typically manifest as unilateral motor signs, hemiparesis, headache, and a decline in mental status or aphasia. Depending on which hemisphere the abscess is in, aphasia or dysphasia may or may not be present in cases of temporal lobe abscesses.

Homonymous hemianopia is a common presentation for patients with occipital lobe abscesses, whereas hemianesthesia, homonymous hemianopia, neglect of one half of the body, alexia, or poor spatial perception are typical symptoms of parietal lobe abscesses. Pituitary abscesses can mimic a tumor and manifest as endocrine abnormalities and defects in the visual field. Facial weakness, fever, headaches, hemiparesis, dysphasia, and vomiting are common symptoms of brain stem abscesses. The differential diagnosis includes a wide range of other CNS infections, such as meningitis, subdural empyema, epidural abscess, viral encephalitis, and non-infectious causes, such as migraine, intracerebral and subarachnoid hemorrhage, venous sinus thrombosis, or malignancy.

7.3.4. Diagnosis

The most reliable method of diagnosing a brain abscess is neuroimaging. The size, location, and stage of the abscess, as well as the degree of surrounding edema and the existence or absence of mass effects, such as midline shift, hydrocephalus, and imminent herniation, are all revealed by an MRI, which is more sensitive than a CT scan. There are several distinct stages in the development of bacterial brain abscesses: early cerebritis, late cerebritis, early abscess, mature abscess, and, ideally, resolution.

Since each of these stages lasts for about four days, the intra-axial brain abscess rule of four days applies. The development of brain abscesses is based on a healthy immune system, which is not the case in an immunocompromised host. The abscess cavity's progressive reduction in cross-sectional diameter serves as a gauge for treatment success. The abscess wall's radiologic alterations, i.e., edema surrounding it, thickness and contrast enhancement, or the condition of the interior contents, are not trustworthy indicators of treatment outcome. A ring-enhancing lesion in CT or MRI scans, with a hypodense center reflecting the necrotic center of the abscess encircled by a variable zone of edema, is a characteristic finding of a brain abscess.

CT imaging studies prove particularly valuable in delineating contiguous pathology within the head and neck, serving as a potential source of infection. High-detail CT imaging excels in detecting bone lysis associated with aggressive sinusitis and otomastoiditis, outperforming MRI in this regard. CT is also superior in defining bone dehiscence resulting from previous trauma, which may contribute to intracranial infections. Both MRI and CT offer comparable capabilities in characterizing retropharyngeal abscesses and chronic fungal sinus and skull base infections. However, CT exhibits lower sensitivity than MRI in discerning the stages of cerebritis and abscess formation and in ruling out alternative causes of intra-axial necrotic masses in the brain. MRI, particularly when employing diffusion brain imaging sequences, maintains a high level of sensitivity and specificity, as discussed subsequently. Nevertheless, certain abscesses may persist in a chronically sequestered state, posing challenges in differentiation from tumors. These cases fall within the category of tumefactive lesions, which also include sequestered infarcts, thrombosed giant aneurysms, and the Balo variant of multiple sclerosis, among others.

The primary challenge associated with neuroimaging investigations, particularly CT imaging, is its ability to accurately distinguish abscesses from tumors, including neuroblastomas and metastatic lesions. In one study, the first diagnosis for 8 out of 26 patients who had a brain abscess was that of a tumor. Another study found that the initial findings on CT scans of 100 patients with confirmed brain abscesses could not be radiographically separated from those characteristics of a malignancy in 18% of the cases.

Compared to CT scanning, MRI scanning offers better soft tissue resolution and detail, and although the cost is significantly higher, there is no exposure to ionizing radiation. Brain abscesses appear hypointense and exhibit ring enhancement on T1-weighted MRI scans after the contrast agent gadolinium is administered. The central region of necrosis appears hyperintense on T2-weighted sequences, and it is encircled by a distinct capsule of hypointense tissue and a clearly visible region of low-density tissue that represents cerebral edema. The capacity of MRI imaging studies to identify the cerebritis stage prior to the formation of an abscess with a fully developed capsule is another significant benefit. The diffusion techniques are the most useful MRI sequence. This technique shows the restriction of water movement within the forming fibrous abscess capsule and is most useful once central necrosis has occurred. Other techniques, like magnetic resonance spectroscopy (MRS), can identify byproducts of bacterial metabolism like pyruvate, acetate, and lactate, which may help distinguish brain abscesses from cancer.

Radionuclide brain scans using Indium-111-labeled leukocytes do not provide any advantage over conventional neuroimaging techniques. During the past several years, positron emission tomography (PET) with 18F-fluorodeoxyglucose (FDG) imaging has been playing larger roles in the diagnosis and management of patients with suspected brain abscesses.

Routine laboratory studies lack significant diagnostic utility in identifying brain abscesses. Approximately 40% of patients exhibit a normal white blood cell count, while around 60% show an elevated erythrocyte sedimentation rate, as well as elevated C-reactive protein levels although not consistently. Monitoring the sedimentation rate over time can be valuable to documenting therapeutic responses if elevated. In patients with a space-occupying lesion, lumbar puncture is strictly contraindicated unless prior MRI or CT scans indicate a low risk of herniation post-LP and there is a clear clinical suspicion of meningitis or meningeal carcinomatosis, justifying the associated risks. CSF analysis in brain abscess patients typically reveals findings similar to other parameningeal infections—pleocytosis with mixed neutrophils and lymphocytes, elevated protein levels, normal glucose levels, and a negative gram stain. CSF cultures are generally sterile unless there is an anatomical connection between the abscess and spinal fluid, which may occur in cases secondary to trauma or postoperative complications; blood cultures are positive in 10–20% of patients. While reasonable empiric therapy can be designed for common brain abscesses, optimal identification of causative microorganisms requires culturing material under strictly anaerobic conditions. Additionally, a biopsy can be obtained for pathological evaluation to rule out malignancy, fungal invasion, and to detect unusual microorganisms using special stains.

7.3.5. Treatment

A combined medical and surgical approach is necessary for the treatment of brain abscesses. The collection is drained and specimens for gram stain, culture, and histology tests can be obtained by stereotactically guided needle aspiration of pus. When an organism isolated from culture is resistant to antibiotics or when antimicrobial therapy is not working well, an open craniotomy may be an option. Patients with multiple abscesses that do not respond well to surgical drainage or those with smaller abscesses, but stable neurologic function may be candidates for antimicrobial therapy alone.

The range of microbiological agents that are known to cause brain abscesses and the extent to which a particular antimicrobial can cross the BBB and enter the abscess cavity itself influence the choice of antibiotics. It may be assumed that mixed aerobic and anaerobic flora are present in brain abscesses that develop in close proximity to frontal sinus infections. In this case, treatment should consist of metronidazole 7.5 mg/kg IV every 6 hours or 15 mg/kg IV every 12 hours, along with high-dose penicillin 10–20 million units per day, even if anaerobic bacteria are not recovered. If there is a possibility that the abscess originated from a dental focus, it is recommended to maintain anaerobic cultures for 7–14 days to identify Actinomyces species. However, penicillin-based standard therapy should be effective in treating actinomycosis. Antimicrobials covering anaerobes, Enterobacteriaceae, and *Pseudomonas* spp. should be used in combination to treat brain abscesses associated with chronic otitis media and mastoiditis.

Therefore, in this clinical scenario, cefotaxime, ceftazidime, or ceftriaxone plus metronidazole would be an effective combination. Even though anaerobes may not always grow in bacterial cultures, especially if the organisms are picky such as when the lack of growth of Enterobacteriaceae or *Pseudomonas* spp is observed. To rule out these specific organisms as the cause of infection, abscess material cultured from a patient who has not received intravenous antimicrobial therapy previously can be trusted. In a similar vein, the lack of *S. aureus* growth in the abscess matter culture would also be strong evidence against this agent's involvement in the pathophysiology of the abscess. *S. aureus* is generally much more likely to be connected to endocarditis, CNS metastases, trauma, or wound infections following surgery. Vancomycin should be a part of the empirical therapeutic regimen if a brain abscess is linked to a neurosurgical procedure to treat both coagulase-negative *Staphylococcus* spp. and MRSA. A 6- to 8-week course of parenteral antimicrobial therapy plus regular follow-up computed tomography scans or MRI for at least 3 months to evaluate the therapeutic response is recommended. The antimicrobial regimen can be modified once antimicrobial susceptibility testing results become available. The dosage of third-generation cephalosporins is 2 g IV every 4 h for ceftazidime and 2 g IV every 12 h for ceftriaxone, and therapy is required for a minimum of 6 weeks. Patients with a brain abscess caused by *Nocardia* spp. should be treated with higher doses of trimethoprim/sulfamethoxazole (15 mg/kg/day of the trimethoprim component) in three to five divided doses until the infection is controlled;

thereafter, the dose can be reduced to one double-strength trimethoprim/sulfamethoxazole tablet orally twice daily for 3–6 months in non-immunocompromised patients and up to a year in the immunocompromised person. In severely immunocompromised patients due to advanced AIDS, lifelong treatment for Nocardia CNS infections may be required. The method of surgical intervention depends on the patient's clinical status and the neuroradiographic characteristics of the abscess.

7.4. Spinal Epidural Abscess

The epidural space, as defined earlier, is the area between the dura and the vertebral column posterolateral to the spinal cord. The midthoracic and lumbar regions have the largest amount of this space, which stretches from the foramen magnum to the sacrum. Small arteries, loose fatty tissue, spinal nerve roots, and lymphatics are all found in the epidural space. A collection of pus between the dura and the spinal column is called an epidural abscess. ASspinal epidural abscess is a medical emergency due to the possibility of resulting in spinal cord compression and the potential for irreversible paraplegia or quadriplegia.

The incidence of spinal epidural abscesses peaks in the sixth and seventh decades, and they are more common in the elderly. The illness usually affects patients whose comorbid conditions predispose them to immunocompromised states, and it is uncommon in children. The elderly, IV drug users, people with HIV infection-related immunosuppression, and people undergoing spinal surgery are among the other risk groups.

7.4.1. Pathophysiology

Spinal epidural abscesses can develop either spontaneously or as a result of the direct introduction of pathogens into the epidural space. The most prevalent cause of spontaneous infection in the epidural space is hematogenous spread from distant sources (50%), such as skin and oral cavity infections, pneumonia, other respiratory tract infections, endocarditis, intra-abdominal and pelvic sepsis, and UTIs. Other factors contributing to spontaneous abscess formation include direct extension (contiguous spread) from preexisting discitis or osteomyelitis in an adjacent vertebral body, extension from a decubitus ulcer or paraspinal abscess, blunt spinal trauma, or penetrating injuries. Secondary causes encompass postoperative infections (constituting 16% of all spinal epidural abscesses) and infections associated with epidural anesthesia catheters. An epidural hematoma resulting from trauma may also become secondarily infected, progressing to an epidural abscess. In most cases, the underlying cause of an epidural abscess dictates its location within the spinal canal. Epidural abscesses secondary to preexisting vertebral osteomyelitis are typically limited to the anterior spinal canal, whereas most spontaneous spinal epidural abscesses resulting from hematogenous spread of bacteria are typically located posteriorly within the spinal canal. Septations in the epidural fat are assumed to be the secondary cause of the segregation and isolation of abscesses to the anterior or posterior spinal canal.

The anterior and posterior compartments of the epidural space are separated by these septations, which also divide the space longitudinally. Epidural abscess formation is typically restricted to a maximum of four vertebral levels due to the longitudinal septations. Due to the disruption of the epidural septations, postsurgical spinal epidural abscesses frequently involve multiple compartments extending several levels and circumferentially around the spinal cord. The presence of pus and granulation tissue in the epidural space can compress the spinal cord and also reduce and compromise arterial blood flow, which in turn can cause spinal cord ischemia. The neurologic aftereffects of the formation of an epidural abscess can either be extremely acute or gradually progressing, and in the latter case, total paralysis may happen in a few hours. It is believed that both ischemia and compression of the neural elements of vascular thrombosis are secondary causes of neurological injury.

7.4.2. Risk Factors

Most patients with a spinal epidural abscess have one or more known risk factors in common. These include osteomyelitis, discitis, diabetes, alcoholism, IV drug abuse, degenerative joint disease of the spine, immunodeficiency states, cancer, and chronic renal failure. Comparing reports from other large case series, the range of risk factors is rather constant. Patients who suffer from comorbid conditions like alcoholism and diabetes are more vulnerable to developing a spinal abscess due to their weakened immune systems. More direct influences are responsible for the development of spinal epidural abscesses than other risk factors. In order to cause an epidural infection, pathogens that cause discitis and bacteremia linked to IV drug abuse directly seed the epidural space.

7.4.3. Microbiology of Spinal Epidural Abscess Formation

S. aureus is the predominant microorganism found in spinal epidural abscesses, with gram-negative organisms, particularly *E. coli* and *Pseudomonas* spp., accounting for 18%. Other contributors include gram-positive organisms such as *Streptococcus* spp. (10%) and anaerobes (2%), with polymicrobial growth observed in 5–10% of cases. *M. tuberculosis* has been identified in various instances, particularly in economically less-developed countries. Less frequently implicated pathogens in spinal epidural abscesses are inclusive of *Brucella* spp., Actinomyces, *Cryptococcus* spp., and *Aspergillus* spp.

7.4.4. Clinical Features and Diagnostic Considerations

Back pain and fever are the typical clinical presentation of a patient with a spinal epidural abscess, and nerve root pain frequently follows, which is brought on by nerve root compression from a ruptured intervertebral disc. If spinal cord compression worsens, it can cause paralysis, limb weakness, bowel and bladder problems, and motor weakness. In actuality, there is a great deal of variation in the presentation; additional common clinical findings include fever (61%), paresis (53%), bladder or bowel dysfunction (36%), sepsis (17%), radiculopathy (12%), and plegia (14%). Due to the general and nonspecific nature of the symptoms and signs, patients may occasionally receive an incorrect initial diagnosis. About 25% of patients have point tenderness over the involved vertebral levels, which is linked to underlying skeletal involvement. Although lumbar involvement is the typical site of spinal epidural abscess formation, thoracic and cervical involvement are also frequent.

It is not always the case that the time interval between the onset of symptoms and their presentation corresponds well with the results of surgery. At the time of presentation, most patients have neurological deficits found on physical examination, and both abrupt and chronic neurological decline can happen in a matter of hours or months.

An almost constant elevation in the erythrocyte sedimentation rate (ESR) is the most consistent laboratory abnormality. Studies have shown that ESR and C-reactive protein are highly sensitive and moderately specific in identifying patients in emergency rooms with spinal epidural abscesses. Approximately 75% of patients have leukocytosis.

The CSF analysis results vary, from normal to frank pus, and up to 60% of cases have been reported to have positive blood cultures. In many facilities, contrast-enhanced MRI scans are the preferred diagnostic procedure because they provide superior resolution of soft tissue, the spinal cord, and the epidural space when compared to CT myelography. On T1-weighted MRI scans, an epidural abscess manifests as a low-intensity image.

One of the most sensitive, precise, and accurate imaging techniques for identifying and characterizing the presence of a spinal epidural abscess and pinpointing its location is still gadolinium-enhanced magnetic resonance imaging. In the absence of MRI services, myelography ought to be done. A lumbar puncture to measure CSF protein concentrations is not necessary for diagnosis and shouldn't be done because it could cause meningitis by introducing bacteria into the subarachnoid space.

7.4.5. Treatment

The foundation of therapy for spinal epidural abscess involves a surgical intervention to remove pus and granulation tissue, followed by an extended course of parenteral antimicrobials. In cases where neurological signs are present at the onset, immediate surgical decompression of the spinal cord is imperative.

Pending the availability of culture results and considering the common involvement of *S. aureus* in spinal epidural abscesses, the treatment regimen should incorporate an antistaphylococcal penicillin, a first-generation cephalosporin, or vancomycin along with an agent effective against gram-negative organisms, such as a third-generation cephalosporin. If MRSA is suspected or implicated, vancomycin is the recommended choice. In instances following a neurosurgical procedure, a combination of an antistaphylococcal penicillin, a third-generation cephalosporin, and an aminoglycoside is prescribed. Spinal epidural abscess is associated with a high mortality rate and significant long-term consequences, including paralysis.

The estimated mortality rate is 14%, and 35–40% of patients experience neurological sequelae, such as residual weakness or permanent paralysis. The prognosis hinges on the clinical and neurological condition of the patient at the time of presentation, with higher mortality and long-term morbidity rates in cases presenting with sepsis or plegia.

Medication therapy has been the only treatment for spinal epidural abscesses. The bulk of these patients, however, fit into one of three groups:

- (i) panspinal infections that were not treatable with drainage;
- (ii) surgical candidates who had a history of poor health and coexisting illnesses, like long-term lung or cardiac disease; or
- (iii) total paralysis lasting longer than 24 hours.

To treat patients without surgery, the physician must be willing to conduct repeated neurological examinations, track the effectiveness of treatment with repeated MRI scans, and obtain the microorganisms responsible by alternative methods, such as blood culture or needle aspirate. On the other hand, non-operative treatment of spinal epidural abscesses should be done with caution.

7.5. Parasitic Infections of the CNS

7.5.1. Cerebral Malaria

Despite its eradication from North America and Europe, malaria continues to afflict over 2.5 billion people worldwide and is responsible for 1 to 3 million deaths annually. The disease is caused by five different Plasmodium species: *Plasmodium vivax*, *Plasmodium ovale*, *Plasmodium malariae*, *Plasmodium knowlesi*, and *Plasmodium falciparum*. The latter, *P. falciparum*, is the main culprit behind most deaths and serious complications of malaria, particularly those involving the CNs. Female Anopheles mosquitoes transmit malaria sporozoites to humans during a blood meal. Sporozoites swiftly reach the liver, where they multiply in about a week, either becoming tissue schizonts or remaining dormant hypnozoites produced by *P. vivax* and *P. ovale*.

Infected liver cells eventually burst, releasing numerous merozoites. Each merozoite infects red blood cells, leading to symptomatic infection through repeated cycles of maturation and rupture of red cells, releasing more merozoites. Some parasites during this process develop into sexual forms called gametocytes, which do not cause symptoms but can circulate for an extended period.

Ingestion of these gametocytes by Anopheles mosquitoes initiates the sexual reproduction cycle, resulting in motile sporozoites invading the mosquito's salivary glands. These sporozoites can then be transmitted back to humans during the mosquito's next blood meal. Economically less developed nations—especially those in sub-Saharan Africa, Central America and the Caribbean, South America, the Middle East, the Far East, and Indonesia—are heavily affected by malaria. It is highly recommended that readers visit the CDC website to obtain the most recent information available regarding the distribution and drug resistance of *Plasmodium* spp. individually for every nation.

P. falciparum is the cause of the most malignant form of malaria and is associated with almost all serious complications associated with the infection. Cerebral malaria, in particular, is the most prominent and serious of these complications. Attributable mortality remains relatively high (20%) and is often associated with delays in diagnosis and treatment. As *P. falciparum* trophozoites mature in the red blood cells, they induce the formation of small knobs on the surface of the red cell. These knobs bind to adhesion molecules (also known as intercellular adhesion molecule-1) on the microvascular endothelial cells and lead to sequestration.

Sequestration refers to the process wherein erythrocytes containing mature forms of *P. falciparum* adhere to microvascular endothelial cells, leading to a significant reduction or disappearance of these cells from circulation. The sequestration of erythrocytes in small blood vessels and the resulting obstruction of microcirculatory flow are specific characteristics of *P. falciparum*, playing a crucial role in causing coma and death in cerebral malaria. Another essential factor in the pathogenesis of cerebral malaria is the increased production of cytokines. In an effort to control the infection, the host immune system initiates a robust proinflammatory response, prompting cells of the macrophage-monocyte series to release various cytokines, including tumor necrosis factor (TNF)-α, interleukin (IL)-1, IL-6, and IL-8. However, this response may also lead to complications such as severe anemia, hypoglycemia, and cerebral malaria.

The production of cytokines, specifically TNF-α, causes the adhesion molecules to be upregulated in malaria. Moreover, rosetting occurs when parasitized erythrocytes attach themselves to nearby uninfected cells. In addition, the normally flexible cell becomes more spherical and rigid as the parasite matures inside the erythrocyte. The rosetting and stiffening of the parasitized erythrocytes cause the erythrocytes to become stuck in the capillaries.

The result of cytoadherence, rosetting, and rigidity is the enhancement of sequestration of

P. falciparum-parasitized erythrocytes in the cerebral vasculature, stagnation of the cerebral blood flow, and secondary ischemia leading to tissue hypoxia, lactic acidosis, hypoglycemia, and prevention of delivery of nutrients to the tissues. High concentrations of TNF-α can precipitate cerebral malaria by increasing the sequestration of parasitized erythrocytes. Although all tissues potentially can become involved, the brain is the most profoundly affected.

This process in the CNS causes delirium, altered consciousness, convulsions, paralysis, coma, and, in the end, a swift death if treatment is not received. Severe falciparum malaria can cause systemic symptoms such as disseminated intravascular coagulation, pulmonary edema, lactic acidosis, hypoglycemia, anemia, and adult respiratory distress syndrome. It is noteworthy that most patients do not exhibit cerebral edema, and the pathophysiology of malaria does not involve vasculitis or inflammatory cellular infiltration in or around the cerebral vasculature. Rather than brain swelling brought on by cerebral edema and capillary leakage, elevated intracranial pressure most likely results from an increase in the total volume of cerebral blood. In most cases, elevated intracranial pressure is not linked to coma in malaria. The clinical characteristics of Fever and chills (83%) altered sensorium (48%) jaundice (27%), anemia (75%), cerebral involvement (45%), thrombocytopenia (41%), and renal failure (25%) are among the symptoms of *P. falciparum* malaria.

Consider the diagnosis in individuals exhibiting altered consciousness, fever, and pertinent travel history, which is crucial to obtain. It is essential to inquire about the patient's compliance with or use of prophylaxis for malaria. The travel location is of particular significance, given that *P. falciparum* typically displays resistance to chloroquine. Resistance to trimethoprim/sulfamethoxazole, mefloquine, and other agents has been reported in various regions, especially Southeast Asia and sub-Saharan Africa. Unlike *P. vivax* and *P. ovale*, *P. falciparum* does not have a latent form in the liver. Therefore, cases of *P. falciparum* malaria should manifest clinically within a month after departing from an endemic area.

The laboratory diagnosis of malaria is performed by the examination of the blood smear. Thick and thin blood smears continue to be the gold standard for laboratory diagnosis of malaria in current practice, despite the fact that delays are frequent due to the time required for their preparation and reading. Even though there are quick diagnostic tests based on lateral-flow immunochromatography that allow doctors to identify malaria parasite antigens from finger-prick blood specimens in as little as 10–15 minutes, microscopic analysis of blood smears is still the most economical method for diagnosing malaria, given that the results are promptly communicated to the relevant parties.

Kits for rapid diagnostic testing based on molecular platforms that have a high negative predictive value and sensitivity for *P. falciparum* would be especially helpful in acute care settings in low malaria endemicity areas where blood smear reading and diagnosis are not possible due to a lack of laboratory expertise. Finally, quick diagnostic testing can help critically ill patients by quickly confirming or ruling out a malaria diagnosis and enabling timely treatment. Due to their limitations, rapid test kits for malaria cannot soon replace microscopy of blood smears, and additionally have the inability to distinguish between the four species of Plasmodium and to determine parasitemia quantitatively.

Penetral malaria is lethal if left untreated. Notwithstanding the initial interpretation of the blood smear, the patient in cases of severe malaria involving the CNS must be treated as though they have falciparum malaria. Blood should be obtained for diagnostic testing as soon as it is available, and parenteral antimalarial medication should be started empirically, advises the CDC, if severe malaria is highly suspected but a laboratory diagnosis cannot be made at that time. Parenteral quinidine gluconate should begin as soon as it is thought that the diagnosis is likely. As part of the recommended therapeutic regimen, a loading dose of 6.25 mg base/kg (= 10 mg salt/kg) is infused intravenously over a period of 1–2 hours, and then 0.0125 mg base/kg/min (= 0.02 mg salt/kg/min) is continuously infused. An alternate treatment plan entails an intravenous loading dose of quinidine gluconate (15 mg base/kg; 24 mg salt/kg) infused over 4 hours. This is followed by 8 hours of incremental infusions of 7.5 mg base/kg (12 mg/kg salt) every 8 hours. The combination of clindamycin, tetracycline, or doxycycline with quinidine gluconate therapy is recommended. Intravenous clindamycin (5 mg base/kg every 8 h) or doxycycline (100 mg every 12 h) may be administered if the patient cannot tolerate oral therapy until oral therapy can be started. Parenteral artesunate, one of the artemisinin derivatives that have been demonstrated more recently to significantly lower mortality in African children suffering from severe malaria, is recommended by the authors to take the place of quinine as the preferred treatment for severe falciparum malaria globally.

Parenteral quinidine gluconate has the potential to cause hyperinsulinemic hypoglycemia and is cardiotoxic. Thus, it is necessary to get a baseline EKG before starting therapy and to keep a careful eye on glucose levels. Continuous cardiac and blood pressure monitoring is part of critical care management, along with appropriate supportive care for coexisting medical conditions that are frequently linked to severe malaria. These conditions include convulsions, renal failure, adult respiratory distress syndrome, disseminated intravascular coagulation, lactic acidosis, hypoglycemia, abnormalities in fluid and electrolytes, circulatory collapse, acute renal failure, secondary bacterial infections, and severe anemia.

Intravenous corticosteroids are completely contraindicated and are linked to unfavorable results. Although it is frequently observed in adult cerebral malaria patients, brain swelling on CT scans is unrelated to survival or the depth of coma. When used as an adjuvant treatment for adult cerebral malaria, mannitol therapy lengthens the duration of coma and may be hazardous. Research on antipyretics, anticonvulsants (phenobarbitone), anti-cytokine/anti-inflammatory drugs (pentoxifylline, dexamethasone, anti-TNF antibodies), iron chelators, and hyperimmune sera has not shown any promise in terms of bettering patient outcomes.

With treatment, almost all patients with CNS malaria recover completely if they survive the acute episode. However, globally, overall mortality in children and adults remains unacceptably high. Approximately 12% of patients with cerebral malaria may have lasting neurologic sequelae, including cortical blindness, tremor, cranial nerve palsies, and sensory and motor deficits, although approximately 50% of these sequelae resolve with time.

7.5.2. Amoebic Meningoencephalitis

When free-living amoeba species like *Naegleria fowleri* and *Acanthamoeba* species infect humans, the result is a striking and nearly always fatal primary meningoencephalitis. Living freely, *N. fowleri* are widely distributed in nature, especially in shallow freshwater in warm climates or the upper surface layers of lakes. *Acanthamoeba* species are typically found in fresh and brackish water as well as soil. The southeastern states account for the majority of cases in the US, which usually involve children or young adults. Clinically, patients experience headaches, photophobia, and a sudden high fever; obtundation develops rather quickly. In warm, freshwater lakes, swimming and waterskiing have typically a long history.

The amoebae infiltrate the nasal cavity through blood vessels associated with the olfactory nerves, traversing the cribriform plate to reach the frontal lobes and surrounding meninges. This process leads to the rapid development of a highly necrotizing, purulent, and destructive encephalitis. Olfactory involvement may result in alterations of smell or taste. Otherwise, nonspecific symptoms such as confusion, irritability, restlessness, and seizures manifest, progressing quickly to delirium, stupor, and coma. CSF analysis typically reveals a bloody appearance, leukocytosis with a predominance of neutrophils, low glucose levels, and elevated protein. When the diagnosis is strongly suspected, examining unstained CSF with a slide warmer can reveal the characteristic, mobile, amoeboid motion of the trophozoites. Gram stain and culture results are usually negative. The CDC has developed a PCR assay for Naegleria, Acanthamoeba, and Balamuthia.

Frontal lobe involvement is easily visible on MRI, but due to the condition's rarity and lack of obvious symptoms, diagnosis is frequently delayed. The pathogens are susceptible to amphotericin B, which is administered to patients *in vitro*, and only a small number of patients have been reported to have survived. Although the best course of treatment for this illness is unknown, some authors advise taking maximum systemic doses of amphotericin B along with doxycycline and rifampin as an intracisternal amphotericin B adjunct. Surgery to treat hydrocephalus typically entails shunting and the implantation of a reservoir for intrathecal amphotericin B.

7.5.3. Neurocysticercosis

The most prevalent helminthic infection of the nervous system and a major global contributor to acquired epilepsy is neurocysticercosis. Mexico, Central America, South America, Africa, Southeast Asia, India, the Philippines, and Southern Europe are among the regions with a high prevalence of cysticercosis. According to more recent data, it is becoming a bigger issue in Europe. Adult cases of neurocysticercosis arise from brain infections caused by larval cysts of the pork tapeworm cestode *Taenia solium*. Two distinct mechanisms cause human infection: either the eggs are consumed and subsequently fertilize, or the intestinal wall is penetrated and the cysticerci are transported hematogenously to various tissues, mainly the brain and muscles, where they encyst and remain potentially infectious for an extended time. On the other hand, eating undercooked pork can cause humans to consume the cysticerci. In the second case, the cysticerci develop into the common tapeworm, which clings to the intestinal wall and can reach lengths of up to 3 meters while having a 25-year lifespan. It creates proglottids, or egg-filled segments, during this time, which are expelled in the stools. When these proglottid eggs are consumed, the patient may sometimes develop neurocysticercosis as a result of autoinfection with their intestinal tapeworm.

When cysticercal cysts enlarge in the brain parenchyma over months or years, it can cause symptoms of neurocysticercosis. People with neurocysticercosis, which was contracted 30 years ago after traveling to an endemic region of the world, may exhibit seizures when they arrive in the US. Depending on the quantity, the size, and the anatomical location of the cystic lesions, the clinical signs can vary and are nonspecific, with frequent presenting symptoms including headaches and seizures. Headache, nausea, vomiting, changes in vision, dizziness, ataxia, and confusion are symptoms of elevated intracranial pressure (ICP) that may arise if the cysts obstruct the flow of CSF. It is possible for chronic meningitis to develop when the cysts are situated in the meninges. Cysts proliferating at the base of the brain cause an uncommon form of cysticercosis known as "racemes" cysticercosis, which can cause severe illness, including mental decline and even death. Again, the location and size of the cysts determine how severe the symptoms are. Intraspinal cysts are common and can cause symptoms of cord compression.

Seizures (64%), symptoms linked to elevated intracranial hypertension, and meningism are the most common clinical presentations. Up to 50% of patients have intracranial calcifications that are suggestive of cysticercosis, according to radiological studies of the skull. Increased pressure, elevated lymphocyte and eosinophil counts, elevated protein levels, and decreased glucose levels are all consistently observed in CSF analysis. Neuroimaging (CT scanning or MRI) studies that show multiple cysts of different sizes and stages are a simple way to diagnose neurocysticercosis. Both the parasites and the modifications they cause to the nervous system may be visible on an MRI. For patients with multiple cysts, serological testing is available with sensitivity levels as high as 94%, however, for patients with a single cyst, the sensitivity is much lower. More mature cysts are observed to frequently calcify. The greatest sensitivity (95.9%) is found in PCR assays, while specificity varies (80–100%) based on the controls employed. Serology is typically accessible at some national commercial laboratories or through the CDC. However, due to the low specificity and sensitivity of existing tests, the identification of specific antibodies and antigens is currently only used to support the diagnosis.

7.5.3.1. Treatment

CNS lesions are categorized as either active or inactive neurocysticercosis based on neuroimaging studies. The effectiveness of antiparasitic medications in patients with inactive parenchymal neurocysticercosis is still restricted because these patients typically show no signs of viable or degenerating parasites. These patients should receive standard anticonvulsive therapy with either carbamazepine, phenytoin, or phenobarbital because they have an increased risk of seizures. Ventriculoperitoneal shunts must be used to treat patients who develop hydrocephalus.

Anticonvulsants are required for the treatment of seizures, which almost all patients with active neurocysticercosis experience. Since the cysticerci usually undergo complete degeneration over 1 to 2 years, most of these patients can probably be treated symptomatically and then followed up with an MRI. This process leaves patients with either calcified, and inactive cysticerci that still cause seizures and necessitate anticonvulsant therapy, however in most cases including a normal MRI, in which case anticonvulsants can be tapered as long as the patient doesn't have any more seizures. The prognosis of this condition has been significantly improved with cysticidal drugs such as albendazole and praziquantel. These medications can be administered together, with praziquantel given at doses of 50–100 mg/kg/day for 15–30 days or albendazole at 10–15 mg/kg/day for 8 days. Trials comparing the efficacy of these drugs have shown albendazole to be superior to praziquantel. An additional advantage of albendazole is its ability to destroy subarachnoid and ventricular cysts. In cases with large subarachnoid cysts, higher doses (up to 30 mg/kg/day) or more prolonged, and occasionally repeated, courses of albendazole may be necessary. While these agents effectively eliminate cysticerci, some controlled trials have not demonstrated any clinical benefit over symptomatic treatment alone. Praziquantel's main adverse side effect is the worsening of neurologic function, leading to symptoms such as headaches, dizziness, seizures, and increased intracranial pressure. This is likely due to an increase in the host inflammatory response and cerebral edema resulting from larval death. There is a consensus that anti-cysticidal drugs are not recommended for patients with only calcified lesions. Patients with single enhancing lesions generally fare well without antiparasitic therapy. However, antiparasitic therapy is indicated for patients with multiple subarachnoid cysticerci or giant cysticerci, while it is contraindicated in patients with cerebral edema (cysticercal encephalitis).

In particular, hydrocephalus and intraventricular cysts require surgical intervention for effective management of the disease. For patients with ventricular cysticerci, endoscopic removal is still the recommended course of treatment. Surgical excision of cysts obstructing CSF flow has been the standard treatment for ventricular neurocysticercosis. Recent research has shown that treating these patients with antiparasitic medications results in fewer shunt failures. A prominent inflammatory arachnoiditis is linked to cysticercosis affecting the basilar cisterns, which can be exacerbated by vasculitis, leading to lacunar infarctions, and cysticerci invasion into larger vessels, causing strokes. Therefore, some writers have suggested treating patients with cisternal cysticercosis with corticosteroids in addition to other medications.

A consensus guideline panel headed by Garcia and coworkers underscored four major tenets of managing neurocysticercosis: (i) individualize therapeutic decisions, including whether to use antiparasitic drugs, based on the number, location, and viability of the parasites within the CNS; (ii) actively manage growing cysticerci either with antiparasitic drugs or surgical excision; (iii) prioritize the management of intracranial hypertension secondary to neurocysticercosis before considering any other form of therapy; and (iv) management of seizures that are a result of secondary seizures due to an organic focus that has been present for a long time.

7.5.4. Echinococcus

Tapeworms, which frequently infect dogs, cats, wolves, and other carnivores, are the cause of echinococcal disease. While it is widespread throughout the world, it is especially prevalent in the nations that border the Mediterranean, some regions of East Africa, Russia, and South America. Although there isn't much echinococcal disease in the US, it's vital to understand that wolves, foxes, and bears in Canada and Alaska frequently carry this parasite. When an animal eats an infected egg, the oncosphere inside is activated, breaks through the gut wall, and travels through veins or lymphatics to different parts of the body where it forms hydatid cysts. This is how the disease is caused. About 10% of cysts are found in the lungs and up to 80% are found in the liver. CNS involvement is rare, occurring in less than 2% of cases. Cysts can be single or multi-layered at all anatomic locations.

Of the four species that infect humans, *Echinococcus granulosus* and *Echinococcus multilocularis* account for the vast majority of cases. CNS disease is commonly characterized by slowly enlarging solitary cysts in the brain. Depending on the size and location of the cyst, the patient may remain asymptomatic. However, as the CNS lesion enlarges in size, symptoms may arise from the local effects of the lesion itself or secondary to raised ICP, resulting in headache, nausea and vomiting, seizures, hemiparesis, dysarthria, and cranial nerve palsies. The diagnosis may be suspected from the radiographic appearance of the cyst itself seen on CT scanning or MRI. Classic radiographic features include a sharp, spherical border lacking a rim of enhancement or surrounding edema, although a fine rim of peripheral enhancement with perilesional edema may be seen if active inflammation is present. CT is superior for the detection of extrahepatic disease, while MRI does not appear to add any diagnostic benefit.

The CDC offers immunodiagnostic testing, which has a sensitivity range of 60 to 90% and is very sensitive for liver cysts but less sensitive for brain cysts. Therefore, cerebral echinococcal disease is not completely ruled out by a negative test. The chance of diagnosing echinococcus is also increased by a history of travel to or residence in an endemic area, particularly if there has been contact with sheep. Individuals who have intracranial hydatid cysts typically exhibit elevated intracranial pressure as a result of CSF flow interference along with a focal neurological deficit. Hydatid cysts are treated surgically, to remove the cyst entirely without rupturing it to avoid an allergic reaction or recurrence. For four months, albendazole therapy is administered three times a day at a dose of 10 mg/kg. This oral antihelminthic medication has a broad spectrum of action and works by preventing the larval and adult worms from absorbing glucose. As a result, the glycogen stores are exhausted, which lowers the production of ATP and causes the parasite to die. Large cysts can shrink, and smaller cysts can go away when using albendazole.

7.5.5. Strongyloidiasis

Small nematodes called *Strongyloides stercoralis* can be found in soil in free-living forms, but parasitic forms (the male does not enter the intestinal mucosa, and instead are expelled in stool, as compared to the adult female) reside within intestinal crypts in the duodenum, the jejunal mucosal villi, or in the submucosa. The adult worms typically pierce the mucosa to release their eggs, which then defecate with the stool. The female may deposit eggs that hatch into rhabditiform larvae that pass out in stool after entering the intestinal lumen. These organisms typically release eggs that mature in the soil and give rise to more rhabditiform larvae.

These larvae change into filariform infectious larvae in the environment, which can pierce human and other mammal skin directly. For unclear reasons, in certain patients, the transformation from rhabditiform to filariform infective larvae can also happen in the perianal or lower bowel before the larvae passing out in the stool. Autoinfection is the term for the process by which the filariform larvae burrow through the intestinal wall and perianal skin to re-infect the patient. The filariform larvae burrow through the skin, reach the lymphatics, and then the venous system, where they are transported to the capillaries in the lungs. Here, they move up the airways, down the esophagus, and into the small bowel by passing through the alveoli after leaving the blood vessels. Pulmonary symptoms, urticarial symptoms, and ground itch are among the presenting symptoms. An intestinal worm burden may be the cause of a malabsorption syndrome. Up to 30 years after their return to the US and the UK, World War II veterans who were held as prisoners of war in the Pacific theater were found to have autoinfection and chronic strongyloidiasis.

The most detrimental effect of *S. stercoralis* infection is massive autoinfection brought on by immunosuppression, e.g., people receiving steroid therapy, organ transplant recipients, those with HTLV-1 coinfection, cancer patients, or those who have recently received corticosteroid or cytotoxic drug treatment for lymphoma, leukemia, or leprosy. In the hyperinfection syndrome disorder, the invasive form of the filariform larvae hematogenously spreads to all organs, including the liver, lungs, and brain, and the autoinfection cycle intensifies to produce massive infection with millions of parasites throughout the entire intestine.

Immunocompromised patients may experience headache, altered mentation, meningismus, focal or generalized seizures, or motor weakness as a symptom of this hyperinfection syndrome. Strongyloides larvae in the meninges can cause pyogenic meningitis and encephalopathy, which are both frequent conditions. The possibility of meningitis and septic shock from *E. coli* is a distinctive feature of the hyperinfection syndrome. Other gram-negative enteric bacteria like *E. coli* may be present.

These gram-negative infections are believed to be brought on by enteric organisms carried on the larvae or in their guts during their migration through the tissues, which, once the CNS is invaded, causes bacterial meningitis. Due to pre-existing immunosuppression (usually from corticosteroids), eosinophilia is almost never observed in patients with hyperinfection syndrome, despite being common in strongyloidiasis. Eosinophilia is a sign of poor prognosis, where the lower the eosinophil count, the worse the prognosis. Finding the larvae in sputum, stool, or duodenal aspirate can be a helpful aspect of the diagnosis. Treatment with thiabendazole 25 mg/kg twice a day for 10 days has been found to be an effective for massive strongyloidiasis. The hyperinfection syndrome has also been successfully treated with ivermectin therapy.

7.5.6. Toxocariasis

Nematodes called *Toxocara canis* and *Toxocara cati* cause intestinal infections in dogs and cats, respectively. The eggs of these organisms are widely dispersed in the soil that humans may come into contact with as a result of the infection residing in domestic animals. Human infection typically results when eggs are consumed and hatch in the small intestine. Following this, the larvae pass through the intestinal wall and into different bodily tissues, where they typically appear as visceral larvae migrans (VLM). Hepatomegaly, anorexia, nausea, abdominal pain, vomiting, lethargy, behavioral abnormalities, pneumonia, cough, wheezing, lymphadenopathy, or fever are among the symptoms. The disease is characterized by striking eosinophilia, and unilateral loss of vision may occur in older children, adolescents, or young adults, where ophthalmoscopy reveals a lesion resembling a retinoblastoma.

When eosinophilia is observed in young children (2–4 years old), a clinical diagnosis of VLM is easily suggested. CNS involvement can present as optic neuritis, meningoencephalitis, myelitis, dementia, cerebral vasculitis, or epilepsy, though these conditions are extremely rare. Patients with VLM may also exhibit encephalopathy and seizures as a sign of CNS involvement. Meningoencephalitis, transverse myelitis, and psychiatric disorders are some additional symptoms.

Treatment consists of either 400 mg of albendazole taken twice a day for five days or 2 mg/kg of diethylcarbamazine taken orally three times a day for 10 days. Steroids are recommended for eye conditions and might be required if there is significant lung, heart, or CNS involvement. A random migration of *Angiostrongylus cantonensis* and Gnathostoma species into the CNS can cause meningitis, which is included in the differential diagnosis of parasitic eosinophilic meningitis.

A Closer Look

Illuminating the Brain

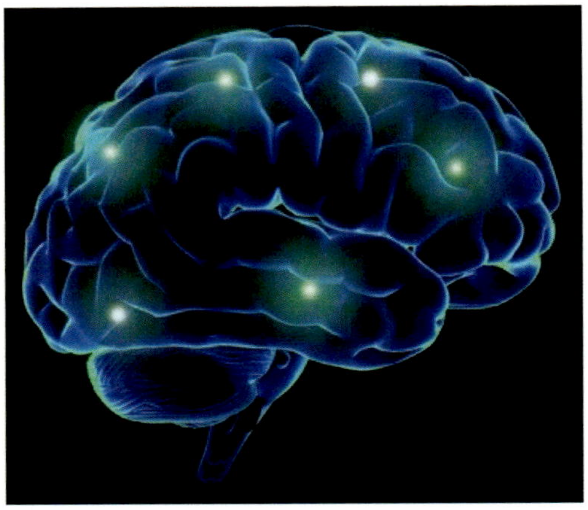

The human brain contains roughly 100 billion neurons, each of which is a part of complex networks that regulate our emotions, thoughts, and behavior. A single neuron's message can have profound effects on different parts of the brain, but current technology makes it challenging to understand these connections.

To facilitate the mapping of these networks, a group of researchers from MIT, Harvard, Boston University, and Tufts University has now created a method that uses functional magnetic resonance imaging (fMRI) to scan the brains of awake mice by selectively activating neurons with light and monitoring the resulting activity in different brain regions.

Through the comparison of this data with fMRI brain scans of humans, scientists may be able to gain important insights into the brain circuits at the root of conditions like epilepsy, schizophrenia, autism, and PTSD.

The new method, known as opto-fMRI, expands on optogenetics, which is the genetic engineering of light-responsive cells that enables researchers to selectively activate or deactivate specific nerve cells. Target cells are genetically modified to produce channelrhodopsins, which are proteins that are located in the cell membrane and allow cells to be controlled by light. These channels regulate how charged molecules called ions enter the cell. A neuron is activated when its voltage is altered by pumping positive ions into it.

Blood flow in the brain is visible to scientists using functional magnetic resonance imaging (fMRI), which shows activity in specific brain regions. It is used by neuroscientists to pinpoint the areas of the brain that are affected by neurological disorders or active during specific behaviors. The ability to measure activity across the awake brain is made possible by fMRI, which offers the rare chance to evaluate the entire functioning brain at once. The primary sensory cortex of the brain, which interprets touch and pain sensations, is where the researchers introduced channelrhodopsins into neurons. They discovered through fMRI that following the activation of those neurons by light, the primary motor cortex, which regulates movement, and the secondary sensory cortex, which processes additional sensory information, also became active. That outcome is in line with a previously identified neural circuit.

Summary

- Acute infections of the central nervous system (CNS) are medical emergencies that, if left untreated, can have fatal consequences or cause severe long-term effects that severely impair the affected person's quality of life.
- The Cerebellum and cerebrum of the brain, spinal cord, and covering membranes of the optic nerves comprise the central nervous system (CNS). The inflexible walls of the skull and the spinal canal of the vertebral column shield these structures.
- Acute CNS infections are classified into three main categories: meningitis, encephalitis, and abscesses. These infections are typically caused by the microorganisms that cause them to spread through blood.
- The definition of bacterial meningitis is an inflammatory reaction to pyogenic bacterial invasion of the pia mater, arachnoid membranes, and the area around the central nervous system.
- A common result of bacterial infections in the paranasal and otomastoid sinuses is phlebothrombosis of the nearby draining cortical (cerebral) veins.
- Pneumococcal meningitis varies in risk with age, but it is much more common in infants than in adults and young children. The incidence increases once more to roughly double the average incidence for young and middle-aged adults over the age of 70.
- Individuals with diabetes, a history of alcohol abuse, hepatic cirrhosis, or chronic urinary tract infections are particularly vulnerable to this condition.
- Colonization of the nasopharynx or respiratory tract is a crucial prelude to infection by any of the three microorganisms (*S. pneumoniae*, *N. meningitides* as well as *H. influenzae*) are most frequently linked to meningitis contracted in the community.
- Acute CNS infection is a medical emergency, and it may be necessary to distinguish between bacterial meningitis and other conditions that affect the central nervous system, such as encephalitis, brain abscess, subdural empyema, and aseptic meningitis.
- The blood–brain barrier keeps larger proteins out, which is why CSF protein levels are typically less than 40 mg/dL. CSF protein tends to rise and increases with disease duration before starting therapy when the barrier breaks down during meningitis.
- Brain abscesses begin as small-scale cerebral inflammation (i.e., poorly defined regions of encephalitis), which at first included inflammation, edema, and bacteria in the brain parenchyma.
- CT imaging studies prove particularly valuable in delineating contiguous pathology within the head and neck, serving as a potential source of infection.
- The range of microbiological agents that are known to cause brain abscesses and the extent to which a particular antimicrobial can cross the blood-brain barrier and enter the abscess cavity itself influence the choice of antibiotics.
- Back pain and fever are the typical clinical presentation of a patient with a spinal epidural abscess; nerve root pain frequently follows, which is brought on by nerve root compression from a ruptured intervertebral disc.

- Nematodes called *Toxocara canis* and *Toxocara cati* cause intestinal infections in dogs and cats, respectively. The eggs of these organisms are widely dispersed in the soil that humans may come into contact with as a result of this infection in domestic animals.

References

1. Carpenter, R. R., & Petersdorf, R. G., (1962). The clinical spectrum of bacterial meningitis. *Am. J. Med., 33*, 262–275. doi: 10.1016/0002-9343(62)90024-4.
2. Durand, M. L., Calderwood, S. B., Weber, D. J., et al., (1993). Acute bacterial meningitis in adults. A review of 493 episodes. *N. Engl. J. Med., 328*, 21–28. doi: 10.1056/NEJM199301073280104.
3. Feigin, R. D., & Shackelford, P. G., (1973). Value of repeat lumbar puncture in the differential diagnosis of meningitis. *N. Engl. J. Med., 289*, 571–574. doi: 10.1056/NEJM197309132891108.
4. Filippidis, A., & Fountas, K. N., (2009). Nasal lymphatics as a novel invasion and dissemination route of bacterial meningitis. *Med. Hypotheses, 72*, 694–697. doi: 10.1016/j.mehy.2008.10.031.
5. Fishman, R. A., (1992). *Cerebrospinal Fluid in Diseases of the Nervous System*. Philadelphia: WB Saunders Co.
6. Flierl, M. A., Rittirsch, D., Huber-Lang, M. S., & Stahel, P. F., (2010). Pathophysiology of septic encephalopathy – an unsolved puzzle. *Crit. Care, 14*, 165. doi: 10.1186/cc9035.
7. Fothergill, L. D., & Wright, J., (1933). Influenzal meningitis: Relation of age incidence to bacterial power of blood against causal organism. *J. Immunol., 24*, 273–284.
8. Gorse, G. J., Thrupp, L. D., Nudleman, K. L., Wyle, F. A., Hawkins, B., & Cesario, T. C., (1984). Bacterial meningitis in the elderly. *Arch. Intern. Med., 144*, 1603–1607. doi: 10.1001/archinte.1984.00350200107016.
9. Hausdorff, W. P., Feikin, D. R., & Klugman, K. P., (2005). Epidemiological differences among pneumococcal serotypes. *Lancet Infect Dis., 5*, 83–93.
10. Hayden, R. T., & Frenkel, L. D., (2000). More laboratory testing: Greater cost but not necessarily better. *Pediatr. Infect. Dis. J., 19*, 290–292. doi: 10.1097/00006454-200004000-00005.
11. Helbok, R., Broessner, G., Pfausler, B., & Schmutzhard, E., (2009). Chronic meningitis. *J. Neurol., 256*, 168–175. doi: 10.1007/s00415-009-0122-0.
12. Herndon, R. M., & Brumback, R. A., (1989). *The Cerebrospinal Spinal Fluid*. Boston: Kluwer Academic Publishers.
13. Hill, D. J., Griffiths, N. J., Borodina, E., & Virji, M., (2010). Cellular and molecular biology of *Neisseria meningitidis* colonization and invasive disease. *Clin. Sci. (Lond)., 118*, 547–564.
14. Hsu, H. E., Shutt, K. A., Moore, M. R., et al., (2009). Effect of pneumococcal conjugate vaccine on pneumococcal meningitis. *N. Engl. J. Med., 360*, 244–256. doi: 10.1056/NEJMoa0800836.
15. Joffe, A. R., (2005). Prognostic factors in adults with bacterial meningitis. *N. Engl. J. Med., 352*, 512–515. doi: 10.1056/NEJM200502033520519.
16. Joffe, A. R., (2007). Lumbar puncture and brain herniation in acute bacterial meningitis: A review. *J. Intensive Care Med., 22*, 194–207. doi: 10.1177/0885066607299516.
17. Join-Lambert, O., Morand, P. C., Carbonnelle, E., et al., (2010). Mechanisms of meningeal invasion by a bacterial extracellular pathogen, the example of *Neisseria meningitidis*. *Prog. Neurobiol., 91*, 130–139. doi: 10.1016/j.pneurobio.2009.12.004.

18. Kallstrom, H., Blackmer, G. D., Albiger, B., Liszewski, M. K., Atkinson, J. P., & Jonsson, A. B., (2001). Attachment of Neisseria gonorrhoeae to the cellular pilus receptor CD46: Identification of domains important for bacterial adherence. *Cell Microbiol., 3*, 133–143. doi: 10.1046/j.1462-5822.2001.00095.x.

19. Kallstrom, H., Liszewski, M. K., Atkinson, J. P., & Jonsson, A. B., (1997). Membrane cofactor protein (MCP or CD46) is a cellular pilus receptor for pathogenic *Neisseria. Mol. Microbiol., 25*, 639–647. doi: 10.1046/j.1365-2958.1997.4841857.x.

20. Kim, K. S., (2010). Acute bacterial meningitis in infants and children. *Lancet Infect. Dis., 10*, 32–42. doi: 10.1016/S1473-3099(09)70306-8.

21. Mason, E. O., Jr, Kaplan, S. L., Wiedermann, B. L., Norrod, E. P., & Stenback, W. A., (1985). Frequency and properties of naturally occurring adherent piliated strains of *Haemophilus influenzae* type b. *Infect. Immun., 49*, 98–103.

22. May, M., Daley, A. J., Donath, S., & Isaacs, D., (2005). Early onset neonatal meningitis in Australia and New Zealand, 1992–2002. *Arch. Dis. Child Fetal Neonatal Ed., 90*, F324–327. doi: 10.1136/adc.2004.066134.

23. Mein, J., & Lum, G., (1999). CSF bacterial antigen detection tests offer no advantage over Gram's stain in the diagnosis of bacterial meningitis. *Pathology, 31*, 67–69. doi: 10.1080/003130299105601.

24. Mook-Kanamori, B. B., Geldhoff, M., Van, D. P. T., & Van De, B. D., (2011). Pathogenesis, and pathophysiology of pneumococcal meningitis. *Clin. Microbiol. Rev., 24*, 557–591. doi: 10.1128/CMR.00008-11.

25. Mulks, M. H., & Plaut, A. G., (1978). IgA protease production as a characteristic distinguishing pathogenic from harmless *Neisseriaceae. N. Engl. J. Med., 299*, 973–976. doi: 10.1056/NEJM197811022991802.

26. Negrini, B., Kelleher, K. J., & Wald, E. R., (2000). Cerebrospinal fluid findings in aseptic versus bacterial meningitis. *Pediatrics, 105*, 316–319. doi: 10.1542/peds.105.2.316.

27. Neuman, M. I., Tolford, S., & Harper, M. B., (2008). Test characteristics and interpretation of cerebrospinal fluid gram stain in children. *Pediatr. Infect. Dis. J., 27*, 309–313. doi: 10.1097/INF.0b013e31815f53ba.

28. Nigrovic, L. E., Kuppermann, N., & Malley, R., (2008). Children with bacterial meningitis presenting to the emergency department during the pneumococcal conjugate vaccine era. *Acad. Emerg. Med., 15*, 522–528. doi: 10.1111/j.1553-2712.2008.00117.x.

29. Nigrovic, L. E., Kuppermann, N., Macias, C. G., et al., (2007). Clinical prediction rule for identifying children with cerebrospinal fluid pleocytosis at very low risk of bacterial meningitis. *JAMA, 297*, 52–60. doi: 10.1001/jama.297.1.52.

30. Oliver, W. J., Shope, T. C., & Kuhns, L. R., (2003). Fatal lumbar puncture: Fact versus fiction – an approach to a clinical dilemma. *Pediatrics., 112*, e174–176. doi: 10.1542/peds.112.3.e174.

31. Pfister, H. W., Fontana, A., Tauber, M. G., Tomasz, A., & Scheld, W. M., (1994). Mechanisms of brain injury in bacterial meningitis: Workshop summary. *Clin. Infect. Dis., 19*, 463–479. doi: 10.1093/clinids/19.3.463.

32. Pichichero, M. E., Loeb, M., & Anderson, S. D. H., (1982). Do pili play a role in pathogenicity of *Haemophilus influenzae* type B? *Lancet, 2*, 960–962. doi: 10.1016/S0140-6736(82)90161-1.

33. Prevention CfDCa, (2005). Prevention and control of meningococcal disease, recommendations of the Advisory Committee on Immunization Practices (ACIP). *MMWR Recomm Rep., 54*, 1–21.

34. Rouphael, N. G., & Stephens, D. S., (2012). Neisseria meningitidis: Biology, microbiology, and epidemiology. *Methods Mol Biol., 799*, 1–20. doi: 10.1007/978-1-61779-346-2_1.

35. Sarff, L. D., McCracken, G. H., Schiffer, M. S., et al., (1975). Epidemiology of *Escherichia coli* K1 in healthy and diseased newborns. *Lancet, 1*, 1099–1104. doi: 10.1016/S0140-6736(75)92496-4.

36. Sarff, L. D., Platt, L. H., & McCracken, G. H. Jr., (1976). Cerebrospinal fluid evaluation in neonates: Comparison of high-risk infants with and without meningitis. *J. Pediatr., 88*, 473–477. doi: 10.1016/S0022-3476(76)80271-5.

37. Schiffer, M. S., Oliveira, E., Glode, M. P., McCracken, G. H. Jr., Sarff, L. M., & Robbins, J. B., (1976). A review: Relation between invasiveness and the K1 capsular polysaccharide of *Escherichia coli. Pediatr. Res., 10*, 82–87. doi: 10.1203/00006450-197602000-00002.

38. Schuchat, A., Robinson, K., Wenger, J. D., et al., (1997). Bacterial meningitis in the United States in 1995. Active surveillance team. *N. Engl. J. Med., 337*, 970–976. doi: 10.1056/NEJM199710023371404.

39. Skipper, B. J., & Davis, L. E., (1997). Ascertaining hypoglycorrhachia in an acute patient. *Am. J. Emerg. Med., 15*, 378–380. doi: 10.1016/S0735-6757(97)90131-5.

40. Song, J. H., Dagan, R., Klugman, K. P., & Fritzell, B., (2012). The relationship between pneumococcal serotypes and antibiotic resistance. *Vaccine, 30*(17), 2728–2737. doi: 10.1016/j.vaccine.2012.01.091.

41. Tattevin, P., Bruneel, F., & Regnier, B., (2002). Cranial CT before lumbar puncture in suspected meningitis. *N. Engl. J. Med., 346*, 1248–1251. doi: 10.1056/NEJM200204183461615.

42. Thigpen, M. C., Whitney, C. G., Messonnier, N. E., et al., (2011). Bacterial meningitis in the United States, 1998–2007. *N. Engl. J. Med., 364*, 2016–2025. doi: 10.1056/NEJMoa1005384.

43. Toleman, M., Aho, E., & Virji, M., (2001). Expression of pathogen-like Opa adhesins in commensal *Neisseria*: Genetic and functional analysis. *Cell Microbiol., 3*, 33–44. doi: 10.1046/j.1462-5822.2001.00089.x.

44. Tunkel, A. R., & Scheld, W. M., (1993). Pathogenesis and pathophysiology of bacterial meningitis. *Clin. Microbiol. Rev., 6*, 118–136.

45. Unhanand, M., Mustafa, M. M., McCracken, G. H. Jr., & Nelson, J. D., (1993). Gram-negative enteric bacillary meningitis: A twenty-one-year experience. *J. Pediatr., 122*, 15–21. doi: 10.1016/S0022-3476(05)83480-8.

46. Van, C. H., Hijdra, A., & De Gans, J., (2002). Lumbar puncture and the risk of herniation: When should we first perform CT? *J. Neurol., 249*, 129–137. doi: 10.1007/PL00007855.

47. Verghese, A., & Gallemore, G., (1987). Kernig's and Brudzinski's signs revisited. *Rev. Infect. Dis., 9*, 1187–1192. doi: 10.1093/clinids/9.6.1187.

48. Ward, M. A., Greenwood, T. M., Kumar, D. R., Mazza, J. J., & Yale, S. H., (2010). Josef Brudzinski and Vladimir Mikhailovich Kernig: Signs for diagnosing meningitis. *Clin. Med. Res., 8*, 13–17. doi: 10.3121/cmr.2010.862.

49. Weisfelt, M., Van De, B. D., Spanjaard, L., & De Gans, J., (2007). Nosocomial bacterial meningitis in adults: A prospective series of 50 cases. *J. Hosp. Infect., 66*, 71–78. doi: 10.1016/j.jhin.2007.02.017.

50. Wurzner, R., Orren, A., & Lachmann, P. J., (1992). Inherited deficiencies of the terminal components of human complement. *Immunodefic. Rev., 3*, 123–147.

Chapter

INFECTIONS OF THE EYE

8

Contents

Unit Introduction

An eye infection is a condition affecting the eyes that is brought on by a bacterium, virus, or fungus. Conjunctivitis, or pink eye, is the most typical eye infection, and while most pink eye cases are caused by viruses, it can also be a result of bacterial infection. Antibiotics are not effective in treating viral infections, as they are only used in treating infections caused by bacteria.

One or both eyes may become infected with an eye infection, and certain infections are not dangerous. There are typically other medical emergencies that may result in blindness. Almost any part of your eye can be affected by an eye infection, including your eyelid, cornea, conjunctiva, or external eye structures (Figure 8.1).

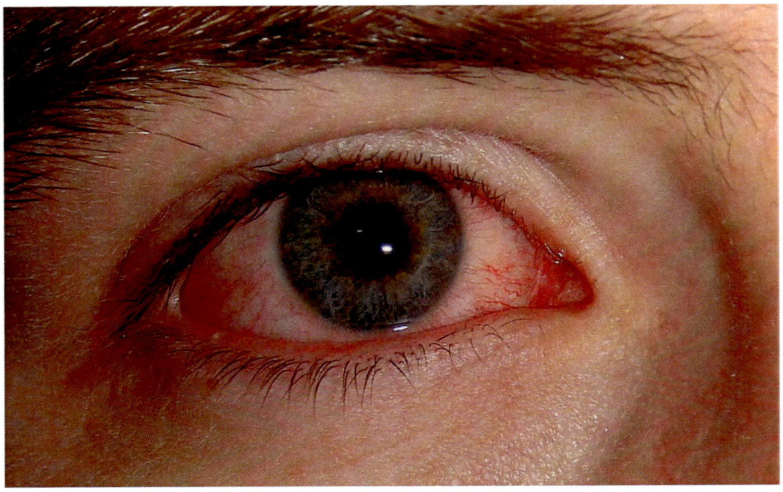

Figure 8.1. *Microorganisms cause infections in one or both eyes, with pink eye (conjunctivitis) being the most common eye infection.*

Source: By P33tr at English Wikipedia – Transferred from en.wikipedia to Commons, Public Domain, https://commons.wikimedia.org/w/index.php?curid=2930985.

Orientation and Directional Terms

Terms	Definition	Illustration
Conjunctivitis	Conjunctivitis, more commonly known as pink eye, occurs when blood vessels in the conjunctiva become infected with a virus or bacteria. In its microbial form, pink eye is highly contagious (there is also a non-contagious allergic form).	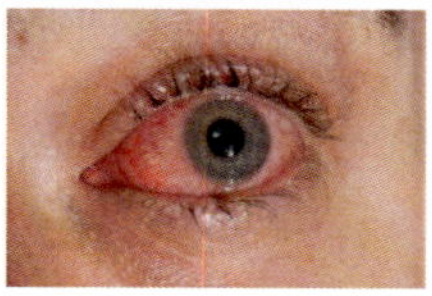
Sty	A sty is a small bump or pimple that grows on the outer edges of your eyelid. It is caused by a bacterial infection of the oil glands that exist in that part of the eye.	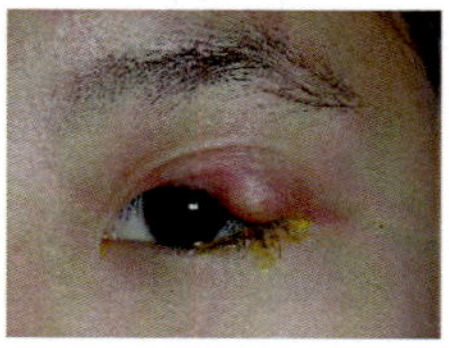
Keratitis	Keratitis is a viral, bacterial, or fungal infection of the cornea. It can also result from an eye injury. Contact lens wearers are especially susceptible to contracting keratitis.	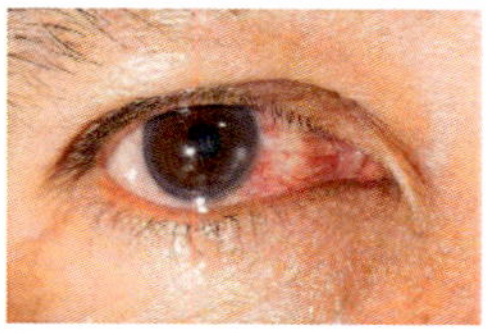
Blepharitis	Blepharitis is a bacterial inflammation of the eyelids. As with sties, the condition has its origin in the clogging of oil glands at the base of the eyelashes.	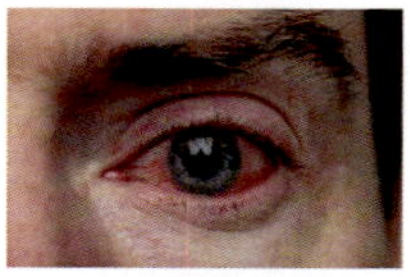
Uveitis	Uveitis is an infection of the uvea, the pigmented layer of the eye, including the iris and choroid. Causes include viral infections, eye injuries, or immune-system deficiencies.	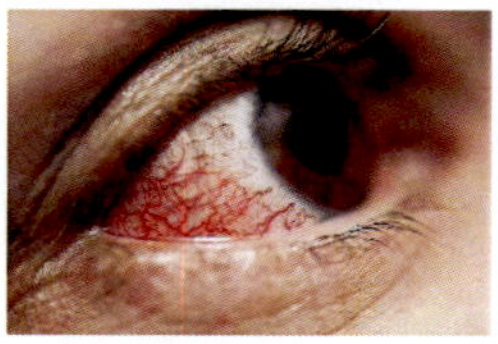
Cellulitis	Cellulitis is an eyelid infection. It generally occurs when a scratch or minor eye injury becomes infected with some form of bacteria (e.g., Staphylococcus or staph).	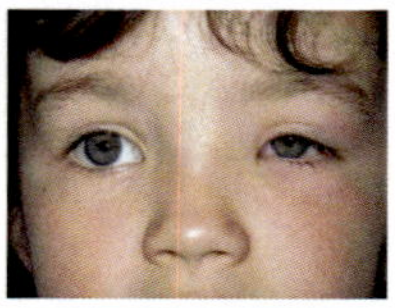
Endophthalmitis	Endophthalmitis is a severe inflammation of the inside of the eye. It results from a bacterial or fungal infection, most often from Candida or yeast fungus.	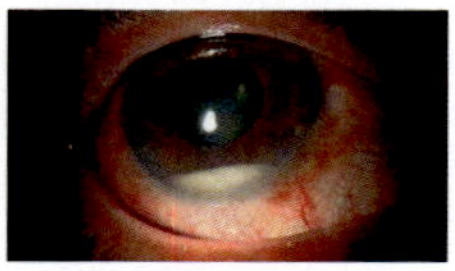
Dacryocystitis	Dacryocystitis is a blockage of the tear ducts. It can be congenital (present from birth) or acquired, typically through bacterial infection.	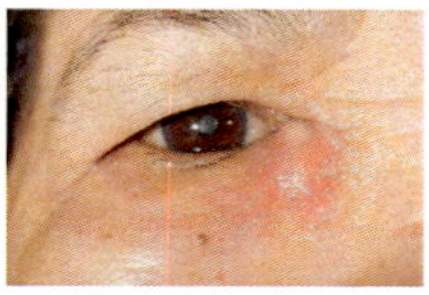
Ocular herpes	Ocular herpes is an infection of the eye by the herpes simplex virus (HSV-1). It is spread by contact with other persons carrying the virus (though not sexually like HSV-2, another herpes virus).	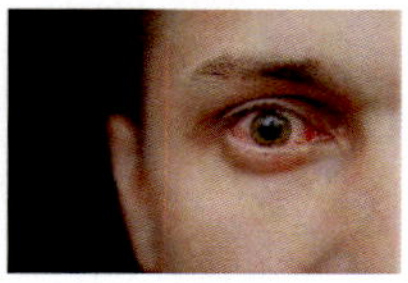

8.1. Common Eye Infections

An infection in your eyes is probably the cause if you've experienced any discomfort, swelling, itching, or redness. Treatment for eye infections varies depending on the cause, which can be viral, bacterial, or fungal.

The good news is that you can get treatment quickly because eye infections are easy to identify. This is all the information you require to identify the cause and treat the eight most prevalent eye infections.

8.1.1. Conjunctivitis/Pink Eye

Pink eye, or infectious conjunctivitis, is one of the most prevalent infections of the eyes. It occurs when bacteria or a virus infect the blood vessels in the conjunctiva, the thin membrane that surrounds your eyeball. Your eyes consequently become irritated and turn pink or red (Figure 8.2).

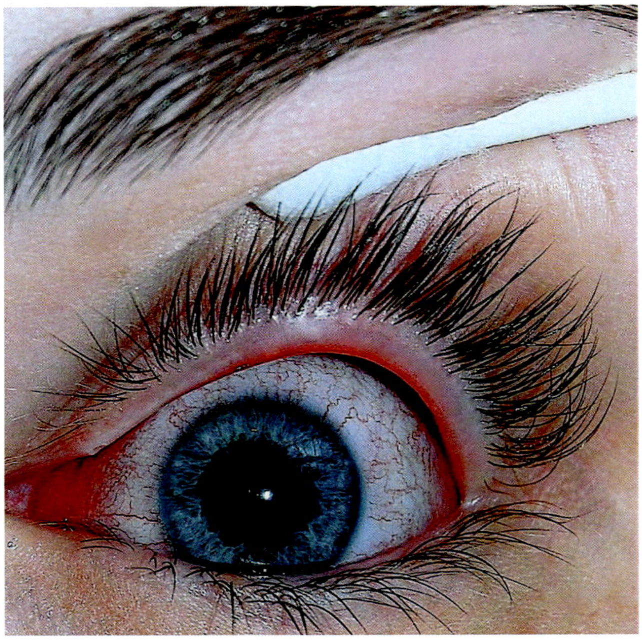

Figure 8.2. *Infectious conjunctivitis.*

Allergies or exposure to chemicals, such as chlorine in swimming pools, can also cause this infection. It is very common for conjunctivitis to be brought on by bacteria or viruses, and for up to two weeks following the onset of the infection, you can still spread the infection. If you experience any of the following symptoms, get in touch with your doctor right away so they can be treated:

- a pinkish or reddish hue in your eyes.
- a thick, watery discharge from your eyes that is most noticeable in the morning.
- itching or a persistent sensation of something in your eyes.

- shedding more tears than usual—especially if one eye is affected.

Conjunctivitis caused by bacteria and viruses can travel quickly from one person to another, whereas contagious allergic conjunctivitis does not exist.

8.1.1.1. Viral Conjunctivitis

The most prevalent kind of conjunctivitis is viral conjunctivitis. Due to its high contagiousness, this particular form of pink eye frequently spreads throughout crowded areas like schools. Usually, it results in watery discharge and red, burning eyes. The same virus that gives people the common cold runny noses and sore throats also typically causes viral conjunctivitis (Figure 8.3).

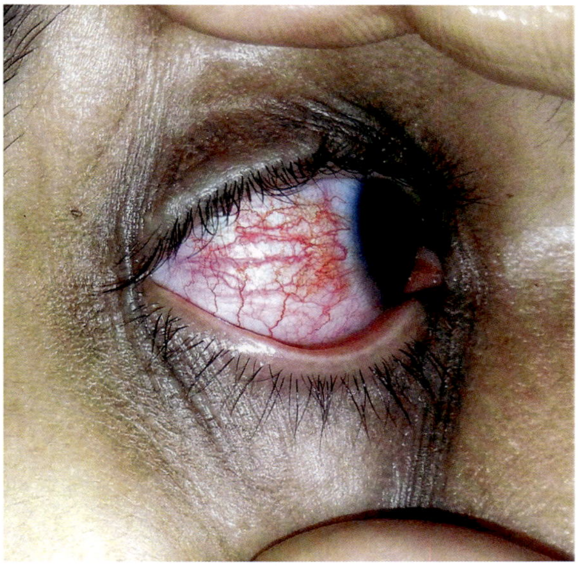

Figure 8.3. *Viral conjunctivitis.*

Source: By Banswalhemant – Own work, CC BY-SA 4.0, https://commons.wikimedia.org/w/index.php?curid=90397215.

8.1.1.2. Bacterial Conjunctivitis

Even more easily spread is bacterial conjunctivitis. Your eyes will be red, painful, and filled with sticky pus if you have bacterial conjunctivitis. On the other hand, certain bacterial infections might not produce any discharge at all. Pink eye and strep throat can occasionally be caused by the same bacteria (Figure 8.4).

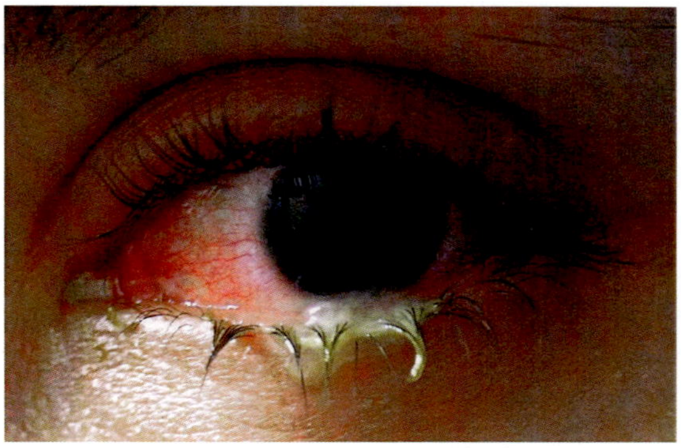

Figure 8.4. *Bacterial conjunctivitis.*

Source: By Tanalai at English Wikipedia, CC BY 3.0, https://commons.wikimedia.org/w/index.php?curid=3646869.

8.1.1.3. Allergic Conjunctivitis

A form of pink eye known as allergic conjunctivitis is caused by an allergic reaction to pollen, animals, smoke from cigarettes, chlorine from swimming pools, fumes from cars, or other environmental triggers. It is not transmissible, and your eyes may get puffy and become red, watery, and itchy (Figure 8.5).

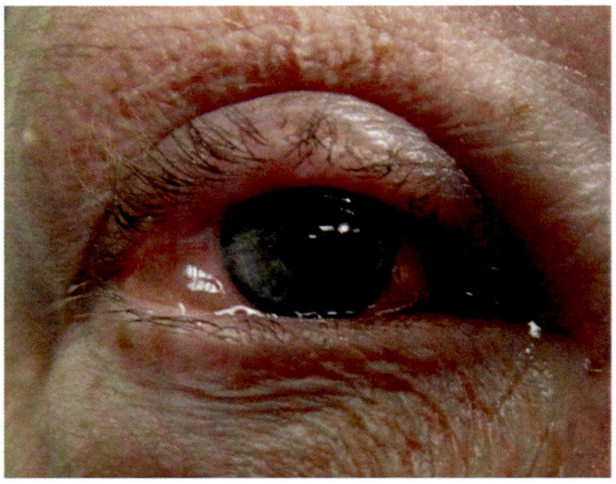

Figure 8.5. *Allergic conjunctivitis.*

Source: By James Heilman, MD – Own work, CC BY-SA 4.0, https://commons.wikimedia.org/w/index.php?curid=40647835.

8.1.1.3.1. Symptoms

With the previously discussed causes, symptoms differ. In addition to mild redness, allergic symptoms include clear and watery discharge. Itching may or may not happen, sometimes to a great extent. Bacterial infections usually cause little pain, but they can also look quite dramatic, with moderate redness and almost always a yellow-green discharge, sometimes to an extreme degree. In addition to causing swelling and redness on the eyelids, this discharge can adhere to the lashes and give the appearance of crustiness.

Patients who wear contact lenses may be more susceptible to severe bacterial infections. Wearers of contact lenses also run the risk of developing a bacterial corneal ulcer, which would cause excruciating pain and light sensitivity. Infections with viruses are typically painful and can also result in moderate redness. Usually, the pain feels gritty and sandy, as if something might be in the eye, and there there may be additional mild to severe photosensitivity.

8.1.1.4. Keratitis

An infection of the cornea results in infectious keratitis, or corneal swelling. Your iris and pupil are covered in a clear layer called the cornea. Keratitis can be caused by an eye injury or an infection (viral, fungal, bacterial, or parasitic), however it is not always contagious.

Depending on its causes, keratitis can be classified into two main categories – infectious and non-infectious.

8.1.1.4.1. Infectious Keratitis

Listed are commons factors behind the cause of infectious keratitis (Figure 8.6):

1. **Bacteria:** *S. aureus* and *P. aeruginosa* are the two most prevalent species of bacteria that can cause bacterial keratitis. Most often, it appears in those who misuse their contacts.
2. **Fungi:** *Aspergillus*, *Candida*, or *Fusarium* spp. are the culprits behind fungal keratitis. Fungal keratitis is more common in people who wear contact lenses, similarly to bacterial keratitis. On the other hand, these fungi can also be encountered outside.
3. **Parasites:** The prevalence of an organism known as Acanthamoeba in Americans who wear contact lenses has increased. The parasite can be acquired by swimming in a lake, hiking through a forest, or getting contaminated water on your contact lenses. It is an outdoor parasite. The name for this kind of infection is Acanthamoeba keratitis.
4. **Viruses:** The main cause of viral keratitis is the herpes simplex virus, which first causes conjunctivitis before moving on to keratitis.

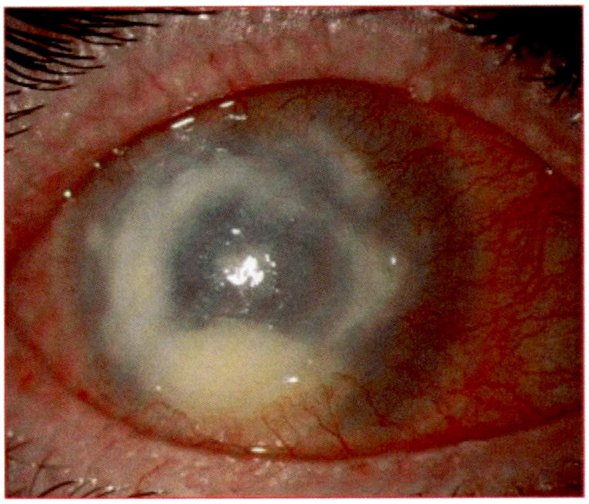

Figure 8.6. *Parasitic (acanthamoeba) infection.*

Source: Eyewiki.

8.1.1.4.2. Noninfectious Keratitis

Some non-infectious reasons for keratitis could be (Figure 8.7):

- Extending the wear of your contacts.

- Using contacts with extended wear.
- While swimming, keep your contacts on.
- Residing in a warm climate, which raises the possibility of corneal damage from plant materials.
- A weakened immune system
- Exposure to strong sunlight, sometimes known as photokeratitis.

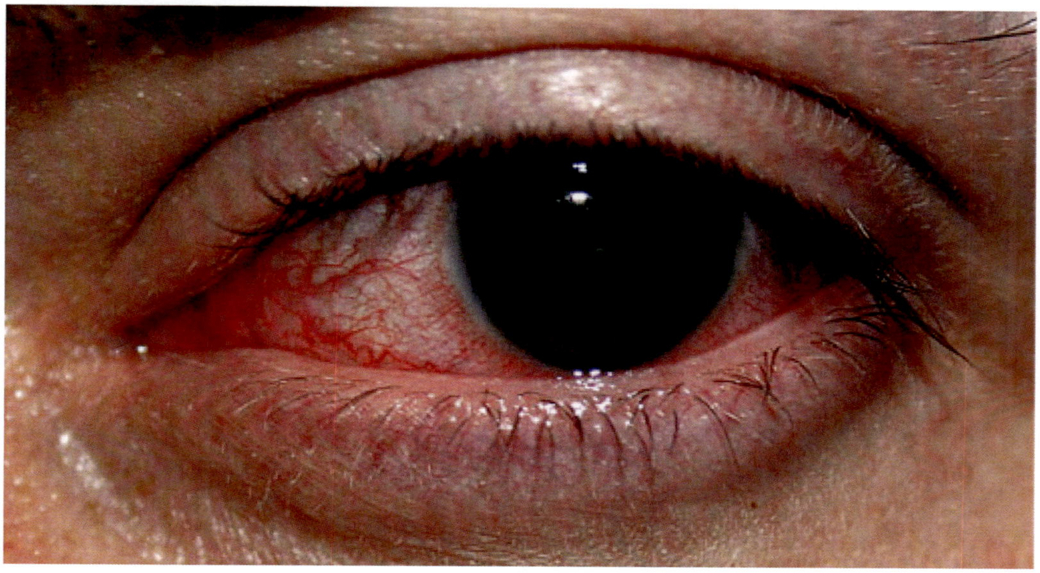

Figure 8.7. *Non-infectious keratitis.*

Source: By Eddie314 at the English-language Wikipedia, CC BY-SA 3.0, https://commons.wikimedia.org/w/index.php?curid=5412067.

Symptoms of keratitis can include:

- Redness and swelling in your eye;
- Eye pain or discomfort;
- Producing more tears than usual or an abnormal discharge;
- Pain or discomfort when you open and close your eyelids;
- Loss of some vision or blurry vision;
- Light sensitivity;
- Sensation of having something stuck in your eye.

You're more likely to develop keratitis if:

- You wear contact lenses;
- Your immune system is weak from another condition or illness;
- You live somewhere that's humid and warm;
- You use corticosteroid eyedrops for an existing eye condition;

- Your eye is injured, especially by plants with chemicals that can get into your eye.

If you have any signs of keratitis, see your doctor right away so the infection can be treated. Treatments for keratitis can include the following:

- **Bacterial:** A keratitis infection can typically be resolved with antibacterial eye drops in a few days. More serious infections are usually treated with oral antibiotics.
- **Fungal:** Antifungal eye drops, or medication will be necessary to eradicate the fungal organisms causing your keratitis. This may need several weeks or months.
- **Viral:** Within a few days to a week, the infection can be stopped with oral antiviral drugs or eye drops. Even after treatment, viral keratitis symptoms can recur, as a virus cannot be completely eradicated.

8.1.2. Endophthalmitis

A bacterial or fungal infection can cause endophthalmitis, a severe inflammation of the internal organs of the eye. The most frequent cause of endophthalmitis is fungal infections caused by *Candida* spp. (Figure 8.8).

Although it is uncommon, this ailment can develop following specific eye surgeries, such as cataract surgery. It could also occur if something pierces your eye. Symptoms to be aware of, particularly following surgery or an eye injury, include the following:

- Mild to severe eye pain;
- Partial or complete vision loss;
- Blurry vision;
- Redness or swelling around the eye and eyelids;
- Eye pus or discharge;
- Sensitivity to bright lights.

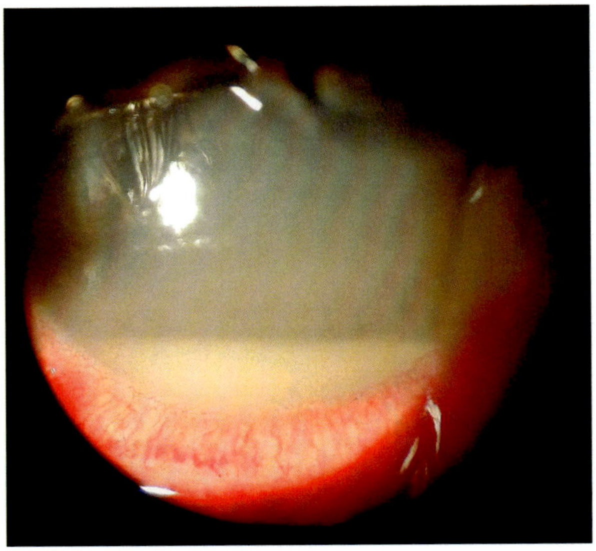

Figure 8.8. *Endophthalmitis.*

Source: By Imrankabirhossain – Own work, CC BY-SA 4.0, https://commons.wikimedia.org/w/index.php?curid=59072356.

The course of treatment is determined by the infection's cause and severity. To help treat the infection, you will first need to have an injection of antibiotics directly into your eye using a specialized needle. To reduce inflammation, a corticosteroid shot might also be administered to you.

Any foreign material that has gotten into the eye must be removed immediately if it is the cause of the infection. In these situations, get emergency medical help; never attempt to extract an object from your eye on your own.

Within a few days of receiving antibiotics and having the object removed, your symptoms should start to improve.

8.1.3. Blepharitis

An inflammation of the skin folds covering your eyes is called blepharitis. The most common cause of this kind of inflammation is blockage of the oil glands located beneath the skin of your eyelids, at the base of your lashes. Bacteria may be the cause of blepharitis (Figure 8.9).

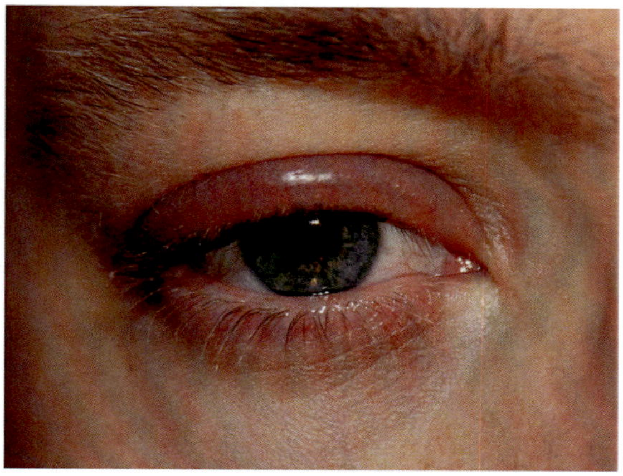

Figure 8.9. *Blepharitis.*

Source: By clubtable – Self-photographed, Public Domain, https://commons.wikimedia.org/w/index.php?curid=20138102.

Symptoms of blepharitis include:

- Eye or eyelid redness, itchiness, swelling;
- Eyelid oiliness;
- Sensation of burning in your eyes;
- Feeling like something's stuck in your eyes;
- Sensitivity to light;
- Producing more tears than usual;
- Crustiness on your eyelashes or corners of your eyes.

You're more likely to develop blepharitis if you:

- have scalp or eyebrow dandruff;
- are allergic to your eye or face makeup;
- have oil glands that don't work properly;
- have lice or mites on your eyelashes;
- take certain medications that affect your immune system.

Treatments for blepharitis include:

- Cleaning your eyelids with clean water and applying a warm, wet, clean towel to your eyelids to relieve swelling.
- Using corticosteroid eye drops or ointments to help with inflammation.
- Using lubricating eye drops to moisten your eyes and prevent irritation from dryness.
- Taking antibiotics as oral medications, eye drops, or ointments applied to your eyelids.

8.1.4. Sty

A sty (also known as a hordeolum) is a bump on the outside corners of your eyelids that resembles a pimple. These glands can become clogged with debris, oils, and dead skin, which promotes the overgrowth of bacteria, and a sty is the resultant infection (Figure 8.10).

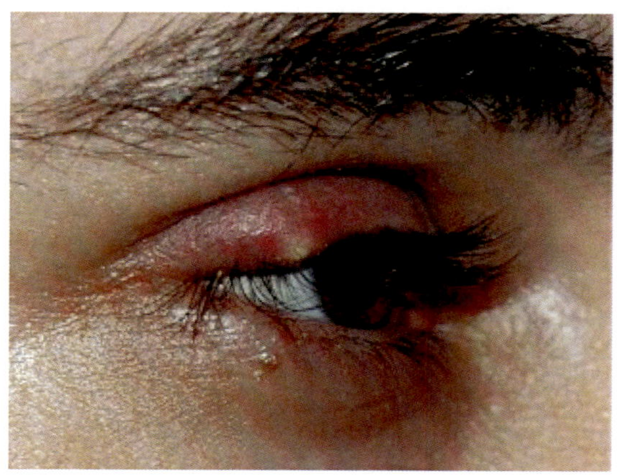

Figure 8.10. *Stye.*

Source: By Andre Riemann – Own work, Public Domain, https://commons.wikimedia.org/w/index.php?curid=670483.

An obstruction of one of the oil glands in the eyelids results in a stye. This permits bacteria to proliferate within the clogged gland. Styes resemble typical acne lesions that appear on other parts of the skin. It's possible for you to have multiple styes simultaneously.

Most styes take a few days to develop. They could exhaust and recover by themselves. When an inflamed oil gland completely obstructs, a stye may develop into a chalazion. Your vision may be affected if a chalazion grows to a significant size.

Demodex is a mite that is frequently found on human skin and can cause blepharitis and can exacerbate styes. Styes are more likely to occur if you have blepharitis.

Other possible common eyelid bumps include:

- Xanthelasma: elevated yellow patches on your eyelids, which are a common aging sign. These are not harmful, though occasionally they may indicate elevated cholesterol.
- Papillomas: skin-colored or pink pimples. While they are not harmful, they may slowly spread, obstruct your vision, or cause you discomfort due to appearance. If so, surgery can be used to remove them.
- Cysts: Small fluid-filled sacs that can affect your vision.
- Tenderness of the eyelid

Sty symptoms include:

- Pain or tenderness;
- Itchiness or irritation;
- Swelling;
- Producing more tears than usual;
- Crustiness around your eyelids;
- Increased tear production.

Some treatments for sties include:

- Applying a fresh, warm, moist cloth to your eyelids several times a day for 20 minutes at a time.
- Wash your eyelids with water and a mild, fragrance-free soap.
- Using over-the-counter (OTC) painkillers to treat pain and swelling, such as Acetaminophen (Tylenol).
- Removing makeup and contact lenses until the infection clears up.
- Applying creams containing antibiotics to aid in the infectious overgrowth's death.

Consult your physician if, despite treatment, the pain or swelling worsens. In roughly 7 to 10 days, a sty should go away. If it doesn't work, find out what other options your doctor has.

8.1.5. Uveitis

The retina is the portion of your eye that sends images to your brain, and the uvea is the central layer of your eyeball that carries blood there. Uveitis results when an infection causes your uvea to become inflamed.

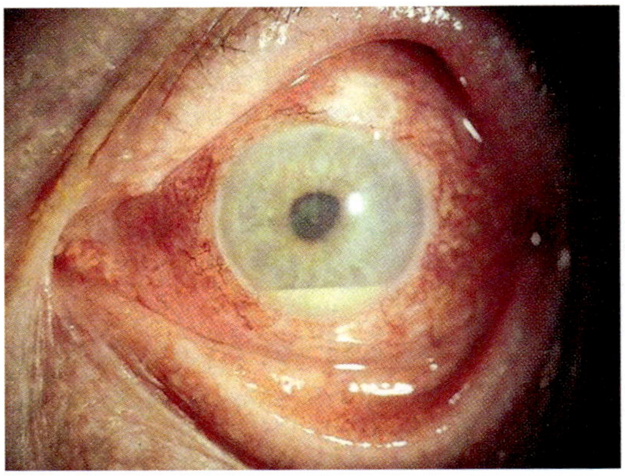

Figure 8.11. *Anterior uveitis often affects the colored part of the eye, i.e., the iris.*

Source: By EyeMD (Rakesh Ahuja, M.D.) – Own work., CC BY-SA 2.5, https://commons.wikimedia.org/w/index.php?curid=1229578.

Viral infections, eye trauma, and immune system disorders are common causes of uveitis. Long-term issues are rare with uveitis, but blindness may result from untreated severe cases (Figure 8.11).

Uveitis comes in three varieties, and they depend on the area of the uvea that is impacted. Anterior uveitis is the term for swelling of the uvea close to the front of the eye, where the symptoms can appear suddenly and persist for several weeks. While some types of anterior uveitis resolve on their own, others can recur.

Intermediate uveitis is the term used to describe swelling of the uvea in the middle of the eye. From a few weeks to many years, symptoms may persist, and this form may experience cycles of improvement followed by deterioration.

The term "posterior uveitis" refers to uveal swelling that moves toward the back of the eye. The duration of symptoms may be years, and they may appear gradually.

In severe cases, all layers may be involved, and uveitis causes are not always known to doctors. You run a higher risk of developing uveitis if you currently have or have had:

- Illnesses like Lyme disease, shingles, herpes simplex, syphilis, and parasites like toxoplasmosis.
- A systemic inflammatory disease like lupus, rheumatoid arthritis, or inflammatory bowel disease (IBD).
- An eye injury.

The risk of developing uveitis is further increased by smoking (cigarettes, cigars, or pipes). Uveitis symptoms can include:

- Eye redness;
- Pain;
- "Floaters" in your visual field;
- Sensitivity to light;
- Blurry vision.

Treatment for uveitis may include:

- Wearing darkened glasses;
- Eye drops that open up your pupil to relieve pain;
- Corticosteroid eye drops or oral steroids that relieve inflammation;
- Eye injections to treat symptoms;
- Oral antibiotics for infections that have spread beyond your eye;
- Medications that subdue your immune system (severe cases).

Treatment for uveitis typically begins to improve after a few days. If an underlying condition is the cause, posterior uveitis, which affects the back of the eye, can take longer to heal—up to several months.

8.1.6. Orbital Cellulitis

An infection of the muscles and fat surrounding the eyes is called orbital cellulitis. It impacts the cheeks, brows, and eyelids. It could start out abruptly or be the result of an infection that gets worse over time (Figure 8.12).

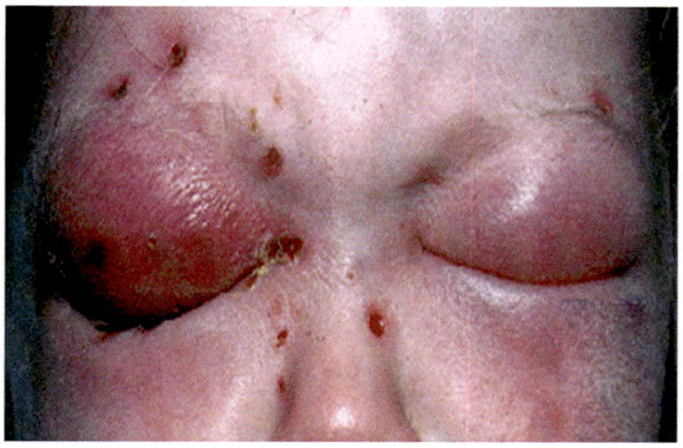

Figure 8.12. *Orbital cellulitis.*

Source: By Jonathan Trobe, M.D.– University of Michigan Kellogg Eye Center – The Eyes Have It, CC BY 3.0, https://commons.wikimedia.org/w/index.php?curid=16115960.

An infection as dangerous as orbital cellulitis can have long-term effects. Orbital cellulitis is distinct from periorbital cellulitis, which affects the skin surrounding the eyes or the eyelid. In kids, it typically begins as a sinus infection caused by bacteria like Haemophilus influenza. The infection used to affect young children, under the age of seven, more frequently, however thanks to the development of a vaccine that aids in infection prevention, it is now uncommon.

Orbital cellulitis can also be brought on by beta-hemolytic streptococci bacteria such as *S. pneumoniae*, and *S. aureus*.

Immediate medical attention is imperative as orbital cellulitis infections in children can rapidly deteriorate, and potentially cause visual impairments or even loss of sight.

Symptoms may include:

- Painful swelling of the upper and lower eyelid, and possibly the eyebrow and cheek;
- Bulging eyes;
- Decreased vision;
- Pain when moving the eye;
- Fever, often 102°F (38.8°C) or higher;
- General ill feeling;
- Difficulty with eye movements;
- Double vision;
- Shiny, red, or purple eyelid.

Tests commonly done include:

- CBC (complete blood count);
- Blood culture;
- Spinal tap in affected children who are very sick.

Other tests may include:

- X-ray of the sinuses and surrounding area;
- CT scan or MRI of the sinuses and orbit;
- Culture of eye and nose drainage;
- Throat culture.

Generally, a hospital stay is required, and the most common form of treatment is the intravenous administration of antibiotics. Surgery might also be required to remove pressure from the area surrounding the eye or to drain the abscess.

An infection with orbital cellulitis can rapidly worsen, therefore an individual with this illness needs to be examined every few hours.

8.1.7. Ocular Herpes

Uncomfortable symptoms of eye herpes include redness, sensitivity to light, and the sensation of a foreign object in the eye. Additionally, some people may get sores on their eyelids.

Eye herpes, ocular herpes, or herpetic eye disease are terms used to describe HSV symptoms that impact the eyes.

Recurrent infections may raise the possibility of sequelae like detachment of the retina, secondary glaucoma, and corneal scarring.

8.1.7.1. Types

There are two major types of HSV (Figure 8.13):

- **Type 1:** Herpes type 1 (HSV-1) can cause symptoms like fever blisters, which some people call cold sores, or it can be asymptomatic.
- **Type 2:** The virus that is spread through sexual contact is known as herpes type 2 (HSV-2). Although the genitalia are the primary site of symptoms, the eyes may also be affected.

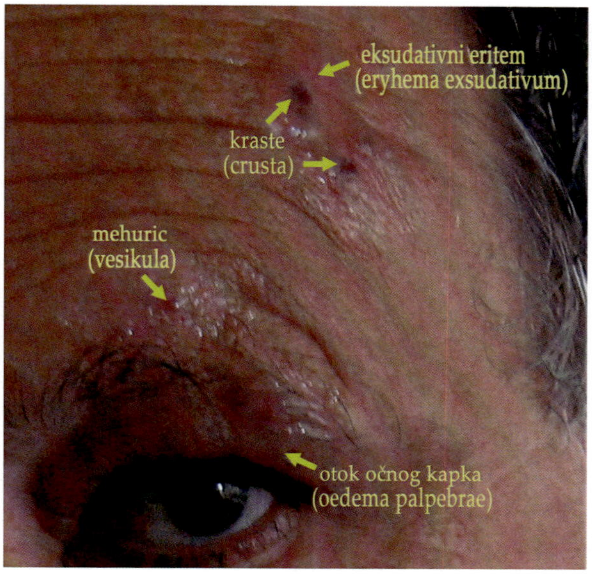

Figure 8.13. *Ocular herpes.*

Source: By User: Milorad Dimic MD – Own work, CC BY-SA 3.0, https://commons.wikimedia.org/w/index.php?curid=12120471.

The American Academy of Ophthalmology (AAO) states that HSV-1 is more likely to cause eye infections than HSV-2.

Usually, skin-to-skin contact with an individual who already has herpes will result in the transmission of either form of the virus. When the virus is activated, it can move from its dormant state in the nerve cells to the eye by traveling through the nerves.

According to the AAO, 90% of individuals will at some point in their lives have been exposed to HSV-1, usually as young children.

8.1.7.2. Symptoms

Herpetic eye disease can cause a person to have a wide range of symptoms. These can affect one eye more than the other, but they can happen in both.

Depending on which area of the eye is afflicted, some symptoms may vary. These are a few instances of these symptoms:

- The feeling of something being in the eye;
- Headaches;
- Light sensitivity;
- Redness;
- Tearing;

On top of the eyelids, herpes sores can also occur occasionally, and could seem like a blistered rash. After the blisters form crusts, they usually heal in three to seven days.

A person's vision may change if the herpes virus damages the retina, the cornea, or the inside of the eye. Even though a person's eye may appear painful, eye herpes usually does not cause much pain.

8.1.7.3. Conditions with Similar Symptoms

Ocular symptoms of HSV may resemble those of the varicella-zoster virus, which is the cause of chickenpox.

Shingles, or herpes zoster, can result from the varicella-zoster virus reactivating. This results in vesicles, or tiny blisters, on the scalp and forehead that may extend to the corresponding eye. Another ailment that may present with comparable symptoms is pinkeye, or conjunctivitis.

8.1.7.4. Causes

A person infected with the herpes virus can transmit it through their spit or nasal secretions. When someone is experiencing a cold sore, the chance could be increased.

The body's nerves, including those in the eyes, may then be penetrated by the virus found in the secretions. Sometimes the virus infects the body without causing any issues or symptoms, which is said by medical professionals to be dormant. A dormant virus may begin to replicate in response to specific stimuli, resulting in ocular irritation. These triggers include, for instance:

- Fever;
- Major surgical or dental procedures;
- Stress;
- Sunburn;
- Trauma or severe injury.

The herpes virus has the potential to spread widely, however not everyone who gets the herpes virus or comes into contact with it, will develop eye herpes.

8.1.7.5. Diagnosis

Herpetic eye disease is diagnosed by ophthalmologists, or eye doctors, by obtaining a patient's medical history and inquiring about their symptoms. Questions are obtained from the patient regarding when they first took notice of their symptoms, and whether any improvements or deterioration of their condition have occurred.

The eye will be physically examined by the ophthalmologist. A slit lamp, a type of special microscope, may be used during the examination to view the surface of the eye and possibly the eyelid because HSV causes dendrites, a branching pattern, on the cornea.

By examining the sores, these experts can typically make an accurate diagnosis of eye herpes. To measure the eye pressure, they will need to use specialized equipment if the infection has spread to the deeper layers of the eye, where examination is also recommended.

It is rare to do HSV of the eye laboratory testing. Typically, eye herpes primarily affects the front of the transparent eye. We call this disease epithelial keratitis.

Stromal keratitis is the term used when eye herpes reaches the deeper layers of the cornea. This condition is particularly concerning for eye doctors as it has the potential to result in corneal scarring, and lead to permanent vision impairment for the individual.

8.1.7.6. Treatments

The degree of herpes keratitis determines how it should be treated. Antiviral medications, both topical and oral, are typically used by doctors to treat mild infections.

- **Eyelids:** Physicians may advise patients to apply topical ointments, like an antiviral ointment, sparingly to their eyelids.
- **Outer Eye Layers:** In the event that the eye herpes solely impacts the external layers of the eye, a physician might recommend an antiviral eye drop or an oral antiviral drug, like acyclovir (Zovirax). These lessen the impact of the virus and may shorten the time that symptoms last.

People should always consult an ophthalmologist, though, as some eye drops have the potential to exacerbate symptoms.

- **Deeper Eye Layers:** An ophthalmologist may recommend antiviral eye drops and oral medications if the herpes virus has impacted the deeper layers of the cornea.

In addition, they might recommend steroid eye drops, as they can aid in lowering ocular inflammation, which may result in elevated intraocular pressure.

However, because steroids can exacerbate herpes in the body, the AAO emphasizes that people must take antiviral medication in addition to steroid eye drops.

8.1.7.7. Prevention

Some doctors may advise taking antiviral medications on a regular basis to lower the risk of developing eye herpes again because the condition can lead to secondary infections.

Doctors work to prevent recurrence of herpetic eye infections because they can cause more damage to the eyes. Some preventive advice is as follows:

- Avoid touching the eyes;
- Wash hands thoroughly;
- Practice good hygiene;
- Attend regular eye exams;
- Use contact lenses as an eye doctor instructs.

8.2. Organisms of Eye Infection

Figure 8.14 illustrates the microorganisms relevant to eye infections, including commensal, colonizing, and exogenous bacteria. Among these, *P. aeruginosa* and the protozoal parasite Acanthamoeba can be acquired from domestic water supplies and can lead to keratitis in contact lens wearers. If *P. aeruginosa* is detected in samples from a hospitalized patient, it is important to consider a potential water source (Figure 8.15).

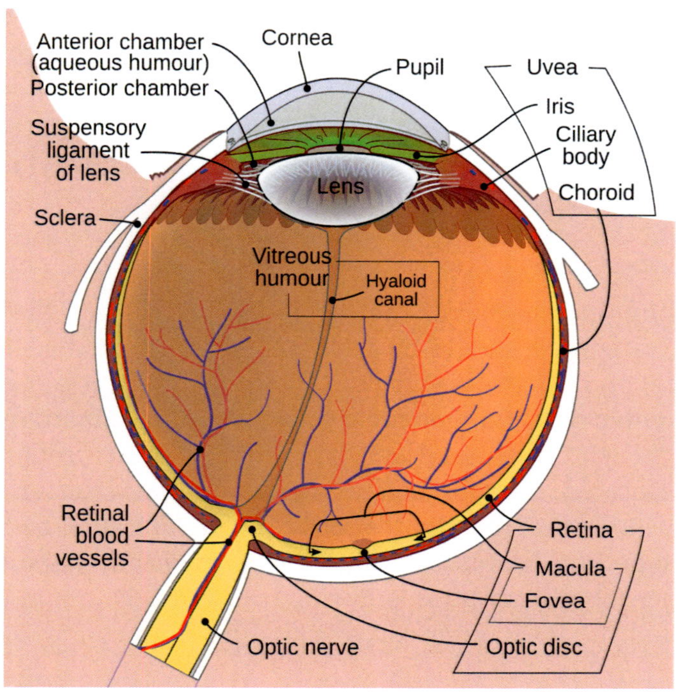

Figure 8.14. *The structure of the eye and adjacent tissues.*

Source: By Rhcastilhos. And Jmarchn - Schematic_diagram_of_the_human_eye_with_English_annotations.svg, CC BY-SA 3.0, https://commons.wikimedia.org/w/index.php?curid=1597930.

	Bacterial phyla	Skin (%)	Lid margin (%)	Ocular surface (%)	Fornix conjunctiva (%)
	Proteobacteria	31.6	77.4	44.6	90
	Firmicutes	32.9	4.1	36.3	4.4
	Actinobacteria	23.5	8.7	8.7	0
	Bacteroidetes	7.4	3.4	3	1.3
	Deinococcus-Thermus	0.3	0	5.6	0
	Bacterial genera	**Skin (%)**	**Lid margin (%)**	**Ocular surface (%)**	**Fornix conjunctiva (%)**
Proteobacteria	*Acetobacter*	0	0	6.9	0
	Neisseriaceae	9.6	5.1	6.8	1.5
	Acinetobacter	1	0.5	12.3	3.9
	Sphingomonas	0.3	0.1	2.5	0.4
	Pseudomonas	5.8	65.1	2.1	80.7
Firmicutes	*Staphylococcus*	15.2	1.8	3	1
	Aeribacillus	0.3	0	11.3	2
	Streptococcus	6	0.3	2.3	0
	Bacillus	0.4	0.2	5.9	0.3
	Veillonella	5.1	0	1.6	0
	Thermoanaerobacterium	0	0	4.5	0.3
	Geobacillus	0	0	2.8	0.5
Actinobacteria	*Corynebacterium*	12.2	7.8	4	0
Deinococcus-Thermus	*Deinococcus*	0.1	0	3.8	0

Figure 8.15. *Surface microbiota on the eye.*

Source: Chiang, M. C., & Chern, E., (2022). Ocular surface microbiota: Ophthalmic infectious disease and probiotics. Front. Microbiol., 13, 952473. doi: 10.3389/fmicb.2022.952473.

8.3. Pathogenesis

The red eye inflammation and discharge that go along with it are the hallmarks of bacterial conjunctivitis. Particular attention should be paid to a severe infection that manifests as severe hyperemia, eyelid edema, and a profuse purulent discharge. *Neisseria meningitidis* and *Neisseria gonorroheae* are two possible bacteria that could be active in this situation. The cornea is harmed by the massive release of lytic enzymes from dying and dead neutrophils. When the cornea is injured or becomes perforated, microorganisms can enter the anterior chamber and then the vitreous humor, which can lead to endophthalmitis (Figure 8.16). *P. aeruginosa* can also cause an aggressive keratitis type in a hospital setting. This is especially important for patients in the ICU who have had superficial corneal trauma during treatment. Pain and vision loss are common symptoms of keratitis, and the ICU patient is typically unable to communicate these symptoms.

An infection of the vitreous humor known as endophthalmitis can cause pain, headaches, photophobia, and loss of vision. After penetrating trauma, organisms can enter the posterior eye; therefore, it is important to take into account soil-derived organisms like *Bacillus cereus*. Unusual environmental bacteria can be isolated when plant material causes a penetrating injury. Particularly important are the coagulase-negative staphylococci in postsurgical endophthalmitis. Additionally, organisms may enter the posterior chamber through the blood, and endocarditis is a likely intravascular source. A liver abscess brought on by *Klebsiella pneumoniae* is another example, as is candidemia resulting from an infected central venous catheter. You need to get in touch with the ophthalmologist right away.

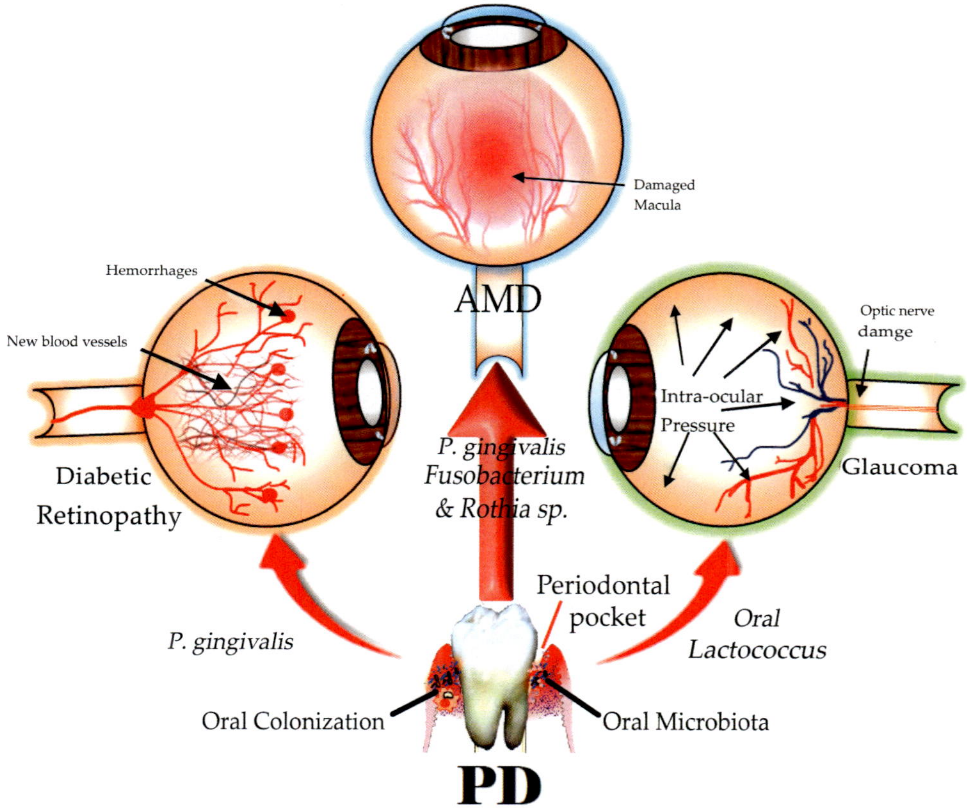

Figure 8.16. *Abrasion of the epithelium allows organisms to invade the cornea and beyond.*

Source: Arjunan, P., & Swaminathan, R., (2022). Do oral pathogens inhabit the eye and play a role in ocular diseases? Journal of Clinical Medicine, 11(10), 2938. https://doi.org/10.3390/jcm11102938.

It might be challenging to differentiate between cavernous sinus thrombosis and orbital cellulitis. Cellulitis typically develops from an infection that spreads from a nasal sinus into the orbit. Trauma can easily damage the thin tissue that divides the ethmoid air cells from the orbit. The symptoms of orbital cellulitis include fever, headaches, and dark red skin around the eyes. There is also pain when moving the eye, which is indicative of inflammation in the orbital cavity's surrounding soft tissue. Proptosis, or forward displacement of the eye, is caused by space constraints within the cavity. The extension of thrombophlebitis in the facial veins causes cavernous sinus thrombosis. The patient has a severe fever, chills, and headache. The diagnosis may be aided by bilateral signs and palsies of the IIIrd, IVth, and VIth cranial nerves, even though it may be challenging to differentiate the illness from orbital cellulitis. Eyelid abscesses, like styes or chalazion, are purulent infections of the lid's glands, and infections of the lid as a whole are typically unilateral and arise in front of the orbital septum. Figure 8.17 shows the lacrimal glands. This entity differs from orbital cellulitis in that, although pain, swelling, and erythema may occur, eye movement is typically painless and normal.

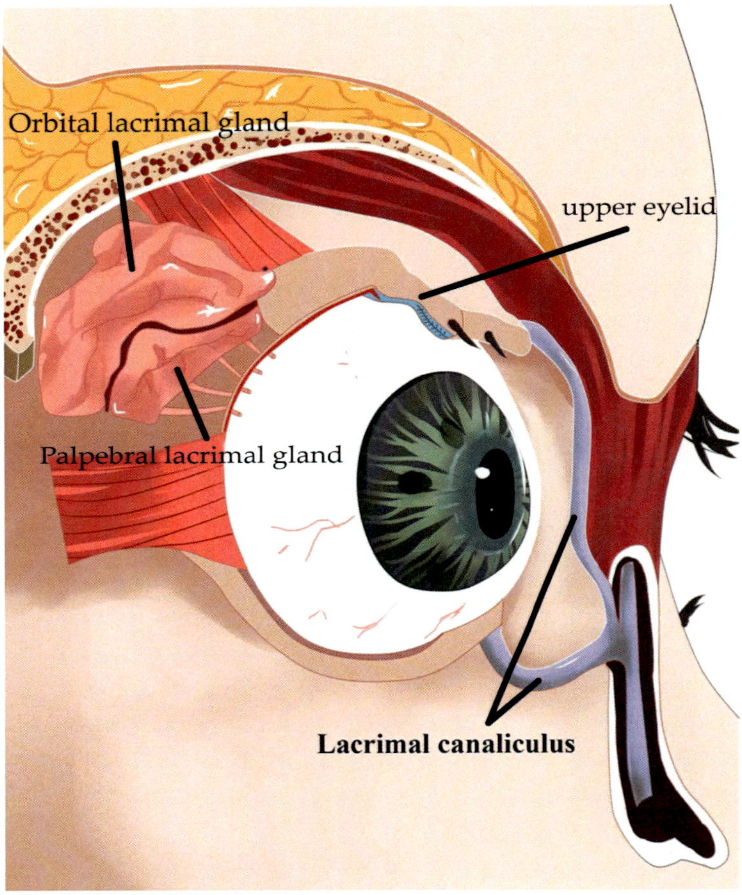

Figure 8.17. *The structure of the lacrimal glands.*

Source: Lin, Y., Zhang, Y., Shi, K., Wu, H., & Ou, S., (2023). Advances in clinical examination of lacrimal gland. Front. Med., 10, 1257209. doi: 10.3389/fmed.2023.1257209.

Infections of the lachrymal gland and nasolachrymal duct are referred to as dacrocystitis and canaliculitis, respectively (Figure 8.18). Although *S. pyogenes* and *Pneumococcus* are common pathogens that typically cause infections, *Actinomyces israelii* can also cause chronic infections. A nodule is created when the duct becomes inflamed. It is made up of an outer layer of fibrous tissue that encloses a purulent group of neutrophils, which in turn surround "sulfur granules." When these granules are found in an excised nodule, they can be used as a diagnostic tool. They are composed of conglomerations of actinomycete bacteria.

	Purpose	Advantage	Disadvantage
Anatomical tests: Palpation CT/ MRI Ultrasound	Check the morphology and tissue changes of the lacrimal gland	Intuitive and repetitive, it can compare the morphological and tissue changes caused by lacrimal gland diseases.	More detailed differential diagnosis of diseases with similar symptoms, medical history, and morphology is required, and pathological tissue examination requires multidisciplinary collaboration.
Invasive examination puncture	Check the pathology of lacrimal gland disease	If standard tests are inconclusive, a more precise and sensitive test may be needed to diagnose the issue.	To avoid causing harm and complications, it's crucial to perform the examination using sterile techniques.
Tear function test: Schrimers Testing TMH	Check the amount of lacrimal gland secretion to check the lacrimal gland secretion function.	Fast, simple, and enables preliminary screening for some eye diseases with too much or few tears.	Tears secretion is less repetitive and affected by external stimulation.
Tear film stability tests: TBUT Tear osmolarity The component of the tear	The quality of the lacrimal gland secretion was determined by detecting the stability of the tear film.	The quality of tears that lacrimal glands secretion is known under the influence of eye surface diseases such as dry eye disease, Sjogren's syndrome.	The environmental factors and the invasive inspections will affect the results.

Figure 8.18. *Infections of the lacrymal gland and nasolacrymal duct.*

Source: Lin, Y., Zhang, Y., Shi, K., Wu, H., & Ou, S., (2023). Advances in clinical examination of lacrimal gland. Front. Med., 10, 1257209. doi: 10.3389/fmed.2023.1257209.

8.4. Diagnosis and Management

The resident flora of the external ocular surface consists of commensal organisms, including species of *Staphylococcus*, *Corynebacterium*, and *Propionibacterium*. Any environmental organism has the potential to appear as a fleeting flora in the eye. However, the tissues and spaces inside the eye are sterile. Since the cornea is avascular and the conjunctiva is protected by blood flow, different kinds of organisms may infiltrate these tissues. Any organism that penetrate the inside of the eye and infect the intraocular tissues can do so because they are comparatively immune-privileged. An important risk factor for infections of the cornea and other intraocular tissues is trauma. Even though exogenous infections are more frequent, hematogenous infections or infections that spread from nearby organs can also cause eye infections.

Bacteria, fungi, parasites, and viruses are the possible causes of ocular infections, and each of these pathogens can result in a variety of diseases. Based only on clinical features, it is typically difficult to identify the causative agent because their features may or may not be distinctive. It may frequently be impossible to distinguish between infectious and non-infectious conditions. Furthermore, a multitude of factors influence the prevalence and distribution of the different types of infectious agents linked to eye infections. *In vivo* techniques like corneal confocal microscopy have made significant progress recently in solidifying clinical diagnosis, particularly in cases of fungal keratitis and amoeba. Aside from its restricted use, the equipment might not be accessible in all environments. Therefore, the gold standard for etiological diagnosis continues to be confirmed through microscopic examination and culture of the clinical samples. These days, molecular diagnosis adds speed, sensitivity, and specificity—factors that were previously lacking in traditional microscopy and culture methods.

8.4.1. In Vivo Corneal Confocal Microscopy

This technique is a compelling non-invasive method that provides image contrast enhancement and magnifications of up to × 200 to × 500, enabling the visualization of corneal details even in cloudy corneas. It makes it possible to make repeated observations that support the diagnosis, treatment, and ongoing monitoring of microbial keratitis cases. Even though confocal microscopy has been shown in multiple studies over the past 10 years to be effective in the diagnosis of Acanthamoeba, fungal, Nocardia, and Microsporidia keratitis, the diagnostic accuracy has only recently been documented. Four observers, who were blind to the tissue diagnosis, evaluated confocal images twice, and diagnostic accuracy indices were computed in one of the studies that used positive tissue diagnosis as the reference. With agreement ratings ranging from fair to moderate, the authors reported the greatest positive likelihood ratio of 2.94 and the lowest negative likelihood ratio of 0.59. It was not advised to use confocal microscopy alone to diagnose microbial keratitis. The purpose of the other study was to ascertain variations in the interpretation and analysis of confocal microscopy results between and among observers.

8.4.2. Conventional Microbiological Methods

Clinical samples from the infection site are required for the diagnosis of eye infections. Seldom can serum samples be used to diagnose eye infections. With the exception of virus or chlamydia isolation, the sample that is typically available is very minute and needs to be processed directly without the use of transport media. Nonetheless, after being stored for 24 hours at room temperature, the use of Amies transport medium without charcoal was demonstrated to be equally effective as processing corneal scrapings directly from the patient for the purpose of culturing bacteria and fungi. Most media should be incubated for a minimum of one to two weeks to support the growth of slow-growing or picky organisms. The types of clinical samples that are typically obtained to diagnose different types of eye infections are enumerated in Table 8.1.

Table 8.1. Type of Sample and Recommended Procedure for Sample Collection in Various Eye Infections

Type of Infection	Type of Sample	Recommended Device/Procedure for Sample Collection
Blepharitis	Scales/discharge from the lid margin.	Forceps/cotton swab.
Conjunctivitis	Fluid/discharge from the lower conjunctival sac.	Calcium alginate/cotton swab.
Dacryocystitis	Fluid/discharge from the lower conjunctival sac.	Calcium alginate/cotton swab.
Keratitis	Corneal scraping.	Kimura spatula, No. 15 surgical blade, bent needle.
Uveitis	Anterior chamber fluid.	Paracentesis (anterior chamber tap) with tuberculin syringe.

Endophthalmitis	Anterior chamber fluid Vitreous aspirate vitreous biopsy.	Paracentesis (anterior chamber tap) with tuberculin syringe tuberculin syringe vitrectomy.
Panophthalmitis	Vitreous biopsy evisceration contents.	Vitrectomy evisceration.
Deep seated stromal infiltrate in keratitis	Corneal biopsy	Lamellar biopsy
Non-healing keratitis requiring keratoplasty	Corneal buttons	Penetrating keratoplasty
Contact lens-associated keratitis	Contact lenses, lens cases, and lens solution.	Aseptically removed from the eye. Aseptically collected.
Postoperative endophthalmitis following intraocular lens implantation.	Intraocular lens	Surgical removal
Eye injury with iris prolapse/ incarceration.	Iris tissue	Surgical removal

Source: https://www.ncbi.nlm.nih.gov/pmc/articles/PMC3272189/.

8.4.3. Processing of Clinical Samples From the Eye

Ocular samples need to be processed directly at the patient's side and with particular care. In the event that the hospital's microbiology lab is unavailable, the necessary slides and media can be obtained in advance and stored for use. When the samples are collected, the slides or media can be brought to the lab in safe boxes. Products that can be sent straight to the lab for processing include contact lens cases and solutions.

Table 8.2. *Direct Smear Examination Methods Used for the Diagnosis of Eye Infections*

Type of Sample	Type of Organism/Antigen to be Detected	Staining Methods for Smears
Conjunctival swabs/scrapings	Bacteria, fungi, parasites (microsporidia), viral antigens.	Gram, Giemsa, KOH + Calcofluor white, Kinyoun stain direct/indirect immunofluorescence or immunoperoxidase.
Corneal scrapings	Bacteria, fungi, parasites (*Acanthamoeba*, microsporidia), viral antigens.	Gram, Giemsa, KOH + Calcofluor white, Lactophenol cotton blue, Gomori methenamine silver, Ziehl-Neelsen stain, Kinyoun stain direct/indirect immunofluorescence or immunoperoxidase.
Aqueous/vitreous fluids/biopsy	Bacteria, fungi, viral antigens	Gram, Giemsa, Calcofluor white, Gomori methenamine silver Direct/indirect immunofluorescence or immunoperoxidase.

Source: https://www.ncbi.nlm.nih.gov/pmc/articles/PMC3272189/.

For most samples, the common culture media and direct smear examination techniques used for the isolation of bacteria and fungi are similar, though the inoculation technique may differ. Specific protocols are needed for sample collection to detect viruses and parasites. Samples like corneal buttons/ biopsies, eviscerated contents, or any other tissues must be examined by histopathology concurrently in order to look for a correlation that will lead to a valid diagnosis. The direct microscopy techniques that can be applied to identify different organisms from ocular samples are listed in Table 8.2. Contact lenses, contact lens solutions, intraocular lenses, and corneal biopsies are examples of materials that are typically not used to make smears.

The majority of samples, with the exception of fluids for PCR, are put in sterile phosphate buffered saline pH 7.2, and are sent to the lab. Prior to being tested, the samples may be kept at 4°C for 24 hours. Should the testing be postponed, storage at – 20°C is advised. It is possible to isolate DNA directly from aqueous and vitreous fluids, and can be kept at 4 or –20°C prior to further testing. The culprit organisms can be identified in less than 24 hours using PCR. Given the low sensitivity of traditional culture methods, it is thought to be helpful in the diagnosis of both fungal and bacterial endophthalmitis (Propionibacterium acnes). Possible reasons for low sensitivity include a small number of organisms, potential localized infection in the capsular bag, fastidious nature of the organisms, and previous antibiotic therapy. P-specific primers are used in PCR. Acnes has been applied to vitreous specimens that have been found to be negative in smear and culture but positive in PCR using eubacterial primers. In many culture-negative cases of endophthalmitis, the causative organism can be identified by DNA sequencing of the universal (eubacterial) nested PCR product. In addition, PCR has proven to be helpful in diagnosing.

8.4.4. Direct Clinical Sample Microscopy Analysis

The majority of microbiology labs offer a prompt diagnosis that aids in starting a particular treatment early in the course of the illness based on the preliminary smear analysis of the clinical samples. It is a good laboratory practice to deliver the preliminary microscopy results as quickly as feasible. When smears are properly stained and examined under a microscope, an etiological diagnosis can frequently be made without the need for additional culture. The most widely used stain for identifying bacteria, fungi, and parasites is called gram stain. The identification of bacterial and fungal elements in corneal scrapings is said to be influenced by the disease's stage, with both the sensitivity and specificity of Gram stain and potassium hydroxide with calcofluor white being higher in advanced stages. It's been demonstrated that bacilli that are either partially or not stained can reveal information about Mycobacterium infection in corneal scrapings. The presence of an acid-fast organism would be discovered upon staining the smear with Ziehl Neelsen stain, which would prompt the immediate start of therapy with 2.5% amikacin. The corneal slit lamp images of patients' corneas are shown in Figure 8.19. An infection with Nocardia would be identified by the presence of acid-fast filaments in the Kinyoun stain, which is a modified Ziehl Neelsen stain with 1% H_2SO_4. Therefore, based on the results of the initial smear analysis of the clinical sample, a treatment protocol can be developed, particularly in cases of microbial keratitis.

On the other hand, due to its low sensitivity, the use of smear examination in the diagnosis of infectious endophthalmitis is not very encouraging. On the other hand, early intravitreal antifungal therapy administration can be aided by the identification of fungal elements in vitreous samples. There aren't many studies that discuss how smear exams help start treating other ocular infections early on. On the other hand, a positive therapeutic outcome greatly benefits from the identification of *N. gonorroheae* in the conjunctival secretion smear Gram stain. Every ocular sample that is submitted to our laboratory undergoes a direct smear examination using either the Gram stain or potassium hydroxide with calcofluor white (KOH+CFW) protocol. When necessary, special stains for Giemsa, Ziehl Neelsen, Kinyoun, and Gomori methenamine are carried out.

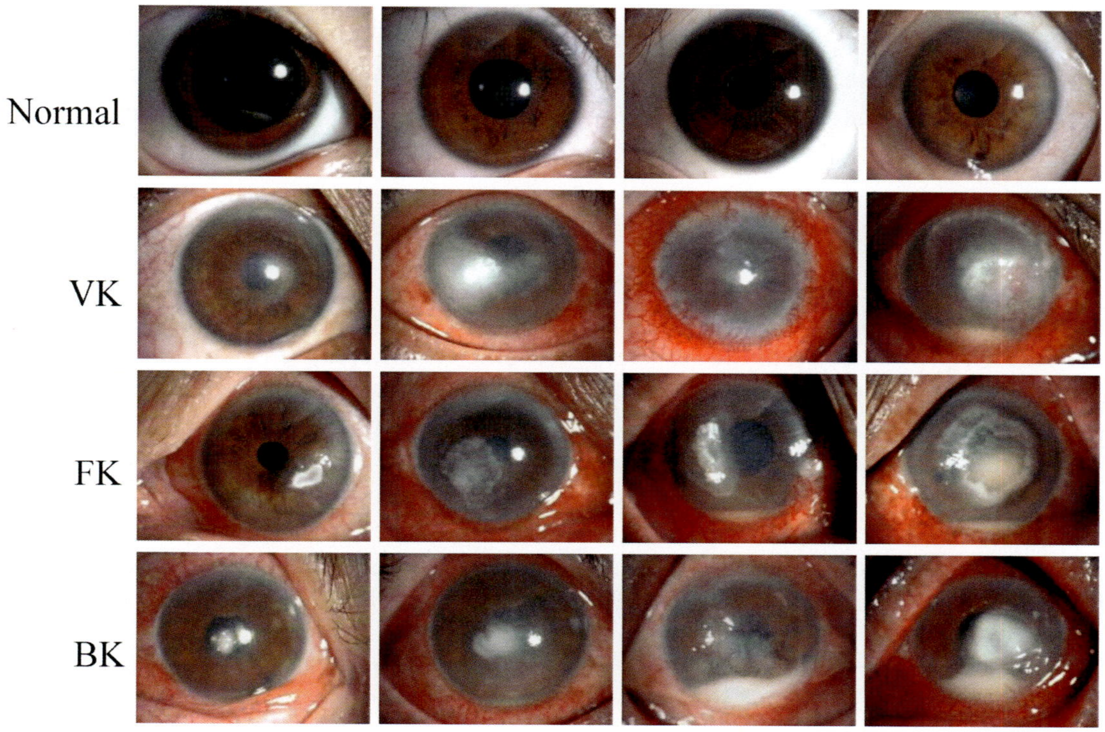

Figure 8.19. *Representative slit lamp images of the normal cornea (normal), viral keratitis (VK), fungal keratitis (FK), and bacterial keratitis (BK), from top to bottom.*

Source: Hu, S., Sun, Y., Li, J., Xu, P., Xu, M., Zhou, Y., Wang, Y., Wang, S., & Ye, J., (2023). Automatic diagnosis of infectious keratitis based on slit lamp images analysis. Journal of Personalized Medicine, 13(3), 519. https://doi.org/10.3390/jpm13030519.

Centrifuged deposits of aqueous/vitreous fluids (cytospin), conjunctival scrapings/swabs, or stained smears of corneal scrapings can all be used to quickly diagnose viral infection. Nonspecific staining methods like Giemsa, Papanicolaou, and hematoxylin-eosin stain can be used to achieve this. These methods facilitate the visualization of various inflammatory cells, primarily lymphocytes, intranuclear/intracytoplasmic inclusions, koilocytic changes, and multinucleated giant cells.

Giemsa stain is useful for identifying different cell types, but Papanicolaou stain is more effective at revealing intranuclear inclusions in smears. Even though these staining methods are quick and affordable, they frequently provide poor sensitivity and are nonspecific when it comes to diagnosing viral infection. For instance, these stains are unable to distinguish between the varicella zoster virus (VZV) and HSV intranuclear inclusions. Certain cytology methods that imply the presence of viral antigens in the clinical sample are employed in the indirect diagnosis of viral infections. Viral keratitis can be diagnosed with great benefit if cell-associated viral antigen is found in a corneal or conjunctival scraping. HSV, VZV keratitis, and adenoviral keratoconjunctivitis can all be diagnosed with direct and indirect immunofluorescence as well as indirect immunoperoxidase assays. As long as the test system is equipped with appropriate monoclonal or purified polyclonal antibodies, both of these tests are quick, sensitive, and specific. The indirect immunofluorescence (IF) assay is not as advantageous as the indirect immunoperoxidase (IP) assay. While the latter has the inherent issue of quenching (fading) of fluorescence and necessitates an expensive and sophisticated fluorescence microscope, the former offers a permanent preparation for records and makes use of a standard light microscope. Furthermore, while the IF technique yields better results with frozen tissue sections, the IP technique can be applied to paraffin-embedded tissue.

8.4.5. Techniques for Culturing Fungi, Bacteria, and Parasites (Acanthamoeba)

Inoculation of the sample on suitable culture media is the first step in the processing of the culture process. The type of media to be used, including its differing incubation conditions, can be chosen with the help of prior knowledge about the expected microorganisms. Most samples are processed in order to separate the fungi and bacteria. Typically, the fungi linked to eye infections are saprophytic, quickly growing fungi that can thrive on media intended for bacteria, like chocolate agar and blood. For the culture of bacteria, fungi, and Acanthamoeba from corneal scrapings, a single protocol is advised. However, the culture for Acanthamoeba is excluded from situations where only bacteria and fungi are anticipated (endophthalmitis). The various media that are used to cultivate common organisms from ocular samples are listed in Table 8.3.

Table 8.3. *Media Used for Culture of Bacteria, Fungus, Acanthamoeba from Ocular Samples*

Type of Sample	Culture Media	Expected Organisms
Lid margin scales	Sheep blood agar Brain heart infusion broth Sabouraud dextrose agar[a]	Bacteria Fungi
Conjunctival swab	Sheep blood agar Sheep blood chocolate agar Brain heart infusion broth Sabouraud dextrose agar[a]	Bacteria Fungi
Corneal scrapings	Sheep blood agar (aerobic, anaerobic) Sheep blood chocolate agar Brain heart infusion broth Sabouraud dextrose agar[a] Thioglycollate broth Non-nutrient agar with *E. coli*	Bacteria (aerobic, anaerobic) Fungi *Acanthamoeba*
Aqueous/vitreous	Sheep blood agar (aerobic, anaerobic) Sheep blood chocolate agar Brain heart infusion broth Sabouraud dextrose agar[a] Thioglycollate broth[a]	Bacteria (aerobic, anaerobic) Fungi
Corneal biopsy/ buttons	Sheep blood agar (aerobic, anaerobic) Sheep blood chocolate agar Brain heart infusion broth Sabouraud dextrose agar[a] non-nutrient agar with *E. coli*	Bacteria (aerobic, anaerobic) Fungi *Acanthamoeba*

Contact lenses	Sheep blood chocolate agar (aerobic, anaerobic) Sabouraud dextrose agar[a] non-nutrient agar with *E. coli*	Bacteria (aerobic, anaerobic) Fungi *Acanthamoeba*
Contact lens solutions	Sheep blood chocolate agar (aerobic, anaerobic) Sabouraud dextrose agar[a] non-nutrient agar with *E. coli*	Bacteria Fungi *Acanthamoeba*
Intraocular lens/ iris tissue	Sheep blood agar	Bacteria Fungi

[a]With antibiotics (gentamicin or chloramphenicol) but without cycloheximide. Potato dextrose agar may be used in addition to Sabouraud dextrose agar for better sporulation.

Depending on the samples' availability, fewer media may be used. Except for Sabouraud dextrose agar, which requires an incubator for BOD of 25–27°C, all media are incubated at 37°C. Blood agar needs an anaerobic chamber or an anaerobic jar with gas packs for anaerobic culture, while chocolate agar is incubated in 3–5% CO_2 in a candle jar or CO_2 incubator. Every other medium undergoes aerobic incubation.

Culture media are checked daily for growth and are incubated for one to two weeks prior to being disposed of. Atypical mycobacteria, Canthamoeba, and Nocardia species are examples of slow-growing bacteria that need a long incubation period. Even though the majority of fungi linked to eye infections are saprophytes and develop in a week or so, they might need to be incubated for two to four weeks to properly sporulate and enable identificatoin.

While it is possible to examine bacterial and fungal colonies with unaided eyes, a microscope is necessary to observe the growth of Acanthamoeba. Under the ×4 objective lens of the microscope, non-nutrient agar plates (with the lid on) are examined for the presence of trophozoites near the inoculation mark on the medium's surface. On the *E. coli* lawn, one might be able to see the distinctive track marks left by the trophozoites' migration. Acanthamoeba doesn't create colonies. In liquid media, bacterial growth manifests as turbidity that needs to be Gram stained and subcultured to be identified. When bacteria or fungi grow confluently (more than 10 colonies) on solid media after being inoculated, and is visible in smears, or can be grown in multiple media, it is deemed noteworthy.

8.4.6. Antibiotic Susceptibility Testing

The most effective medication for treatment can be chosen with the aid of susceptibility testing. The Clinical Laboratory Standards Institute (CLSI) has established a reliable standard for determining the MIC of antibacterial agents. Guidelines for the disc diffusion assay (CLSI M02-A10, 2009), broth dilution, and agar dilution methods (CLSI M07-A8, 2009) are also available. Due to the widespread availability of commercial antibiotic discs, the disc diffusion method of testing for bacterial susceptibility is widely used in microbiology laboratories and is highly standardized. The drug level that is achievable in the serum, as opposed to the tear film, cornea, or intraocular space through standard topical or intraocular therapy, is what is contained in the antibiotic discs. Thus, even in cases involving the eyes, organisms considered resistant might be susceptible. Apart from minimum MIC, broth dilution procedures can determine minimum lethal concentration or minimum bactericidal concentration, while the disc diffusion method classifies an organism as susceptible, resistant, or intermediately susceptible. This is particularly clinically significant.

For yeasts and filamentous fungi, susceptibility testing to antifungal medications is carried out using the disc diffusion method and broth or agar dilution techniques, which determine the MIC. Disc diffusion method is available for yeasts (CLSI M44-A, 2009) and some filamentous fungi that are not dermatophytes (CLSI M51-A, 2010). It is comparable to bacterial susceptibility testing. Amphotericin B, ketoconazole, miconazole, fluconazole, itraconazole, and 5FC (flucytosine) are among the medications that are frequently tested. There have only been a few documented antifungal susceptibility tests of ocular isolates. For yeast and filamentous fungi, there are also several antifungals available for e-testing. But unlike bacterial isolates, fungal isolates have not yet been routinely tested for drug susceptibility to antifungals.

8.4.7. Culture of Ocular Samples for Viruses

All samples (apart from smears) for viral diagnosis must be obtained and sent to the lab in the proper transport medium. Transport techniques would change depending on the kind of sample. You can use either Hank's balanced salt solution or 2 sucrose phosphate broth.

Different techniques can be used to process samples in a virology laboratory, depending on the type of sample and the specific virus being tested for. Most of these techniques can be conducted in a moderately equipped laboratory. However, not all available laboratory techniques for diagnosing viral infections can be used in a single laboratory. The choice of technique is based on considerations such as their advantages, disadvantages, cost-effectiveness, and overall usefulness. Certain established cell lines like HeLa, Vero, HEp 2, and MRC-5 have been traditionally employed for isolating HSV from corneal scrapings and other ocular samples. However, a recently discovered immortalized human corneal epithelial cell line has proven to be highly sensitive in isolating HSV.

Viral growth in the cell lines can be verified by IF or IP techniques, which identify viral antigens in the infected cell lines, or by cytopathic effect (CPE) or characteristic cellular changes. CPE may take several days to manifest, but antigens can be found well in advance of CPE, making the latter approach faster. Viruses can be grown on cover slips in vials (shell vial) or in cell lines kept in tubes (tube culture). Viral isolation has been superseded in recent years by viral molecular diagnostic techniques that show viral DNA in clinical samples. Since virus isolation takes time, requires specialized equipment, and is expensive, molecular methods are the best choice for diagnosing viral infections.

8.4.8. Molecular Methods in the Diagnosis of Ocular Infections

Molecular techniques, particularly PCR, are widely used in viral diagnosis and the detection of hard-to-culture organisms like Microsporidia, *Propionibacterium acnes*, and *Toxoplasma gondii*. This is due to their high sensitivity and specificity, or that develop slowly, like Mycobacterium tuberculosis. PCR is a quick, accurate, and sensitive method for diagnosing bacterial and fungal endophthalmitis. The diagnosis of viral infections of the eye has been made possible by the widespread use of PCR-based methods along with various modifications, and are typically used to confirm conjunctivitis or keratoconjunctivitis brought on by adenoviruses, herpes simplex virus, chlamydia, or microsporidia. Both multiplex and uniplex PCR approaches are used to diagnose viral retinitis.

Numerous researchers have shown the value of PCR techniques in enhancing the diagnosis of ocular fungal infections. It has been demonstrated that panfungal PCR with ITS primers is highly sensitive in the diagnosis of fungal endophthalmitis. In order to diagnose fungal keratitis, a recent study compared three different panfungal primers and found that ITS primers have a higher sensitivity for PCR than 18 S rDNA and 28 S rDNA primers. Xcyton Diagnostics in Bangalore, India has developed DNA technology in the form of a DNA chip, which offers a platform for the application of multiplex PCR and hybridization for the simultaneous diagnosis of multiple ocular infections. One major benefit of real-time PCR is that it is quantitative, and reports of its use in the diagnosis and monitoring of various ocular viral infections have been made. Genome fragment sequencing frequently aids in the identification of organisms that are challenging to identify using traditional techniques. Recent studies have linked new microorganisms to eye diseases. These adaptable methods have made it clear that there is still a great deal we don't know about ocular infections.

8.5. Treatment and Prevention

In most cases, viral conjunctivitis resolves on its own in a few days. Most cases of bacterial conjunctivitis or keratitis can be treated with broad-spectrum antibiotic eye drops, whereas specific antibiotics are needed to treat chlamydia and gonorrhea. Curing many of these illnesses is possible.

Most fungal and parasitic infections can also be treated with a variety of drugs. The exception is histoplasma, which we know exists in the retina but cannot even be seen there. The macula, the center of the retina, can only be severely slowed down by laser cauterization, which is the only treatment available at this time. Although there is a chance that this procedure will result in some additional vision loss, the goal is to preserve the current vision. Although new surgical techniques are being studied, it is still not possible to repair the damage already done.

Herpes simplex cannot be completely cured, but topical (applied topically) or oral (ingested) antiviral drugs can frequently prevent ocular flare-ups. If the infection causes severe scarring or vision loss, a corneal transplant may be required. Before eye issues get better, serious illnesses like toxoplasmosis, syphilis, and tuberculosis must be treated holistically.

When it comes to preventing a disease like histoplasmosis, your only real option is to stay away from endemic areas, which are regions where the fungus is prevalent, like river valleys. You should refrain from engaging in any activity that is known to be linked to histoplasmosis if you are in those areas and have a compromised immune system. Examples of such activities include cleaning or demolishing old buildings, exploring caves, and excavating in soil that may contain bird or bat droppings. It's also worth noting that a significant number of eye infections are side effects of genital or STDs like hepatitis B, chlamydia, gonorrhea, crab lice, herpes simplex, thrush, and syphilis. If you have an active cold sore or blister and you have herpes simplex, do not touch your eyes.

Hand washing is a critical step in stopping the spread of pathogenic microorganisms. In order to stop the spread of eye infections, never share towels, pillowcases, washcloths, or makeup.

Practicing safe sexual behavior can reduce your chance of contracting an eye infection as well, and this entails using condoms and, ideally, having fewer sexual partners. Additionally, it's critical to get screened for STIs on a regular basis because many of these illnesses can go undetected until they cause harm and spread to others around you. Keep your hands away from your eyes and clean if you do have one of these conditions. Cold sores, shingles, chickenpox, measles, mumps, the flu, and the common cold all follow this same pattern. Spots, rashes, or mucus containing the organism are symptoms common of these diseases. Avoid touching your eyes and wash your hands often. Never allow children to wipe their noses with an upward hand motion, instead, keep a close eye on them.

For every cleaning, use fresh facecloths and towels and separate linens if you or a family member has an eye infection. Avoid cosmetics if you have eye issues, as they may be a source of recurring infections. Make sure to cleanse the area around the eyes, particularly if there is any discharge coming from the eyes or before applying any medication.

If you wear contact lenses, make sure you take care of them according to the manufacturer's instructions and the advice of your eye doctor, and make sure to wash your hands prior to using them when installing contact lenses.

While strolling in the woods, keep an eye out for twigs and tree branches. Infection with fungus of the eye can also occur from scratches in the eye caused by organic matter.

Lastly, wear sunglasses to protect your eyes from too much sun exposure, which can erode their protective layer.

A Closer Look

Viral Conjunctivitis

A viral conjunctivitis infection is likely the most frequent infection seen in the office of an ophthalmologist. The transparent lining that covers the white portion of the eye is called the conjunctiva. This infection is occasionally referred to as an eye cold.

This kind of infection can be brought on by dozens of viruses. Only the eye may become infected at times. Other times, the eye ailment is a symptom of a wider issue, like a cold or the flu.

Usually, though maybe not always, both eyes are affected. Symptoms are typically not severe and are mild. Occasionally, though, the complaints related to the eyes are so bothersome that they are incapacitating. A broad range of complaints is indicative of viral conjunctivitis. Characteristics include conjunctival swelling, redness, tearing, and a transparent discharge. One notable symptom that may also exist is light sensitivity. Occasionally, the virus causes a lymph node on the cheek in front of the ear to enlarge. (A crucial indicator that the patient's conjunctivitis is viral rather than bacterial).

Visibility may become blurry if the cornea—the transparent front window of the eye—is affected. Fortunately, there are rarely any lasting effects from this blurriness, which goes away in a few days to weeks.

Rarely does the patient experience severe ocular pain along with swelling of the lids, and there is very little chance of bleeding into the lids.

The goal of treatment in the initial days is to ensure the patient's comfort. Painkillers and eye drops can help with the discomfort, but time and rest are the most effective treatments. Cool compresses can also help soothe the eyes and lids. Driving and working should only be done very carefully and cautiously if there is a significant amount of blurriness in the vision. Cortisone eye drops can occasionally be very helpful in managing this infection's symptoms.

Preventing the spread of this disease is crucial because of its high contagiousness. Viral conjunctivitis only takes one or two days to incubate, which makes rapid spread relatively simple. Hand washing is essential in the office to prevent the infection from spreading to other patients. It is best to avoid making direct contact with the infected eye. Care should be taken to prevent indirect contact with hand towels, washcloths, and clothing.

Patients may experience discomfort for a few days, much like with a cold, but eventually, the infection is defeated by our immune systems. For nearly all patients, full resolution is expected. Seldom do symptoms continue to cause vision impairment and scarring.

Summary

- Eye infections fall into three specific categories based on their cause: viral, bacterial, or fungal, and each is treated differently.
- Infectious conjunctivitis, or pink eye, is one of the most common eye infections. It happens when blood vessels in the conjunctiva, the thin outermost membrane surrounding your eyeball, become infected by bacteria or a virus.
- Infectious keratitis happens when your cornea gets infected. The cornea is the clear layer that covers your pupil and iris. Keratitis results from either an infection (bacterial, viral, fungal, or parasitic) or an eye injury. Keratitis means swelling of the cornea and isn't always infectious.
- Endophthalmitis is severe inflammation of the inside of your eye resulting from a bacterial or fungal infection. Candida fungal infections are the most common cause of endophthalmitis.
- Blepharitis is an inflammation of your eyelids, the skin folds covering your eyes. This type of inflammation is usually caused by clogging of the oil glands inside the eyelid skin at the base of your eyelashes. Blepharitis may be caused by bacteria.
- A sty (also called a hordeolum) is a pimple-like bump that develops from an oil gland on the outer edges of your eyelids. These glands can get clogged with dead skin, oils, and other matter and allow bacteria to overgrow in your gland. The resulting infection causes a sty.
- Uveitis happens when your uvea gets inflamed from infection. The uvea is the central layer of your eyeball that transports blood to your retina — the part of your eye that transmits images to your brain.
- Eyelid cellulitis, or periorbital cellulitis, happens when eye tissues get infected. It's often caused by an injury like a scratch to your eye tissues that introduces infectious bacteria, such as Staphylococcus (staph), or from bacterial infections of nearby structures, such as sinus infections.
- Ocular herpes happens when your eye is infected by the herpes simplex virus (HSV-1). It's often just called eye herpes.
- Pseudomonas aeruginosa and the protozoal parasite Acanthamoeba are acquired from domestic water supplies, and can cause keratitis in the contact lens wearer (CLW).
- Bacterial conjunctivitis is characterized by an inflamed red eye and associated discharge.
- The external ocular surface harbors commensal organisms, such as Staphylococcus species, Corynebacterium species, and Propionibacterium species, which form the resident flora. Given a chance, any environmental organism can become a transient flora in the eye.

References

1. Rahul Bhargava, Prachi Kumar, Hemant Phogat, Avinash Kaur, and Manjushri Kumar, (2015). Oral omega-3 fatty acids treatment in computer vision syndrome related dry eye. *Contact Lens and Anterior Eye, 38*(3), 206–210. https://doi.org/10.1016/j.clae.2015.01.007.
2. Bullimore, M. A., S. L., & Jordan, L., (2013). The risk of microbial keratitis with overnight corneal reshaping lenses. *Optometry and Vision Science: Official Publication of the American Academy of Optometry, 90*(9), 937–944. https://doi.org/10.1097/OPX.0b013e31829cac92 DOWNLOAD.
3. Cheng, D., S. K., & Woo, G. C., D. B., (2014). Effect of bifocal and prismatic bifocal spectacles on myopia progression in children three-year results of a randomized clinical trial. *JAMA Ophthalmology, 132*(3), 258–264. https://doi.org/10.1001/jamaophthalmol.2013.7623.
4. Chia, A., L. Q., & Tan, D., (2016). Five-year clinical trial on atropine for the treatment of myopia 2: Myopia control with atropine 0.01% eyedrops. *Ophthalmology, 123*(2), 391–399. https://doi.org/10.1016/j.ophtha.2015.07.004. DOWNLOAD.
5. Cho, P., C. S., & Edwards, M., (2005). Longitudinal orthokeratology research in children. *Current Eye Research, 30*(1), 71–80. https://doi.org/10.1080/02713680590907256.
6. Davis, R. L., E. S., Bennett, E. S., K. B., & Wohl, L., (2015). Stabilizing myopia by accelerated reshaping technique (SMART)-study three-year outcomes and overview. *Advances in Ophthalmolgy & Visual Systems, 2*(3). https://doi.org/10.15406/aovs.2015.02.00046 DOWNLOAD.
7. Leslie Donovan, Padmaja Sankaridurg, Arthur Ho, Thomas Naduvilath, Earl L. Smith III, and Brien A Holden, (2012). Myopia progression rates in urban children wearing single-vision spectacles. *Optometry and Vision Science: Official Publication of the American Academy of Optometry, 89(1):27-32*. https://doi.org/10.1097/OPX.0b013e3182357f79.
8. Downie, L., L. R., (2013). Corneal reshaping influences myopic prescription stability (CRIMPS): An analysis of the effect of orthokeratology on childhood myopic refractive stability. *Eye & Contact Lens: Science & Clinical Practice, 39*(4), 303–310. https://doi.org/10.1097/ICL.0b013e318298ee76.
9. Flitcroft, D. I., (2012). The complex interactions of retinal, optical, and environmental factors in myopia aetiology. *Progress in Retinal and Eye Research, 31*(6), 622–660. https://doi.org/10.1016/j.preteyeres.2012.06.004.
10. French, A. N., M. I., Burlutsky, G., M. P., & Rosa, K. A., (2013). Prevalence and 5- to 6-year incidence and progression of myopia and hyperopia in Australian schoolchildren. *Ophthalmology, 120*(7), 1482–1491. https://doi.org/10.1016/j.ophtha.2012.12.018.
11. Gifford, K., (2016). Myopia control with contact lenses in practice. *Mivision*, (113).
12. Jung, S. K., L. J., & Kakizaki, H., J. D., (2012). Prevalence of myopia and its association with body stature and educational level in 19-year-old male conscripts in Seoul, South Korea. *Investigative Ophthalmology & Visual Science, 53*(9), 5579–5583. https://doi.org/10.1167/iovs.12-10106 DOWNLOAD.
13. Kangari, H., E. M., Sardari, S., K. H., Eftekhari, M. H., Sardari, S., Hashemi, H., Salamzadeh, J., Ghassemi-Broumand, M., et al., (2013). Short-term consumption of oral omega-3 and dry eye

syndrome. *Ophthalmology, 120*(11), 2191–2196. https://doi.org/10.1016/j.ophtha.2013.04.006 DOWNLOAD.

14. ller, T. A., L. M., & Wildsoet, C. F., (2016). Myopia control with bifocal contact lenses: A randomized clinical trial. *Optometry and Vision Science: Official Publication of the American Academy of Optometry, 93(4)*, 344–352. https://doi.org/10.1097/OPX.0000000000000808.
15. N Monnerat, W Bossart, M A Thiel, (2006). Povidone-iodine for treatment of adenoviral conjunctivitis: An *in vitro* study. *Klinische Monatsblätter für Augenheilkunde, 223*(5), 349–352. https://doi.org/10.1055/s-2006-926633.
16. Mutti, D. O., S. R., & Friedman, N. E., Z. K., (2000). Peripheral refraction and ocular shape in children. *Investigative Ophthalmology & Visual Science, 4*(5), 1022–1030. DOWNLOAD.
17. Portello, J. K., Rosenfield M, & Chu, C. A., (n.d.). Blink rate, incomplete blinks, and computer vision syndrome. *Optometry and Vision Science, 90*(5), 482–487. https://doi.org/10.1097/OPX.0b013e31828f09a7.
18. Rose, K. A., M. I., Ip, J., K. A., Huynh, S., S. W., & Mitchell, P., (2008). Outdoor activity reduces the prevalence of myopia in children. *Ophthalmology, 115*(8), 1279–1285. https://doi.org/10.1016/j.ophtha.2007.12.019.
19. Sankaridurg, P., D. L., Varnas, S., H. A., Chen, X., M. A., Fisher, S., L. Z., Smith, E. L. 3rd. G. J., & Holden, B., (2010). Spectacle lenses designed to reduce progression of myopia: 12-month results. *Optometry and Vision Science: Official Publication of the American Academy of Optometry, 87*(10), 631–641. https://doi.org/10.1097/OPX.0b013e3181ea19c7 DOWNLOAD.
20. Tetsuhiko, K., T. H., & Tetsuro, O., (2011). Influence of overnight orthokeratology on axial elongation of childhood myopia. *Investigative Ophthalmology and Visual Science, 52*(5), 2170–2174. https://doi.org/10.1167/iovs.10-5485.
21. Walline, J. J., G. K., McVey, M. E., & Lisa A Jones-Jordan, (2013). Multifocal contact lens myopia control. *Optometry and Vision Science: Official Publication of the American Academy of Optometry, 90*(11), 1207–1214. https://doi.org/10.1097/OPX.0000000000000036.
22. P Wutzler, A Sauerbrei, R Klöcking, J Burkhardt, M Schacke, R Thust, W Fleischer, K Reimer, (2000). Virucidal and chlamydicidal activities of eye drops with povidone-iodine liposome complex. *Ophthalmic Research, 32*, 118–125. https://doi.org/DOI:10.1159/000055600.

INDEX

FSC
www.fsc.org
MIX
Papier | Fördert gute Waldnutzung
FSC® C083411

Kolibri 360 GmbH
Ferdinand-Jühlke-Straße 7
99095 Erfurt, Deutschland
produktsicherheit@kolibri360.de